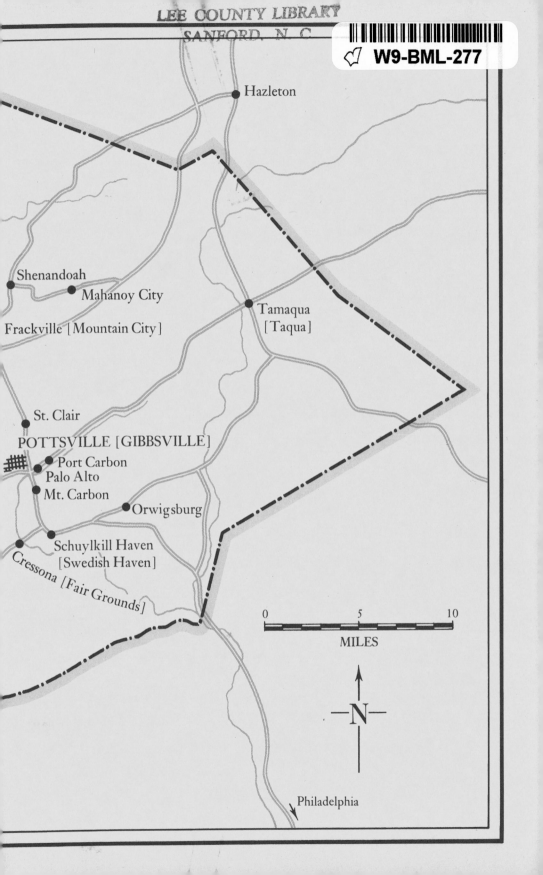

W9-BML-277

Hazleton

Shenandoah

Mahanoy City

Frackville [Mountain City]

Tamaqua
[Taqua]

St. Clair

POTTSVILLE [GIBBSVILLE]

Port Carbon
Palo Alto
Mt. Carbon

Orwigsburg

Schuylkill Haven
[Swedish Haven]

Cressona [Fair Grounds]

0   5   10
MILES

—N—

Philadelphia

The Composition of *Tender Is the Night*

As Ever, Scott Fitz
  (editor, with Jennifer Atkinson)

Profile of F. Scott Fitzgerald (editor)

F. Scott Fitzgerald in His Own Time
  (editor, with Jackson Bryer)

F. Scott Fitzgerald: A Descriptive Bibliography

F. Scott Fitzgerald's Ledger (editor)

The Great Gatsby: A Facsimile of the Manuscript
  (editor)

Apparatus for a Definitive Edition of
  The Great Gatsby

Bits of Paradise: 21 Uncollected Stories by F.
  Scott and Zelda Fitzgerald (editor, with Scottie
  Fitzgerald Smith)

The Romantic Egoists (editor, with Scottie
  Fitzgerald Smith and Joan P. Kerr)

Fitzgerald Newsletter (editor)

Ernest Hemingway, Cub Reporter (editor)

Ernest Hemingway's Apprenticeship (editor)

Hemingway at Auction (editor, with C. E.
  Frazer Clark, Jr.)

Fitzgerald/Hemingway Annual
  (editor, with C. E. Frazer Clark, Jr.)

Raymond Chandler: A Checklist

Kenneth Millar/Ross Macdonald: A Checklist

Chandler Before Marlowe (editor)

Lost American Fiction (series editor)

Pittsburgh Series in Bibliography (series editor)

John O'Hara: A Checklist

THE O'HARA CONCERN

It was a Concern, in the Quaker sense of the term. . . . which was the name given to the obsessive act or thought, or both, of a religious nature.

—*The Lockwood Concern*

THE

O'HARA
CONCERN

A Biography of John O'Hara

BY

MATTHEW J. BRUCCOLI

Random House
New York

Library of Congress Cataloging in Publication Data
Bruccoli, Matthew Joseph, 1931–
The O'Hara concern.
"John O'Hara's works": p.
Bibliography: p.   Includes index.
1. O'Hara, John, 1905–1970. I. Title.
PS3529.H29Z59   813'.5'2 [B]   75-9736
ISBN 0-394-48446-0

Grateful acknowledgment is made to the following for permission to reprint previously published material:

Chappell & Co., Inc.: For two lines of lyrics from "Bewitched"
(page 166). Copyright © 1941 by Chappell & Co., Inc. Copyright renewed. All rights reserved. Also for two lines of lyrics
from "In Our Little Den" (page 166). Copyright © 1950 by
Chappell & Co., Inc. All rights reserved. Used by permission.

Field Newspaper Syndicate: Column by Earl Wilson which
appeared in the New York *Post*, March, 1948.

Charles Scribner's Sons: F. Scott Fitzgerald's letter to John
O'Hara dated 18 July 1933 from page 503 of *The Letters of
F. Scott Fitzgerald*, edited by Andrew Turnbull. Copyright ©
1963 by Frances Scott Fitzgerald Lanahan.

FOR

Katharine Barnes O'Hara

and

FOR

Marisa Bisi Erskine

CONTENTS

ILLUSTRATIONS

FOREWORD

. . . Yet it is to clippings and letters that biographers turn for informa-tion. The biographer of a novelist will presumably read his subject's novels with some care, and more than likely treat them as romans à clef, *a hazard in itself. . . . The Boswell will have as many personal inter-views as possible with people who were acquainted with the subject, and there is the hazard there that the interviewee may have a faulty memory or a desire to distort the facts in favor of or against the subject. The Boswell himself may be tempted to make prejudicial selections, to reject or dismiss whatever may contradict his opinions. But assuming that the biographer is out to write about his subject and not merely to demonstrate his own superior talent, cleverness, honor, and intellect, he is in for a hard time.* No matter how good his intentions, the biographer is almost certain to discover that there is no such thing as a reliable source.[1]

ON SATURDAY, 11 April 1970, I was in Pittsburgh driving to Brooks Brothers with my friend Frederick Hetzel when the death of John O'Hara was announced over the car radio. John Harris, Mrs. Hetzel's grandfather, had fired O'Hara from the Tamaqua *Courier* in 1927, and O'Hara had been managing editor of the Pittsburgh *Bulletin-Index* in 1933. These connections initiated my thinking about this book.

I never met John O'Hara, but we exchanged letters about my bibliographical research on his work. Although neither of us knew that I would become his biographer, one of my letters marked the remote inception of this project. In 1964 I asked O'Hara about the missing final chapter in the Avon paperback edition of *Hope of Heaven*, and he turned my letter over to Albert Erskine, his editor at Random House, which led to a correspondence and a friendship with Mr. Erskine. After the death of John O'Hara, Mr. Erskine was recep-tive to my proposal that I undertake this biography. He arranged a meeting with Katharine Barnes O'Hara, the author's widow, who granted me her approval.

My book comes under the category of "critical biography": an attempt to establish O'Hara's stature in terms of an account of his life and work. It is therefore a *career study*, a study of John O'Hara as professional author. Although this is a scholarly work, it has not been written primarily for academia. Literature belongs to the people who read it—most of whom reside off campus. Indeed, literature is too important to be left entirely in the hands of professors and critics.

Obviously, then, my book is not impartial. I do not believe that an impartial biography has ever been written, for the biographer rigs his work—consciously and unconsciously—in thousands upon thousands of ways. For the record, *The O'Hara Concern* is intentionally biased by my conviction that John O'Hara was a major writer who was underrated by the critical-academic axis sometimes called The Literary Establishment. We never have so many great writers that we can discard one because his aims and standards are unfashionable.

The title for this biography is an obvious reference to *The Lockwood Concern*, conveying the idea that John O'Hara was obsessive about his work. It is not meant to imply any similarity between George Lockwood and John O'Hara. The Lockwood concern proved self-destructive; the O'Hara concern impelled him to mastery.

In simpler times, students were taught three questions for judging literature: (1) What is the author trying to do? (2) How well does he do it? (3) Is it worth doing? These guidelines provide an approach to John O'Hara's concern. He was trying to tell "the truth about his time." He did it "better than anyone else." Of course it was worth doing.

F. Scott Fitzgerald was right: "There never was a good biography of a good novelist. There couldn't be. He is too many people, if he's any good." I have written a biography of the John O'Hara I was able to understand from my research. John O'Hara was also right in stating that "there is no such thing as a reliable source." Nevertheless, a biographer must work from sources, and I have therefore relied heavily on John O'Hara's letters, which are the most reliable source.

I began this book under the misapprehension that the research would be relatively easy, for I assumed that John O'Hara had done much of my work for me already. It seemed a foregone conclusion that this great social historian had been a self-historiographer—that there would be diaries, scrapbooks, albums and immense files of correspondence. I promptly discovered that, unlike F. Scott Fitzgerald, he saved very little. There was one small file of incoming letters and the scrapbooks of reviews that his widow had maintained, beginning with *Ten North Frederick*. O'Hara's daughter, Wylie, saved his letters to her and had photo albums, which she generously permitted me to use. Belle O'Hara—the author's second wife—was known to have compiled scrapbooks, but they cannot be found. Some of the items I had expected to find among John O'Hara's archives are unlocatable—in particular his school writings, if any, and his apprentice journalism on the Pottsville *Journal*. No file of the paper survives for 1924–26. The disappearance of this material resulted in the most serious hole in my research.

It is also worth noting that most of O'Hara's friends predeceased him. By the time I began work, all of the following were gone: Wolcott Gibbs, Robert Benchley, Dorothy Parker, Clifford Odets, John McClain, Wilder Hobson and Philip Barry. Bennett Cerf, Alfred Wright and Walter Farquhar died while I was still researching.

I have been extremely fortunate in the generous help of many people. It is impossible for me to rank my debts, but certain people merit special acknowledgment. My greatest obligation is to Katharine Barnes O'Hara, who freely offered me privileges that I could not have asked for. Albert Erskine, my superb editor, gave me all the help I needed when I asked for it, and knew when to leave me alone. Lynn Strong and James Wilcox at Random House made useful suggestions for revision. My old friend Charles Mann, Curator of Rare Books (and keeper of the John O'Hara Papers) at the Pennsylvania State University Library, helped me in many, many important ways; this book could not have been written without his assistance. Joseph I. O'Hara, Martin O'Hara and Kathleen O'Hara Fuldner—the brothers and sister of the author—were always ready to answer just one more question; along the way they became valued friends, as well as valuable sources. Don A. Schanche generously turned over to me his notes for a biography of O'Hara. The law firm of Carter, Ledyard & Milburn, attorneys for the Estate of John O'Hara, provided substantial assistance. The late George Frazier was the one who first urged me to undertake this book, and I still owe him for many favors. Alden Whitman of the New York *Times* was particularly generous with help. Authorial acknowledgments to wives are *pro forma*, but my Arlyn is special: nothing I write satisfies her.

I am indebted to the saintly staffs at the McKissick Library, University of South Carolina (especially Elizabeth Pugh, Beverly Brooks, Mary E. Goolsby and Claudia Drum) and at the Pattee Library, Pennsylvania State University (especially Marilyn Warnick, Catherine Sauer Grigor and Christine Trower). The copying and photographic work was done by Richard Taylor, who is a marvel of competence and patience. R. L. Samsell and Jeanne Bennett did much of my California research for me. I am particularly indebted to student research assistants at the University of South Carolina who worked with me: Margaret Duggan, Richard Layman and Thomas Blumer. The index was prepared by Mrs. Linda Berry. And where would I be without Katharine Wade, Ruth B. Lalka, Mrs. Marie Willing and Linda Watts?

The following sources are listed in alphabetical order, and I hope they understand the extent of my gratitude: George Abbott, Mrs. Franklin P. Adams, Charles Addams, Robert Alberts, D. C. Allard, Carleton W. Alsop, John K. Amrhein, Wodrow Archbald, Prof. Carlos Baker, Mr. and Mrs. Chad Ballard, Barry & Jenkins, Mrs. Philip Barry, Prof. Charles Bassett, Harvey Batdorf, Jonathan P. Batdorf, Father Francis Beatty, Nathaniel Benchley, Mrs. Lewis E. Bennethum, James H. Bennett, Mrs. Raydelle H. Berger, B. A. Bergman, Irving Berlin, Marshall Best, Mrs. Suzanne Beves, Judge John Biggs, Jr., Clay Blair, Jr., George F. Blum, Richard Boeth, Adm. J. F. Bolger, Dr. William Bond, Gardner Botsford, Nancy Hale Bowers, John Braine, Mr. and Mrs. Gerald Bramwell, David Brown, Prof. Joe Brown, Pearl Kroll Brown, Louisa Browne, Adm. Arleigh Burke, Noel Busch, James M. Cain, Anson Campbell, Donald Carr, the late Bennett Cerf, John Chamberlain, Ronald Ciavolino, Alexander Clark, C. E. Frazer Clark, Jr., Jon Clark, Ray S. Cline, Earle Coleman, Mrs. Saxe Commins, Marc Connelly, Charles W. Corkran, Prof. Hamilton Cottier, Malcolm Cowley, James Gould Cozzens, Joan Crawford, Bing Crosby, John Crosby, Samuel B. Cross, Peter DeVries, Mr. and Mrs. James Dickey, Howard Dietz, Mrs. B. K. Dillingham, the late Richardson Dilworth, Dr. William S. Dix, Ed Donahue, Honoria Murphy Donnelly, Wylie O'Hara Doughty, Philip Dunne, Charles Einfeld, Dr. Frank Elliott, Adm. William E. Ellis, Dr. William Emerson, Elspeth Eric, Burtt Evans, Faber & Faber, the late Walter Farquhar, Ben Finney, Henry Fonda, Michael V. Forrestal, Edward Fox, Marion Franciosa, Barrett Gallagher, Dr. Donald Gallup, Mr. and Mrs. Henry Gardiner, Artemus L. Gates, Peter P. Mc N. Gates, Felicia Geffen, Brendan Gill, Goldsmith & Rosen, Dan Golenpaul, Sheilah Graham, Prof. Sheldon Grebstein, Russ Green, Jane Gregory, Robert E. Grim, Mrs. A. Whitney Griswold, Richard Grossman, Dean Josef G. Gutekunst, Mrs. Nevin Haas, Emily Hahn, Virginia M. Hall, Mr. and Mrs. Ben Hamilton, Mrs. C. W. Handwerk, Vernon Harbin, Robin Harris, Geoffrey Hellman, Mrs. Ernest Hemingway, John Hersey, Mr. and Mrs. Frederick A. Hetzel, Serrell Hillman, Al Hine, the Historical Society of Pennsylvania, the Historical Society of Schuylkill County, Mrs. Wilder Hobson, Mrs. Newton Hockaday, Hodder

& Stoughton, William Hogan, Mrs. Bob Hope, Prof. Carl Hovde, Arthur Hornblow, Jr., Edwin P. Hoyt, Mrs. Merritt Hulburd, Ralph Ingersoll, Zita Johann, Bruce W. Jones, William Jovanovich, John Keats, Gene Kelly, Mr. and Mrs. Morley Kennerly, Robert R. Kirsch, Henry Kisor, Donald S. Klopfer, Robert Kriendler, Margaretta Archbald Kroll, Louis Kronenberger, Richard Lampl, Roy Larsen, Arthur P. Lawler, Dr. William T. Leach, Prof. Rensselaer W. Lee, Warren Leslie, Sheilah Levine, Richard Lockridge, Henry Cabot Lodge, Kenneth Lohf, Stephen Longstreet, William Lord, Mr. and Mrs. Robert A. Lovett, James W. Lowe, Clare Booth Luce, Prof. Richard M. Ludwig, G. Hilmer Lundbeck, Horace S. Manges, Mrs. Herman Mankiewicz, Ada R. Mann, William Maxwell, Father George McAleer, Bruce McClellan, St. Clair McKelway, Charles Mercer, Burgess Meredith, Lewis Milestone, Mrs. David Miller, Gilbert Millstein, Alice-Leone Moats, I. F. Mogavero, Anne M. Murphy, Prof. Andrew Myers, Hoke Norris, Patrick O'Connor, Mary O'Hara, the late Thomas O'Hara, George Oppenheimer, Joseph W. Outerbridge, Roger Palmer, Anita Pfouts, Harold Pinter, Adm. Robert B. Pirie, the late Charles Poore, Mr. and Mrs. Henry C. Potter, Louis A. Rachow, David Randall, Mrs. Wanda Randall, Ruth Sato Reinhardt, the Pottsville *Republican*, James J. Reynolds, Harvena Richter, Allen Rivkin, Reginald Rix, Gilbert Roland, Richard Rodgers, the late Michael Romanoff, Cesar Romero, Robert Root, Anthony Rota, Mrs. Ann Salvani, William Saroyan, J. Paul Scheetz, Edgar Scott, the late Robert T. Simonds, Father Arthur Shea, the late Vincent Sheean, Dr. Donald Sheehan, Oscar Shefler, Leonard Sillman, the Sisters of St. Joseph (St. Patrick Convent), Frances Fitzgerald Smith, Mrs. Kyrie Smith, Red Smith, Sir Charles Snow, Benjamin Sonnenberg, Prof. Robert E. Spiller, Judge Walter K. Stapleton, Vernon Sternberg, Mr. and Mrs. Donald Ogden Stewart, Lawrence D. Stewart, Caskie Stinnett, Frank Sullivan, W. A. Swanberg, H. N. Swanson, the Swedish American Line, Herbert Bayard Swope, Jr., Harold B. Synder, David Thomson, Mrs. James Thurber, Rita Vaughan, Mrs. Phyllis Cerf Wagner, Theodore Wagner, Graham Watson, Richard Watts, Jr., Alec Waugh, Hobart Weekes, Jerome Weidman, Glenway Wescott, Mrs. J. F. Wesoski, Dame Rebecca West, Dr. Neda Westlake, Katharine Angell White, Alden Whitman, Mrs. Robert Whitmer, Thornton Wilder, Charles H. Williams, Mildred Gilman Wohlforth, the late Alfred Wright, Prof. Andrew Wright, James Wyman, Collier Young, Katharine Young, Frank Zachary and Mr. and Mrs. Thomas Zehner.

The following alumni of Fordham Preparatory School responded to my circular letter: Raymond J. Connolly, Francis P. Dolan, George

J. Kearns, Godfrey P. Schmidt, Joseph Russell Sherlock and Frank Walsh.

The following alumni of Keystone State Normal School responded to my circular letter: Mrs. James Hull Aiken, Mrs. Keefer Baum, Mrs. Lewis E. Bennetham, Nellie Bergan, Thomas P. Bordner, Robert Brown, Anna E. Campbell, Mrs. Chester M. Cloud, Lee Eck, Henry M. Frankenfield, Robert E. Grim, Mrs. Charles Kehl, Mary B. Keith, L. Harry Kershner, Blanche M. Leiby, Mrs. Nelson Lessig, Ruth N. Morse, Earl W. Moyer, Mrs. R. C. Nickum, Mrs. G. A. Nunemacher, John D. Rauch, Mrs. Joseph Reinheimer, Emily M. Schaeffer, J. Paul Smith, Mrs. Ryrie Smith, Audrey M. Spurr, Prof. J. Maurice Stratton, Kathryn Wagner and Harold M. Yehl.

Some of the time to work on this book was provided by a grant from the John Simon Guggenheim Foundation. The English department of the University of South Carolina provided substantial research aid under the headships of Professors Calhoun Winton and the late John Welsh. Dean John Guilds, former Vice Provost for Liberal and Cultural Disciplines, made help available at several key points.

M.J.B.
The University of South Carolina
21 August 1974

Katharine Barnes O'Hara died at Princeton on 7 December 1974. At that time this book was in the copy-editing stage at Random House. Since I wanted to surprise her, she had not seen the dedication page.

After John O'Hara's death Sister showed her loneliness, but she carried on well. Without ever behaving like the keeper of the flame, she competently handled the responsibilities of his literary estate. She was largely responsible for the construction of O'Hara's study at the Pennsylvania State University Library, and her pride at the dedication ceremony was obvious.

Sister O'Hara was good to me. She patiently submitted to my probings; she read the working draft of this biography and made suggestions, but she never in any way tried to control my work. More than anything else, she encouraged me. She made a point of telling me that she had confidence in me—thereby giving me the confidence that I did not feel as an apprentice biographer. This book achieved its final form when she suggested that I spend a night working in John O'Hara's study at "Linebrook."

Sister O'Hara charmed without seeming to make any effort to do so. She enjoyed harmless absurdities, and her quick laughter was often directed at herself. She was honest, wise, unpretentious, warm, strong, generous.

CHRONOLOGY

31 January 1905	Birth of John Henry O'Hara at 125 Mahantongo Street, Pottsville, son of Dr. Patrick H. and Katharine Delaney O'Hara.
1912–1920	Attends Miss Carpenter's School and St. Patrick's School.
February 1920–June 1921	Attends Fordham Preparatory School, Bronx; dismissed.
September 1921–June 1922	Attends Keystone State Normal School, Kutztown; dismissed.
Summer 1922– Summer 1923	Works at various jobs, including stint with White Engineering Co.
September 1923– June 1924	Attends Niagara Preparatory School, Niagara, N.Y.; chosen as valedictorian but not allowed to graduate. Falls in love with Margaretta Archbald.
July? 1924–late 1926	Reporter and columnist on Pottsville *Journal*.
18 March 1925	Death of Dr. Patrick H. O'Hara.
January–March 1927	Reporter on Tamaqua *Courier*.
June–July 1927	First trip to Europe, as waiter on *George Washington*.
October 1927	Hitchhikes from Pottsville to Chicago in unsuccessful search of newspaper work.
February 1928	Leaves Pottsville for New York City.
March–August 1928	Reporter and rewrite man on New York *Herald Tribune*. Meets Dorothy Parker, Robert Benchley and Wolcott Gibbs.

5 May 1928	First *New Yorker* sketch, "Alumnae Bulletin," published. Becomes regular contributor.
August 1928–March 1929	Reporter on *Time*, covering sports, religion, theater; also checker.
Spring 1929	Reporter on *Editor & Publisher*.
July 1929	Rewrite man on New York *Daily Mirror*.
Early 1930	Works for Heywood Broun.
May–July 1930	Movie critic and radio columnist ("Franey Delaney") for New York *Morning Telegraph*.
28 February 1931	Marries Helen Ritchie Petit ("Pet") in New York.
April–June 1931	Works for New York publicity department of Warner Brothers.
Summer 1931	Bermuda. Writes "The Hofman Estate" and plans novel.
Fall 1931	Reporter for *The New Yorker*. Works for Benjamin Sonnenberg's public relations firm.
1932	Works for New York publicity department of RKO.
Spring 1933	Separates from Pet.
May–August 1933	Managing editor of Pittsburgh *Bulletin-Index*. Stops drinking 3 July.
15 August 1933	Helen O'Hara obtains divorce in Reno.
August 1933	Returns to New York and begins writing *Appointment in Samarra*. Friendship with F. Scott Fitzgerald.
March 1934	Editor of ship's paper during Caribbean cruise of *Kungsholm*.
9 April 1934	Completes *Appointment in Samarra*.
June–August 1934	Hollywood. Works for Paramount.
16 August 1934	Publication of *Appointment in Samarra* by Harcourt, Brace.
September 1934	Returns to New York.

21 February 1935	Publication of *The Doctor's Son* by Harcourt, Brace. Florida trip.
April 1935	Works on *Butterfield 8* in East Sandwich, Mass. Meets Barbara Kibler in Berkshires.
July–August 1935	Resumes drinking 4 July. Visits Italy and France. Completes *Butterfield 8* in Paris.
17 October 1935	Publication of *Butterfield 8* by Harcourt, Brace.
Early 1936	Engagement to Barbara Kibler broken.
April 1936–Spring 1937	Hollywood. Appears in *The General Died at Dawn*. Works for Goldwyn and MGM. Writing "So Far, So Good" (*Hope of Heaven*). Plans dramatization of *In Dubious Battle*.
Spring 1936	Meets Belle Mulford Wylie.
Spring 1937	Returns to New York; summers at Quogue.
3 December 1937	Marries Belle Wylie in Elkton, Md.
17 March 1938	Publication of *Hope of Heaven* by Harcourt, Brace.
April–August 1938	Visit to France and residence in London.
22 October 1938	"Pal Joey" appears in *The New Yorker*.
March–April; September– December 1939	Hollywood. Works on *In Name Only* for RKO and *I Was an Adventuress* and *He Married His Wife* for Twentieth Century–Fox.
21 September 1939	Publication of *Files on Parade* by Harcourt, Brace.
January–April 1940	Hollywood. Works on *Down Argentine Way* for Twentieth Century–Fox.
July 1940–February 1942	Writes "Entertainment Week" column for *Newsweek*.
Fall 1940	Writes book for *Pal Joey* musical in New York.
October 1940	Publication of *Pal Joey* stories by Duell, Sloan & Pearce.

25 December 1940	*Pal Joey* opens on Broadway.
March–July 1941	Hollywood. Writes *Moontide* screenplay for Twentieth Century–Fox.
1941–1943	Attempts to join armed forces; works for Office of Inter-American Affairs; OSS training. Works on unproduced plays.
Summer 1944	*Liberty* correspondent attached to Task Force 38 in Pacific, aboard *Intrepid*.
24 March 1945	Publication of *Pipe Night* by Duell, Sloan & Pearce.
14 June 1945	Birth of Wylie Delaney O'Hara in New York.
August 1945– January 1946	Hollywood. Works on *Cass Timberlane* screenplay for MGM.
November 1945	Death of Robert Benchley.
June 1946	Works on *A Miracle Can Happen* for United Artists.
9 August 1947	Publication of *Hellbox* by Random House.
1948–1949	Writing *A Rage to Live*.
16 August 1949	Publication of *A Rage to Live* by Random House. Break with *The New Yorker*.
September 1949	Moves to Princeton, N.J. Friendship with Pat Outerbridge commences.
Summer 1950	Working on unpublished nonfiction book, "Observation Car."
10 September 1950	Review of *Across the River and into the Trees*.
8 November 1951	Publication of *The Farmers Hotel* by Random House.
January 1952	Broadway revival of *Pal Joey*.
May 1952	Production of *The Searching Sun* in Princeton.
4 August 1953	Publication of *Pal Joey* play by Random House.

20 August 1953	Ulcer hemorrhage; hospitalized at Harkness Pavilion. Stops drinking permanently.
December 1953–June 1954	Writes "Sweet and Sour" column for Trenton *Sunday Times-Advertiser.*
9 January 1954	Death of Belle Wylie O'Hara at Princeton Hospital.
February 1954– September 1956	Writes "Appointment with O'Hara" column for *Collier's.*
July 1954	Tryout of *The Farmers Hotel* at Fishkill, N.Y.
18 October 1954	Publication of *Sweet and Sour* by Random House.
31 January 1955	Marriage to Katharine Barnes Bryan ("Sister").
Spring–Summer 1955	Hollywood. Writing screenplay for *The Best Things in Life Are Free* for Twentieth Century–Fox; completing *Ten North Frederick.*
24 November 1955	Publication of *Ten North Frederick* by Random House.
February 1956	*Ten North Frederick* receives National Book Award.
16 August 1956	Publication of *A Family Party* by Random House.
1956–1957	Writes two unproduced screenplays for Twentieth Century–Fox (*The Bravados* and *The Man Who Could Not Lose*).
January 1957	Detroit suppression of *Ten North Frederick.*
14 January 1957	Library of Congress lecture.
May 1957	Induction into National Institute of Arts and Letters.
Fall 1957	Completion of Princeton home, "Linebrook."
December 1957	Albany suppression of *Ten North Frederick.*

August 1958	Death of Wolcott Gibbs.
27 November 1958	Publication of *From the Terrace* by Random House.
September–November 1959	Commences regular trips to Britain.
27 February 1960	Publication of *Ourselves to Know* by Random House.
17 September 1960	Publication of "Imagine Kissing Pete" in *The New Yorker*.
24 November 1960	Publication of *Sermons and Soda-Water* by Random House.
11 August 1961	Publication of *Five Plays* by Random House.
November 1961	Resignation from National Institute of Arts and Letters.
23 November 1961	Publication of *Assembly* by Random House.
13 May 1962	Death of Katharine Delaney O'Hara.
29 May 1962	Publication of *The Big Laugh* by Random House.
29 November 1962	Publication of *The Cape Cod Lighter* by Random House.
2 March 1963	Publication of "The Glendale People" in *The Saturday Evening Post*.
4 June 1963	Publication of *Elizabeth Appleton* by Random House.
28 November 1963	Publication of *The Hat on the Bed* by Random House.
20 May 1964	Presentation of Award of Merit for the Novel by American Academy of Arts and Letters.
26 November 1964	Publication of *The Horse Knows the Way* by Random House.
October 1964– October 1965	Writes "My Turn" column for *Newsday*.
December 1964	Hospitalized for jaw pains.

25 November 1965	Publication of *The Lockwood Concern* by Random House.
14 April 1966	Publication of *My Turn* by Random House.
10 September 1966	Marriage of Wylie Delaney O'Hara to Dennis Holahan in New York.
September 1966– May 1967	Writes "Whistle Stop" column for *Holiday*.
24 November 1966	Publication of *Waiting for Winter* by Random House.
May 1967	Speaks at Foyles book luncheon in London.
23 November 1967	Publication of *The Instrument* by Random House.
December 1967	Last visit to Pottsville.
26 October 1968	Birth of Nicholas Drew Holahan.
10 November 1968	Injured as result of fall in Philadelphia.
28 November 1968	Publication of *And Other Stories* by Random House.
September 1969	Hospitalized for throat problem; diabetic condition discovered.
30 September 1969	Birth of Belle Holahan.
27 November 1969	Publication of *Lovey Childs* by Random House.
9 February 1970	Finishes *The Ewings*.
13 February 1970	Starts sequel to *The Ewings*.
11 April 1970	Death of John O'Hara at "Linebrook."
28 February 1972	Publication of *The Ewings* by Random House.
23 November 1972	Publication of *The Time Element* by Random House.
16 August 1974	Publication of *Good Samaritan* by Random House.

I

"Tel Arbre, Tel Fruit"

o'hara, *John (Henry), author; b. Pottsville, Pa., Jan. 31, 1905; s. Patrick Henry (M.D.) and Katharine Elizabeth (Delaney) O'H.; grad. Niagara Prep Sch., Niagara Falls, N.Y., 1924; m. Belle Mulford Wylie, Dec. 3, 1937 (dec. Jan. 1954); 1 dau., Wylie Delaney (Mrs. Dennis J. D. Holahan); m. third, Katharine Barnes Bryan, January 31, 1955. Named hon. citizen City of Philadelphia, 1961. Mem. Nat. Inst. Arts and Letters, Loyal Legion (Pa. commandery), The Silurians, Sigma Delta Chi. Clubs: Nat. Golf Links of Am. (Southampton, L.I., N.Y.); Nassau (Princeton); Field (Quogue, L.I.); Century Assn., The Leash (N.Y.C.); Nat. Press (Washington), Racquet (Phila.); Kew-Teddington Observatory Society, Hessian Relief Society (both Princeton). Author: Appointment in Samarra (novel), 1934; The Doctor's Son and other Stories, 1935; Butterfield 8 (novel), 1935; Hope of Heaven (novel), 1938; Files on Parade (short stories), 1939; Pal Joey (short stories) 1940; Pipe Night (short stories), 1945; Hellbox (short stories), 1947; A Rage to Live (novel), 1949; The Farmers Hotel (novel), 1951; The Searching Sun (play), 1952; Sweet and Sour (essays), 1954; Ten North Frederick (novel), 1955; A Family Party (novella), 1956; From the Terrace (novel), 1958; Ourselves to Know (novel), 1960; Sermons and Soda-Water (3 novellas), 1960; Assembly (short stories), 1961; Five Plays, 1961; The Cape Cod Lighter (short stories), 1962; The Big Laugh (novel), 1962; Elizabeth Appleton (novel), 1963; The Hat on the Bed (short stories), 1963; The Horse Knows the Way (short stories), 1964; The Lockwood Concern (novel), 1965; writer libretto for mus. play Pal Joey, 1940, 52 (winner N.Y. Critics Circle and Donaldson awards, best musical, 1952); (essays) My Turn, 1966; (short stories) Waiting for Winter, 1966; (novel) The Instrument, 1967; And Other Stories (short stories), 1968. Recipient Nat. Book award for Ten North Frederick, 1956; Gold Medal Award of Merit, Am. Acad. Arts and Letters, 1964. Home: Linebrook, R.D. 2, Princeton, N.J. Office: care Random House, 457 Madison Av., N.Y.C.*

—*Who's Who in America*, 1970–1971

THUS the final entry for John O'Hara in a reference work he found endlessly interesting and useful. He read *Who's Who in America* the way a fundamentalist reads the Bible and once claimed to know all the people listed in it—or somebody who knew them. It is noteworthy that the entry for O'Hara, John (Henry)—which he had the opportunity to revise regularly—is not entirely reliable. It omits his first marriage and his newspaper and Hollywood work, but it includes a private joke: the Kew-Teddington Observatory and the Hessian Relief Society were "toy societies" created by O'Hara and a friend.[1]

John O'Hara never expected to make old bones and anticipated an early death during his entire maturity. Many of his friends recall announcements at various stages of his life that he expected to die soon. Certainly his sense of borrowed time spurred him during his period of greatest productivity after his ulcer hemorrhage in 1953. As an old newsman, in 1958 he took the trouble of supplying the *Herald Tribune*, the first New York paper he worked on, with a fact sheet for his obituary.[2]

O'HARA would call his part of the state "my Pennsylvania protectorate." Local people referred to it as "The Region"—probably as a short form for the anthracite region—which encompassed the area within a thirty-mile radius of Pottsville, including all of Schuylkill County and Lykens in Dauphin County.

Pottsville in the early years of the twentieth century was an unusually prosperous small city, for it was situated in the heart of the richest anthracite coal fields in the world ("The best site in the anthracite"). Coal was king until the 1925 miners' strike. Coal brought the railroads, and the largest coal-loading facilities in the world were outside Pottsville. The greatest financial—and political—power in Schuylkill County was exercised by the Philadelphia and Reading Coal and Iron Company, situated in an impressive building at the foot of Mahantongo Street. The "P&RC&I," or "The Coal & Iron," had been instrumental in breaking the Mollie Maguires, a terrorist Irish labor group, in the 1870's. The Girard estate held 18,000 acres of coal and timberland and was managed by Col. James Archbald, whose daughter Margaretta became John O'Hara's first great love. Another holding of coal and land and wealth was the Sheafer estate.

The population of Schuylkill County in 1920 was 217,745, of which Pottsville had 21,876. The total of all productions for the county that year was $162,000,000. The principal communities of the county were Shenandoah, Tamaqua (Tacqua in O'Hara's Lantenengo County) and Mahanoy City (pronounced "Mack-annoy"). Clustered around Pottsville were the towns of Minersville (Collieryville), Port Carbon, Schuylkill Haven (Swedish Haven), Mount Carbon, Frackville, Ashland, Palo Alto, Mechanicsville, St. Clair, Orwigsburg and Cressona (Fair Grounds). In addition to the towns, the county was pockmarked with patches—company shacks clustered around a mine. The miners drank hard. Saloons and roadhouses abounded before and during Prohibition. Some of the roadhouses were brothels—one of which actually called itself the Pussy Cafe—and brothels also operated openly in Pottsville.

17 April 1958

BIOGRAPHICAL MATERIAL ON JOHN O'HARA, AUTHOR

Born, January 31, 1905, Pottsville, Pa.; son of Mrs. Patrick Henry O'Hara and the late Dr. O'Hara. Oldest of eight children.

Graduated Niagara Preparatory School, Niagara Falls, N. Y., 1924.

Reporter, rewrite man, sportswriter on Pottsville Journal, Herald Tribune, Morning Telegraph, Daily Mirror, Time magazine, Editor & Publisher. Managing editor, Bulletin-Index, Pittsburgh, Pa. Drama and movie critic, Newsweek magazine. Columnist, Trenton, N. J., Times-Advertiser, with column called "Sweet & Sour" and for Collier's magazine "Appointment with O'Hara." Contributor of short stories to numerous magazines.

Author, beginning 1934, of Appointment in Samarra (novel); The Doctor' Son & Other Stories; Butterfield 8 (novel); Files on Parade (short stories); Hope of Heaven (novel); Pipe Night (short stories); Hellbox (short stories); Pal Joey (short stories); The Farmers Hotel (novel); A Rage to Live (novel); Sweet and Sour (essays); Ten North Frederick (novel); A Family Party (novella).

1940,
Wrote libretto of musical play Pal Joey, with score by Rodgers & Hart.
miss
married/Helen Ritchie Petit, of Brooklyn, 1931, divorced 1933; married miss Belle mulford Wylie, 1937, died 1954; married mrs. Katharine Barnes Bryan, 1955. One daughter, miss Wylie O'Hara.

Clubs: Century Assn., and The Leash; Nassau, Princeton; Racquet,Philadelphia; National Press, Washington, D. C.; The Beach, Santa Monica, Calif.; Field, Quogue, L. I.

Also member Authors Guild, Dramatists Guild, Writers Guild of America. The Silurians, Sigma Delta Chi. Elected to National Institute of Art and Letters, 1957. Received National Book Award for "most distinguished work of fiction in 1955" for Ten North Frederick, and Donaldson Award and Critics Circle Award for revival of musical play Pal Joey, 1952.

At present completing novel, From the Terrace, for 1958 publication.

Home, Pretty Brook Road, Princeton, N. J., and Quogue, Long Island.

John O'Hara

Obituary notes prepared by O'Hara for New York *Herald Tribune*.

Dr. Patrick Henry O'Hara at age forty-seven, 1915.

The gentry were of English or Welsh descent, and were Episcopalians or Presbyterians. There was a German or Pennsylvania-Dutch sub-aristocracy. The unskilled and dangerous work in the mines was done by the Irish, followed by waves of Polish, Lithuanian and Italian laborers. Schuylkill County voted Republican, and the two principal Pottsville newspapers—the *Republican* and the *Journal*—were firmly of that political persuasion.

Fortunes had been made in coal, and the well-off were cosmopolitan. Philadelphia was a hundred miles away and was served by frequent trains on both the Pennsylvania and Reading lines. There was a strong prep school contingent, as well as a sizable Ivy League delegation. The younger set prided itself on the fact that Pottsville was a great party town during the Christmas holidays. In an age of great and glamorous autos, Pottsville was a bit car-crazy. Besides Cadillacs, Packards and Pierce-Arrows, the streets were dotted with

Katharine Delaney O'Hara at age thirty-five, 1916.

Loziers, Stutzes, Marmons, Mercers, Jordans and Scripps-Booths.[3] It was a time when the rich did not feel guilty. Servants were cheap and plentiful. As the state trooper remarks in *A Rage to Live*, "These bastards know how to live."

THE MARRIAGE OF Dr. Patrick Henry O'Hara and Katharine Delaney at Our Lady Help of Christians Church in Lykens, Pennsylvania, on 18 November 1903, had the overtones of a royal wedding, for it joined two leading Irish-Catholic families in the anthracite region. The bride and groom were the children of self-made entrepreneurs in an area where the Irish-Catholics were mostly part of the laboring force in the mines. Lt. Michael O'Hara[4] had come to Shenandoah in Schuylkill County during the Civil War to marry well into the Franey family and set himself up in the livery, undertaking and construction businesses. His small empire eventually included a theater and a share of a circus, and he became Chief Burgess of Shenandoah. The Major— as he was called—was a teetotaler, having sworn off after a drunken escapade in which he injured a friend. One version of this incident is that he pinked the friend with a sword while celebrating their discharge from the army. When his son Martin was killed as a result of falling in front of a train while drunk, Michael O'Hara made Patrick take the pledge; and Patrick remained a permanent enemy of alcohol.[5]

Joseph Israel Delaney, a Protestant orphan raised by a family named Blum, owned a general store and lumberyard in Lykens, Dauphin County. He had been born Israel Delaney and could trace his roots to pre-Revolutionary settlers; when he converted to Catholicism at the age of fourteen he took the name Joseph. By the time of the Civil War he was in a position to send a substitute. He married Alice (Liza) Roarke.[6] A prosperous businessman, Delaney had risked bankruptcy by giving the coal miners credit during their 1902 strike. Although he became a member of the board of directors of the Miners Bank, his family believed that Masonic and anti-Catholic pressure blocked his election as bank president.

The O'Hara and Delaney families were both staunchly Catholic, and the prosperous fathers were able to provide their children with uncommonly good educations for that time. Patrick O'Hara, born in 1867 (possibly 1865),[7] attended Niagara University before taking his degree in medicine at the University (by which Pennsylvanians meant the University of Pennsylvania) in 1892. Katharine Delaney, born in 1880, was some thirteen years younger than her husband, which was considered a suitable age difference at that time. An O'Hara family tradition is that Patrick had chosen Katharine as his future wife when she was a girl and waited for her to reach a marriageable age. This report seems unlikely in view of the fact that she was twenty-three at the time of the wedding. She had been valedictorian at the Convent of the Sacred Heart, Eden Hall, in Torresdale, where she had excelled in French and music. The "Sacred Heart girls" considered themselves to be a sort of aristocracy within the Church. That she had studied piano with Zederhaly, a student of Franz Liszt, was a matter of family pride. It was Katharine's lifelong habit to attend Mass every day.

After practicing briefly in Shenandoah and for eighteen months in New Orleans, Dr. O'Hara settled in Pottsville, the seat of Schuylkill County, eleven miles from the Shenandoah, and enjoyed rapid success. He did not return to his hometown of Shenandoah because there was bad feeling in the family after the death of the Major—probably result-ing from the division of his estate. Dr. O'Hara had an almost Sicilian feeling about grudges, which he was later to pass on to his oldest son.

The Doctor soon made a reputation for integrity as superintendent of the Schuylkill County Alms House and Insane Asylum, a position he assumed in 1893, by canceling a kickback deal that had existed be-tween the institution and a local liquor dealer named Nichter. He gave up this position because his real professional interest was in surgery. At least once—in the summer of 1905—and perhaps twice, he went to Europe to study operating techniques,[8] and it was his custom to go to Philadelphia once a week to observe the great John B. Deaver operate. As a bachelor, he lived at the Pottsville Club on Mahantongo Street (pronounced "Mahan-tung-go" or "Mock-ann-tango"), and opened an office on Mahantongo, the best street in town. In 1896 he became the first resident surgeon at the Pottsville Hospital. Dr. O'Hara was regarded as the best surgeon in Pottsville, specializing in trephinings and other operations required by mining accidents. Eventually his reputation extended beyond Schuylkill County. Dr. O'Hara was among the first to use oxygen in pneumonia cases; he may have performed the first tracheotomy in America on his son Joseph, letting another doctor take the credit. Surgeons referred to "the O'Hara method" for gall bladder removal, a refinement of the operation to avoid excessive cutting. He was an intensely proud man who insisted on the respect due his profession. He dressed well, had a military bearing and lived by the gentleman's code. The concepts of honor, duty and pride regulated his life. At the same time he was impetuous—especially with money—and had a fierce temper.

He brought his bride to live over his office at 125 Mahantongo Street, in a building he had recently bought, and their first child, John Henry O'Hara, named for the Pottsville physician John Henry Swav-ing, was born there on 31 January 1905. It was said of Dr. O'Hara that the things he loved best were medicine, horses and Johnny-boy. The first-born is a miracle, especially when he is the son of a man who achieves fatherhood late in life. Although seven more children followed in fourteen years—Mary, Joseph, Martin, Thomas, James, Eugene, Kathleen—Johnny-boy was the Doctor's delight and later his despair. He was the one chosen to follow his father's calling. Dr. O'Hara had a religious feeling about his profession and assumed that his first-born would become a doctor. The children were trained to believe in the dignity of the medical profession, and the boys were required to tip their hats to priests and doctors—and whenever they passed a Catholic

Mahantongo Street, Pottsville. Birthplace of John O'Hara. At left, Dr. O'Hara's office at No. 125.

church. It is almost certain that the Doctor had dynastic ambitions. He talked about an O'Hara Brothers Polo Team, and he probably hoped for a flock of O'Hara doctors—perhaps an O'Hara Hospital. The Mayos had done it.

Dr. O'Hara was doing well. He earned probably about $25,000 a year, a good deal of money in those days, and believed in buying the best of everything for his family. He had a rule about traveling through life first-class. In 1913 he bought the Yuengling residence at 606 Mahantongo, an acquisition that brought particular satisfaction; the address inevitably generated jokes about "the magic bullet" and Salvarsan, since 606 was the formula number for the standard syphilis remedy at the time. The Yuenglings had the oldest family-owned brewery in America and were Pottsville aristocracy; their house at Number 606 had been modeled on a New York City town house. In moving to Sixth and Mahantongo and into the Yuengling house in 1916, Dr. O'Hara was literally improving his family's position. It is impossible to determine how early John became aware of the elements of social stratification, but only a dull boy could have missed the neat geography of caste and class in Pottsville: Mahantongo (Lantenengo in Gibbsville) was the best street, with upper-middle- and upper-class families; Norwegian Street (Christiana), one block away, was clearly middle- and lower-middle-class; and everything on the other side of the tracks was unfashionable, except for part of North George Street (North

Frederick). Indeed, there was even significance attached to where a family lived on Mahantongo.

Doctors' sons often think they are special. Their fathers have the power of life and death, and the children share in the respect that doctors enjoy. Even Dr. O'Hara's close friends—as well as his wife—addressed him as "Doctor" because he loathed both "Patrick" and "Pat." He kept the best horses—including five ponies for his children —and a small fleet of Buicks and Fords (to the dismay of John, who longed for more glamorous vehicles). He was quick with his fists; carried a pistol in his medical bag when necessary; could make himself understood in Italian (he was the only doctor in town who spoke that language), Pennsylvania Dutch, and Polish; and feared no man. In addition to the two buildings on Mahantongo Street, he acquired the 160-acre Oakland Farm near Cressona in the Panther Valley— about six miles from Pottsville—where he raised Jersey cattle and into which he poured money. His family summered there, and the Doctor's attempts to make it a model farm may have cost him $10,000 some years—to the wonder of the thrifty Pennsylvania Dutch neighboring farmers.

Doctor O'Hara was a man who generated legends. Convinced at the Dempsey-Willard fight, when he helped Jess Willard from the ring, that Jack Dempsey's hands were encased in plaster of Paris, he developed a hatred for the champion that prompted him to lose $1,000 on Carpentier in the 1921 Dempsey-Carpentier fight. (The Doctor's mood was not improved when he returned home after this fight to discover that sixteen-year-old John had taken out one of the cars without permission and dented a fender.)[9]

In white tie and tails Dr. O'Hara crawled under a trolley to treat an injured child. Katharine O'Hara's account, written up some forty years later, shows the memory for detail that impressed her oldest son:

"How vividly I recall awaiting the Mauch Chunk trolley, when the unmistakable clatter of a runaway horse, always startling, seemed more ominous than ever and, in an instant, that beautiful flaxen-curled child sat on the tracks at the wheels of the suddenly-stopped trolley.

"Less than a minute before, I had remarked at the loving looks of devotion that were exchanged as she gazed into the tall man's eyes. He seemed to idolize the little daughter. And then it happened. The Hay's horse, habitual runaway, stood by. The rest is as you told it. Someone said, 'Did you see Doc vault that railing?'

"I saw him on the ground and heard him shouting incriminations to all trolleys in the world, if a jack could not be found in that Miners-

ville car. (A few months before a man had died under a car because a jack was not available.) The trolley was commandeered and the rest you know.[10]

Later in his life, when he sometimes used two sets of glasses at once, he became involved in a traffic dispute with a teamster who called him a "four-eyed Irish bastard"; the Doctor knocked the man unconscious and left him in the street.

He established a model of personal conduct for his oldest son while less successfully apprenticing him to the realities of medical practice in the coal fields. From an early age John accompanied his father on calls, and the boy witnessed bloody accidents. Dr. O'Hara took his son with him when there was a train wreck at Molina Junction, where John held the hands of the dying because the nurses were busy. This exposure did not take. John threw up while watching one operation. Although he retained a lifelong respect for doctors, he just didn't want to study medicine.

John showed early verbal promise. He taught himself to read before he was four by working out newspaper headlines, and his parents delighted in his boast, "I know my letters up to ten." The annual Christmas gift of an English volume, *This Year's Book for Boys*, started his Anglophilia. "I took to reading, and writing, as the child Mozart took to music. When I was about six someone gave me a hand-printing set, and I had my introduction to moveable type."[11] His schooling began in Miss Katie Carpenter's private classes, not at parochial school. Miss Katie was a gifted teacher who was able to give her pupils a great deal of individual attention because the school had an enrollment of less than fifteen. John loved both the school and his teacher. He remained at Miss Katie's until, the story goes, his mother became disturbed by the fact that he knew more Protestant than Catholic hymns and transferred him to St. Patrick's School across from the O'Hara residence on Mahantongo Street. O'Hara later informed Charles Poore: "The O'Hara children did not go to Mrs. Thurlow's; we had gone to Miss Katie's, conducted by Miss Katie Carpenter, but Mrs. Thurlow did not take Catholics, even though they had been to Miss Katie's, a *much* sweller school."[12] In 1958 he acknowledged his affection for his first teacher in the dedication of *From the Terrace*: "*TO*: MISS KATIE CARPENTER/*GOD BLESS HER*." At St. Patrick's he had to overcome the initial handicap of being regarded as a "ristycrat" by his schoolmates; but he could take care of himself, for he was a fighter and had been given boxing lessons by his father's Negro hostler, Arthur Woodward. The records at St. Patrick's show that John O'Hara entered in 1910 and went through the eight grades of grammar school. (There is a discrepancy here, for he was only five years old in 1910 and had attended Miss Katie's School first.) At St. Patrick's Church, John was for a time a reluctant altar boy at 6 A.M. Mass, which raised his mother's hopes that she had produced a priest.

The Pottsville O'Haras were not on close terms with the Shenandoah branch of the family partly because the Doctor's sisters resented his choice of a wife; but Katharine's children were always welcome at the Delaney house in Lykens. Eugene Delaney, a mining engineer who had graduated from Notre Dame, was John's favorite uncle, and John was fond of his maiden aunt Verna, a good storyteller. The bearded patriarch, Joseph Israel Delaney, loved his grandson, who would describe him as "the nicest man that ever lived, bar none."[13] Grand-

Mr. and Mrs. Joseph I. Delaney with relatives at 635 North Main Street, Lykens.

mother Liza Delaney, a strong-willed woman, seems to have had her reservations about this grandson, however. John enjoyed his visits to the Delaney home at 635 N. Main Street, and particularly liked playing in his grandfather's store and lumberyard and accompanying the deliveryman Ambrose Bupp on his rounds punctuated by stops at the saloon. Some forty years later John could write about the Delaney general store with loving fidelity, remembering "the barrel of dill pickles and the Gail & Ax and the beautifully made chests of Number 50 cotton and the Hecker's catalogue-almanacs and the brass tacks for measuring muslin and the Dietz lanterns and the dried figs and sugar cocoanut (that I used to pretend was Miner's Extra chewing tobacco)." He remembered hearing "my grandfather tell a miner that Stiney now had enough money saved up so he could send to the Old Country for his woman" and "the sights I saw when I delivered groceries on Polish Row."[14] He subsequently re-created Lykens as Lyons in *Ourselves to Know* and affectionately pictured his grandfather as Jeremiah MacMahon.

John was probably driving for his father when he was twelve, and confirmed a taste for reading while waiting in the car between calls. The first writers who impressed him during his early teens were Owen Johnson, Ring Lardner, William Dean Howells, Booth Tarkington, F. Scott Fitzgerald and Sinclair Lewis. Johnson's Lawrenceville and Yale stories fostered his own dreams of prep school and college success; but Tarkington and Lardner impressed him with their technique. Even as a young reader, John worked out the principle that character is the most important element in successful fiction and that realistic characters depend on realistic speech. Fitzgerald introduced him to the glamorous and romantic worlds outside of Pottsville that John aspired to join. Writing about *This Side of Paradise* in 1945, he remarked: "I took the book to bed with me, and I still do, which is more than I can say of any girl I knew in 1920" (O'Hara was fifteen in 1920).[15] The author of *Main Street* was an influence on a budding social historian, a boy who noticed—and remembered—more things than other boys. His appetite for information was prodigious. Christian creeds, college life, jazz, fraternity rituals, railroads, cars and the details of social stratification were some of his particular interests.

Pottsville—like virtually all American towns fifty years ago—was full of "characters." It was a time when eccentricity flourished. John O'Hara encountered and remembered Eggy the Boy Engineer, who carefully dressed in excellent hand-me-downs; Violets, the Pottsville first-nighter and embezzler who killed himself; Dory Sands, the streetcleaner who ran for mayor; Schwartzy, a boy who was terrified of scissors; Jack Kantner, a drunk who was arrested so frequently that the jail became known as the Hotel Kantner.[16] Most children do not notice much; or, if they do, they do not retain it. There was a boy in Pottsville who would retain almost everything he saw.

One of John's boyhood friends was David Randall, the son of a mine superintendent in Minersville and Lykens. The boys once ran away by hopping a freight and got as far as Reading before they were returned home.* Randall, who became manager of the Scribner rare book department and then librarian of the Lilly Library at Indiana University, recalls Katharine O'Hara's interest in John's reports of his experiences. If John told her that he had quarreled with a companion over something that was said to him, Katharine would ask, "How did he say it?" Randall is convinced that John's ear for speech was partly trained by his mother, a view that John shared.

Careless or hostile critics have made the easy—but misleading—key to John O'Hara's career that he was a poor Mick who suffered a trauma or wound from his rejection by the rich Protestants and so used his work to get back at them. O'Hara attempted to rebut this theory about his deprived childhood in a 1962 letter to the New York *Herald Tribune*:

> *Well, my father did own five cars at the same time: three Buicks and two Fords. . . . the chief distinction of the farm was that we owned Noble of St. Mary's . . . a Jersey bull of good lineage. We also had four mules, a team of sorrels, a bay carriage horse, a black carriage horse, five ponies (two of them registered Shetlands) and, for me, a five gaited mare that my father purchased from the Kirby Horse Farm in Bowling Green, Kentucky.*
>
> *. . . my father was a member of the Pottsville Assembly (I never was; I attended the Assemblies, but I was never a member) . . . we had a family membership in the old Outdoor Club, which was a great deal more exclusive than its successor the Schuylkill Country Club. . . . I learned to read and write at Miss Katie's; I learned to dance at the Misses Linder's and at Miss Charlotte Brooks' and Miss Marie Hill's dancing classes. . . .*
>
> *Lay off, Sumps. In 1918, in a store on Chestnut Street in Philadelphia, my old man bought me a pair of riding boots for $55 and the first pair of wing-tip brogues I had ever seen, for $26.50. He paid cash, and we didn't have to thumb it home. That didn't last, but don't say it never happened.*[17]

---

* This was probably the source for Julian English's similar escapade in *Appointment in Samarra*.

When this statement appeared, some literary commentators interpreted it as clear evidence of John O'Hara's social trauma; his insistence on his family's possessions and his touchiness on the subject were regarded as demonstrating that although the O'Hara's had things, they were insecure about their position. But, clearly, any wounds young John O'Hara suffered were not financial.

The theory about John O'Hara's hatred for the upper crust of Pottsville is related to a contradictory interpretation of his career—that he compensated for his social deprivation by snobbishly identifying with the rich. This view holds that he claimed a bogus social status and manifested an unwarranted identification with the upper class in order to make up for his childhood sense of exclusion. All the biographical evidence goes counter to this interpretation. As a child John enjoyed a sense of security. Doctor O'Hara's family had everything that money could buy, and they believed that nobody was better than they were. There were obviously richer men in Pottsville, but they weren't *Doctor* O'Hara. That feeling did not last for John. His life began to go sour in his early teens, as his great expectations began to collapse. After his father died he suffered from a sense of failure, but by then he was in his twenties.

At this remove it is impossible to place the O'Haras accurately in the social hierarchy of Pottsville. The place to start such an inquiry is with the problem of how much anti-Catholic prejudice obtained in Pottsville during the first decades of this century. Pottsville today is at pains to assure visiting scholars that there was little or no such prejudice, but this claim is patently false. That Dr. O'Hara was referred to as "the Irish doctor" was probably something more than a convenient identification. His move from the Pottsville Hospital and his participation in the organization of the A. C. Milliken Hospital (now the Good Samaritan Hospital) almost certainly involved an element of religious bias. The Masons were powerful in The Region's business and politics, and the K.K.K. and its offshoots were active through the Twenties. Pottsville Catholics used the acronym APA for the American Protestant Association; it was a much stronger term than WASP, for the APA was thought to be an actual Protestant-supremacy organization. That the O'Haras were indisputably Irish and Catholic could not have been ignored by the "better element" for whom the Micks were drunken miners or homicidal Mollies or Democrats under orders from the Pope of Rome. Al Smith's religion was an issue in 1928, and before John F. Kennedy it was a commonplace remark that a Catholic could never be President. The narrator of *Butterfield 8*, the semi-autobiographical Jimmy Malloy, states: "Now it's taken me a little time to find this out, but I have at last discovered that there are not two kinds of Irishmen. There's only one kind. . . . I'm pretty God damn American, and therefore my brothers and sisters are, and yet we're not American. We're Micks, we're non-assimilable, we Micks."[18] The less prosperous Pottsville citizens, both Catholic and Protestant, no doubt resented the life style of the O'Haras—in particular, the arrogance of Dr. O'Hara's kid with his expensive mare and his fancy riding clothes.

Then there were all those children, which probably set the O'Haras apart from the planned families on Mahantongo Street.* John had little or no cause to be jealous of his brothers and sisters, for as the first-born he enjoyed special privileges. Nonetheless, it is often the case that the first-born resents his siblings, for each new child means a diminution of the attention he has received. John was not particularly close to his brothers and sisters, although he enjoyed his position as oldest boy and regarded himself as the head of the children. He took charge of them on outings, and he taught his brothers horsemanship. He showed Mart how to make a five-pony hitch and to drive the miniature Conestoga wagon the Doctor had ordered custom-built. John sought his closest friendships outside of the family, and a good deal of his time was devoted to solitary riding and to reading.

The enduring experiences an author draws upon for his work are almost always encountered before he is twenty, and frequently these are childhood experiences. He observes and develops for the rest of his life; but the great emotions to which he returns are the emotions of early youth. In the case of John O'Hara the biographer cannot point, as Edmund Wilson has done for Dickens and Hemingway, to a single traumatic experience like labor in a blacking factory or a war wound. But there are discernible patterns of experience in the youth of O'Hara that shaped his attitudes, the most important of which appear to be the conflicts with his father. As a child he enjoyed the position of daddy's boy, the favored son of a loved and feared father. But in his early teens he experienced a series of rejections by this authority figure and responded by behaving in ways that could only aggravate the problem. Father and son disappointed each other; and disappointment became resentment.

---

* John may have resented the population explosion in his family, for in a 1967 London speech he commented: "My father was a surgeon and presumably knew what caused babies, but it didn't seem to make much difference. In New York, by the way, there is a young and pretty actress who has six children, and when someone said to her that she must be either Catholic or a sex maniac, she replied that she was both. Like my father."[19]

Father and son were alike in many ways—both were stubborn and proud—which led to open conflict. As early as his fourteenth year John had rejected a career in medicine, for at this time he declined his father's offer to put $10,000 in the bank for him in return for a solemn promise to go to medical school. Things were never the same between them after that, and the story "It Must Have Been Spring" (1934) perfectly expresses the frustrations of a strong-willed father and son who love each other. The doctor-father in this story remarks that his son is the "best horseman in Eastern Pennsylvania"—a statement Dr. O'Hara made about John, adding "but apart from that he isn't worth a damn."[20] John compounded his father's disappointment by manifesting an early attachment to alcohol and tobacco, both of which the Doctor personally eschewed and professionally condemned. By the time he was sixteen, John was drinking and occasionally showing signs of intoxication. When he saw his father with a questionnaire from *Who's Who in America*, John was amazed to hear that the Doctor had no intention of filling it out. He boasted that he'd be in *Who's Who* before he was thirty, and his father replied that John would be dead before then. There were bitter conflicts as both refused to yield. Once Dr. O'Hara broke a chair over his son; another time, he knocked him down and kicked him. As his disappointment in John grew, the Doctor began to shift attention to his second son, Joseph—four years younger than John—who adored his father.

The spoiled relationship with his father was certainly not the only factor in John O'Hara's development into a writer. He was born sensitive—easily hurt and painfully aware of human cruelty. That he seemed both shy and arrogant during his adolescence and young manhood is an indication of his trying to find ways to deal with his acute awareness of the cruelties and injustices of human conduct. It is profitless to speculate about whether John O'Hara chose his material or if the material shaped him. The writer and his material coalesced in Pottsville, Schuylkill County, Pennsylvania, between 1905 and 1928. He would later find new subjects in the world outside of Pottsville, but his basic responses to life—his standards of judgment, as well as his major themes—were permanently established before he left The Region.

The volatility and occasional brutality of the father was mitigated by the remarkable mother. Katharine Delaney O'Hara had an excellent mind, in addition to her considerable ability as a pianist. She was well-read and witty, kind and devoted to her family. A gifted mimic, her accounts of the local Delphian Society meetings delighted her children and later yielded a series of *New Yorker* sketches for her son. The children admired and respected their father, but they loved their mother. She made it a musical household. Although he had an excellent ear and loved music, John escaped music lessons. He did, however, become a self-taught banjo player and a local authority on jazz. His instrument was the banjo-mandolin (a banjo tuned like a mandolin to carry the melody), with the Greek alphabet hand-lettered around the edge of the head. The O'Hara family, headed by well-matched, devoted parents, was very different from the family of Dr. C. E. Hemingway in Oak Park, Illinois, in which Ernest learned to hate his domineering mother and be ashamed of his weak father. John and Katharine O'Hara often seemed more like close friends than son and mother. They spent a great deal of time talking together: John particularly valued her recollections of The Region before his time, for Katharine was an accurate anecdotist. When she told a story, she included the details and imitated the speech of the people.

THE YEARS OF World War I were an exciting time for John. He and a friend wrecked the cabin of a German-American club on the theory that it was a hideout for spies. He rose from private to colonel in the Thrift Army by selling $1,000 worth of Thrift Stamps; and he won a spiked German helmet in a county-wide patriotic essay contest—and later lost it in a crap game at prep school. He also won a prize at St. Patrick's for the best drawing of an American flag. John was a confirmed night person by the time he was in his early teens. He liked to stay up late reading and writing in his top-floor room while consuming Uneeda Biscuits and drinking milk that had come from the Jersey cow Dr. O'Hara kept in town for his family. (In later life John credited his survival of ulcers and years of hard living to all the milk he had consumed as a boy.) His earliest writings are all lost, and there is no record of this self-apprenticeship except for family memory of a fanciful piece based on the wallpaper design in the house. In 1918 and 1919 came the great flu epidemics, which hit men with miners' lungs particularly hard. John's experiences driving his father during these epidemics later provided his first long story, "The Doctor's Son" (1934). Pottsville resembled a war zone as the armory and private residences were converted into emergency hospitals. Dr. O'Hara drugged himself with quinine and worked around the clock. When he finally collapsed, he had to sleep with a revolver to protect himself from hysterical men whose families were choking to death.

In later life O'Hara recognized that his awareness of death—both in his work and privately—seemed exaggerated to some observers. In

1961 he explained to William Maxwell, his editor at *The New Yorker*, that for a doctor's son in Pottsville death was a familiar occurrence:

I grew up one Christmas day, stopping to pick up the priest in my governess cart so that he could take Holy Viaticum to Stink Schweikert's father, who was lying on a railway track with a leg mashed off. I grew up when I had to take something, I don't remember what, to a Mrs. Murphy's house, a widow with one daughter a few years older than I, and I had to stand there and mutter to the girl, alone with her, and then a year or so later I heard that the girl had become a whore, but that day I was alone with the girl and her dead mother and I did not know what I was feeling till I got the same feeling reading DUBLINERS.[21]

The O'Hara boys were required to help take care of the livestock, for the horses and ponies had to be groomed every day. John never displayed any enthusiasm for physical labor, but Julia was his mare and he did most of the caring for her. He spent a great deal of time in the saddle and claimed that he could ride thirty-five miles a day—to which he attributed the back trouble from which he suffered in his later years. John was allowed to ride with Troop C of the Pennsylvania State Police and boasted that he once rode a horse that the troopers wouldn't mount. He played tennis and golf, but had little interest in playing team sports. Pottsville was the home of one of the early pro football teams, the Maroons, which he followed; and he was interested in college football, but probably more as an expression of his fascination with college life than as an indication of his pleasure in the game itself. Baseball did not particularly interest him, and he later remarked, "Don't go to a Jesuit school if you don't like baseball."[22]

John was far more interested in girls and jazz than in sports. These interests coalesced in dancing. At this time his three ambitions were to own a coonskin coat, have a Stutz Bearcat and lead his own jazz band—only the first of which he achieved. John had attended three private dancing classes and was an excellent dancer.[23] His first dancing partner was Augusta Yuengling, who came to take him to dancing class in her family's chauffeur-driven Lozier. Later, his favorite partners were Alexandrine Hill and Gladys Suender of Frackville (he called her "the Creole" because of her olive complexion and Spanish shawl). He was popular with girls who responded to his wit, but some found him sarcastic.

After he completed the academic program at St. Patrick's in 1918, John's parents felt that he was not ready to go away to school and he was greatly disappointed when they sent him back across the street to St. Patrick's for a commercial course—where he learned shorthand, which he never used. In the summer of 1920 he worked as a callboy for the Pennsylvania Railroad and "tied up the whole Sunbury Division" by failing to call several train crews. Then Dr. O'Hara decided to expose John to Jesuit discipline at Fordham Preparatory School in the Bronx. Moreover, because Katharine's sister, Mary McKee, lived in East Orange, New Jersey, John would have a place to go on weekends. Located on the campus of Fordham University, the prep school was largely populated by Irish boys, with a sprinkling of Italians and a few more exotic Latin types. Although the school had certain social pretensions—two of Al Smith's sons went there—it was a far cry from Owen Johnson's Lawrenceville stories. John knew it wasn't the real thing—the thing that led to a successful career at Yale.

O'Hara seems to have been a confirmed Yale man by the time he started prep school. In view of this lifetime preoccupation it would be interesting if one man or some special event triggered his Yalephilia, but that does not seem to have been the case. He selected Yale because in his youth it was the objective correlative for all the things he admired, which may be summed up in the word *class*. Harvard was

Fordham Preparatory School, 1921. O'Hara seated third row, second from right.

effete or intellectual; Princeton was agreeably social; but Yale represented power and an automatic assumption of privilege and style. It
was the best, and John was a boy who believed in the difference between first class and no class.

Fordham Prep had two graduations a year, and John entered with
the second class of 1924, in February 1920. The first night at Fordham
he was egged into fighting a boy named Tony Tessaro, an amateur
champion. John fought him to prove himself and "got the shit beaten
out of me." Classes met six days a week—with half-days on Wednesday and Saturday, a schedule that gave the students a chance to hit
the matinees at the local Keith, Loew's and Orpheum circuit theaters
which combined vaudeville and movies. The neighborhood had more-
or-less open beer saloons and speakeasies that catered to the collegians,
and John O'Hara may have started drinking in these places.

The Jesuit discipline did not take. The fathers regarded John as
willful, and he resisted their assumption of infallibility. Already a
waning Catholic, he lost his faith at Fordham: "The priests ruined it
for me." His resistance to discipline was compounded by his indifferent
academic performance. He earned passing grades for the 1920–21
academic year: Latin, 81%; English, 83%; ancient history, 66%; ele-
mentary algebra, 73%. But his grades for the first semester of his
second year (February–June 1921) were bad: Latin, 67%; English,
76%; English history, 59%; intermediate algebra, 49%; biology,
49%. Since 60% was the passing mark, he had failed three out of
five courses; and his transcript notes that he was "honorably dismissed." Although he later stated that he was president of his class,
none of John's locatable classmates has a clear memory of him. He
acted the role of constable in Lady Gregory's play *The Rising of the
Moon*; and he may have written for a mimeographed school publication called the *Ramkin*, of which no copy survives. He appears to
have felt the lure of The Great White Way and to have made for-
bidden visits to Manhattan nightspots, including the Pre Catalan, a
favorite resort of Ivy Leaguers. John was well known to the Prefect
of Discipline, Father Arthur Shea, S.J., who wrote to him after his
success and attempted to restore him to the Church.

The Doctor was predictably outraged by his son's failures at Fordham and kicked him when he came home with the dismissal notice.
A double punishment was decreed: a summer of physical labor
followed by enrollment at Keystone State Normal School at Kutztown,
about twenty-five miles from Pottsville. At sixteen John was big
enough for hard labor: he was six feet tall and had strong hands (perfect
hands for a surgeon, Dr. O'Hara lamented). The record of John's jobs

around Pottsville during the next years cannot be reconstructed with any certainty, but the summer of 1921 was probably when he had the filthy and dangerous job of greasing locomotives. Katharine O'Hara ordered her son to quit. Although the family anticipated an angry reaction from the Doctor, none followed.

Keystone State was a cruel punishment for a boy with a keen sense of class, and he warned his father that he'd be dismissed. It was a hick teachers college with a preparatory school department, both presided over by the all-powerful principal, Amos C. Rothermel, a man of great moral earnestness. Many of the students were day students, and the girls outnumbered the boys. John O'Hara was an exotic presence at Kutztown, more sophisticated and better dressed than the other students, most of them from small towns and farms, who were trying to qualify for a teaching license. He soon acquired a glamorous reputation. Because he wore an officer's cap and a blue suit, the story went around that he had been dismissed from Annapolis. Apparently "Jack," or "Doc" O'Hara allowed the story to stand uncorrected. Although he was not enrolled in the college program, he was elected to the Keystone Society, one of the two literary-social clubs. The other society was the Philomatheans, and forty years later O'Hara recorded the social distinctions that obtained at KSNS with the remark of a character in "All Tied Up" (1964): "Oh, how we hated those Keystones. They were full of Catholics, the Keystones. A Catholic couldn't get into Philo when I was there." With Robert Brown and Lee Eck he formed the "Jolly Trio," which gave jazz performances at Keystone meetings; O'Hara played the banjo-mandolin. He tried unsuccessfully to organize a football team and is said to have been one of the few students who had a full football outfit.

The people who liked him were impressed by his style and fund of information; others resented his assumption of superiority. Some of the "Dutch" students seem to have been annoyed by the confidence displayed by an Irish Catholic; but it is impossible to assess the extent of such prejudice, for some of it was a specific response to Jack O'Hara. One girl never forgot his remark that she and another girl reminded him of pink chiffon and blue velvet. Some of his classmates found him shy, but others regarded him as arrogant and sarcastic— terms that were applied to him all his life. He was reputedly a drinker, and his temper was explosive. On St. Patrick's Day 1922, his close friend Maurice Howell appeared with an orange peel on his lapel, which irritated O'Hara so much that a fistfight resulted. The faculty considered him a discipline problem. When, for example, Prof. Dietrich arrived at his chemistry class and discovered that his experiment setup had been tampered with, he rightly concluded that O'Hara was responsible. "Nobody could have done that except Jack O'Hara," he shouted in his Pennsylvania Dutch accent. "Get out!" Jack left the classroom without protest.

Keystone State did not permit open affection between male and female students, but John acquired a steady girl, Euphemia (Famie) Shumberger of Allentown. Some of his courtship had to be conducted in writing, and classmates were pressed into service carrying messages to her. One classmate recalls John as a perfect Joe College type, wearing a raccoon coat and driving Famie in one of the family cars he sometimes managed to bring to Kutztown.

Although the school had no publications except for its yearbook, *The Keystonia*, O'Hara is remembered by his classmates as showing intense interest in his theme-writing assignments. Apart from that, he manifested no commitment to his course work and is best remembered for his activities outside the classroom, which involved a great deal of conversation. He spent a lot of time at Dewey Hauck's restaurant in Kutztown, which was the closest thing to a student hangout, and also put in a good deal of time in the dormitory reception rooms —"holding court," as one alumna recalls. His academic performance was unexceptional. During the first semester of 1921–22 his grades were: chemistry, 52%; Cicero, 76%; plane geometry, 80%; zoology, 87%. The second semester was worse: Cicero, 60%; trigonometry, 54%; higher English, 70%; chemistry, 55%; plane geometry, 72%. When John was dismissed in June 1922, disciplinary as well as academic causes were involved, for he defied Principal Rothermel's orders to stay away from Famie, whose father was a trustee of the school. Rothermel may have announced John's dismissal in chapel. (O'Hara had his revenge in *From the Terrace* when he named the corrupt Tom Rothermel.) Once again Dr. O'Hara raged, and further punishment was devised. John would have to work for a year in order to qualify for a chance to attend Yale.

IN THE TWENTIES the famous bands made one-night stands all over The Region. The best dance spots were Lakewood Park and Lakeside Park, both near Mahanoy Plane, and Maher's in Shenandoah. Paul Whiteman's elaborate arrangements were considered the acme of jazz, and John, who shared this judgment, particularly admired the trick ending of "Stairway to Paradise." "When Hearts Are Young" (1922) was his "personal anthem." A greatly esteemed local band was the Scranton Sirens, featuring the Dorsey brothers from Mahanoy Plane and Jack Gallagher, a celebrated one-armed singer about whom John later wrote "The Pioneer Hep Cat." There were other dances at the country club, and at Pottsville's Hollyroof and Charlton Hall. The New Year's Assembly was the big dance of the year.[24] For the rest of his life he recalled the excitement of Christmas holidays with pleasure:

It was a rare night when we could drive without chains, and at the club dances there were frequent calls for hot water for frozen radiators. Most cars were roadsters or phaetons that needed side curtains and buffalo robes, and galoshes were a necessity for both sexes, not merely a collegiate affectation. The sounds of chains slapping and curtains flapping are as much a part of those Christmases as the rather prettier Do It Again and Lady of the Evening and When Hearts Are Young.[25]

The social system required that a boy belong to some set or group in order to be included in the fun—all the apparatus of arranging for transportation to dances and assuring an adequate supply of girls. John's closest friends were Ransloe Boone, the son of a Mahantongo Street doctor; Fred Hoefel, a roofing contractor's son (the senior Hoefel had a supply of pre-prohibition whiskey, which John and Fred raided); Deacon Deisher; Bob Root; and his best friend, Bob Simonds, the son of a school principal, also residing on Mahantongo. John was called "Doc" or "Johno." The group constituted itself "The Purity League"—an ironic reference to their shared interest in girls and alcohol. They liked to think of themselves as drinkers, and Doc was the most serious bottle man in the group. Their greatest prank occurred when they made a trip to New York during which they placed red lanterns and a traffic stanchion in the vestibule of Gen. Cornelius Vanderbilt's mansion at 640 Fifth Avenue. One Christmas Eve they deposited their empties on the porch of a Pottsville pillar of respectability for the early churchgoers to see. On another occasion Bob Simonds had a difficult time keeping an intoxicated Doc out of the hands of the law after he broke crockery in a local diner. At least once John did spend a night in jail sleeping off a drunk.[26] Although they were not the best crowd, the members of the Purity League were not a collection of outsiders banded together for mutual protection. They were rather self-consciously defiant—in contrast, say, to the imperious behavior of young aristocrats who confidently assume that whatever they do is right.

In 1922–23 Bob Simonds was a freshman at Dartmouth, and John wrote to him regularly during his own year of penance. A recurring subject was John's attempts to reorganize the Purity League into a drinking fraternity with key and constitution, a plan that never developed. John's letters between 1923 and 1927 are a record of his ambitions and disappointments—college plans and job prospects interspersed with plans for leaving home, ideas about working on a jungle plantation or joining the Foreign Legion. It is noteworthy that John, the prep school failure, was giving Simonds advice about his college career; and that nearly all of the work-travel plans required somebody from Pottsville going with him. These letters discuss writing, but there is little about books. John recommended Galsworthy's *In Chancery* and Christopher Morley's plays; but, surprisingly, he rejected Balzac and Charles Norris' naturalistic novel, *Brass.*[27]

There were several short-term jobs during 1922–23, including a period in the Philadelphia & Reading freight office. The best job from John's point of view was that of "evaluating engineering" with the J. G. White Engineering Co., which meant traveling around the coal region with a crew to take inventory at mines and power installations. This job kept him away from home and—since his meals were paid for by the company—allowed him to invest his $60-per-month salary in clothes. The work provided an excellent experience for a writer who would later be called "the Pottsville Boswell."

John began dating Margaretta Archbald in 1923, when he was eighteen. She was tall, had a memorable smile, was Protestant and four years older than John—having graduated from Bryn Mawr in 1921. Forty years later he would describe her as "one of the most attractive creatures that ever drew breath."[28] "Winter Dance" (1962) is a moving account of the early stages of their love: the prep school boy in this story has fallen for a college girl, which makes him a target for ridicule, but she treats him with kindness. The Archbalds lived at 1509 Mahantongo. Col. James Archbald, a Yale man, managed the Girard estate and was an elder in the Presbyterian Church. He could not have been pleased with the match, simply on the grounds that John had a reputation for wildness and no prospects. The speculation that Col. Archbald opposed his daughter's interest in this unlikely suitor because of religious bias seems unfounded. John's religion may have been a contributing factor, but it was no more than that.

A decade later, while he was working on *Appointment in Samarra,* John wrote to his brother Tom: "I kept a diary once, in 1922–23, and I'll never forget that year. That was a great year; I was home from school, between Kutztown and Niagara, and it was the first year Marg and I were in love. I haven't seen that diary for a long time, but I can remember movies, tunes, clothes, slang, parties—everything."[29]

In the spring of 1923, while Doctor O'Hara was threatening to cut off further funding for his first-born's education, John—with two prep school dismissals behind him—was planning his college career in letters to Simonds. He associated the college experience with success and recognition, for college was to be his first assault on the great world of power and prestige.

"When I get to college" I want to rate a good* national social, a drinking club, a minor varsity letter, varsity play, and "The Lit." I would also like to be a political boss. There's a peculiar attraction in politics for me. Perhaps in future years the wielding of my masterful pen will spell defeat for more than one seemingly likely candidate. (Opposing candidate, of course) I would like the minor letter to show to my son as he matriculates at my college: I crave athletics for the fun I get out of them. I don't deny that I'd not refuse a tennis or golf cup, but I start out by liking tremendously both sports. I would like the place in a play or something because of the trips involved. I would like "The Lit," because it's an honor and because I like "Lit," and the only sincerely unselfish feeling I'd have would be fraternity spirit (in its campus sense) All the other "points" I have spoken of are inspired by a motive purely for "me" and not "for the good of the college." Frankly, I think that stuff is horse-shit and the man who flaunts that flag to the breezes is either old Joe Athlete who is sure of his letters and gold footballs or he's Joe's brother, Tom Politician who for himself or one of his clique is sending thrills thru' the freshmen's spines and incidentally thereby getting said frosh vote. (I don't claim that Juniors and Seniors are immune to that applesauce.)[30]

In the fall of 1923 the Doctor, an alumnus of Niagara University, was able to get John accepted at the Niagara University Prep School, near Buffalo. Niagara was a far cry from Lawrenceville, but it was certainly an improvement over Kutztown. Since the prep school was on the campus of the college, John felt that he was at least in a grown-up world again. The atmosphere, however, was pious, and the discipline strict. Prayer meetings, novenas and retreats were regular features of campus life; and the college literary magazine, ominously called *The Index* (to which John did not contribute), ran to religious essays.

At Niagara John roomed in the O'Donohue Memorial. Almost every afternoon he took a solitary walk to the village of Lewiston, and sometimes he walked to Fort Niagara, where one of his father's former chauffeurs, Foxie Cole, was a sergeant.[31] This time the Doctor's plan succeeded—until the last day of the school year. Despite his apparent indifference to study, John performed brilliantly in his year at Niagara, achieving top grades in English and Spanish. He also began

---

* This eliminates Bus Suender & Brethren ΣN [O'Hara's note].

to enjoy some reputation as a writer, serving as sports correspondent and ghosting love letters for classmates; he remained indifferent to athletic competition, but he later claimed that fooling around in practice he once broke the school shot-put record. John's best friend at Niagara was a college student, Francis Beatty, who was preparing to enter the priesthood. Father Beatty recalls that "Jack did spend most of his time in my room, sitting on the window sill, smoking his everlasting pipe, devoting little time to studies. . . . His literary idol at that time too, was Clarence Budington Kelland.* To my recollection Kelland was the only author he ever lauded to the skies."[32]

The commencement program for the Niagara Prep class of 1924 lists John Henry O'Hara as Class Poet ("The Parting of the Ways") and Valedictorian and gives the title of his senior essay as "Damnation as Procrastination." Then came 15 June 1924, the night before graduation: a place in the Yale class of 1928 was within touching distance,†

NIAGARA UNIVERSITY, N. Y.
ACADEMIC DEPARTMENT

Graduation Exercises
Class of 1924
UNIVERSITY AUDITORIUM
June 16, 1924 at 8 P. M.

Class Motto
" Palma Non Sine Pulvere "
(I have gained the palm, but not without labor.)

Class Colors — Purple and White
Class Flower — White Carnation

Class Officers
President, James William Lowe
Vice-President, Bernard Thomas Lynch
Secretary, Gerald Edwin Madden
Treasurer, Thomas Andrew McCarthy
Testator, Roger John Howard
Poet, John Henry O'Hara
Toast Master, Gerald Joseph Howard

VERY REV. WM. E. KATZENBERGER, C. M.,
Presiding

Chorus of Class Song
Niagara we'll never forget you,
In memory we'll cherish your name;
The old scenes will rise up before us,
And thrill us again and again.
The days will seem years, since we left you,
We'll long for your friendship so true,
But though far away, still we'll love you,
Niagara our cherished N. U.

John O'Hara, John Meehan and Jim McPhillips at Niagara University, 1924.

* Kelland, the creator of Scattergood Baines, was a popular contributor to the slick magazines; however, he seems an unlikely idol for John O'Hara.

† It is not clear whether O'Hara had passed the Yale entrance exams and had actually been accepted.

and his proud parents were en route from Pottsville to see him receive his honors. Everything was sewed up, and John went celebrating with some friends. The details of this binge have become distorted, but they got hold of whiskey—possibly in Canada—and somewhere along the line encountered a couple of policemen who got drunk with them. John returned to campus early on commencement morning, his graduation suit muddied and torn, to be pulled in through a window by Frank Beatty. The Valedictorian-designate was awakened by a faculty member accompanied by a furious Dr. O'Hara. He was not allowed to graduate, and the Doctor did not let him return to Pottsville on the same train with his parents.

There was to be no Yale that fall. Dr. O'Hara decreed that John would again have to prove his seriousness by working for another year before going to college. There was another summer of odd jobs. Between 1920 and 1924 he worked as a freight agent, a soda jerk at Hodgson's drugstore, a meter reader, a switchboard operator, a railroad callboy, a steel mill laborer and a guard in an amusement park. In the fall of 1924 the Doctor surprisingly arranged a tryout for John as a cub reporter on the Pottsville *Journal*—exactly what his son wanted. If Dr. O'Hara still had any lingering hopes that John would study medicine, placing him on a newspaper was a blunder. Perhaps he had written off his oldest son as a wastrel, for John later said that his father never really talked to him after Niagara. It is possible, though, that Dr. O'Hara had formed the plan of letting the boy get a taste of real newspaper work so that the glamour would be destroyed. If so, the plan didn't work. John loved being a newspaperman.

The Doctor spoke to Harry Silliman, the publisher of the *Journal*, and John reported to 215 South Centre Street for a trial at no salary. After about a month he went on the payroll at $6 per week. The *Journal* is no longer being published, and there is no file or microfilm of the paper for 1924–26. John O'Hara's early newspaper work is lost, but his career on the *Journal* can be reconstructed from two of his feature articles. When the paper celebrated its hundredth anniversary on 2 May 1925, he wrote "A Cub Tells His Story." This article—the only surviving example of his *Journal* work—is about what would be expected from any twenty-year-old reporter with eight months on a small paper. It is overwritten and self-conscious. The recognizable O'Hara touches are the confidence (or boasting, as it probably seemed in 1925) and the interest in recognition, success and prizes. The pointed identification of F.P.A. "for the benefit of the uninformed" indicates that the cub had his eye on the big town and the big time.

Staff of *Journal*, 1925. General manager H. G. Rhoads and owner H. I. Sill-man seated. O'Hara's face visible between two girls at left.

A CUB TELLS HIS STORY

Soaked in the Atmosphere of the Office for a Time and Then
Went Out on Stories—Of Course He Will Write
Great American Novel

(By John O'Hara)

A desire to write should be the only real motive inspiring a young man to enter a newspaper office. A desire to write first became manifest in me when I was at the tender age of two.

I had tired one day of the philosophing and of the sedentary life one leads at that age; my philosophy had an insatiable craving for expression and when I found that the language which I spoke was either misunderstood or misinterpreted, I decided that I had perforce to express myself in some other way. My metier of expression had, as I have said, up to that time been oral. But on this memorable day I had seen that lady who had occasionally carried me around push a small piece of wood across a sheet of paper and I observed that wherever the wood had passed, there remained marks on the paper. Always, even at that age, one to experiment, as soon as the lady left the room, I crawled to the table and gained my objective, the piece of wood. Grasping it firmly in my powerful grip, I emulated the lady, but instead of paper I chose the spotless white wood work which ran along the bottom of the wall in my apartments.

This was my first attempt at writing and mine was the reward of genius, but at least and at last I had discovered a splendid method of expression.

Since that time I have gone into the matter more deeply. The handwriting on the wall has been supplanted by the Remington (advt.) on the paper. I have used, variously, pencils, pens, crayons, chalk and the typewriter—anything, in fact, that would follow my guiding hand. Whether or not I had anything to write mattered little: the thing was to write, for I have always loved it.

It was only logical, therefore, that as soon as I could after finishing school, I applied for a job on the newspaper of my choice. My only previous experience in the work had been at school where I was press correspondent of the athletic association. I had written a few things for the school paper and I had even received a rejection slip from Life to show for my contribution to American Humor. But on the whole, you will agree that I was raw material.

For a month after coming to The Journal I did very little writing. Mr. Silliman told me to come to the office and to allow the atmosphere to soak in. I had home-work assigned me: Mr. Silliman advised me to read the Bible and the works of Shakespeare because therein are contained the best models from which to learn newspaper style. At the office I did absorb much of the atmosphere and a few words on it will not be amiss.

The first thing I noticed about the office was that it almost came to my expectations which had been formed by seeing newspaper offices in the cinema. There was paper on the floor; the tobacco smoke was very much in evidence; the typewriters banged away like machine guns—especially Kit Bowman's.

After a day or two I noticed that the expression, "newspaper family," is not used indiscriminately. There really is a camaraderie in a newspaper office which is seldom found in, for example, a bank. Walter Farquhar and Ransloe Boone were the only members of the staff whom I had known before I came to The Journal, but it was not long before I was taken in and made by the rest of the staff to feel that I was one of them. There is a certain intangible informality about a staff room—an insouciance which is not found elsewhere. There is a certain large office in Pottsville which is called, even by the employes, "the school-room." Not so here; the work is done but not under military or pedagogical discipline. If Kit Bowman wants to tell the world our little world, about a book she has read, we need not fear that Mr. Yocum, the News Editor, will rap on his desk with a ruler;

if Walter wants to try a new nickname on someone, he need not fear a profane-not-the-temple-of-business elevation of the eyebrows; Curtis Sterner has his politics to talk about, and Percy Knowlton has such a wide range of interests, from orchestras to office-holding that he always has plenty to say. But I am getting a Nurmian lead on my story and a mile-wide digression from it.

After I was here for a very short time I was sent out on my first story. William DeWitt, of Port Carbon, had shot his father in defense of his mother. The first thing I was told by Mr. Kehoe, then News Editor, was, "Get the facts and get details." I hopped over to Port Carbon and proceeded to people who, I was told, were friends of The Journal. I managed to get about three versions of the shooting but finally I heard what I thought to be the true story. I called on teachers, business men and the doctor who had attended Mr. DeWitt before he died. From all these people I was able to get a fair amount of details, quite a large amount, I thought. I had been told not to see the immediate family as the boy had been taken to the state police barracks and later to prison, and it would have been futile to have tried to get a story from the wife and daughter of the dead man, for coherence is so often lacking after a shock of this kind.

I returned to the office and Mr. Kehoe told me that he would give me as much time as I wanted to write the story and that I was to bear in mind that a newspaper in a case like this simply records happenings, the actual events in order not to influence a jury. I finished the story after about four false starts and turned it in. I could hardly wait until four o'clock to see my first effort in print. I grabbed a first edition and lo! that it was, double-column and in the top center of the first page. I was highly elated until the next day when the Editor told me that the story was good, quite nice, but that it was lacking in sufficient detail. Even that did not detract entirely from my kick at knowing that at least the story was good enough to be printed, the damning faint praise notwithstanding.

The DeWitt story was my start. I have been writing everything except ads, editorials and stories having to do with political policy of the paper. Walter needed a man to help him in sports: I became that man. There was a hectic period. Inexperienced, Saturday found me covering a high school game; Sunday, a professional game; Sunday night, feverish pounding of the typewriter, trying to write a presentable account of the games I had seen. The worst part of writing football stories was the fact that my offerings appeared on the same page as Walter's. If they could have been printed on the woman's page they might have looked more like real football stories. As it was, they suffered by comparison, for they were separated from Walter's by only at the most, three columns.

"Approach" and "presence" are also required of tyros at this well-known "newspaper game," so I was given that box in the south-east corner of the first page, His First Job. There was a task for you— rather you than me, for frankly I did not like it. (Mr. Silliman told me when I started this that I was to tell the whole truth.) I suffer from an inferiority complex and because of this I never chose strangers to be subjects of, or subject to these intriguing write-ups. The daily agony continued until after numerous rebuffs and innumerable supposed humorous remarks, I became discouraged and told Mr. Kehoe that people do not want to have their first jobs printed for public view. I found that many people who are successful were, for the first time in their lives, overcome with modesty and reticence, while those who had not risen much higher than their first jobs did not like the fact broadcast.

Ransloe Boone relinquished for a time The Inquiring Reporter and I took it. This was a little easier for most people of intelligence have formed opinions on the questions which are asked and they are only too willing to answer. Within a month after I first took The Inquiring Reporter I was quite willing to have that star remain in Mr. Boone's crown.

Not a bad job at all is my present one, rewrite man. I read about fifteen papers every day and from them I glean juicy bits which might interest Pottsville people. In the course of my adventures in this job I have clipped enough bad breaks to allow F. P. A. to sit back and take a long, long rest. F. P. A., for the benefit of the uninformed, is the best columnist in the country, and the breaks I have clipped would furnish material aplenty for him to comment upon.

A lovely time was had by all when Mr. Silliman told us more or less rookies that we would collaborate on a Christmas story. At first it was right good fun, kidding each other about what part belonged to whom and why, if any. We spent no little time in conference, discussing the plot, the title and in deciding where each of us would start and end his part. The story appeared and with it the announcement that to anyone who was able to guess where each of us began and ended, five dollars would be given.

This collaborating is on the debit—or is it credit?—side of our ledgers if only for its value as experience. I have helped to write sketches for school papers and a vaudeville show, but never had I collaborated on a piece of fiction until "The Girl at Dryser's." The O. Henry Memorial Prize Committee apparently thought nothing of it.

And so it has gone. I have not been named as the twenty-year-old sensation for anything I have written in my brief career in journalism. My hopes were never quite as sanguine as that, but there is time. I have every hope of winning a Pulitzer Prize, and if I ever get to it, I intend to write The Great American Novel. Newspapermen are notorious in that respect, I have heard tell. The achievement of that *distinction is the ambition of them all, but somehow they never find the time.*

To my practiced eye, the foregoing paragraphs look like over 2000 words and that, as the old lady said, is the limit. This, you know, may one day be a valuable story. There's no telling how soon I'll be famous or notorious and if I should get on the front page, you, dear and patient reader, can go to your safe deposit box and finding your Anniversary edition, musingly say, "Hm, I suspected as much," or, "I knew he had the stuff in him." The striking likeness may come in handy, too.

And now look around and choose the nearest exit, for that's all until 2025.

Twenty-five years later the author of *Appointment in Samarra* and *A Rage to Live* wrote a memory piece for the *Journal*:

FAMOUS AUTHOR WRITES

OF HIS EARLY DAYS ON JOURNAL;

IS NOW BIG LITERARY FIGURE

One hundred years ago I was on The Journal when it celebrated its twenty-fifth anniversary. Or, to put it another way, twenty-five years ago I was on The Journal when it celebrated its one-hundredth anniversary. (I have just finished playing golf, and I am not at all ready to swear that it wasn't a century ago that I was a cub reporter.)

When I first went on The Journal I was almost entirely among strangers. It is one of the curious things about Pottsville that it was possible for me, a reasonably gregarious individual, with a fairly wide acquaintance in Schuylkill, Dauphin, and Carbon counties, to go to work on a newspaper and find that I knew well only three persons. But then my getting on The Journal was pretty strange in itself.

My father was not exactly bosom pals with Harry Silliman. They had had what may be referred to as their "differences." Nevertheless, when I indicated that I wanted to be a newspaper man and not a surgeon, my father spoke to Mr. Silliman—at a meeting of the Schuylkill County Fair directors, I believe it was—and I got a job. Pay: zero a week to start.

Ransloe Boone, my oldest and one of my best friends, already had a year's experience on the paper. Walter Southall Farquhar, who had not yet invented the sportitorial, was not a crony, but he was not an enemy. When Walter coached Pottsville High I used to ride out to Dolan's Park every afternoon (it's hard even for me to believe that I once owned a saddle horse), and every afternoon Coach Farquhar would call to me: "Get that blank-blank horse off the field." As against that, though, Walter and I had had many a shot together at the

Assembly and the club dances, so we were about even. My other friend when I went on the paper was Fran Keenan, who was prettier than Farquhar and Boone put together, which is not giving her any of the best of it.

The city editor in those days was Bill Kehoe, an easy-going fellow who caught me using the word protege when I meant cortege. Percy Knowlton, one of the most painstaking newsgatherers I ever knew, was the top reporter. Curt Sterner wrote and planned politics and policies. Bill Ent, always with a half pound of Imschweiler's home-made caramels in his pocket, covered the Court House. And Kit Bowman, who later married the man who had taught her English in high school, ran the Society page and wrote the guess-who sketches for the Saturday paper.

They were a wonderful group, professionally and as the friends they soon became. I never did get to know Kehoe, but from Percy I learned to respect A Fact, and to spell names correctly. Percy was a Mayflower descendant who augmented his income by playing cello in Seltzer's Orchestra and by getting elected to City Council, all of which adds up to a well-rounded man. Curt Sterner, who we were all sure had a million bucks stashed away, was correspondent for several Philadelphia papers, and from him I learned condensation (and padding, too). I also learned an invaluable simile: of a certain group of people he once said: "They're as immoral as flies." From Bill Ent I acquired a working cynicism about everything and everybody that in Bill's case—and possibly in my own—covered up an abundant sentimentality.

From Kit Bowman I learned the Charleston.

One wintry morning as Kit and Boone and I were leaving to go on our rounds, the editor said: "I know one thing about this paper. I'll bet it's the only paper that has three reporters that wear 'coonskin coats." It certainly was true that at nine-thirty every morning the three of us would depart together as though for a football game, but actually for Buehler's for The New York World, Hodgson's for a malted milk and pretzels, and thenceforth to the Centre Street stores and the other news sources.

One afternoon, after the paper had gone to press, the editor paid a surprise visit to our part of the building and discovered Boone and me taking lessons in the Charleston. The instructress was that esteemed Phi Beta Kappa from Mount Holyoke, Miss Catherine Davis Bowman. "For God's sake," said Silliman—and fled.

It wasn't all fun, of course. Newspaper men and women have more fun for a very obvious reason: if they didn't, they'd go crazy. It's an old and forgotten maxim that every piece of news hurts some-body. (Irvin Shrewsbury Cobb, not necessarily John O'Hara, although I'll go along with him most of the way.) The deeper meaning of the statement is that when an item of news is "nice" about somebody,

somebody else is hurt because it wasn't about him. But I could—and won't—tell you about covering a mining accident for The Journal. The bell rang, the signal that a car was coming up, presumably with the injured or dead. The car came up, and all that was on it was a foot, a human foot in a miner's Pac boot. Or another time when we got a tip that a murder had been committed "somewhere near Auburn" and Bud Rhoads and I took off in the Oakland coupe and "somewhere near Auburn" we came upon the body of a Negro, lying deep in a ditch. He had been murdered all right, with a knife, and it was a very hot day.

And somewhere between the fun and disaster, the sense and satisfaction of a job well done. I will say right here and now that I am pretty sore at Schuylkill Haven. I never have worked so hard in my life as when I covered the Schuylkill Haven celebration ever so long ago, all by myself. Heber Felix and Mel Bamford knew that, but I wasn't invited to the recent festivities. And I think the Pulitzer Prize people should have known that it was my stories—and the investigation behind them—that led to the proper punishment of the mobbies who set fire to Father Fleming's rectory in Mahanoy Plane. (Credit where credit's due: to help me in that investigation I had a friend, no longer in Pottsville and never a newspaper man, whose initials are R. T. S.)*

I parted company with The Journal in 1926, for the best possible reason. I had A Date; it was the lady's last night in town before taking a long trip. My Lutheran friends will forgive me, but I had the choice of covering a church supper or quitting the paper. If I remember correctly, and I usually do, the Rev. Emil Weber would have approved the decision I made. So the next day I was out of a job and on my triumphant way to the Tamaqua Courier, where I soon exhausted the patience of the Harris Brothers.

A small paragraph here about my friends the Messrs. Meredith and Stewart of the Courier, and Russ Green, of the Mahanoy City Record-American. Now, in 1950, I don't know what's happened to either one of them. Not even Nat Holman knew more about basketball than Bob Meredith. Stewart, who was an Older Man, would pay for my morning slugs of applejack when I didn't even have lunch money. Russ Green, who also was called Bob, was an alert, flip-cracking sports writer who didn't have to take any back-talk from any sports writer in the business. I like Red Smith, but he's no surprise to newspaper men who knew Don Skene and Bob Green.

---

* The arson case referred to in this article was the June 1926 burning of Holy Rosary Rectory at Mahanoy Plane in retaliation for Father Fleming's denunciation of the Tilly-Billy brothel. A detailed account of the case in the Tamaqua *Courier* ("Ask New Trial in Arson Case," 7 February 1927) may have been written by O'Hara. When the story broke in 1926 John enlisted the aid of Bob Simonds in covering it and believed that his efforts had something to do with the prosecution of the arsonists.

In the years after the Harris brothers gave me my walking papers, I found employment—however brief—on the New York Herald Tribune, Time magazine, Editor & Publisher, the New York Daily Mirror, The Morning Telegraph (twice, yet!), Newsweek magazine, The New York Journal-American, and International News Service. (If I have slighted anybody, it's deliberate.) I have seen the color of the money of The Brooklyn Eagle, The New York Times, the Pittsburgh Bulletin-Index, the London Express, and most of the major magazines. I have seen things I wrote appear in alphabets that did not include 26 characters. Professionally, I have had an interesting career, which began across the street from Joe Nichter's and Mootz's. Joe Nichter, with his Pierce-Arrow, and Mootz's with those butter creams.

Right now, what is most interesting to me is another line of endeavor. I am wondering. Clint Sheafer with those iron shots. Dr. Boord's putting. Jack Pepper's drives. Mr. Frank Rosebery's hit-and-run technique. Dan Slattery and his short game. Bert Knittle and his Bulger Brassie. Jimmy Schroeder and his take-two-and-hit-to-right. Bill McQuail and his 2-iron. Not to mention the ladies, most of whom came from Frackville.

If there is any piece of advice that I may impart to the youth of Schuylkill County it is this: keep your eye on the ball, and take it easy.

As a matter of fact, the best advice to the youth and age of the world is: take it easy.

Easy may do it.

But I doubt it.[33]

John's *Journal* salary was eventually raised to $25 per week, and in addition to straight news coverage he filled in where needed. He also wrote a weekly feature story. The *Journal* was an afternoon paper —causing John trouble because he always found it difficult to function in the morning—and one chore was to phone around the county for leads (forty-eight calls twice a day). In this way be became friendly with Russ Green of the Mahanoy City *Record-American* fifteen miles away, as obituary items yielded to conversation about Franklin P. Adams and Heywood Broun of the *World*. Friday was payday, and Green and O'Hara began meeting Friday nights to drink beer—usually at Maher's in Shenandoah. Green was impressed by the attention John paid to what was going on around them and by the fact that his observations were uncommonly acute. On occasion John was taken with drink; once Green had to deal with him when he lurched across the dance floor waving a condom. Green had the impression that John was deliberately storing up material in his saloon sessions.[34] Another drinking companion, Bob Simonds, was rebuked for not paying attention to what went on in saloons: "These people are real," John said.

During the busy football season John was assigned to help sports editor Walter Farquhar. A Pottsville institution who wrote for the *Journal* and the *Republican* for more than fifty years, Farquhar was probably the first person to recognize John O'Hara's literary promise. He nursed John through his outbursts or sulks and encouraged him to leave Pottsville. "Walter Farquhar knew what the rest of us didn't," Russ Green admits. The high school football games were important news, but the big football story was the Pottsville Maroons. O'Hara sometimes went on the road with Farquhar, and once they wrote their stories of a wet game sitting in their underwear in the Providence Biltmore while their clothes were being dried. The *Journal* was not generous with by-lines, so it was an exciting day when John received his first for a story on the Maroons. Under Farquhar he became a serious football fan, and the two men prepared elaborate charts of the Maroon games for the coach. Another tutor at the *Journal* was Fred Hohman, a compositor who gave John lessons about type that he always remembered.

Better at feature writing than straight news, John wrote two articles that were noticed and remembered by Pottsvillians: an account of the closing of Hodgson's drugstore and an imaginative piece about a day the sun didn't rise, which compared the effect to the darkness of a mine. His favorite assignment was his own column, "After Four O'Clock," which began on 2 April 1925. An imitation of "The Conning Tower," it was so titled because it was written after the presses rolled. This column was signed "Trewq"—the five letters on the upper left of a typewriter keyboard. John received no extra pay for the column, but he loved it. Indeed, he conceived the idea of expanding it county-

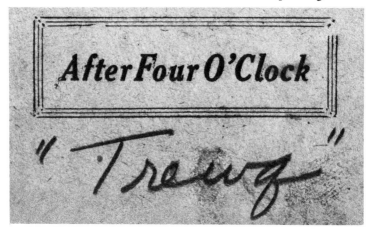

Proof of O'Hara's first column in *Journal*, 2 April 1925.

wide and unsuccessfully tried to enlist Farquhar and Green in the
project. John was intensely proud of "After Four O'Clock." Green
recalls:

I remember him gloating once. He had a sharp observation on a na-
tional item, and F.P.A. had it practically word for word in the next
morning's World. *O'Hara promptly crowed, in his column, that he*
had it first. I said, "What the hell, John. You had a P.M. edition crack
at it; F.P.A. couldn't go until the next morning": He drew himself
up—the only time I ever remember him angry with me—his eyes closed
into slits, and he practically hissed at me—"Well, goddammit, I was in
print first."[35]

The effect of newspaper training on future novelists has been
widely argued, but O'Hara felt that the discipline was valuable: "It
teaches economy of words. It makes you write faster. When you're on
rewrite as I was, you can't fool around at half-past nine trying to
write beautiful lacy prose."[36]

In the winter of 1924–25 Dr. O'Hara, now fifty-seven, was showing
signs of fatigue. The barber who shaved him every morning told John
that his father was falling asleep in the chair and that his skin didn't
feel right. In early March 1925 the Doctor took a Florida vacation, but
he wired that he was returning on the twelfth.

About twenty-five years ago a man got off a Pullman car in a
small town in Pennsylvania. He was wearing a polo coat and a tweed
cap and he was accompanied by a porter. I had a small roadster waiting
at the station, and when I saw the man I went to him and kissed him
because he was my father.
    I took him by the hand and led him to the little car and drove him
home. I got him upstairs and helped him undress—he had no luggage
on the train—and put him to bed. In a week's time, less one day, he
died.
    What he died from was overwork.[37]

Joe O'Hara recalls that he went with John to the station and that their
father made John ride home on the running board because the car
was crowded.
    Dr. Patrick O'Hara died of Bright's disease at 606 Mahantongo
Street at 1 a.m., 18 March 1925. He knew he was dying, of course.
During his final days he warned John that he had a lung spot, which
later worried John and increased his sense of impending death. The

Doctor's last words to his oldest son were "Poor John." The night his father died John went to the Alco restaurant on Centre Street, where he overheard a Pottsville doctor comment on Dr. O'Hara's death: "Well, he wasn't much good anymore." John knocked him down. The funeral at St. Patrick's was "as big as a politician's." More than twenty priests were present, and forty cars were in the cortege.[38]

Dr. O'Hara died intestate. His estate was appraised at $49,649.60:

125 Mahantongo	*$10,000*
stable	*250*
606 Mahantongo	*8,000*
2 tenements	*6,000*
farm	*3,500*
cash, investments &	
personal property	*21,899.60*
	$49,649.60

He left no insurance, and had less than $1,000 in the bank. A $1,500 trust fund had been established for each of the eight children. There was a safe-deposit box full of worthless German marks that the Doctor believed would come back. Patients owed him a great deal of money —perhaps as much as $60,000—but patients didn't pay dead doctors. Under the laws of Pennsylvania one-third of the estate of people dying intestate went to the State, which consumed the securities and ready cash. Since all of the children were minors, they became wards of the orphans' court, and their shares of the estate were held in trust by the Berks County Trust Company in Reading—which failed during the Depression. Katharine had something of her own ("Delaney money," possibly $60,000, which her husband had refused to touch), but this was also lost when the Lykens bank failed. The farm had to be sold; the horses and ponies went; all the cars except one Buick went. Santa Claus was dead. The O'Hara family went from prosperity to genteel poverty—if not overnight, then in the course of months. It takes time for a family to realize that it is in reduced circumstances, so for a while the O'Haras continued to live in something like their usual style.

John, the oldest child at twenty, took little responsibility for the family finances. His salary on the *Journal* was probably never more than $25, and most of that went for alcohol and gasoline. Katharine Delaney O'Hara—with her staunch religious faith and her own resources of character—coped. She managed the income-producing tenements, with the help of Joe and Mart. Somehow she kept the house

O'Hara family after death of Dr. O'Hara in 1925. Standing: Thomas, Martin, John, Joseph. Seated: Eugene, Mrs. O'Hara, Mary, James. Kathleen in front.

at 606 Mahantongo and provided for the children. Her father and brother Eugene were dead; and the O'Hara side did little beyond disposing of the livestock. Eventually the struggle to provide for and educate the younger children became grim, as dollars and quarters began to matter.

The attitude of mixed defiance and pride of the O'Hara children after the Doctor's death is illustrated by an anecdote about Mart O'Hara, a football star at Pottsville High School. After scoring a touchdown in a grudge game against Minersville he ran along the Minersville side of the field thumbing his nose and yelled, "And that goes for your Polack priests, too!" He was removed from the game, but his brothers were delighted.

John O'Hara later claimed that the death of his father and the consequent alteration in family finances put an end to his ambitions for entering Yale in the fall of 1925. In view of his permanent disappointment and concomitant fascination with Yale, the matter deserves exploration. If he had in fact passed the entrance exams, John could have gone to New Haven. His brother Tom later attended Brown during the Depression, and Jimmy attended Lafayette. John could have attended Yale, but he obviously could not have attended in the style he aspired to. He was not an Alger hero. It wouldn't have been the real thing to be a bursary boy who waited on tables while the gentlemen browsed at J. Press and danced at the Fence Club. It had to be the right way or not at all.

Margaretta Archbald at Bryn Mawr, 1921.

Moreover, John liked being a newspaperman and he knew what he wanted to do with his life: he was going to be a writer. Perhaps the attractions that New Haven had held for an eighteen-year-old boy were not the same for a twenty-year-old reporter who knew where the bodies were buried. Moreover, he wanted to marry Margaretta Archbald, and four years at New Haven would delay the marriage.

After graduation from Bryn Mawr (a number of O'Hara characters would go there, including Caroline English), Marg taught at an Indian school in Montana and was in and out of Pottsville between secretarial jobs in Philadelphia and New York. It took John at least a decade to get over Marg. He talked to her or wrote her almost daily between 1923 and 1931. The decision against marriage was Marg's, and it was made on the basis of John's drinking and ungovernable temper—not because of religion,* money or age difference.[39]

The three years in Pottsville after his father's death were a bad time for John. The family was in trouble; even if he was not disposed to help, he was nonetheless keenly aware of his failure to do so. He was in love and couldn't marry the girl—or the girl wouldn't marry him. His local reputation was rapidly deteriorating: "dirty-neck and dirty-mouth O'Hara"; "Dr. O'Hara's good-for-nothing kid, the one that got thrown out of all the schools." Probably worst of all, he wasn't realizing his ambitions. Despite his apparent irresponsibility, he knew he was at a dead end. His ambitions went beyond the *Journal*. Although his newspaper job had become routine, it nonetheless provided freedom, material and the start of a point of view. He was serving an apprenticeship as a social historian—a term he later became disaffected with when it was too freely applied to his work. John was well acquainted with the underworld of the county. He sought employment from the leading bootlegger, Marc Antonio Mosolino (Tony Moss), but was told: "You're too good for this. Go out and get yourself a job and stay away from me."† He was known at the roadhouses, such as the Log Cabin and Amber Lantern (which was also called the Stagecoach) near the Lakewood and Lakeside dance pavilions. He was a regular at Rap Cardin's speakeasy, corner of Mahantongo and Centre, and at the Plaza Cafe, where there was a prominent-eared counterman dubbed "Loving Cup" who would later appear as a character in

* Marg's sister Sarah became a Catholic convert and joined the Order of the Holy Child.

† There are two reports of this encounter, both of which derive from John O'Hara. The other version is that Mosolino offered him a job selling liquor at the country club dances, and that O'Hara turned it down.

43

Appointment in Samarra. One night in 1926 John O'Hara sang "Jazz Me" with the legendary Jack Gallagher in Duffy's saloon, corner of Logan and Norwegian. Jimmy Malloy, the narrator of "Fatimas and Kisses" (1966), remarks that as a young reporter he had the capacity to drink large quantities of alcohol without getting drunk, which was not true of his creator. John was regarded as a difficult drinker at a time when inebriety was a national pastime.

The richest young man in Pottsville was Clinton Whitcomb Sheafer, the heir to a coal and land fortune whom John later dubbed "the local Jock Whitney." The Sheafer counting house was an imposing building at 325 South Centre Street. Clint Sheafer was a Williams graduate with considerable charm and an aristocratic confidence. John envied his popularity and the life style which his wealth permitted. Sheafer had a private squash court, liked to drink, drove Mercers and Marmons. He would keep a dance going by paying the musicians to work overtime or would move the band to his own home. He also owned the Dodge agency and once threw a drink in Bill McQuail's face. McQuail, a successful Irish coal operator, was active at the Schuylkill Country Club. Although the O'Haras could not afford to maintain their membership after the Doctor's death, John seems to have continued to regard himself as a member of the club. On one occasion when he crashed a club dance McQuail told him to leave. These events were remembered by Pottsville readers when *Appointment in Samarra* was published in 1934. The recognition of McQuail as the model for Harry Reilly was automatic; however, the identification of Clint Sheafer with Julian English was inaccurate. There were certain obvious connections between English and Sheafer, but Whit Hofman is the character based on Clinton Whitcomb Sheafer—as the name echo indicates.

WHILE HE WAS on the *Journal* John was writing free-lance material and corresponding with magazine editors, but none of his work was accepted. His attitude toward his *Journal* job had become less than satisfactory to his employers in 1926. When sent to interview Gus Luckenbill, a local weather prophet who employed a goose bone, John returned with the explanation that he couldn't find the man. This act of irresponsibility coming on top of his record of tardiness and insubordination resulted in his dismissal by managing editor David Yocum. After a couple of weeks of unsuccessfully trying to catch on with another paper in the area, John asked to be taken back by the *Journal* and promised to mend his ways. He lasted two weeks before failing to cover a Lutheran church supper on Margaretta Archbald's last night in town, late in 1926. This time he was permanently fired. From the *Journal* he went to the Tamaqua *Courier*, thirteen miles to the northeast. The circumstances of this transfer are now obscure, but one version is that Harry Silliman arranged for John Harris of the *Courier* to hire John because he felt sorry for Mrs. O'Hara.

John started on the *Courier* in the first week of January 1927 at $23, and the pay ledger notes that he was "laid off" on 19 March. There were no by-lines on the *Courier*. John Harris' daughter remembers that he fired O'Hara partly because of the reporter's outspoken support of the Democrats (Al Smith was preparing to run for the Presidency) on a Republican paper, and the same thing is said about his troubles on the *Journal*. Whatever the particular cause was, Harris seems to have had a variety of good reasons to choose from. John's work was good—when he did it—but for part of the time he was commuting to Tamaqua by trolley and arriving late, hung over, or both.

During this period of failure John "got a girl in trouble." She was a Shenandoah girl, and although the matter was kept quiet, some people knew about it. John sought Bob Simonds' advice, and he borrowed $500 from his brother Joe to pay for an abortion in Philadelphia. John did not feel consuming guilt over this pregnancy, but it added to his sense of failure and confirmed his determination to get out of The Region.

After his separation from the Tamaqua *Courier* in March 1927, John tried to catch on with two new magazines, *Time* and *The New Yorker*, working through the Placement Service of the Yale Club of New York, probably with the help of Col. Archbald. At this time he was also trying to sell free-lance articles and offered *Scribner's* magazine a piece on why he was casting his first vote for Al Smith. He was also contributing items to "The Conning Tower," his first known appearance being: "As our about-to-be-assembled book will be compiled from Tower clippings, it is Mr. John O'Hara's suggestion that it be called 'Files on Parade'" (New York *World*, 17 March 1927). F.P.A. did not use this title, but O'Hara saved it for his own use in 1939. O'Hara's first real contribution to the column was a punning letter that appeared on 16 June 1927, when F.P.A. printed "From the Tower's Attention-Caller," a group of jokes and puns. It was a great event for O'Hara because the column had a large following. "The Conning Tower" enjoyed unusual prestige, and successful writers took pleasure in donating items to it. After he crashed the column O'Hara became a steady contributor, with seven appearances in 1927—some of which can be said to adumbrate his later work. On 13 December 1927, F.P.A. used a 500-word imitation of Sinclair Lewis:

A SPEECH BY GEORGE F. GABBITRY AT A CHRISTMAS PARTY, DELIVERED AT,
LET US SAY, SCOTT HIGH, TOLEDO, BEFORE THE ENTIRE SCHOOL

Well boysangirls, or praps I should say young ladies and gentlemen, your principal has asked me to say a few words to you on the Christmas speert. I accepted with uh alacrity, alacrity, I'll tell you, because it isn't often we business men would refuse the opporchunity to address such an intelligent body of clean-cut young men and charming young ladies.

Before I go any further I would ask you to indulge me for a few moments while I tell you a humorous little joke which I heard only a few days ago. It was told to me by the President of a big concern which has branches in Chicago, Illinois; Kansas City, Missouri; Boston, Mass.; Missoula, Montana; Pittsburgh, P A and numerous other cities throughout the globe. This story illustrates the speert of cawoperation, on which, upon which all the basic principles and fundamental conceptions of modern day business is founded.

To get on with the story, then. Seems there was a band concert being given at one of the many public parks scattered throughout the length and breadth of this country. Now it happened there was a rude fellow, a lout, probly a radical at that, in the audience. This fellow apparently didn't like the way one of the musicians was playing so he stood up on his feet and shouted, "My Go- my stars, that piccolo player is awful!"

One of the other musicians heard this outcry and he too stood up and said, "That was no piccolo player, that was my fife."

Now that story may amuse you, but I wonder how many you young people see the underlying meaning in the little anecdote. In other words, how many you young people can see that it was cawoperation and nothing else that made that rude fellow look ridiculous in the eyes of his fellow men? How many you young people reelize that it was what we call in this season the true, sincere Christmas speert? For my dear friends the Christmas speert is nothing but another name for cawoperation. And that statement includes those of you young ladies and gentlemen who come from the Jewish denomination. We have a rabbi in our Boosters' Club and he enners into the Christmas speert with the same vigor and zeal and energy and vim and inthusiasm that we of his brothers do. Tolerance, madear young people, is cawoperation, and we who are out in the world, fighting the battle of existence day after day, reelize the value of tolerance and cawoperation, in short, madear young people, the Christmas speert.

I know you are all anxious ahum to return to your classrooms and get to your studies so I will keep you only a few seconds longer.

And any time you are in the shopping districk doing your shopping don't hesitate to drop in and see me. Just innerduce yourself and I will be glad to drop whatever work I am doing at the time and talk with you. In closing I wanna thank your principal for asking me to address you young folks and I also wanna thank you, madear young people, for listening to the humble words of an old codger like myself.

JOHN H. O'HARA

It is not parody, for O'Hara did not burlesque Lewis; rather, he borrowed George F. Babbitt in order to write like Sinclair Lewis. The piece attracted attention and so impressed James M. Cain, who was editing the *World* editorial page, that he reprinted it in the paper's Christmas Day issue. O'Hara brought back Gabbitry twice again in 1928 with "George F. Gabbitry Stops a Little Early for the Wife at Her Literary Club Meeting" (12 January) and "George F. Gabbitry Settles Once and For All the Democratic Situation—If Any" (13 March). Between these two pieces O'Hara further acknowledged Lewis' influence with "The Man Who Knew Sinclair Lewis" (27 January).

He probably had some temporary jobs in spring 1927 before making his first trip abroad as a waiter on the U.S. Lines *George Washington* in July. This job was arranged by his Uncle Jack McKee (Mary Delaney's husband), who was with the Immigration Service. John had hoped for a wet ship or at least a glamorous dry ship. The *George Washington* was dry and stodgy; a waiter in the third-class dining room did not encounter interesting people or receive generous tips from passengers paying $87.50 fare. His first sight of Europe came at Cóbh as he unloaded laundry bags—a fact John O'Hara recalled with satisfaction in 1965 when he watched his Rolls-Royce being loaded on the *Sylvania* at that port. The last port-of-call for the ship was Bremerhaven, where John was beaten up in a brawl at the Rotesan bar. John was back in Pottsville in August and unsuccessfully trying to obtain the job of assistant purser on the *Leviathan*.

In October 1927 John finally decided to leave Pottsville, bumming his way west looking for newspaper jobs. He reported to Bob Simonds from Ohio:

Well, I've made the break, as you see. When you didn't phone Friday night I definitely decided to go to State with Root. . . . I went with him Saturday, loafed around and left Monday, yesterday.

*Got to Pittsburgh, 160 miles from State, on one ride and immediately
made for Carnegie Tech and Ned Dolan. I left State with six bucks,
of which I now have three. On the morrow I leave for Columbus.
There I'm going to try to get a job. I'll save some (if I get said job)
then hit for Chicago and another job, then points South or West,
depending on how much dough I'll have by that time. My ultimate
aim is Missoula, Montana and I'm going to try to make the Mardi Gras
in New Orleans in February. I know how tough the going will be, but
it will be only physical and not the mental torture I've been entertaining? since I came back from Europe and previous to that jaunt.*

*I have with me only the clothes on my back, shaving kit and one
toothbrush and a towel. I also have a Penn State banner for my back,
which is wet,* of course, but helps with the rides no end.*[40]

There was no newspaper job in Columbus; when he was turned away
by the Salvation Army, a priest got him a meal and a hotel room. In
Herrin, Illinois, the police thought John was a strikebreaker and put
him up for a night in jail before escorting him to the city limits.
Chicago had no newspaper jobs for him, but sympathetic journalists
gave him a few dollars. He lived in a flophouse at 600 West Madison
Street, on skid row. (Some twenty-seven years later John O'Hara
took his daughter by limousine from the Ambassador East to see this
rundown hotel.) Hungry, he tried for a job as a groom, but was turned
down because he was wearing a Brooks Brothers suit.

Chicago was so discouraging that John abandoned his plans for
the West or South. His western destination had been Missoula,
Montana, and it is probable that Marg Archbald was there. He
bummed his way home, and in November 1927 was back in Pottsville
after six weeks, looking for another sea job. "Anything but a whale-
boat and any job but coal-passer. (Birsie Richards passed coal for
eight hours in one stretch, when usually they don't work more than
four.)" His unofficial engagement to Marg had been broken, and John's
prevailing mood was despair. "At my present rate I'll end up in a
joint in Tia Juana with a bullet in my left ventricle. And when that
time comes you'll know that someone else did what I haven't the
courage to do myself."[41] Later in 1927 he wrote again to Simonds: "I
simply must get out of Pottsville or I'll buy a gun and use it. Yes,
it's come to that. I've never been so unhappy, so little enthusiastic
about life, and it's all the fault of this place, and of myself. If I had
some objective, something tangible to look forward to, it wouldn't be
quite so lethal, but as is—"[42]

---

* I.e., corny or fresh.

After graduating from Eden Hall, Mary O'Hara had taken a secretarial course and decided to seek a career in New York. John decided to go too and raised some getaway money by working briefly as a secretary in a briquetting plant and doing jury duty at $20 a week. By March 1928 he was living with the McKees at 538 Central Avenue in East Orange, New Jersey, while looking for work in Manhattan.

II

The Big Town

J OHN O'HARA was twenty-three and on his own in New York in
1928: "To a man who had worked in the small towns of eastern
Pennsylvania the city was inexhaustibly rich with unwritten columns
of wonderful, exciting stuff. . . . and in the excitement of his first
year in the big city he felt the need to live forever."[1] New York was
a journalistic heaven populated with great newspapermen and cele-
brated wits—Herbert Bayard Swope, F.P.A., Stanley Walker, Grant-
land Rice, Heywood Broun, Harold Ross, Ring Lardner, Frank
Sullivan, Robert Benchley, Dorothy Parker. Broadway had *Rio Rita*,
Show Boat, Marilyn Miller in *Rosalie*, Ina Claire in *Our Betters*, the
Astaires in Gershwin's *Funny Face*, Rodgers and Hart's *A Connecticut
Yankee* and *Present Arms*, Barry's *Paris Bound*, DeSylva, Brown and
Henderson's *Good News* and *Hold Everything*, O'Neill's *Strange
Interlude* and *Marco Millions*. The songs of the year were "Button
Up Your Overcoat," "I Can't Give You Anything but Love," "I'll
Get By," "Let's Do It," "Love Me or Leave Me," "Sweet Sue, Just
You," "That's My Weakness Now," "You're the Cream in My Coffee"
and "You Took Advantage of Me." The best-selling novel of 1928 was
Thornton Wilder's *The Bridge of San Luis Rey*. Other successful
American novels of the year were S. S. Van Dine's *The Greene Murder
Case*, Viña Delmar's *Bad Girl*, Booth Tarkington's *Claire Ambler*, Anne
Parrish's *All Kneeling*, Mazo De La Roche's *Jalna*, Louis Bromfield's
The Strange Case of Miss Annie Spragg.

The Big Town was a dream come true for the young man from
Pottsville who pounded the pavements looking for work. He reported
on his job-seeking to Bob Simonds:

*I left Povie [Pottsville] Tuesday after week-ending at Bucknell. I
fussed around N.Y. and the Yale Club, which sent me to* Time. *There
I met Noel Busch and Newton Hockaday. They're about my age and
occupy an office together. I was chatting with Busch, telling him my
record and yes I read* Time *and have had letters printed in it and yes
I understand Time-style. Hockaday, whom I hadn't met said, "Say*

didn't you write about Sherwood? I called Sherwood and asked him point-blank what size shoe he wore." So we were a pleasant trio for a few minutes. Busch then suggested I do these books and bring in my reviews Wednesday.[2]

The letter about Sherwood was in reply to a *Time* reader who wrote to the magazine stating that it would never have anyone big enough to stand in Lindbergh's shoes. O'Hara suggested that *Time* try Robert E. Sherwood, a very tall man. The letter was printed with a note giving Sherwood's shoe size as thirteen.[3] The two books O'Hara was given to review on trial were G. K. Chesterton's *Robert Louis Stevenson* and Bennett Doty's *Legion of the Damned*; neither review was used.

O'Hara phoned F.P.A., who told him there weren't any openings on the *World*, but to try anyhow. O'Hara sent a note to the legendary editor, Herbert Bayard Swope, who wrote on it, "We're loaded." He sent it back with his own comment, "I didn't know it was loaded." Then he went to see F.P.A., who phoned Julian Mason at the New York *Post* and arranged for O'Hara to be interviewed, promised to talk to Harold Ross of *The New Yorker* and told O'Hara: "Don't worry. *I'll* get you somewhere." The back of the envelope for the letter to Simonds—postmarked 8 March 1928—has a note: "Start

F.P.A. (Franklin P. Adams).

Tomorrow on the Herald-Tribune, thanks to F.P.A."* Six years later John O'Hara thanked his patron by dedicating *Appointment in Samarra* to him.

The city editor of the *Trib* was Stanley Walker, a Texan of about thirty who was building the best city room in America. He hired John O'Hara at $35 per week. Livelier than the *Times*, the *Trib* was successfully competing against "the newspaper of record" with the quality of its writing. It was particularly strong in feature and sports writers. Grantland Rice ("The Sportlight") and W. O. McGeehan ("Down the Line") were the stars of the sports section, along with boxing writer Don Skene. Percy Hammond was the drama critic, and Richard Watts, Jr., reviewed movies. Mark Sullivan wrote influential political comment.

By the end of his first week on the *Trib*, O'Hara was able to report to Simonds: "I have gotten drunk, slightly, with the city editor and the asst. c.e. went to the trouble of coming down from his desk to congratulate me on a story. . . ." The world of a New York reporter was full of celebrities:

Here is a list of the people I've met and spoken to, either on assignments or socially: F.P.A.,* Frank Sullivan,* Herbert Asbury,* W. O. McGeehan,* Dick Watts,* Clare Briggs,* Belle Livingstone,* Walter Winchell,* Charles Brackett, Don Skene,* Frank Getty,* Arthur Caesar,* Harold Lloyd* and wife,* father and daughter; Howard Dietz* and spouse,* Tommy Guinan,* Senator George, Dennis Tilden Lynch,* McKay Morris,* George de Zayas,* Mrs. Harry Houdini,* John Haynes Holmes, Wm. Lloyd Garrison—to name but a gross. . . . I have marked with a star the names of people who I think would remember me if they were to see me tomorrow.[4]

The young reporter was eager to make his mark beyond the city room. While he was working for the *Trib* he was trying to moonlight on *Time*.

I saw Luce the other day. When I walked into his office he said, "Well Mr. O'Hara, after all these years of letter-writing!" He wants me to do a fiction book as a specimen of my reviewing that type, but he was pleased (although he did not accept) with the two already written. I am fairly certain I will do that work as a regular thing, which would mean, I understand, an additional $20 a week to my income.[5]

---

* F.P.A. printed this item in his column: "J. O'Hara of Pottsville, Pa., has accepted a position on Ogden Reid's newspaper."

O'Hara had sent Harold Ross ideas for *New Yorker* assignments before he left Pottsville, but from the *Trib* he began bombarding the magazine with suggestions for profiles and "Talk of the Town" pieces, none of which was used. While he was still living in East Orange he wrote Ross:

> *I am pregnant with what I think is a good idea. We spoke, you and I, of the advisability of doing a Profile of Betty Compton. She is a good type and probably excellent copy, but my idea is, how about a twin-profile of Betty Compton and Bobby Arnst, who are almost without a doubt the leading Tiny Tots of New York?*
>
> *"As every (prep) school boy knows," this Bobby Arnst has had a Meteoric Rise, moreso even than Betty Compton's. The idea would be, of course, to give them equal space and more or less subtly to contrast their careers. Incidentally I believe this plan would remove any trace of press-agentry that might dullen (?) a Profile of either one.*
>
> *I shall await, etc.*[6]

Ross's notations on this letter read in part: "Too airy, not enough substance . . . too flip not enough to them." O'Hara obtained an assignment for a profile of Al Smith, Jr., which he submitted; but it was not published.

Joel Sayre, then a reporter on the *Trib*, first encountered O'Hara through a note in his box at the paper: "Dear Sayre: Good piece this morning. Congratulations . . . Since you have expressed your hostility by ignoring me completely, I just want to say that it doesn't bother me in the slightest. NUTS TO YOU, TOO. John H. O'Hara." Almost certainly, this communication was intended as a joke, but it was the sort of thing that added to O'Hara's reputation for extreme touchiness or insecurity. Sayre has described O'Hara's sartorial habits in 1928, singling out a coonskin coat and cane: "Not even the most grizzled veterans on the staff had ever heard of a cub on day-rewrite carrying a cane; but O'Hara carried one."[7] He did, in point of fact, wear his coonskin coat in New York; but not in the spring and summer, when he was on the *Trib*.

It is difficult to differentiate the real from the apocryphal stories about O'Hara's reportorial days in New York. One anecdote, which was told by O'Hara himself, is that when he arrived to cover an important story he would issue orders to the other reporters who didn't know him but assumed he was in charge. When he was identified, O'Hara got a punch in the nose from "some guy from City News who didn't know that I was a sensitive character."[8]

New York was full of watering holes for a thirsty reporter. The closest to the *Trib* was next-door on 40th Street, the Artist and Writers Club—known as Bleeck's—a favorite speakeasy for journalists. His first night on the *Trib*, John was introduced to the proprietor, Jack Bleeck (pronounced Blake) by Stanley Walker, and after a time succeeded in getting credit. It was very heaven to be young and at the bar with "Ring W. Lardner, Grantland Rice, Percy Hammond, Heywood Broun, Henry Cabot Lodge (then an anonymous editorial writer on the *Trib*), Alva Johnston, Russell Owen, and you-name-him."[9] When John saw Lardner he was too shy to introduce himself. Other favorite speaks for writers were the Type & Print Club, an upstairs place on 40th Street; Tony Soma's (Tony's) on West 49th Street and later on West 52nd Street; Matt Winkle's at 53rd and Park; and Dan Moriarty's at 216 East 58th Street, where O'Hara became friendly with Jack Thomas, the young author of *Dry Martini*, who was on his way to an early death from chronic alcoholism. The Type & Print Club was where O'Hara first met John K. Hutchens, a young reporter on the *Times*, and asked if he was related to the editor of the *Daily Missoulian and Sentinel*. When Hutchens replied that he was the editor's son, O'Hara was delighted and explained how much Martin Hutchens' letter of advice had meant to him when he had applied for a job on that paper. O'Hara also regarded himself as an adjunct member of the Yale Club, across from Grand Central Station. Jack and Charlie's Puncheon Club on 49th Street was to remain a favorite resort—especially after it became "21" in 1930—but it was too expensive for O'Hara to patronize regularly in 1928. O'Hara first met H. L. Mencken in a speakeasy and asked him, "Where did you get the idea that if you haven't learned the bass clef you can't appreciate music?"

"Did I say that?"

"You said it all right," replied O'Hara, telling him where.

"I was right," stated the Baltimore antichrist.[10]

O'Hara's first appearance in *The New Yorker*, "The Alumnae Bulletin," came on 5 May 1928, having been accepted by John Mosher, the first reader for "over the transom" submissions. Mosher subsequently rejected a number of O'Hara's stories because he found them "elliptical"—which O'Hara remarked was Mosher's favorite word. Jack Bleeck cashed the $15 check, and humorist Frank Sullivan and boxing writer Don Skene persuaded John to drop the middle initial from his by-line. Sullivan, a *World* columnist and *New Yorker* contributor, became O'Hara's lifelong friend.

"The Alumnae Bulletin" is a 200-word monologue that appeared at the back of the magazine and consists of the comments of a woman reading the class notes in her college magazine.* In 1928 O'Hara became a regular contributor to *The New Yorker*, placing twelve casuals (Harold Ross's term for anything that was not a profile or part of a department). His seventh contribution, "A Safe and Sane Fourth," in the 15 September issue, was the first of a series of fourteen sketches about the Orange County Afternoon Delphian Society published over the next four years. A second series dealing with the Hagedorn & Brownmiller Paint and Varnish Co. was launched on 1 December 1928 with "The Boss' Present"; this series included fourteen sketches over three years. Although these early *New Yorker* appearances anticipate some obvious qualities of O'Hara's later work, they are not particularly significant in themselves. Short monologues relying on the author's ability to characterize people through speech, satirical of social pretensions, they are exercises rather than attempts at short stories. These sketches may be compared with the vignettes of Hemingway's 1924 *In Our Time,* for both are attempts to record—action for Hemingway, and speech for O'Hara. The difference is that O'Hara's early sketches have no stylistic distinction. Nonetheless, the important point is that the twenty-three-year-old reporter placed twelve items in *The New Yorker* during his first year in Manhattan. It was the general opinion that he had a promising future—if drink didn't get him.

By the time O'Hara began appearing in *The New Yorker,* the staff included editors he would work with the rest of his career. Katharine Angell, who had joined the magazine as assistant literary editor in 1925, hired E. B. White in 1926 (and married him in 1929). James Thurber came in 1927. Wolcott Gibbs—who became O'Hara's closest friend at *The New Yorker*—was hired as a copy editor in 1928. Although O'Hara did not become a member of the inner group at the magazine, he found friends (and drinking companions) among the staff: St. Clair McKelway, Joel Sayre, Charles Addams, Hobart Weekes, William Maxwell.

Commuting from East Orange was inconvenient for a young man addicted to late hours, and O'Hara found digs in New York as soon as possible. His first address was probably a rooming house at 107 West 43rd Street (he also stayed at 103 East 46th Street at this time), but he lived all over Manhattan during this period—including a number

---

* This issue of *The New Yorker* included a humor piece by Donald Ogden Stewart, two Peter Arno cartoons, a profile of Dr. Alfred Adler, a poem by E. B. White and a "Reporter-at-Large" piece by Morris Markey.

of places in Greenwich Village. O'Hara's various rooms reflected his disorganized life style, with piles of dirty laundry through which he would search for a wearable shirt. Shortly after joining the *Trib* he acquired a "companionate mistress." She was a reporter, more successful than O'Hara, and emancipated. Their arrangement was in keeping with the new freedom. "She announced the restrictions under which she would continue to see me. The principal one is that if I ever *think* of wanting to marry her, I am bound in honor (☺) never to see her again. There is to be positively *no* claim on the other by either one of us, except that when one of us needs the other he is to call up, whether it's four in the morning or one in the afternoon. Both of us may be unfaithful and have entire freedom."[11]

One evening in New York when O'Hara passed a newsboy shouting the headlines he grabbed a stack of papers and began calling, "Extra! Extra! Herbert Hoover turns Catholic!" It became a favorite gag, and he repeated it on other occasions. After he was a successful novelist he felt that the newspaper book reviews did not receive sufficient attention, so he bought papers from a newsboy and yelled, "Read all about it!"—quoting book reviews.

John O'Hara was well launched in the big time, and at twenty-three had most of the things he wanted—except Marg; but the self-destructive pattern began to repeat itself. He was frequently late at the *Trib* and sometimes too drunk or hung over to do his work properly. Stanley Walker shifted him to day rewrite, which required O'Hara to salvage the previous day's important news and make stories out of information phoned in by reporters. When Walker fired him in August 1928—after six months—O'Hara admitted that the action was justified: "I was a mess. Nobody knew where I was living."[12] Walker's assessment was: "I said goodby . . . to John O'Hara in the conviction that he was sadly misplaced on the paper. While with us he wrote nothing at all of any distinction."[13] His by-line did not appear during his stint on the *Trib*.

It is impossible to determine whether he could not control his drinking in a world that seemed to run on alcohol, or whether he had come to feel that he really didn't want to be a reporter. After all, his ultimate ambition was to write novels; newspaper work was just a way to support himself until he could live on his fiction. Perhaps in some way he understood what he needed to develop as a novelist, and that his development did not require showing up at the *Trib* without a hangover at 10 A.M.

He went directly from the *Trib* to *Time*, stopping at Whitehouse

& Hardy to buy a pair of shoes for $23. He was put to work "doing these fucking newscastings"* under Roy Larsen.[14] O'Hara quit because he disliked both Larsen and the job; but he was kept on at space rates in a variety of capacities: second-string drama critic, book reviewer, sports reporter and, he claimed, religion editor for a brief time. None of his *Time* work can be identified, except for a review of *Polly* (21 January 1929).[15] He was listed on the masthead as a "weekly contributor" from November 1928 to April 1929.

I was known as Super-Checker O'Hara. One day I went through the magazine and made a list of errors. (I was the only name on the masthead who hadn't graduated from Yale or Harvard. No, there was one other; he was graduated from M.I.T. I didn't go to college.) This list was taken to Harry [Luce]. And I was given another job. It was a kind of game. After everything was checked, I went through it on my own. The game was that I was not supposed to look things up, refer to books, etc., but do it on my own, from what I know. Sort of the average-reader approach. I got an extra $15 a day for this. . . ."[16]

Some of O'Hara's alcoholic adventures became legendary anecdotes. One *Time* assignment was to cover a flight that Amelia Earhart was giving the press over New York. O'Hara arrived at Newark Airport too late but persuaded another pilot, who was going to deliver the plane back to Miller Field, to take him along. O'Hara got out when the plane landed at Miller Field, but as the pilot taxied to the hangar O'Hara got the idea that someone was stealing the plane. He ran after it and smashed a window. A mechanic slugged him and he woke up in a ditch. The foregoing seems to be the best version of a story that takes several forms.[17]

The *Time* men O'Hara hit it off with were Noel Busch—who had interviewed him when he first arrived in New York—and Wilder Hobson. Busch was a cousin of Briton Hadden, the co-proprietor of *Time*, and had left Princeton to write theater and movie reviews for the magazine. In the fall of 1928 Busch acquired an additional job covering sports for the New York *Daily News*, requiring car trips to Yale and Princeton on which John accompanied him. It was a good arrangement: O'Hara was fascinated by college life and knew more about football than Busch. Briton Niven Busch, Jr., Noel's brother, was writing very successfully for *The New Yorker* and moonlighting

* "Newscasting" was a daily rewrite of news items in *Time* and other sources for distribution to radio stations.

for *Time*. For a while the Busch brothers allowed O'Hara to use their apartment, but the setup was unsatisfactory because O'Hara would lose his key and cause a commotion to gain admittance. Wilder Hobson impressed O'Hara; he had been voted the wittiest member of the Yale class of 1923 and Most Likely to Succeed, and was a member of Scroll and Key. He and O'Hara had a number of common interests, particularly jazz and what might be called the machinery of snobbery.

The sober John O'Hara of this period has been described as "shy," "kind" and even "humble"; but in his cups he was pugnacious and brash.* People were uneasy around him when he was drunk: "I was a brooder by nature, but by second nature I was a toper, and the brooding that sent me to the bottle lasted only long enough for the whiskey to reach my brain, whereupon it took other forms, such as violence or sex or euphoria or the enjoyment of music."[18] Both patterns of behavior were expressions of a sensitive young man's sense of failure, for in certain ways New York was a repetition of Pottsville after Dr. O'Hara's death, in that he was a have-not surrounded by haves. At *Time* he keenly felt that he was an outsider in an old-school-tie organization. All the successful young men seemed to have Yale and/or family connections with Hadden and Luce. Even if they weren't earning large salaries, they had money behind them. O'Hara was living in cheap rooms and wearing shabby clothes—some of which had been his father's, including a top hat that Cesar Romero borrowed to audition for a job as a ballroom dancer when they were both living in a rooming house on West 43rd Street.[19] His life style fluctuated between disorganized and disastrous: "I have just come off a three-weeks' bender, during which I fell down a flight of stairs, was punched in the face, had a mild attack of d.t.'s and spent about $400."[20] On *Time* he averaged $160 a month, but for December 1928 his pay check was $10. While he was working for *Time*, O'Hara offered to write a series of "Speakeasy Knights" pieces for *The New Yorker*, dealing with saloon characters such as Prince Michael Romanoff; but the project was not encouraged.

John keenly regretted his inability to do things for the younger O'Hara children—especially at Christmas. Kathy, the baby of the family, recalls one Christmas morning in Pottsville when John arrived from New York with a watch for her that he had bought in Philadelphia's Broad Street Station with his last dollar.

Luce and Hadden annually exchanged jobs as business and editorial

---

* Pearl Kroll, one of the *Time* researchers, recalls the "sweet and humble" O'Hara who comforted her when the editors were harsh with her.

heads. O'Hara got along better with Hadden and hoped that when he took over as editor in 1929, Hadden would find a regular staff position for him; Hadden died in February 1929, however, and his cousin John Martin became managing editor. "His first official act was to fire me. We didn't get along at all. I naturally went to Harry about this, but Luce ratified Martin's judgment. . . ."[21] Another version of O'Hara's separation from *Time* has Luce telling him that the magazine had no use for a man who stayed in bed until 10 A.M. O'Hara later remarked that Luce always gave him "that Protestant look."[22] Whether or not anti-Catholic prejudice actually operated against him, O'Hara believed it did.* Luce provided O'Hara with a letter of introduction to James Wright Brown, the publisher of *Editor & Publisher*, who hired him at space rates.

MARGARETTA ARCHBALD WAS WORKING in New York, and the series of breaks and reconciliations resumed. The breaks were occasioned by John's ungovernable temper and drinking. One night he quarreled with Marg at the St. Regis Roof and smashed dishes. Marg was sharing an apartment with her cousin Mary Brooks from Scranton, who was being successfully courted by a Yaleman named A. Whitney Griswold. O'Hara would arrive late and pound on the door, demanding to see Marg. At first Mary and Whit were nonplused by these alcoholic visits, but the two suitors enjoyed talking to each other. In later years O'Hara liked to claim that he always knew that Whit Griswold would become president of Yale.

Wolcott Gibbs became O'Hara's most intimate friend, and other friends said that O'Hara would have died for him. Gibbs has been described as "a New York swell." Connected with old New York families, he was familiar with the status system that fascinated O'Hara. Moreover, Gibbs had not gone to college, which comforted O'Hara. Before he became the drama critic, Gibbs exerted a strong influence on *The New Yorker* fiction. Some of his editorial pronouncements could have been made by O'Hara: "Editorial theory should probably be that a writer who can't make his context indicate the way his character is talking ought to be in another line of work"; "Try to make dialogue sound like talk, not writing."[23] These rules almost certainly resulted from their talks about writing, and it is an open question as

---

* He was convinced that he had been instrumental in encouraging Luce to proceed with *Fortune* by explaining that every small-town banker in the country would have to keep a copy on his desk for prestige.

to whether the editor or author was the stronger influence on the other. Their friendship was commemorated when O'Hara chose the name Gibbsville for the fictionalized version of Pottsville.

It is difficult to reconstruct the friendship between O'Hara and Gibbs in any detail because their personal correspondence has not survived, and there are only thirty-one letters from O'Hara to Gibbs in the files of *The New Yorker* for the periods when Gibbs was filling in as fiction editor between 1933 and 1937. These letters are not strictly business, for they are peppered with wisecracks and in-jokes. Nevertheless, it is clear that both men were in an awkward position because *The New Yorker* was rejecting a good many of O'Hara's stories, and Gibbs had the job of relaying the bad news. Gibbs greatly admired O'Hara's talent, but felt that his work was too difficult for most readers—a view Gibbs held for a long time. The nature of their friendship, as well as Gibbs's editorial judgment on what he regarded as O'Hara's deliberate obscurity, can be seen from O'Hara's May 1932 report to his brother Tom:

Gibbs was very drunk, and as sometimes happens when he gets like that, he got in one of his Brutally Frank moods, in which the idea is to tell people that I know more about him than anyone else in the world; that I never take advantage of his friendship; that I am the God damn best writer The New Yorker has, but that I am stupid because I didn't know what they want; that I am too obscure, and forget that The New Yorker is read by pretty dull people.

Although John O'Hara always resisted editing, his working relationship with Katharine Angell was smooth, partly because she coddled him. She went over his work with him in person, and he made a point of coming to these meetings sober and without a hangover. Mrs. Angell tried to run interference between O'Hara and Harold Ross. Both men had short fuses; moreover, Ross was an extremely unpredictable man with a vast stock of idiosyncrasies. The relationship between O'Hara and Ross was uneasy during the twenty-two years O'Hara wrote for his magazine. Ross was a painstaking editor who read everything that went into each issue and covered the copy and proofs with queries. O'Hara required little querying, but even so Mrs. Angell would try to get Ross to remove some of his notes before the writer saw them. Ross had a list of sexual taboos and banned words that he suspected O'Hara of trying to violate. A famous fiat attributed to Ross was "I'll never print another O'Hara story I don't understand. I want to know what his people are doing."[24] Ross is also supposed to have told O'Hara, "I trust you with nouns, but not with adjectives."[25] In the

Harold Ross.

early days, however, Ross was receptive to his work and encouraged
him to extend the Delphian series.

Although O'Hara was already known as a prickly man, Mrs.
Angell found him unfailingly polite. Even though she had an expense
account, he insisted on taking her to lunch when their editorial meetings required it—preferably at "21," where he could show off a bit
when he was in the money. Mrs. Angell regarded O'Hara as "a lovable
man." His ego seemed an expression of his feelings of failure and
inferiority. "John O'Hara cared about people and was essentially a
kind man and a real friend, which few egotists are."[26] He came to rely
on her for many things. Once he phoned and asked her to get the

best lung specialist in New York for him because he was hemorrhaging to death. Mrs. Angell and Ik Shuman, then managing editor, dispatched a doctor who found O'Hara had vomited so much from a hangover that he had ruptured blood vessels in his stomach and throat. His anxiety about his chest may have resulted from his father's warning that he had a lung spot.

The New Yorker contributor O'Hara was closest to for a long time was Dorothy Parker. A famous wit, Mrs. Parker was a superb writer of self-mocking verse and stories. Her wisecracks—such as "If all the girls who attended the Yale Junior Prom were laid end to end, I wouldn't be surprised"—were widely quoted. She moved among the brightest people in New York and was a member of the Algonquin Round Table group. O'Hara greatly admired her work, from which he had learned something about control of tone. Her best story, "Big Blonde" (1929), may have provided a model for his story technique. Mrs. Parker was one of the first New York people to recognize his great promise. Many of his friends thought he had a minor talent, but she insisted that it was a major talent. He was often in her company. They shared a liking for drinking and late hours at Tony's, and he was delighted to be admitted to her circle of friends.

Mrs. Parker and Robert Benchley were very close friends; they both had liberal political convictions, and had been very active in behalf of Sacco and Vanzetti. Benchley was one of the best-liked men of his time, and O'Hara quickly developed deep affection for the man whose writing he had admired while still in Pottsville. One night Benchley saw O'Hara at the theater with a young lady—probably Marg—and said, "Hello, Mr. O'Hara. I'll bet we're the only ones here wearing pumps."[27] The girl was impressed, and O'Hara never forgot this kind gesture. A man of great personal warmth and a *bon vivant*, Benchley was loved for his kindness and sweetness of character. Unlike Mrs. Parker, his humor did not depend on malice.

Benchley had to deal with Mrs. Parker's suicidal depressions. On one occasion when he visited her after an unsuccessful suicide attempt, he sternly warned her that if she didn't stop trying to kill herself she would injure her health. O'Hara came to have some of the responsibility for taking care of Dorothy Parker. Adele Lovett, the wife of a banker who later became a cabinet officer, was a close friend of Dorothy Parker. When she first met O'Hara at the afternoon drop-ins at Mrs. Parker's apartment, Mrs. Lovett found him shy. Among the competing wits he sat and listened.

Another mutual Parker-O'Hara friend was John McClain, who

Dorothy Parker.

had recently arrived in New York by way of Kenyon College and
Brown, and was working as a ship-news reporter for the New York
Sun. In certain ways McClain represented what O'Hara wanted to
be: handsome, charming, a good drinker, well-dressed, accepted by
influential men and highly successful with women. The perfect image
of the dashing reporter who contrives to live well without money,
McClain was one of the most popular young men in New York. He
was for a time Dorothy Parker's lover in a publicly messy affair. In
his twenties John O'Hara possessed considerable masculine attractive-
ness, despite an acne-pitted complexion and bad teeth. He was successful with women, but by no means in McClain's class. The impression
that O'Hara was a great womanizer is an exaggeration.

Robert Benchley.

Another early admirer of John O'Hara's talent was Betty Dietz, the wife of songwriter Howard Dietz. The Dietzes maintained a salon at their home on 11th Street, where the witty and celebrated gathered to play a trivia game called "Guggenheim." Again O'Hara seemed shy and even countrified to some of these celebrities. One of his triumphs came when he impressed Dietz by perfectly imitating the Whiteman recording of "Washboard Blues" at Tony's.

O'HARA STILL had the problem of supporting himself. After he was fired from *Time* in April 1929, he worked so briefly for *Editor & Publisher* that the magazine has no record of his employment. He also tried to get a reporting job on the *Evening Post*. In the spring of 1929 he spent two weeks in a Princeton dormitory as the guest of an undergraduate friend. By the summer he was a night rewrite man on the New York *Daily Mirror*, a Hearst tabloid, but the martinis at Racky's, where the dayside people gathered at the end of their shift, made it difficult for him to get to work at 6 P.M.

I hated to leave the Mirror. *The city editor had a Pierce-Arrow roadster and wore silk shirts, and while I would have chosen a Lincoln phaeton and buttondown broadcloth, the idea was the same. There was money to be made. Moreover . . . we had quite a bunch of characters. Winchell was there, a striver then, who wrote Broadway and Hollywood chatter and had not yet constituted himself a one-man State Department.*

Helen Nolan, easily one of the most beautiful women in New York, was a reporter. Alma Jane Frankenfelder, later Jane Franklin, was just out of Barnard and taking with good nature some rather rough treatment. Walter Howey, whom Ben Hecht and Charles MacArthur had in mind when they wrote The Front Page, *was there as Hearst's watchdog, and so was Emile Gauvreau, another tabloid giant, if you'll pardon the seeming contradiction in terms.*

Dan Parker, who goes with the lease, was already established as the man to beat if you wanted to be top guy among prize-fight reporters. Gordon Kahn, who subsequently became a commie and wore a monocle, was on day rewrite, and incidentally it was Kahn who told Jimmy Cannon who told me about the Mirror *job. Winchell likes to think he got me the job; he had nothing whatever to do with it. . . . And speaking of by-lines, the first one I got on the* Mirror *was By John F. O'Hara. This must have returned to plague the Archbishop of Philadelphia. It annoyed me because my middle name is Henry, which is annoyance enough in itself.*[28]

An entertaining event of his brief *Mirror* tenure was the plot to sneak a woman into the Yale Club bar. O'Hara and Newton Hockaday —who had interviewed him when he applied for a job at *Time*— dressed Jeanne Atherton in a man's suit and escorted her into the bar. However, the bartender became suspicious, and they were asked to leave. O'Hara ghosted an article for the *Mirror*, "Girl Invades Yale Club Bar, Only for Men."[29]

After his separation from the *Mirror* for tardiness and drunkenness in 1929, O'Hara had a series of short-term jobs which he either quit or was fired from. He tried unsuccessfully to catch on at *The New Yorker* as a "Talk of the Town" reporter and briefly worked for Benjamin Sonnenberg's public relations firm, handling an Ely Culbertson bridge match. On the day the match began O'Hara didn't report for work, and Sonnenberg located him sleeping in a speakeasy known as "The Homeless Dogs." The young man hungry for success and fame was seeking them in his own way.

While he was working for *Time* and the *Mirror* O'Hara was also steadily writing for *The New Yorker*. In 1929—his second year as a contributor—he placed twenty-five casuals, of which six continued the Delphian series and ten continued the Hagedorn & Brownmiller chronicle. This record indicates how hard he was working at writing, for if twenty-five casuals were printed he probably submitted considerably more. Although his 1928–29 published fiction output consisted of short sketches, rather than fully developed stories, it was an impressive body of work to have printed in a magazine with high editorial standards. John O'Hara was not appearing for glory in little magazines; he was selling regularly to *The New Yorker*; he was a professional. *The New Yorker* was the only magazine O'Hara's fiction appeared in before December 1931, and he regarded himself as a *New Yorker* writer. This situation does not necessarily indicate that he was deliberately tailoring his work to the taste of the one magazine; but it is clear that his development as a writer was strongly influenced by his association with *The New Yorker*, simply in terms of what the magazine was accepting or rejecting.

During his first year in New York O'Hara continued his "Conning Tower" contributions. The dialogue in one of his nine 1928 pieces so impressed James M. Cain, then on the editorial staff of the *World*, that he was convinced O'Hara had the makings of a playwright. Cain tried to persuade O'Hara to write a play and offered to secure backing for it. Nothing came of this scheme. Cain later recalled: "O'Hara seemed surprised at my admiration for the piece, indifferent to my idea, and utterly indifferent to me."[30]

O'Hara's only other free-lance appearance in 1929 was a one-shot column on jazz, "Saxophonic Fever," in the Sunday *Trib* for 17 February 1929. In 1930 and 1931 nine more of these columns appeared, three of which were recollections of Pottsville. Of particular interest was "The Pennsylvania Irish," in which he described the influence of Irish speech on the immigrant Polish miners, who spoke with a rich brogue. The 14 December 1930 column praised Louis Armstrong, and in the 1 March 1931 column O'Hara claimed that he was the first "to set down the name of Louis Armstrong." It seems likely that O'Hara hoped these columns would catch on with the public and bring him a regular job as a columnist, an ambition that he pursued with varying degrees of success for the rest of his life.

The October 1929 crash had no direct effect on O'Hara because he had nothing to lose on Wall Street, but it made the job situation tougher because a lot of punctual, sober men were competing for newspaper jobs. Late in 1929 or early in 1930 O'Hara asked Heywood Broun if he could help with the "Give-a-Job-Till-June" campaign that Broun was running. He was put to work answering mail and handling contributions, and was surprised to be put on Broun's personal pay-

Heywood Broun.

roll for $35 a week. In addition to providing lunch, Broun picked up
the tabs when they went out at night. Broun had been one of O'Hara's
heroes from the time he began reading the *World* in Pottsville, and
close contact with Broun strengthened this admiration, for he seemed
to be the ideal example of a successful columnist. Broun was a big
spender, a good drinker and a brilliant writer. O'Hara particularly
admired his ability to turn out good copy against a deadline in the
midst of noisy distractions. He later described Broun as "the best-
writing newspaper man I ever knew of." When Broun died in 1940,
O'Hara wrote a letter of tribute to *The New Republic*:

> *There are men who are everything they are for no other reason
> than that they have about them or attached to them the right things:
> a Richard Whitney, who naturally went to Harvard and was a mem-
> ber of the Pork and the crew, and hunted, and did this and that. Not*

so Broun. Broun honored Harvard by going there, continued to keep it respectable by continuing to like it. He gave the imprimatur to basketball because he had played it at Horace Mann. He gave the horse laugh to food-and-wine purists by simply tossing off a stinger and following it with a whiskey sour. I know I still have a raccoon coat for the excellent reason that at my age Heywood Broun had one too. He made a lot of people seem right by letting it be known they were his friends. He honored me, by God, by letting me sit with him, work for him, drink to him.

Hello, Heywood.[31]

Except for a stint on the *Morning Telegraph* in May–July 1930 some of O'Hara's jobs during that year remain matters of conjecture.* The *Telegraph* (not to be confused with the *Telegram*) was primarily devoted to turf information, with a secondary interest in the entertainment world. O'Hara reviewed movies, the less important plays, and radio programs, and wrote fifteen columns about radio under the by-line "Franey Delaney" (the maiden name of his paternal grandmother and his mother's maiden name). Since he did not own a radio, he worked from radios in bars. In June he was assigned to review movies on Saturday mornings over radio station WMCA. He found his first appearance an ordeal, and after a couple of broadcasts he stopped coming to the station. He never heard anything further from WMCA, and for a long time wondered if there was a Saturday morning period of radio silence.

The year 1930 was O'Hara's hardest year in New York. He was often broke and sometimes hungry. At one point he went three days without eating. His sister Mary had a secretarial position at the *Daily News* and was always good for a meal, but a lecture went with it. It was probably at this time that he worked as night switchboard operator at a disreputable hotel-cum-whorehouse, which gave him time to write on the job.† He firmly warned Mary never to come see him at this establishment. The financial hardship was accompanied by problems with Marg, and O'Hara wrote Bob Simonds: "If I had had sense enough to break it off early in 1928, or if she had had sense enough to let me alone in 1929, we'd have been spared 1930, the worst year in my life."[32]

---

* In his 1950 *Pottsville Journal* article O'Hara said that he had worked for the *Telegraph* twice; only one period of employment has been identified. He also stated that he wrote for the *New York Journal-American*, but this stint has not been traced. In 1929 or 1930 O'Hara wrote for *Today—in New York*, a publication that was distributed in hotels; no copy has been found.

† This job is later held by Eddie Brunner in *Butterfield 8*.

Some of John O'Hara's experiences during his early years in New York would be repeated by his character Jimmy Malloy, who also shares O'Hara's attitudes. Although Malloy is an autobiographical figure, it is misleading to regard Malloy and O'Hara as the same person. O'Hara rarely wrote straight autobiographical fiction: Malloy is a fictional character, many of whose experiences came from the author's life.

The otherwise bad year was productive for the twenty-five-year-old writer, for he placed twenty-one casuals in *The New Yorker* in 1930, only five of which continued the Delphian and Hagedorn & Brownmiller series. Although they are still quite short—a thousand words or less—stories like "The Girl Who Had Been Presented," "New Day," "The Man Who Had to Talk to Somebody" and "On His Hands" represented a clear advance in O'Hara's work and are immediately recognizable as his.* The stories—or sketches—still have very little plot. Their effect depends almost entirely on characterization, which is usually developed through speech. At this stage O'Hara was still relying on dramatic monologues, as in "On His Hands." These early stories typically involve some point of snobbery or status-seeking; and they adumbrate the major themes of O'Hara's work: social cruelty, human isolation, the need for love and the hell of loneliness.

The style is bare, for O'Hara resisted simile and metaphor—except in speech. Although he came to be regarded as an author who freighted his work with detail, these stories employ only selected details as characterizers. There are no nonfunctional details. The labels and brands are specified in the stories because they matter to the characters; the characters' awareness of and response to these details characterize themselves. The Princeton undergraduate in "On His Hands" is the kind of person who notices that the family of a girl he is interested in has a "1921 Pierce limousine" and attempts to evaluate their position accordingly. He is also the kind of person who has run up a $400 bill with his tailor; clothes matter to him, and it is therefore in character for him to refer to Wetzel. The details work, not because the author is fascinated by them, which he is, but because they matter to the characters. They are the right details.

Critics have complained that O'Hara's use of such details limited the audience for his work when it was originally published and

---

* These four stories plus a Delphian story, "Ten Eyck or Pershing? Pershing or Ten Eyck?" were the earliest stories included in *The Doctor's Son*, O'Hara's first collection.

diminishes that audience even more now. How many readers in 1930 knew that Wetzel was an expensive New York custom tailor? How many readers in 1975 know that the Pierce-Arrow was the American equivalent of the Rolls-Royce? The meaning of some details is clear from context, as with the Pierce-Arrow; but in other cases O'Hara is writing for readers who know what he is talking about.

The economy of these early stories is remarkable. By focusing on a particular point in the character's life, O'Hara is able to project the reader backward and forward. In "New Day" the account of Mrs. Brown's empty morning miniaturizes her empty life. This morning is every morning. The story ends with a favorite O'Hara device, the underplayed tag line: "The telegram was unsigned." Mrs. Brown's relationship with her husband is such that she doesn't sign her telegrams to him: she is as isolated from him as she is from everyone else. The tag lines in some stories puzzled readers who were accustomed to more authorial guidance.

The role of the author in a story in which he is not a character is detached. He does not intrude in his own voice, and he does not explain to the reader. This quasi-reportorial point of view has led to the easy and misleading assumption that John O'Hara belonged to the hard-boiled school—with the further assumption that he was a disciple of Ernest Hemingway. The hard-boiled writers, as exemplified by Dashiell Hammett, were studiously unemotional and relied heavily on violent action. O'Hara's work is emotional and frequently senti-mental. The reader perceives O'Hara's responses to his material, for the author is emotionally involved. There is surprisingly little violent action in O'Hara, apart from drunken conduct, but there is consider-able violence of speech. "The boys in the black mask" tried to employ the real speech of their criminals and detectives; but in most cases it came out as distorted toughness, or even self-parody. The speech of O'Hara's characters is always believable. Hemingway's influence on O'Hara has been exaggerated. Both writers endeavored to treat sex truthfully, but they had little or no material in common. Although both wrote a bare style, O'Hara did not imitate the rhythms of Hemingway's prose. The influence existed, but it manifested itself in less obvious ways. O'Hara read *A Farewell to Arms* so carefully that he could visualize the pages, and learned from it techniques of para-graphing. Hemingway's chief influence on John O'Hara was as a model of literary craftsmanship and professional discipline.

Assessing his literary debts for the foreword to the Modern Library *Appointment in Samarra* (1953), O'Hara stated:

In the matter of influences, here they are: Fitzgerald, Sinclair Lewis, Galsworthy, Tarkington, Owen Johnson, but chiefly Fitzgerald and Lewis. If Hemingway influenced me the influence is not apparent to me, and I can see countless instances of the effect of my reading Fitzgerald and Lewis. (I am speaking now of the novel: my short stories, the early ones, did owe something to Hemingway, Dorothy Parker, and Lardner, until, as Wolcott Gibbs has pointed out, I got going on my own. What the stories owed Hemingway was form; what they owed Mrs. Parker was point of view; what they owed Lardner was my discovery from him that if you wrote down speech as it is spoken truly, you produce true characters, and the opposite is also true: if your characters don't talk like people they aren't good characters. It's a point, or rather two points, that most critics do not appreciate when they speak so airily of the Good Ear, the Rhythms of American Speech. Sometimes I almost feel that I ought to apologize for having the ability to write good dialog, and yet it's the attribute most lacking in American writers and almost totally lacking in the British.)

John O'Hara has been credited with having invented "the *New Yorker* story," a comment which probably means, if anything, that his stories established the kind of lightly plotted, oblique story that appeared frequently in the magazine. He was certainly the best and most prolific writer of such stories; however, Katharine Angell White, Wolcott Gibbs and Harold Ross had a great deal to do with formulating and establishing this story type. One result of the apparent identification of O'Hara's stories with *The New Yorker* was that it was almost impossible for him to place his work in other quality magazines.

LATE IN 1930 John O'Hara met Helen Ritchie Petit at an Equity ball. She was small and blond, with deep blue eyes, and was considered a beauty at Wellesley, where her classmates were struck by her "Alice-in-Wonderland air" and "child-like manner." Other friends described her as "uptight and jumpy" and said that her conversation was hard to follow. She was a disorganized and untidy girl; women noticed that her clothes were often stained. Pet—as John called her—was twenty-two, three years younger than he. Her family situation was interesting, for she was the only child of an appalling woman whose husband had left her. Pet and her mother lived comfortably in Brooklyn with her wealthy bachelor uncle, David M. Mahood, a successful inventor who was devoted to his niece. After graduation from Wellesley in 1928, she studied at the Sorbonne and took an M.A. at Columbia. She taught briefly in a New York City high school, but she was stage-struck. In 1960 O'Hara described her through Jimmy Malloy in "Imagine Kissing Pete": "She was nice. Pretty. Wanted to be an actress. I still see her once in a while. I like her, and always will, but if ever there were two people that shouldn't have got married. . . ."[33] Mrs. Petit detested John.

At Christmas time, 1930, broke and without a job prospect, O'Hara returned to Pottsville. His brother Joe, who was living with the McKees in East Orange and coming home on weekends, describes him as "memorizing *A Farewell to Arms*" and mailing out stories which didn't sell. O'Hara had made a contact with Kyle Crichton, an editor at *Scribner's* magazine, and through him was trying to open up a new market for his stories. On Washington's birthday in 1931 O'Hara drove back to East Orange with Joe; and on 28 February he and Pet were married at the Municipal Building after six days of partying. He had to borrow money to set up housekeeping, and the note was co-signed by Dick Watts and Joe O'Hara. O'Hara thought that he had arranged for Jimmy Walker to perform the marriage, but "the late Mayor of New York" failed to appear, so the deputy city clerk married them.[34]

Joe O'Hara was with John and Pet the day before their wedding, and urged his brother to phone their mother. O'Hara said he would, but didn't. Katharine O'Hara learned about her son's marriage from Walter Winchell's radio program. Pet was Protestant, but it is unlikely that this circumstance accounted for John's reluctance to inform his mother, for he had long since ceased to be a practicing Catholic. Katharine O'Hara had been deeply troubled by John's loss of faith and wrote anguished letters about his drinking and womanizing to Francis Beatty, his Niagara University friend who was about to be ordained. After his marriage O'Hara wrote Simonds, "I haven't heard from my family as I am still without the Roman fold, entirely through my own fault as Pet has urged me to come around but I haven't quite got to it."[35] It has been remarked that no Irishman leaves Holy Mother Church without some sense of guilt. When Beatty was ordained on 7 June 1931 O'Hara attended the Solemn Mass and spoke about his marriage outside the Church. Father Beatty urged him to talk to one of the priests at St. Patrick's Cathedral and see what could be done. Pet was not with O'Hara, and Father Beatty never saw him again.

The reunion with Beatty provided the idea for the 1938 story "No Mistakes," in which a young man and his pregnant wife attend the first High Mass of his college friend. When the priest learns that the wife is Protestant, he cuts them. This story provides a good example of the way O'Hara converted life into fiction. Although he worked extremely close to life, O'Hara rarely transcribed it. In "No Mistakes" the basic situation—O'Hara's attendance at Father Beatty's first High Mass—comes from the author's experience; the rest was imagined.

The newlyweds set up housekeeping in a small apartment at 41 West 52nd—convenient to Tony's and, when they were flush, to "21." Pet received an allowance of $100 per month from her family. O'Hara found a job in the New York publicity department of Warner Brothers through a tip from John McClain. His duties involved contacting the press and setting up interviews when stars like Constance Bennett, Richard Barthelmess, Ann Harding, Marilyn Miller, Bebe Daniels and John Barrymore came to New York.[36] O'Hara's boss, Charles Einfeld, was impressed with his originality and assigned him to write a series of special ads for James Cagney's film *The Public Enemy*. The first ad, which appeared on 22 April 1931, read in part:

There exists today a world within our world that we dare not ignore. And monarch of this unlicensed kingdom is "The Public Enemy."

He is here! We know he is here! Behind locked doors—in expensive motors—brushing your shoulders—touching your life. But what is he? Why is he? Who is he?

Thursday morning you will meet him face to face. Thursday morning you will witness a new milestone of cinema accomplishment —a slice of today's life—quivering!—real!—unadorned!—astounding!

If this ad represents John O'Hara's unadorned work, he must have laughed like hell while writing it.[37]

In the spring of 1931 O'Hara's career again intersected with that of James M. Cain, when Cain was managing editor of *The New Yorker*. One of the policies Cain tried to enforce was that all advances had to be cleared with him so he could keep the records straight. When Harold Ross made a small advance to O'Hara without clearing it, Cain forced a showdown with Ross—not about O'Hara, but about the policy. The result was that Ross rescinded the advance. Cain felt so guilty about it, knowing O'Hara needed the money, that he quit *The New Yorker* and went to Hollywood.[38]

In June Pet's "Uncle Dee" gave the O'Haras $1,000 for a belated honeymoon. France was rejected in favor of Bermuda because the money would last longer there. By late June they were in a cottage called "Greenway" at Paget East, where O'Hara cut down on his drinking and wrote his first extended fiction while producing stories

Pet and John in Bermuda, 1931.

and starting a play. In July, Kyle Crichton paid $75 for "Alone" for *Scribner's*, which was O'Hara's first acceptance outside of *The New Yorker*. The story appeared in December 1931, and O'Hara believed that its publication marked a turning point in his career because it made *The New Yorker* regard him as a more valuable contributor. "Alone" is a stream-of-consciousness sketch about a young man on the morning of his wife's funeral and does not represent any departure from O'Hara's other work at that time. Encouraged by this sale, he began bombarding Crichton with stories—some of them *New Yorker* rejects—but did not succeed in selling another story to *Scribner's* until "Early Afternoon" was accepted in 1932.

The most important effect of the sale of "Alone" was that it started him thinking in terms of the Scribner's short-novel contest. In 1930 the magazine began a competition for a $5,000 prize to be awarded to a short novel. The contest was particularly appealing to writers because the magazine published, and paid for, the best submissions—not just the winning story. At the beginning of August 1931 O'Hara reported to Crichton that he was "working like hell on my one-fifth Minor American Novel (one-fifth finished)." By 18 August he sent the short novel, "The Hofman Estate," noting that "the pace is mine and the piece has been written so fast (it's really journalistic) that there hasn't been much time for Influences."[39] The idea for "The Hofman Estate" derived from Pottsville's Sheafer Estate. It is possible that a visit to Bermuda by Bob Simonds and his fiancée, Catherine Melley of Coaldale, served as a catalyst for this work. The three Pennsylvanians talked about the Pottsville area; and although nothing survives of the short novel, it was about The Region. It is not extravagant to claim that "The Hofman Estate" was the inception of *Appointment in Samarra*—and, perhaps, of the entire Gibbsville cycle. However, the author who became such a productive novelist had trouble structuring his material at this point. His *New Yorker* pieces were still only sketches, and he had yet to publish a plotted short story. Now his first novel was really a long story. On 28 August Crichton returned "The Hofman Estate" with the explanation that the sexual material was too strong for *Scribner's*. Then on 1 September Crichton wrote urging John to make it into a big novel: "By elaborating on it, making more of the ramifications of that interesting family and making the erotic story a subsidiary rather than an all-enveloping thing, I think you could turn out a book which would establish you. . . . The more important thing is that the book department here is interested in you a great deal."

On 16 September John and Pet left Bermuda and spent a hellish two weeks with her mother at 24 Monroe Place, Brooklyn, until he raised enough money to rent an apartment at 19 West 55th Street. Mrs. Petit had been under the impression that O'Hara was on leave from his Warner Brothers job, but he had quit. Shortly after returning to New York, O'Hara went to Scribner's to see about an advance for rewriting "The Hofman Estate" into a novel. Maxwell Perkins, the legendary Scribner's editor who had spotted Fitzgerald, Hemingway and Wolfe, was not convinced that the long story "could be made into a satisfactory book," so there was no advance. No typescript of "The

Hofman Estate" survives, and John and Pet told Joe O'Hara they threw it down a sewer after Perkins declined the advance.

The job O'Hara found in the fall of 1931 was as a "Talk of the Town" reporter on *The New Yorker*, with a drawing account of $75 per week. Since top price for a "Talk" piece was $35, he was expected to turn in two or three usable pieces each week. Editors B. A. Bergman and Ralph Ingersoll thought well of his work, but Harold Ross was convinced that O'Hara was strictly a writer of casuals. Bergman particularly liked a piece about a ride over New York in the Goodyear dirigible, *Columbia*, which Ross killed. The only O'Hara appearance in "The Talk of the Town" listed in the magazine records is "Home in the Mud" (5 December 1931), about a Hudson River houseboat colony, which the magazine's records credit to O'Hara and McConnell. It was subsequently attributed to Jimmy Malloy in *Butterfield 8*. O'Hara was also hoping to fill in for Morris Markey with the "Reporter at Large" department. After two weeks Ross decided to dismiss O'Hara, although Bergman and Ingersoll tried to dissuade him. Since Ross never did his own firing, Bergman had to do it; but he also tried to find a Hollywood job for O'Hara.

The dismissal from *The New Yorker* hurt. Soon after, Ingersoll was at a fancy-dress ball when O'Hara staggered up to the table and sat down.

"What's *your* name?" asked the very drunk O'Hara.

"For Christ sake, you know me—I'm Mac Ingersoll."

Whereupon O'Hara lurched to his feet and punched Ingersoll, knocking him out of his chair. Ingersoll was so surprised that he sat on the floor and said, "Now what was that all about?"

"I've been waiting to catch up with you. You're the son of a bitch who fired me from your goddamn magazine."

"You're the goddamn son of a bitch that doesn't know what he's talking about, because at the meeting at which you were fired I voted in your favor."

"Well, I'll be goddamned. I owe you a drink."

A drunken conversation ensued in which O'Hara talked about his troubles at length.[40]

Bergman received much the same treatment. After Bergman had ceased to be the wonder man Ross was always searching for and had gone to work for Hearst, the author of *Appointment in Samarra* encountered Bergman in a restaurant and said, "You fired me, you son of a bitch. Now look at you and look at me!"—accompanied by the O'Hara glare.[41]

Authors are notoriously given to destroying works of which they have another copy, which seems to have been the case with "The Hofman Estate." In the fall of 1931 O'Hara was rewriting it. But in the meantime he had written another long story, "The Doctor's Son," which he submitted for the *Scribner's* magazine contest by 12 January 1932. Almost immediately he began pressing Crichton for a decision to publish and kept it up through the spring. On 23 May he sent Crichton a telegram at 4:26 A.M.:

PLEASE READ LIBERTY MAY 21 STOP MY STORY SUPERIOR BUT IF YOU DISAGREE BURN MANUSCRIPT BECAUSE DASHIELL WEBER BRIGHTON THOUGHT MINE DECENT PIECE AND IF THEY WERE WRONG I MAY BE WRONG STOP I THINK STORY IS WORTH DECENT BREAK STOP IF YOU THINK NOT ITS TIME TO DECIDE

OHARA

This telegram was prompted by Conrad Richter's story "Her People of the Patch," set on Pottsville's Mahantongo Street and in a mining patch. Richter lived in Pine Grove, near Pottsville, and O'Hara was disturbed to find that another writer was using The Region. It must have seemed to him that his very own material was being preempted.[42]

"The Doctor's Son" was not one of the stories published in the 1931–32 *Scribner's* contest; and in August 1932 judges Burton Rascoe, William Soskin and Edmund Wilson awarded the prize jointly to "The Big Short Trip" by John Herrman and "A Portrait of Bascom Hawke" by Thomas Wolfe.[43] O'Hara considered entering *College Humor's* novel contest.

In November 1931 Ogden Nash, then an editor for Farrar & Rinehart, read "The Hofman Estate" and tried to get his firm to give an advance on it; but the plan fell through. O'Hara also tried William Morrow, without success. On 31 January 1932 ("I am twenty-seven years, three hours, old; and God! I hate it"), O'Hara informed Simonds, "I've been slaving away at the rewriting of The Hofman Estate, which I suddenly began the other night." As he worked on the novel, O'Hara realized how much he had forgotten about The Region and planned to return to Pennsylvania, "Pet notwithstanding," for research. He would revive this plan but never act on it.

At the close of 1931 O'Hara was again unemployed. During the year he had appeared sixteen times in *The New Yorker* and once in *Scribner's*. Two of the casuals were the final items in the Delphian series; and in May and June he published four sketches about the

Idlewood Country Club, which was all he did with that subject. These series sketches were easy to write, but O'Hara took no satisfaction from them and abandoned the form until "Pal Joey." None of the 1931 stories represents an advance in his work, although at least two are particularly good—"Mary" and "Mort and Mary." "Mary" was inspired by a locally famous beauty of The Region, who would appear again in *Appointment in Samarra*. The story describes her transition from miner's daughter to high-class call girl. The other noteworthy story, "Mort and Mary," chronicles the successful and happy life of an Irish saloonkeeper's son who marries a beautiful Cuban and prospers in her father's business. The meaning of the story is entirely implied, for by now O'Hara was confident enough of his skills to underplay his stories. "Mort and Mary" ends with a seemingly approving statement—"There will never be any scandal in that family. Real, dependable people."—but the meaning of the story is that they are utterly dull.

O'Hara achieved his first book appearance in 1931 when "Ten Eyck or Pershing, Pershing or Ten Eyck" (Delphian) and "The New Office" (Hagedorn & Brownmiller) were included in *The New Yorker Scrapbook*—putting him in excellent company which included Fitzgerald and Hemingway. The following year "Early Afternoon" was reprinted in *Best Short Stories of 1932.** His work was beginning to attract attention, but he was a long way from being able to support himself by writing fiction. On 20 May 1932 he wrote his brother Tom: "Incidentally, I never told you that Dorothy Parker told me I would never be happy because I am a genius, and that she'd bet if Hemingway saw the Scribner's story ["Alone"] he wanted to cut his throat. I am sorry to be compelled to add that Mrs. Parker was tight, but I understand she has told other people the same thing about me."

By the middle of 1932 O'Hara was working for the New York publicity department of RKO, but was fired "only because I missed, on the average, a day a week from hangover trouble."[44] When he saw Frank Buck's *Bring 'Em Back Alive* he warned RKO that it would be a flop; it was a great success. At one point in 1932 O'Hara applied for the job of editing the magazine for the Crescent Athletic Club. He had ambitious writing plans for the year, which he explained to Simonds:

* Edward J. O'Brien, the editor of the *Best Short Story* volumes, accorded honorable-mention stars to a number of O'Hara's stories in the Thirties.

I have two plays to write, which have been slithering (how's that for a word?) within me for some time past. One of the ideas you'll be liking. Do you remember the old Christmas tree parties at the Boones'? Well, I would start my play with a sort of reunion of such: a wealthy guy decides to get the old bunch together, after ten years, just as they were in 1922; that is, the same people, the same furniture. The play would be an exposition of what had happened to them all in the intervening decade, and what would happen the night of the reunion. I think it's a hot idea—and a lousy one if it doesn't come off. But we must watch and pray. The other play is much in the Philip Barry tradition, and is too New Yorky for words. I don't want to start it till I've spoken for Katharine Hepburn and Pat O'Brien, whom I see in the leading roles, and no one else do I see. In addition, there is the item known as Novel, which I do want to get over and done with. I still may go to Hollywood for RKO, as a dialogroller (awful!), and I'd like to get an awful lot done before that happy day.[45]

At the end of 1932 O'Hara sent Simonds another projection.

You remember The Hofman Estate and The Doctor's Son, the two pieces I submitted in Scribner's contest? Well, I now have an idea about them which sounds sound. I showed the Doctor's Son to Howard and Betty Dietz, and I hear, from other sources, that they have gone around praising it to pretty influential people, among them Guinzburg, of the Viking Press. My idea is this: make a few changes in both stories; that is, give them a definite common locale (such as referring to Pottsville by a fictitious name, but using the same name in both stories), and writing a third story, also with the same locale, and putting them in one book together. I would write a third story, about someone like Puss or Furdummt, to complete what might inaccurately be called a trilogy. It would be a post-war picture of The Region, from the standpoint of the three classes: the Sheafer aristocrats, the middle class O'Haras, and the Schwackie gangster type. You'd have the three classes and the predominating races in just about the right periods. Don't you think it sounds good? All I'd have to do would be to make the simple changes in the stories I have, and write the third. Which is where you come in.

As soon as I get some money, and we can arrange it, I want to see you. . . . Pet gets bored when I talk about The Region, and I get sore when she gets bored, and so on. . . . You see, I would like to sit around and chew the fat, sort of to refresh my memory about the roundheader boys and to Study Conditions. You and I might even go for a spin in the general direction of Pottsville, although not in it, to be sure. . . .

Getting back to the book (never very far away from it, I'll agree), what do you think of this idea? In the book about the Sheafers ["The Hofman Estate"], I brought them up to about the time of the crash, but, of course, did not refer to it. The Doctor's Son was left hanging, as it were, at about the age of 14, just after the war. Now the third story, about the Schuylkill County gangster, could be built around a guy like that Malloy (if that's the name), but not an Irishman. He would have to be a Schwackie. The gangster might be a sort of hanger-on at a roadhouse which was occasionally visited by the Pottsville country club set. I would bring the doctor's son up to date, as of 1930; a drinker, roustabout, etc., playing around with the Sheafers. The roadhouse could either be a place like Turin's, or the Log Cabin. The third story most likely would be told through the eyes of the gangster, whose job would be that of assistant manager (at a place like Turin's), or, if we decided on a lower-scale dump, the gangster could be just one of those mysterious pimps or bootleggers, whose source of income is never very definite, so far as you and I can be sure. He would be attractive, in a common way, and we could have Polly falling for him, the doctor's son either picking a fight or being a pal, and Clint being friendly but superior. In the first two stories there would be only slight relationship between the two: a common locale, and names of towns and streets and people would appear now and then in both stories, but in the third story the people would really get together in the same roadhouse barroom. It might be effective to have the whole story take place over a period of one night; from the time the gangster comes around, early in the evening, to "go to work," until dawn the next morning, when the night's festivities had ended. This would give me an opportunity to give a complete picture of the roadhouse, with a lot of behind-the-scenes stuff, such as the arrival of the liquor in a Reo speed-wagon (Turin's, I really think, would be the best place), and a few unimportant people having dinner, and Papa and the gangster talking business, and a small orchestra setting up their instruments, getting ready for the nightly brawl, etc., etc. If you and Kate could have us for a week-end, or even if I could come over alone, and you could tell Papa in advance what I have in mind, I think the atmosphere would be all set. You and I could go up there early in the evening, or late in the afternoon, and just hang around and watch things. You could assure Papa that I have no designs on his place, that I'm not a Prohi agent, and that I would not libel him.[46]

This plan includes most of the elements of *Appointment in Samarra*, with the crucial exception of Julian English. The role of the doctor's son, Jimmy Malloy, was cut down to a mention as that story was preserved for separate publication, and the gangster type became Al Greco. Again, it is noteworthy that O'Hara was still not confident of his ability to construct a novel and was planning to fake the structure by stitching together three stories.*

Meanwhile the marriage was going bad. O'Hara's drinking and inability to keep a job aggravated the problems with Mrs. Petit, who was continuing Pet's allowance. When she became pregnant in February 1933, Pet had an abortion at her mother's insistence. Things were never right between John and Pet after that, and for a long time he felt guilty about consenting to the abortion. There were other problems. He didn't take Pet's theatrical ambitions very seriously— or perhaps it is more accurate to say that he didn't take acting seriously. Pet was beginning to drink heavily too; and O'Hara's violent behavior when drunk became a familiar topic among their friends, who talked about his physical abuse of Pet. It was said that he threw her out of a moving cab. He developed suspicions—apparently ground- less—about her interest in other men. There were violent scenes followed by spells of remorse.

O'Hara's published story production for 1932 fell to eleven, but among them were the three best stories he had written so far: "Ella and the Chinee," a description of a stupid and mean waitress; "I Never Seen Anything Like It," an account of a stickup; and "Mr. Cass and the Ten Thousand Dollars," which is a masterpiece of condensation. The account of Cass's clumsy attempts to share his day of success with two former classmates implies a biography of a diligent college outsider who succeeds—as well as of the popular boys who fail. The 1932 publications included his second appearance in *Scribner's*, "Early Afternoon," and a *New Yorker* profile, "Of Thee I Sing, Baby," for which O'Hara received $175—his largest writing check to date. The *New Yorker* piece is unusual in that the subject, a chorus girl, is not identified, and it is in the form of a story rather than an interview- biography. He subsequently reclassified it as a story and included it in *The Doctor's Son*.

As O'Hara became surer of his short-story technique, his attitude toward editorial interference correspondingly hardened. One day in 1933 Jerome Weidman, then a twenty-year-old writer, was leaving the *New Yorker* building after a difficult editorial meeting with Harold Ross on one of his stories. O'Hara saw him in the lobby, and noticing his depression, invited him out for coffee. When he recounted his problems with Ross, O'Hara gave him what Weidman calls "the only lesson I ever had in how to write a short story." O'Hara told him,

---

* It is just possible that he picked up this scheme from Faulkner's 1929 book, *The Sound and the Fury*.

"Once you have finished a story, there's only one way to improve it: tell the editor to go to hell."[47]

In the spring of 1933 O'Hara and Pet separated. He took the break hard. Even though he realized that his marriage had been a mistake, O'Hara felt guilty about its collapse. When Mildred Gilman encountered him in front of the 49th Street Trans-Lux he informed her, "Mildred, you will be the last person to see me alive." Since he seemed reasonably sober, she took him seriously and persuaded him to go into the theater with her. They sat in the back row, and he talked about his depression over his failed marriage.[48]

Interesting—sometimes dangerous—things happened to O'Hara when he was drinking. One night at a gangster party in the Village he encountered a woman who became convinced that he had stolen her jewelry. He began receiving threatening phone calls, which sounded authentic. O'Hara handled the problem by checking out of his hotel and walking through Grand Central Station carrying his bags. He left the station and checked into a nearby hotel. The calls stopped. On another occasion he got involved with a mobster who thought O'Hara was asking too many questions about Mickey Coll. O'Hara toured the bars with this increasingly menacing companion until they encountered a bartender in the Village who squared him.

Unemployed and drinking heavily after the separation, O'Hara decided to get out of New York and applied for the job of managing editor of the Pittsburgh *Bulletin-Index*, which he saw advertised in a trade publication. The *Bulletin-Index* was a struggling amalgam of *Time* and *The New Yorker* that had been salvaged and assembled from several Pittsburgh social magazines. It sold for 10¢ and had a circulation in the early Thirties of perhaps 2,000 copies per week. The boss, J. Paul Scheetz, who appeared on the masthead as "Adv. Mgr.," was a little younger than O'Hara and a graduate of the University of Missouri School of Journalism. His brother Henry Scheetz, president of the Fuller Paper and Box Co., was bankrolling the weekly. The Scheetz brothers sent O'Hara a copy of the magazine and invited him to criticize it by way of qualifying for the job as editor.

THE WEBSTER

40 WEST 45

NEW YORK

Dear Mr. Scheetz:

First of all I became a cover-to-cover reader of The Bulletin-Index, without reading sentence by sentence. I tried to get the tone of the book; the rhythm. There is no rhythm. The reason for that is mechan-

ical, typographical. Apparently no one has taken the time to develop a style. I don't mean literary style; that can be acquired. I mean what newspapers call style: 13 W. 44th St., or 13 West Forty-fourth Street— that sort of thing. Another abstract thing which struck me is that apparently too many individuals are being individualistic: Time style here, semi-Winchell style there, semi-Robert Quillan's Paragraphs style yonder. There is not, as with Time, the influence of one person, or a merger of influences, to be more accurate. Time's blatant flippancy came from the late Briton Hadden, who actually spoke conversationally as Time reads. Luce does too, but to a lesser degree. The point is, they did agree, formulate some kind of consistency from which developed the present Time presentation.

Speaking now of general policy, mine would have been to put that swell picture of the nude man posing for the gals on the cover. Caption: ". . . for Fun." (See p. . . . ; or See The Arts.) Even the picture of Dilettante Bailey would have been better on the cover than that of dour Director Denny. Better, because Dilettante Bailey is an interesting face, he is shown in an unfamiliar setting, and that torso on which he is working is a female torso. It's funny, impudent, impertinent. It's Time-ly. (You've no idea how many photos Time goes through each week, trying to get just something like that. I take it Bailey is a semi-big shot in Pittsburgh. Therefore, that picture on the cover would be locally like a Time cover of G. B. Shaw clad only in a bathing towel. Get what I mean?) Frankly, Director Denny's earnest countenance did not make me want to read the book. Time's policy is this: the "cover story" is the most important story of the book that week. I do not mean that it is the most important story of the week from a news standpoint. Far from it. Most always the cover story is planned from one to six months ahead, for obvious reasons. You will notice that the man or woman on the cover of Time always is the subject of a long, exhaustive, comprehensive story. Which is as it should be. If Denny was the big news of the week, write a piece about him; but he hasn't got to be on the cover. It's a good thing to remember that by the time a weekly comes out, the readers are pretty sick of the Big News-boy's goddam face, as Beatrice Lillie would say. Let a story appear, but unless the subject of the story has not been in the news much in the past, his or her picture isn't necessary. Always excepting this: if you have a photo of Senator Reed scratching his ass or Andrew Mellon eating a hot dog, use it. Still, I repeat, not necessarily on the cover.

Lay off humorous drawings unless there is some good reason for running them regularly and in an established spot in the book.

More policy: womanize the book. There are too few photos of some, too many photos of men. I knew this was the case without going through the text; I knew it from the ads. I don't know how you are budgeted, but I say, have more pix of women, a ratio of 2:1 isn't too much. This is my psychology: a man isn't interested in a picture of another man unless he is a) handsome and handsomely turned out; b) ugly; c) in an awkward or exciting pose. By the same token, women are not interested in men other than as I have stated. Advertising agencies have found this out. See Lucky, Camel, Chesterfield ads, from the famed *Blow Some My Way* ad to the latest Camel. The reason is, to be really psychological about it, women are more homosexual than men. Men do not say: "Jones is a handsome man." Women do say: "Grace is lovely." What's more, women like to see what other women are wearing, and here again is psychology; they like to admire or to criticize their own sex. These things you may know, but they have been lost sight of in the editing of the book as I see it. That's the reason the sculping photo would have done on the cover. The man is a male, the girl is a female, and attractive. The man wears the slightest of jock straps, and the girl is almost within arm's reach of him. Really, my *Time*-broken heart bleeds when I think of that wasted photo.

Apropos: I would not try to make your book a collection of feelthy pictures, nor would I make it a Pittsburgh *Woman's Home Companion*. But you know probably better than I do that the more women read your magazine, the more black ink your accountants must use, and you said you're out to make money. Institutional ads are nice, but save only the Peoples-Pittsburgh Trust Company page) dull. They pay, but they are not productive of competing ads. You know what I mean: Macy's takes 21 columns in a paper; Gimbel follows suit. You can make two blades of ad grass grow where only one grew before.

I could point out numerous instances of a lack of consistency in the typographical presentation of the text, but they are self-evident. One flagrant error of commission: some names are in bold face, others are not. Now unless a departmental style is arrived at and decided upon (such as *Time's* People), it is unwise to discriminate, especially where no discrimination is intended. It is all right to be snooty, to blackface the people who are bigwigs in Pittsburgh, but that must be understood by the readers. Consistency. Consistency. Consistency. It is just as important to put the ushers-to-be in bold face as it is ushers-who-were. More, in fact, because such names are more likely to be news. Names of ushers-to-be have not been published so often as those that were. A small point, but significant.

Let me go through the book at random, pick other small points of the sort which could be corrected in copy; on page 3 Mistinguett's name is twice misspelt. Page 7, instead of "Louise Reed," her caption should have been "Looney Jeague?" (I doubt that little story, but it could have been true.) Things like that. They are things which strike the trained eye (mine, for instance), which do not seem important to the average reader who skims through the whole book. Yet, let us suppose that a military-minded man were to read the story of the Boyd-Pennell wedding (page 10). Let us suppose that the man knew that Lieut. Boyd is an infantry officer. Military-minded man then would scoff at the idea of an arch of sabres, for the sabre is a cavalry weapon. In other words, pedantic, picayunish copyreading, leading to an approximation of total accuracy, results in fewer scoffers, more respect for the publication. Every average reader knows a little more about one thing than he does about all others, whether his specialty be philatelics or philology. And when he comes upon a story dealing with his specialty, he wants it to be right. In a well-written ably edited publication, he gets that. If he doesn't quite get it, he ought to get enough of it to cause him to write a letter. And when he writes a letter, his letter gets published, by God. If he pans the hell out of the book, okay. Have you ever noticed that every time a man writes a panning letter to the editor, and the letter is published, the man looks a little foolish? At the same time, the publication acquires a badge of courage (real or spurious).

I wish you had sent me a few more copies of the book; past issues. Up to now, as Al Smith says, I have been mostly critical. I've had to be. You will understand that my criticisms imply change, and therefore my criticisms are, to my mind at least, constructive. I have had, for example, no opportunity to determine whether the anti-Press story is typical editorial-page matter, or whether it had a special purpose. In any case I do not approve of the story as presented. If you had it under the masthead, okay. Or if it were signed by a writer who the readers know is an editor or social critic. As is, there it is, simply a controversial article, definitely opinionated, without any person or the publication standing by to take the rap. It is anonymous in the worst sense. Time "weasels" such things by quoting private opinion directed against the policy of the Press, with "adroitly manoeuvered phrases" tending to direct the reader's opinion into one channel. This story is such a highly special thing that I would rather discuss it with you in person, in order to determine what you have determined as policy on such matters. If I had that story I'd have found out whether all Scripps-Howard papers were attacking the insurance companies. If so the story might have been written like this: "Out of an office high above New York's Park Avenue came last week a ukase, and twenty-six links of a newspaper chain rattled disturbingly in the ears of many an insurance corporation. The ukase: attack insurance officers' high salaries." And so on. Taking the stand that Scripps-Howard's attack was unwarranted, or unjust, I would not have The Bulletin-Index say so; I would have some of the local insurance men call it "cowardly," "undermining public confidence," etc. On the other hand, *if your arrived-at policy should include an editorial page (and I think it should), you could say what you pleased under your own banner line.*

To continue my editing in absentia: the next story is the sculpture yarn. Pretty good reporting, but with too much taken for granted. I mean that the reporter must have thought, oh, everybody knows what George Bailey does for a living, so why say what he manufactures? Well, that's the difference between my point of view and that of the person who wrote the story. Before I could rewrite that story I would insist on knowing just what Bailey-Farrell Mfg. Co. manufactured. Paper dolls? Stoves? Hand grenades? Kotex? Templates? Glassware? Then contrast Bailey's regular work with his new hobby, if there is a contrast, and go on with the story pretty much as written: "To Sarasota, Florida, last winter went, as usual, the lions, snakes, anteaters, giraffes, of the Ringling-Barnum & Bailey Circus. To Sarasota, too, went George Hungerford Bailey, Presbyterian Elder, second-sixteen (Aronimink) golfer, art patron, president of Bailey-Farrell (pots & Pans) Mfg. Co. No novelty to Elder Bailey were the sights and smells of the Ringling menagerie. He anticipated a conventional holiday. But a fortnight after his arrival in Sarasota Elder Bailey & wife gained a new neighbour. She, Sculptress Isadora Goldfarb, clicked with the Baileys, they with her. In Elder Bailey she found a tyro enthusiast for her art. In her art Elder Bailey found manual, aesthetic release. With borrowed knife, scalpel, Elder Bailey quickly became Dilettante Bailey. In six weeks he completed two worthy torsoes, one bas-relief. Returning to Pittsburgh he enrolled at Tech, completed a primary course in anatomy, modelling. Now Dilettante Bailey plans a show in 1935." Etc. then go on with the story pretty much as it is written. But you see what I mean when I say that I would want to do some research or be able to ask someone in the office for the quick dope on Bailey, et al. All those "facts" that I have filled in in the lead as I have written it are the kind of thing I would want to know. Not knowing them, not being able to find them in the stories as they appear in the magazine, I have, as you see, made up "facts" to show how I would handle stories. I think you can see I know my Time style, and there is not much point in going through the whole book and rewriting every story.

I must make this point at this point: if I were to please you sufficiently to warrant your giving me the job, I would not attempt to make over the magazine in one issue. I would begin with a real Time-like cover story, and watch the effect on the other members of the staff. I would make certain changes in lay-out; for instance I would discontinue the humorous drawing and try to have more vignettes (unless the little boy and girl in the drawing are established characters). I would make what changes I deemed necessary week by week until the whole book had changed its complexion. We would have to have a get-together with the printer—you, the printer, myself—and determine a type policy. There probably would have to be some kind of staff reorganization. I am not much of a believer in staff conferences; I think they usually are a waste of time; but I would want to have a couple of light talks with individuals.

I am enthusiastic about the magazine and its chances, now that I have given it some concentrated attention. If you decide I am the man, the sooner I start, the better. I will be in the country next Monday, Tuesday, and Wednesday. My hostess will be Mrs. Wilcox Stires. "Whippoorwill," Chappaqua, N. Y., if you want to get in touch with me. I don't know what her phone number is. I'll be back in New York Wednesday night, and will be ready to go to Pittsburgh at any time after that. I expect my play to be finished and in the hands of the typing service by that night (Wednesday), and then there will be nothing else to hold me here, as I have polished off a couple of New Yorker pieces which were hanging fire.

So there we are—or here I am, and there you are. It's been fun to go over the book. I've enjoyed it. And I trust it will be by no means the last time.

> *With best wishes,*
>
> *Faithfully,*
>
> *John O'Hara*[49]

By mid-May 1933 O'Hara was in Pittsburgh with the duties of managing editor—although his name never appeared on the masthead—and living on a due-bill at the William Penn Hotel. The *Bulletin-Index* needed his skills, and to the copyboys, Burtt Evans and Frank Zachary, he seemed like something out of *The Front Page*: he wore Brooks clothes sloppily (it was a matter of awe that he had $5 ties when a copyboy's salary was $7), kept golf clubs in the office, corresponded with famous writers and editors, and was appearing in *The New Yorker*. His working relationship with the Scheetz brothers was less than happy. While recognizing that he was helping the magazine, they were put off by his personal life and work habits. He came in late and drove the printers crazy with last-minute copy.

John O'Hara's by-line never appeared in the *Bulletin-Index*, but former staffers have clear recollections of some of his work. The first important article by O'Hara was "Joe: Straight Man," a short profile, with *Time* overtones, of Joseph Guffey, the Democratic leader of Pittsburgh, which appeared 18 May 1933. Frank Zachary went with O'Hara to interview Guffey and recalls his tough reporter pose: "Senator Guffey, everything you say will be on the record and used against you."

He is not superstitious, else he would not have taken offices on the thirteenth floor of his great and good friend M. L. Benedum's building in narrow Fourth Avenue. To those offices go the big & the little, for one thing or another, but chiefly for favors. They sprawl in benches in the outer office of the mysterious Japi Co. (which is not listed by Dun & Bradstreet, nor registered in the 'phone book), and ultimately are ushered by one of the Guffey hirelings into the private office. This room looks lived in, comfortable, a bit old-fashioned. In a bookshelf is a reflection of the Guffey taste, which is good: "The Biography of a Virginal Mind," (the story of Mary Baker Eddy, famed Christian Scientist), Denis Tilden Lynch's "An Epoch & a Man," (a Grover Cleveland biography); Walter Liggett's "The Rise of Herbert Hoover"; Brand Whitlock's two volumes of "La Fayette"; a mighty tome called "Athletics at Princeton"; Gann's "Maya Cities." Old news-photos of Woodrow Wilson, newer pictures of Franklin Delano Roosevelt, hang on the walls. The chairs are easy on the buttocks, there are not enough ash trays.

The Jack Pettis orchestra was at the Urban Room at the William Penn Hotel, with a vocalist named Dolores Reade—who later married Bob Hope. John dated her and wrote the 3 August cover story on her, "Torch Singer." During the summer of 1933 the *Bulletin-Index* was peppered with items that can be confidently attributed to O'Hara: for example, " 'Anthony Adverse' has been tapped for membership, will go to its room in Book of Month Club." His presence can be detected in references to *The New Yorker*, to New Yorkers such as Geoffrey Hellman, Dorothy Parker and Lucius Beebe, and to New York clubs —particularly on the Letters to the Editor pages. Some of these letters were no doubt planted by O'Hara so he could reply to them. A question about the tunnel between the Yale Club and Grand Central Station elicited a detailed account of how "a member of the staff of *The Bulletin-Index* walked one night in 1929 from the Yale Club bar to Park Avenue & Fiftieth Street without once coming out in the open."

In 1930 or 1931 O'Hara had initiated a correspondence with F. Scott Fitzgerald, and on 25 June 1933 wrote from Pittsburgh to compliment Fitzgerald on "More Than Just a House," which had recently appeared in *The Saturday Evening Post.** O'Hara revealed a great deal about himself in his letter, for he regarded Fitzgerald as a man who shared his feelings.

---

* O'Hara had probably started sending fan letters to Fitzgerald from Pottsville.

Well;

You've written another swell piece, doing again several of the things you do so well, and doing them in a single piece. Miss Jean Gunther, of the More Than Just a House Gunthers, was one of those girls for the writing about of whom you hold the exclusive franchise, if you can puzzle out that sentence. It was really all told when she told Lew Lowrie, "Well, at least you've kissed one Gunther girl." Not to get too autobiographical about it, she's the type that the Lowries and O'Haras never have been able to cope with, and in my experience I've encountered a complete set of them. Have right here, in this really Fitzgeraldian city, where I am editing a magazine for the upper crust.

And that easily we get to the second thing you've done so well: Lowrie, the climber; and I wonder why you do the climber so well. Is it the Irish in you? Must the Irish always have a lot of climber in them? Good God! I am the son of a black Irish doctor (gone to his eternal reward) and a mother who was a Sacred Heart girl, whose father was born Israel Delaney (Pennsylvania Quaker who turned Catholic to marry an immigrant girl, Liza Roarke). My old man was the first doctor in the U. S. to use oxygen in pneumonia, was recognized by Deaver as being one of the best trephiners and appendix men in the world. But do I have to tell you which side of the family impresses me most? I doubt it. You've guessed it: because Grandfather Delaney's connections included some Haarmons from Holland and a Gray who was an a. d. c. to Washington, and I have some remote kinship with those N. Y. Pells, I go through cheap shame when the O'Hara side gets too close for comfort. If you've had the same trouble, at least you've turned it into a gift, but I suspect that Al Smith is the only Irishman who isn't a climber at heart. Anyhow in Lowrie you've done a sort of minor Gatsby. (By the way, I saw Warner Baxter in a pretty bad movie tonight.)

Another thing you did was to take a rather fantastic little detail—the girl wearing bedroom slippers with Jodhpurs—and put it across by timing it just right. You got the old man's madness with the detail of the $20 he borrowed in 1892, and once again you dabbled successfully in death. Oh, hell. A swell piece.

I read somewhere that you are in Maryland, and I hope things are breaking better for you than they were when I last heard from you, which was from Lausanne. Breaking fine for me. My pretty little wife is rolling out to Reno next week, and the girl I loved from the time I was 17 got married in Haiti last month, to a Byronic lad whom she'd known about two months. And she was the shadow on the wall that broke up my marriage. Oh, my.

John O'Hara[50]

92

On 18 July, Fitzgerald, who was laboring over the final draft of *Tender Is the Night*, wrote O'Hara a now widely quoted letter about his own social insecurities: "So if I were elected King of Scotland tomorrow after graduating from Eton, Magdalene to Guards, with an embryonic history which tied me to the plantagonists, I would still be a parvenue."[51]

O'Hara was frequently depressed in Pittsburgh. He continued to be troubled by his failed marriage; writing to Crichton at *Scribner's* in May he stated, "I now fully realize that I love my wife, and you'll see a story with plenty of depth, kid."[52] Pittsburgh residents hint that a scandal was barely averted in 1933 when O'Hara became involved with a recently married woman. He was unhappy with his job and his life, and his unhappiness often took the form of alcoholic despondency. On the night of 3 July 1933 he contemplated jumping from the window of his hotel room in a mood of drunken despair as he perched on the sill. Instead, he went on the wagon. Pet obtained the Reno divorce—on the ground of extreme cruelty—on 15 August 1933.

At the same time that he was brooding about Pet—and to a certain extent about Marg—he was concerned about the limitations of his fiction. When Crichton complimented him on a story, which *Scribner's* declined, on 2 August, O'Hara wrote back:

I think a lot of what you said is a lot of crap, for the reason that I know so much better than anyone else that I have an inferior talent. The reason I think I have an inferior talent is that when I write I can't sustain an emotion. It isn't that I don't feel things, but when I begin to write out of hate, I find myself being diverted into tolerance; and when I write about love, or from love, I get critical and nasty. Only once in a while can I sustain either of the two, and the pieces in The New Yorker are the ones that start from hate, and here is one that started from love. I can't tell you, though, whether it's a good piece, but it has plenty of feeling in it. But I'm not important, and I never will be. The next best thing is to be facile and clever. But thank you for the analysis and the kind words. I get nothing of the kind here, and I miss them.

The uneasy relationship between O'Hara and the Scheetz brothers steadily deteriorated. There had been difficulties over O'Hara's bar bills at the William Penn, and the owners felt that he was doing his own writing on *Bulletin-Index* time. The break came in early August over O'Hara's objections to having his personal mail opened at the office, and he departed for New York after a scuffle. This event has grown in telling to a fistfight in which O'Hara knocked one of the owners across a desk, but it probably involved only pushing or shoving.

O'Hara and his employers were no doubt equally relieved at his separation from the *Bulletin-Index*. He had done a lot for the magazine, but Paul Scheetz had come to regard him as more trouble than he was worth. O'Hara missed New York and wanted to be near Pet, whom he intended to remarry after he won her respect by publishing a novel. His three-month tenure on the *Bulletin-Index* generated several Pittsburgh legends—in particular, that he wrote or at least started *Appointment in Samarra* there, which is not true. He may have been tinkering with "The Hofman Estate" and "The Doctor's Son"; but the only piece of O'Hara fiction that Pittsburgh can definitely claim is "Hotel Kid," which appeared in the September 1933 *Vanity Fair*—and perhaps the casuals that appeared in *The New Yorker* in September.

By late August 1933 O'Hara was living in an $8 or $9 per week room at the Pickwick Arms Club Residence, a hotel at 230 East 51st Street, between Second and Third avenues. The Pickwick Arms was obviously inexpensive, but it was not a dump—$9 went a long way in the Depression. The picture of John O'Hara living in abject poverty while writing *Appointment in Samarra* is a distortion. He was broke but not starving. He did not find a job and perhaps did not look very hard for one. In the fall of 1933 he was offered the job of press agent for *Tobacco Road* at $40 per week but turned it down because he did not think the play would last. (It became one of the longest running hits in the American theater.) *The New Yorker* published four of his casuals in September–October, which provided eating money; and in November–December O'Hara wrote four columns on Ivy League football for the magazine. A story, "The Public Career of Mr. Seymour Harrisburg," appeared in the *Brooklyn Daily Eagle* in November.

In October he wrote Fitzgerald to compliment him on "Ring," his Lardner obituary-tribute:

October 14-15, 1933

Dear Mr. Fitzgerald:

A little story I have to tell you runs about like this: a bunch of the boys and girls were sitting around Tony's last night, and Jim Thurber began to rave about a piece you wrote in The New Republic. Dottie Parker, who knows about my admiration for your writing, said to me: "Did you hear that, John? Jim just said Scott has a beautiful piece about Lardner in The New Republic." So on the way home I stopped at an all-night newsstand and bought a New Republic, blind, and went into a beanery to read your piece. But it was not the right issue, so I went to another newsstand across the street and said, "Have you got last week's

New Republic?" The man said with a smile: "Why yes, I have, but it's tied up in this bundle (indicating a tightly tied bundle of old magazines). You want it for the article on Lardner I guess." So he got it out for me. He said he had had a lot of requests for that issue of The New Republic, and wondered why, and made a point of finding out. "And so I read it," he said. "It's a wonderful article."

I read the piece over and over, and tonight I gave the magazine to Mrs. Parker. We stopped here, where I am living, while I went upstairs and got it, and then we went to a Baltimore Dairy Lunch (by a coincidence) and she read the piece, and she wept tears. The only thing I could think of to say was "Isn't it swell?" You know. The usual inarticulate O'Hara. Mrs. Parker said: "The Gettysburg Address was good too."

Last night I tried to write to you to tell you what I thought of the piece, but I gave it up, because I told myself that you'd rather not hear what anyone thought of what you thought. But tonight I write regardless. I think you ought to know that I do mean to tell you what I think of the piece. The only thing is, you'll have to guess by my incoherent words. If you never wrote anything else, if you never had written This Side of Paradise, "Ring" would have been a writing [career] enough for anyone. But then if you hadn't written This Side of Paradise you probably wouldn't be the man who did write "Ring." (I [don't] seem to have any consistent style about quotes and titles. Do [you] mind?) I only hope no one else tries to do a piece on Lardner. [You] have said all that should be said. Lardner must have made the [?] First Fridays to get that piece—and I mean that as reverently [as I] can mean anything.

All this from one who has been a frank imitator of Lardner.

Regards.

John O'Hara[53]

Note: The original of this letter is torn, and the bracketed words are inferential readings.

By December 1933 O'Hara was working steadily on his novel. His accounts of the chronology of writing it differ. In 1934 he stated that he had begun writing it in late December 1933;[54] but in the 1953 foreword to the Modern Library *Appointment in Samarra* he said that he had started in September 1933. It may be that both versions are correct: that in September he was reworking the stories but in December was actually starting the novel. His chief problem was whether to stick with his old plan of combining three long stories into an episodic novel, or to start all over again. He decided that if he was going to write a novel, he should really write one. His writing habits were established—he was a night writer, starting after midnight and working for five hours or more. Since his room was too small for a desk, he typed on the bed, using a new portable typewriter. As was his invariable custom, he wrote directly on the typewriter, and there was no carbon copy. When the night's stint was done, he slept through noon and spent the afternoons at the movies or visiting Dorothy Parker or playing backgammon at Ira Gershwin's East 72nd Street apartment. In the evenings he drank coffee at Tony's until it was time to write. On Thursdays he put on his dinner jacket and took Nancy Hale—who was also being courted by Gibbs—dancing at the Algonquin. He saw a good deal of Pet, which they kept a secret from Mrs. Petit, and worried about his failure in marriage. A fictional portrait of John O'Hara at this time is Hector Connolly in Nancy Hale's 1942 novel, *The Prodigal Women*—a heavy-drinking, violent Irish writer tormented by his lost Catholicism and divorce.*

O'Hara remained on the wagon, except for Christmas Eve 1933, when Robert Benchley spotted him sitting alone drinking coffee at Tony's and insisted on making Black Velvets. Benchley ceremoniously mixed the champagne and stout and joked with O'Hara. Two hours later O'Hara went back to the Pickwick Arms singing.[55] It is not clear what being on the wagon meant for O'Hara at this time, for he wrote his brother Tom in October that "the most I have had in any one day since then [July] has been a cocktail and a glass of wine at dinner."

On 5 January 1934 O'Hara sent Harold Ross a report on his association with *The New Yorker*, the obvious purpose of which was to elicit some sort of financial assistance. A $125 check from *Harper's Bazaar* for "All the Girls He Wanted" had helped O'Hara to get through December, but by late January he was some 30,000 words into the novel—with 60,000 more to be written—and had run out of eating money. He sent special-delivery letters to three publishers—Viking, Morrow, and Harcourt, Brace—requesting an advance to complete the book, with the stipulation that his typescript be read overnight. Then he went to the movies. All three publishers telephoned, and the first call was from Charles A. Pearce of Harcourt, Brace. Cap Pearce read the work-in-progress and urged his firm to make the advance. O'Hara went to see Alfred Harcourt, who asked, "Young man, do you know where you're going?" Upon replying that he did know what the rest of the novel

---

* O'Hara's comment on *The Prodigal Women* appeared in his 1953 foreword to the Modern Library *Appointment in Samarra*: "The lady later crucified me in a novel, but she so thoroughly misunderstood me that only a few mutual friends recognized the caricature."

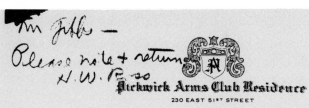

Pickwick Arms Club Residence

230 EAST 51ST STREET

NEW YORK

January 5, 1934

Dear Harold:

I have been going over my history, and I
find that I am approaching a New Year, the seventh
year of my association with The New Yorker. I
have had dealings with The New Yorker in the
years 1928, 1929, 1930, 1931, 1932, 1933. During
that time I have done everything except to sell
a drawing: I have written casuals, a column of
Notes & Comment, several Talk items, newsbreaks,
one department, one Profile, and two tips on
pieces by Frank Sullivan and Robert Benchley. The
association has been uniformly pleasant for me,
and I hope satisfactory to you. I have resented
very few rejections. The good pieces I wrote
have been recognized by O'Brien and other col-
lectors, or recommended by Winchell or Russel
Crouse, and the bad pieces have been forgotten by
my enemies. I have sold more than a hundred
casuals, and so far as I know, caused only one
cancellation of subscription (a football column
brought that about). And so I think it would be
nice if you were to have a medal struck, or did
something else in the way of commemorating what
I believe to be a fact: that in the period beginning 1928 I have contributed more pieces to
The New Yorker than any other non-staff man. This
year I hope not only to sell you a great many
pieces, but also to round out my record with the
sale of a drawing; thus establishing me as one
who has done everything on The New Yorker.

With best wishes,

Faithfully,

John O'Hara

John O'Hara

A dollar bonus on each casual----nice!

To Harold Ross, January 1934.

would do and how it would end, O'Hara was given a contract calling for $400 in $50 weekly payments until 1 April delivery.

Tom O'Hara was at Brown, and John sent him progress reports during the completion of the novel. In February O'Hara wrote that Helen P. O'Hara, "who has the best taste of anyone I know," liked it so far and Mrs. Parker was reading it. Dorothy Parker's encouragement and generosity were important to O'Hara, for he was proceeding with difficulty—working in spurts followed by writing blocks. He did not know how good the novel really was and needed her reassurances. When he wanted to take Pet away for a weekend, Mrs. Parker gave him $50; but Pet was afraid her mother would find out, so he used the money to get his winter coats out of Macy's storage.

O'Hara visited the Simondses in Allentown in February and intended to return for a long visit. But he wrote them from New York on 21 February:

> . . . if I were to leave New York—which is to say the vicinity of Pet—I wouldn't be able to work, and right now the only important thing in my life is work, this novel. . . .
> . . . She is opening in this damn review [New Faces of 1934] in a fortnight or so, and I hate the very thought of it. I think all actors are terrible people. . . . However, there it is in Pet, one of the most intelligent people I've ever known, so I have to take it, and I'm afraid it's going to cause trouble. . . . I have one chance of sanity, and that is to finish the novel and make it good. To have done that will enable me to keep my self-respect, and not only my self-respect, but Pet's respect; she still will believe that a good novel is better than the best performance an actor can give.

> Here is the passage from Spectre and Emanation:
> Let us agree to give up love
> And root up the infernal grove,
> Then shall we return and see
> The worlds of Happy Eternity.

> And throughout all Eternity
> I forgive you, you forgive me.
> As our dear Redeemer said:
> This the wine and this the bread.*

The working title for the novel was "The Infernal Grove." After about 50,000 words—roughly half the novel—were done, O'Hara was

---

* Untitled poem from William Blake's notebook.

having tea in Dorothy Parker's apartment when she showed him a volume of W. Somerset Maugham's plays which included *Sheppey*, a play about the death of a London barber. The book was open to the speech by Death in which she describes to Sheppey the attempts of another man to evade her: "I was astonished to see him in Bagdad, for I had an appointment with him in Samarra."

"There's the title for my book."

"Where?" said Mrs. Parker.

" 'Appointment in Samarra,' " I said.

"Oh, I don't think so, Mr. O'Hara. Do you?"[56]

Alfred Harcourt didn't like the new title either, but the author insisted that the Samarra legend conveyed "the inevitability of Julian English's death." Inevitability would become a major theme of O'Hara's novels.

One of the side benefits of O'Hara's work on *Appointment* is that it put him on a fellow-novelist basis with Fitzgerald, who was coming to New York from Baltimore in January–February 1934 to see *Tender Is the Night* through publication. As always, Fitzgerald was happy to help a young writer who admired him. When O'Hara sought his advice on the novel, "Fitzgerald's first judgment was yes-yes-but-also-no."[57] O'Hara reciprocated by proofreading *Tender*.* One night O'Hara, Fitzgerald, Dorothy Parker and Pet (Helen) went out together. John wasn't drinking, but the others got tight.

Very late, on the way to Helen's apartment, Scott was making heavy passes at Helen and she was not fighting him off. We got to the apartment, which was on Park Avenue and had a doorman and she got out and so did Scott. I couldn't, because I was not supposed to be seeing Helen and she was afraid the doorman would report me to her family. Scott followed her into the foyer as far as the elevator, then she left him. He was assisted by the doorman. Meanwhile Dottie had said to me, "He's awful, why didn't you punch him?" I said Helen seemed to like it and we were divorced (I did not see fit to tell Dottie that I was seeing a lot of Nancy).[58]

In March 1934, with the novel unfinished, O'Hara went on a three-week West Indies Cruise as editor of the ship's paper. The *Kungsholm* of the Swedish American Line left New York on 9 March and stopped at Barbados, Trinidad, Venezuela, Curaçao, Cristobal,

---

* Although O'Hara referred to the proofs of *Tender* as one of his treasured possessions, they were not found among his books after his death. He did, however, have framed in his study seven of Edward Shenton's original illustrations for the novel.

THE KUNGSHOLM CRUISE NEWS

John O'Hara, *Editor*

March 9th, 1934, Cruise

Yoo-hoo! So Long!

Oh, for goodness' sake quit sitting there with a long puss, trying to tell us you wish you didn't have to go home. What about us (and by

---

Jamaica, Haiti and Nassau—docking in New York on 28 March. He produced eight issues of the four-page *Kungsholm Cruise News*, of which one page was canned travel information. The job took about twenty minutes a day, he said. Although he had good intentions for completing the novel aboard the ship, he missed his contractual deadline by a week. He did not accompany a girl on the trip—although he met one onboard—so the reason for this excursion was not sexual. John McClain had accepted the *Kungsholm* job, and O'Hara filled in for him when it was impossible for McClain to go. Since the ship stopped at Haiti, and Margaretta Archbald Kroll was married to the son of the Bishop of Haiti, the speculation arises that O'Hara may have been motivated by a desire to see her. He did try to visit, but discovered that she was away on a cruise. Aboard the *Kungsholm* he learned how to say "Thank you" in Swedish—which he kept ready for thirty-five years.*

When *Tender Is the Night* was published in April 1934, Fitzgerald sent O'Hara a copy inscribed: "Dear John: May we meet soon in equally Celtic but more communicable condition/Scott Fitz." O'Hara was not a book collector; but he kept this copy, and it was in his bedroom bookcase when he died. Fitzgerald preserved O'Hara's thank-you letter in his scrapbook:

---

* The final issue of the *Kungsholm Cruise News* included O'Hara's parody tourist guide to Manhattan: "Until recently the natives shared with other Americans the oppression inflicted by an individual named Volstad or Volsted or Volsteadt or Vollstead, and there was a mushroom growth of clandestine bistros where the natives and visitors to the island might gather to sigh for the days before this tyrant fastened his yoke upon the citizenry, and to watch and pray for the day of liberty." The ship's paper was bound as a souvenir book with the title *Reminiscences from "Kungsholm"*—thereby becoming John O'Hara's first book.59

You helped me finish my novel. I finished it yesterday. The little we talked when you were in New York did it. I reasoned that the best parts of my novel will be said to derive from Fitzgerald, and I think I have muffed my story, but I became reconciled to having done that after talking to you and reading Tender Is the Night in proof. No one else can write like that, and I haven't tried, but the best parts of my novel are facile pupils of The Beautiful and Damned and The Great Gatsby. I was bushed, as Dottie says, and the fact that I need money terribly was enough to make me say the hell with my book until you talked to me and seemed to accept me. So then I went ahead and finished my second-rate novel in peace. My message to the world is fuck* it! I know this is not the right, the classical (as Hergesheimer would punctuate it), attitude, but I can write better than Louis Brom-field, Tiffany Thayer, Kathleen Norris, Erskine Caldwell or Mike Gold, so I am not the worst writer there is.†

During the final week of work on the novel, O'Hara was offered a loan by Fitzgerald, but turned it down because he knew Fitzgerald was strapped. The typescript of *Appointment in Samarra* was delivered to Harcourt, Brace on 9 April 1934—six days late. O'Hara completed the last page with $5.55 in his pocket.

---

* Fitzgerald blue-penciled out this word.

† On 9 April 1934 O'Hara urged his brother Tom to read *Tender*, calling it "one of the great books of the world. I think of it and think of it, and the more I do, the more I'm beginning to believe it's the greatest book I've read, despite certain obvious failings." Evidence of how carefully O'Hara read the novel is provided by the fact that he marked the repetition of the phrase "the compromises of how many years" on pp. 35 and 69 in his copy.

III

Success

WITH *Appointment in Samarra* finished, O'Hara was full of plans; most of which depended on the sale of movie rights. He wanted to visit Russia; he wanted to buy a Ford and tour America gathering material for a reportorial book about "the revolution"; he considered buying a used Rolls-Royce to drive to Hollywood for resale; and he needed a suit.[1] O'Hara asked Philip Barry to read *Appointment* in galleys; Barry's judgment had particular value to him because Barry had achieved all of the things for which O'Hara yearned. When O'Hara was up against it in New York, Barry had *Holiday* and *The Animal Kingdom* on Broadway. The success of his plays allowed Barry to be at home on the Riviera, at Hobe Sound, and at Southampton—where he enjoyed the good life and the best company. O'Hara admired Barry and was proud of their developing friendship, which in itself seemed a form of recognition. Barry, however, was shocked by the novel; but he gave it to Adele Lovett, who thought it was a masterpiece and said so to O'Hara when she encountered him at Tony's. Several years later he made her a present of the original (and only) typescript with instructions to leave it to Yale.[2] Mrs. Lovett's response mattered to O'Hara, for she had great taste and style and was a close friend of Dorothy Parker, who had dedicated a book to her.

Although *Appointment* was regarded as a work of remarkable sexual frankness in 1934, there is no evidence that O'Hara had bowdlerization problems with Harcourt, Brace. The proofs have only two deletions of sexual material: a description of Helene Holman teasing Al Greco with her breasts and a continuation of Julian and Caroline's conversation about the word *masticate*.[3]

Paramount read *Appointment* in galleys and declined to buy it because it was too strong for the movies, but they offered O'Hara a job writing dialogue. He was at Paramount from 12 June to 20 August at $250 per week, and is supposed to have reported for work late with the explanation "You should have seen her." When O'Hara recognized the saddle in a producer's office as a Whippy he was assigned to a

APPOINTMENT
IN SAMARRA

Inscription on galley proof, *Appointment in Samarra*.

cavalry picture for Cary Grant, Richard Arlen and Carole Lombard, which was not produced. He also polished dialogue on other scripts but did not receive a screen credit.

In 1934 Hollywood was a pleasant place for a young writer, but O'Hara missed the East. He took an apartment at 575 North Rossmore and bought his first car—a used Ford, which he soon traded in on a new 1934 Ford V-8 phaeton. There was an abundance of night life, and O'Hara became a regular at the Vendome, Ciro's, the Trocadero, the Brown Derby, Al Levey's and the Coconut Grove. He was lunching with Benchley at the Vendome when he looked around and saw Dolores Del Rio, Mrs. John Lodge, Mrs. Lewis Milestone, Mrs. Donald Ogden Stewart, Marlene Dietrich and Zita Johann: "more beautiful women than any other room in the world."[4]

Every day I made some excuse to stop at a Sunset Boulevard garage owned by Eddie Pullen, the former racing driver, to have a look at a white Rolls-Royce phaeton he had for sale for $1500. It was *a beautiful thing, about ten years old, and I think the only reason I did not buy it was that I was making good money for the first time in my life and had developed a horror of going into debt. I spent every cent I made, of course, and my credit was getting good, but to go into hock for $1500 for a Rolls-Royce would have been to deprive myself of the first real financial freedom I had ever had, and I was enjoying every minute of it. I was twenty-nine years old, divorced, not on good terms with my family, with no commitments or responsibilities, the author of a highly successful first novel, almost two years on the wagon,* and as one girl said, a pullover.*[5]

He was put off by the organization and administration of the studios—what he called "the nephew system." The top executives seemed to have given jobs to all their stupid relatives. The only thing he really liked was the pay, and he returned some fifteen times over the next twenty years for the easy money. As a gesture of his Eastern allegiance he dressed Brooks and bought a new Norfolk suit which he wore as a protest against Hollywood fashions. In August, Paramount renewed his option for another three months at the same salary, but O'Hara asked to be released because he wanted to return to New York.

He was still in Hollywood, however, when *Appointment in Samarra* was published on 16 August 1934.[6] That night the Herbert Asburys—O'Hara knew him from the *Trib* and *The New Yorker*—gave a big party for him at their Beverly Hills home. Among the guests were Nunnally Johnson, Joseph Moncure March and S. J. Perelman. At ten o'clock the butler went to Wilshire Boulevard and bought fifty copies of the Los Angeles *Examiner*, which had William Soskin's rave review that began: "John O'Hara's first novel, Appointment in Samarra, is too good to be true." (This review also appeared in the New York *American*.) The New York *Times* carried a highly favorable notice by John Chamberlain. The novel was widely covered, but reservations were expressed by some reviewers who were disturbed by the sexual material, and there were attempts to demonstrate the influences of Fitzgerald, Hemingway, and particularly Lewis. The most hostile review was Henry Seidel Canby's in *The Saturday Review of Literature*, headlined MR. O'HARA, AND THE VULGAR SCHOOL. Canby was disturbed by the technique, which he called "corrupted Hergesheimerism." The characters he found without values and meaningless except for "a sociological importance if and when they can be proved to be accurate studies of the contemporary American and not

---

* O'Hara had been on the wagon for only one year, having quit drinking on 3 July 1933.

Author of *Appointment in Samarra* (1934).

a sensationalist's half-truths." He concluded by longing for "the good old days of the Restoration."

Canby no doubt helped sales, for his front-page review gave the novel visibility; moreover, it produced a delayed reaction. In October Sinclair Lewis interrupted his review of Canby's *The Age of Confidence* in *The Saturday Review of Literature*—of which Canby was the editor—to attack *Appointment* as "the erotic visions of a hobbledehoy behind the barn." Lewis ridiculed the title as "bad art, atrocious philosophy, and—since it is both meaningless and difficult to remember—shockingly bad box-office." He rechristened the novel "Assignation in Abyssinia." The Sinclair Lewis attack is puzzling, for he had twice commended the novel in print before his *SRL* piece, as Kyle Crichton pointed out in a *Life* article.[7] The explanation that Lewis was polishing his Canby apples seems too simple, for it is likely that his reversal may have resulted from hearing O'Hara compared favorably—in some cases more than favorably—to himself. Even Nobel prizewinners are competitive. It is also possible that Lewis' reaction to O'Hara was related to his recent break with Harcourt, Brace. Some time later they were at adjacent urinals in "21," and Lewis left hurriedly when O'Hara attempted to tell him off. In 1935 O'Hara took revenge in *Butterfield 8* by including in a description of writer Henry White (originally Harry S. Lewis) getting the drunk treatment at "21." Nevertheless, O'Hara retained his respect for Lewis' early work and continued to praise it. In 1959 he wrote Mark Schorer: "Lewis, the only Lewis, saw Babbitt. All the other novelists and journalists and Babbitt himself were equally blind to Babbitt and Zenith and the United States of America until 1922."[8]

Always tardy in those days, John sent the dedication copy of *Appointment* to F.P.A. fourteen months late. The inscription on the free front end paper reads: "To Frank/turn over four pages/from John O'Hara/October 9, 1935." Adams had acknowledged the dedication in his 11 August 1934 "Diary of Our Own Samuel Pepys": "So home, and read all the afternoon John O'Hara's 'Appointment in Samarra,' a carefully written book, with some of the best talk, especially between husband and wife, that ever I read, and I got a great glow of pride when I saw that the book had been dedicated to me, and a great feeling of relief that I thought it a good book." And on the seventeenth—"Boy, I yell for 'Appointment in Samarra'/A dandy novel by John O'Hara."

Although *Appointment in Samarra* was not an immediate or unmitigated critical success, even the unfavorable reviews were the kind that sell copies, for they stressed the shocking qualities of the novel. Moreover, Harcourt, Brace spent money on promotion. Advance paperbound copies were distributed to reviewers and opinion-makers, and there was a good deal of advertising. Dorothy Parker's endorsement was used for an ad:

That this is John O'Hara's first novel seems to me an interesting fact only extraneously; a matter for envy and nothing else . . . It stands, a fine and serious American novel, of shrewd and inevitable pattern and almost unbelievable pace. This swift savage story of Julian English's life, and the lives of those who crowd his way, set down as sharp and deep as if the author had used steel for paper, is, it seems to me, of high importance both as a work of American letters and a document of American history . . . Mr. O'Hara's eyes and ears have spared nothing, but he has kept in his heart a curious and bitter mercy.[9]

One review that had particular significance for O'Hara was *The New Yorker*'s (1 September 1934), since he felt that as a member of the family he deserved serious and respectful treatment. Clifton Fadiman was cautious in that he seemed to hedge his bets. He complained that it was hard to review *Appointment*: "Just about the most sheerly readable novel within miles, its whole meaning lies in that readability, and stops there." It was his contention that the novel is all surface because O'Hara "deliberately has no ideas," that his intention is "to produce no effect at all." This review is significant in view of the difficulty O'Hara's books would have with *The New Yorker* reviewers and Fadiman. A late plug came from Ernest Hemingway in the December 1934 *Esquire*: "In the meantime, since it is Christmas, if you want to read a book by a man who knows exactly what he is writing about and has written it marvelously well, read Appointment in Samarra by John O'Hara."

On 15 August—the day before publication—the *Times* reported that 5,000 of the 7,500-copy first printing had been sold, and that a second printing of 10,000 had been ordered. On 7 October a full-page ad in the *Trib* book section announced the third printing. This ad quoted twenty-six comments, including Fitzgerald's ("John O'Hara's novel indicates the tremendous strides that American writers have taken since the war") and Walter Winchell's ("Orchids to John O'Hara's grand novel!"). Harcourt, Brace ordered five printings in 1934–35, which was impressive for the Depression, when $2.50 was a meaningful figure. Nevertheless, *Appointment* was not really a best seller.*

Predictably, *Appointment in Samarra* disturbed Pottsville, for Gibbsville was undeniably Pottsville. Katharine O'Hara was the recipient of outraged or sympathetic calls—depending upon whether or not the caller recognized himself (more often, herself)—as the game of identifying real-life sources for characters and episodes in the novel commenced. Some details were easy: Lantenengo Street was obviously Mahantongo Street; the Apollo Hotel was the Plaza; the Gibbsville Club was the Pottsville Club; Dr. Malloy was based on Dr. O'Hara; Ed Charney was based on either bootlegger Butch Macdonald

---

* The novel appeared in the *Publishers Weekly* best-seller list only once, as number ten for the month of October.

or Mosolino; Harry Reilly was based on Bill McQuail; and Whit Hofman was based on Clinton Sheafer. Some people thought Sheafer was also Julian English. In 1935 the Danville, Pennsylvania, *Morning News* printed an editorial utilizing a Pottsville girl's comments on the town's shocked reaction to *Appointment* and her commiseration with Mrs. O'Hara: " 'And now he's brought all this disgrace on her after her life of hardship,' sighed our fair informant."

Julian English is the author himself, we were told, in the guise of a young man who owns automobile agencies in Pottsville and Shamokin. And the wife of Julian is the girl John loved as a youth but failed to get and her mother in the book is the real girl's mother as big as life. The Pottsville people like the charitably inclined elderly lady and were particularly incensed at the cruelly clever caricature in the book. . . . He was home last Christmas, she said, but didn't get asked out so very much during his stay.[10]

After *Appointment* was published, Walter Farquhar—who had helped break in John O'Hara as a cub on the Pottsville *Journal*—wrote asking him for help in getting a job on a New York paper. O'Hara was willing to help, but tried to discourage Farquhar because the job situation was tough for sportswriters. He went on to comment bitterly on Pottsville and indicated that *Appointment* was in part motivated by a need to cut himself off from his hometown.

If you're going to get out of that God awful town, for God's sake write something that will make you get out of it. Write something that automatically will sever your connection with the town, that will help you get rid of the bitterness you must have stored up against all those patronizing cheap bastards in that dry-fucked excresence on Sharp Mountain. Stick it out for another year, but in that year go home at night knowing that you've done a thousand words a day toward showing them what you really think of them. You don't love them, any more than I do. You couldn't. You are a snob, but a snob not the way Ed Luther is, but the way I am. The Ed Luther kind can be bought—and lost on Wall Street. I was a snob when I was starving on 43rd Street.[11]

Farquhar remained in Pottsville for another thirty-five years to become a local journalistic institution.* And O'Hara kept returning to it in his fiction for the rest of his life.

---

* Farquhar's copy of *Appointment* was inscribed: "To Walter Southall Farquhar: what they mean when they say gentleman, and what I mean when I say friend.—John."

Readers who looked for a one-to-one relationship between Pottsville people and Gibbsville characters were oversimplifying O'Hara's technique. In the foreword to the Modern Library Edition of *Appointment*, O'Hara wrote:

Nobody ever guessed Julian English right. The quick readers thought they knew because of superficial resemblances between Julian English and some living men (me included), such as financial and social backgrounds, drinking habits, clothes. The truth is that the basic Julian English was from the wrong side of the tracks and never wore a buttoned-down collar in his tragic life. Under cumulative and finally unbearable pressure he killed himself. That's all I'll say about that.

O'Hara never publicly identified the source for Julian English, but in 1962 he wrote Gerald Murphy about *The New Yorker* profile of the Murphys—who were a source for Dick and Nicole Diver in *Tender Is the Night*:

In the case of Julian English, the guy in real life was a fellow named Richards, who was definitely not country-club, but had charm and a certain kind of native intelligence, and who, when the chips were down, shot himself. I took his life, his psychological pattern, and covered him up with Brooks shirts and a Cadillac dealership and so on, and the reason the story rings so true is that it is God's truth, out of life.

O'Hara went on in this letter to contrast his method with Fitzgerald's:

Scott wrote the life, but not the lives. And that is true partly because Scott was always writing about the life. Sooner or later his characters always came back to being Fitzgerald characters in a Fitzgerald world. . . . If I had known the Murphys and been compelled to write about them, I would have started by putting them in, say, Santa Barbara, if only to get away from the very things that Scott most wanted to write about. The life, the way of life.[12]

William Richards shot himself in the head with a .32 caliber revolver at 6:45 P.M., 14 February 1933, at his apartment on Arch Street in Pottsville. Birsie, or Birdsie, Richards had been born in 1905 and was O'Hara's age; he had been recently married. The death certificate gives his "usual occupation" as surveyor, but presumably his real occupation was gambling. His wife attributed the suicide to financial pressures. Thus in his first novel John O'Hara found the fictional technique that he would employ for the rest of his career, a combination of the psychological pattern of one person and the externals ("the life," the way of life) of one or more other persons. It was a matter of some satisfaction to him that readers almost always incorrectly identified the sources for his characters because they regarded his novels as *romans à clef*. There is no single key to his characters. The *roman à clef** is built on the direct correspondence between the work and its real-life sources. Indeed, the readers—some of them, at least—of the *roman à clef* are supposed to make the connections. The author expects the insiders to recognize his characters and action—in *The Sun Also Rises*, for example—and it can be said that this identification is really part of the author's plan. Not so for O'Hara. His background and details are accurately transcribed from life; some of his stories happened; his characters are, to a greater or lesser degree, drawn from actual people. But the fictional construct involves the creation of characters. Although Julian English's characteristics were taken from Birsie Richards plus John O'Hara plus Clint Sheafer plus other people, Julian is none of them. He is O'Hara's invention.[13]

The realism of *Appointment in Samarra* is realism of selected detail —not photographic realism. It is sociological realism in that the author utilizes customs and details to denote social stratification. In the case of some rituals, such as the Ammermann dinner party at the country club, the reader requires the background explanation which the author provides. But for possessions the detail is simply given. You are what you own. Either the reader understands the significance of a make of car or he doesn't. O'Hara is using these details intentionally and meaningfully: a Franklin is not a Buick, and a car is never just a car. Readers who are not aware of these distinctions or who regard them as irrelevant are apt to dismiss O'Hara's details as arbitrary and meaningless. But O'Hara's details are not lost on fit readers.

In the Twenties if you said a man owned a Franklin you would not be talking about the kind of man who owned a Buick, although some Buicks cost the same amount of money as some Franklins. The Franklin-owner would not be wearing an Elks tooth nor a Rotary Club button. He might wear a Masonic pin, but not a Shriner's. The Franklin-owner was more likely to be a tennis player than a golfer, a doctor than a real estate agent, a college man than a non-college man, and a much more independent thinker than the Buick owner. He would also be likely to own more securities than the Buick owner, whose money would be tied

---

*Literally, a novel with a key; that is, a novel based on actual people or real events which are more or less disguised.

up in personal enterprises. Now why is all this so important to the novelist? It is important because character is so important; it would be out of character for a Buick type man to own a Franklin; it would not be quite so much out of character for a Franklin man to own a Buick. In any case, the novelist has told the reader that Jones owns a Franklin, therefore Jones will behave as a Franklin-owning Jones will behave. And if he behaves in a way that is out of character, either the novelist has been wrong in providing him with a Franklin, or he, the novelist, must explain and make credible the acts that are not in character for the Franklin-owning Jones.[14]

What he didn't know, O'Hara researched:

When I wrote Appointment in Samarra I established a dummy garage business, took my papers to a guy I know who is a v.p. at General Motors (who wanted to know when the hell I had run a garage), and he in turn passed me on to a fellow at the Automobile Chamber of Commerce. Not much of that appears in the book, but everything that does appear is accurate and sound. I also boned up on taxicology [sic] with the late Yandell Henderson so that the carbon monoxide suicide would be all right.[15]

He claimed that *Appointment* was the first novel to employ this form of suicide.

For John O'Hara the art of fiction was above all the art of creating character. His rule was that the author who does not write accurate dialogue cannot be "depended on for his understanding of character and his creation of character." Accurate dialogue is governed by the character's social-economic-educational background. However, O'Hara recognized that perfect realistic or naturalistic speech is impossible, although he tried to indicate special inflections with italics. While admitting the futility of trying to duplicate speech rhythms and regional pronunciations, he exercised complete control over vocabulary and grammar—the common upper-class blunder with the objective case, for example, as in "Jimmy didn't come with she and I." Fitzgerald acknowledged O'Hara's mastery of dialogue in his Note-Books: "The queer slanting effect of the substantive, the future imperfect, a matter of intuition or ear to O'Hara, is unknown to careful writers like Bunny [Wilson] and John [Bishop]."

Appointment is a naturalistic novel; that is to say, it is a deterministic work. The metaphor of the title indicates that Julian's death was inevitable, though it is left to the reader to assess the influence of the forces of heredity which operate on him. There is the obvious possibility that Julian's suicide may not be unrelated to his grandfather's.

O'Hara interprets heredity so broadly that it overlaps with environment. In *Appointment* heredity includes such things as the social position and family traditions one is born to. Being born on a certain street to certain parents with certain memberships and allegiances and being impressed with the knowledge that one will be expected to attend certain schools, after which one will honor certain family obligations and marry into a certain social level—these are as deterministic in O'Hara as a taint of idiocy is in Zola. Environment is heredity.

The purpose of the novel is not to protest against the social system—O'Hara was never a reformer—but to show the futility and waste of life within the system. Although his point of view is detached, O'Hara is not indifferent to his characters; nor does he hate his rich characters. He focuses on middle- and upper-class people because their lives are more complicated. The rich are different, and the richer they are, the more different they are. Like Fitzgerald, O'Hara was impressed by the style and grace the rich can achieve; and, like Fitzgerald, O'Hara was frequently disappointed by what they actually do with their lives.

What was assumed to be O'Hara's indifference to his characters—his hard-boiled attitude—was his disciplined authorial point of view, not his emotional insufficiency. He was an unintrusive author, but this is not to say that he was indifferent to his characters. He thinks Dr. William Dilworth English is a cold, murderous son-of-a-bitch, and the reader knows he does. O'Hara avoided open judgment; but the acts of inventing characters and selecting material, of creating speech and action, all involve authorial judgment. The author does not instruct the readers how they are to feel about Julian; but the novel presents Julian as weak and self-indulgent. He is doomed by forces of character and circumstance he cannot cope with. Because Julian does not deserve his wretched end, he wins pity. It has been charged that he is a superficial characterization, that O'Hara did not make the reader understand Julian's suicide. These charges miss the point that the social organization in Samarra-Gibbsville determines the appointment. Julian kills himself because he cannot face life as an outsider.

A significant rare authorial comment occurs when Julian and Caroline have intercourse after he has failed to apologize to Harry Reilly: "It was the greatest single act of their married life. He knew it, and she knew it. It was the time she did not fail him." The reader has to decide how much emphasis to put on the definite article in the last sentence. Does *the time* imply *the only time*? Julian's strong reaction to Caroline's refusal to keep their love-making date at the country club makes the point that this time she does fail him when he desperately needs reassurance and sustenance. (Julian fails Caroline, of course, but he needs her more than she needs him.) Caroline Walker English is the first full-length example of the misogyny that runs through O'Hara's work. He was interested in women and liked them —personally and professionally—but he had an almost Jansenistic distrust for their sexual destructiveness. The English marriage is contrasted with the solid middle-class Fliegler marriage, which opens and closes the novel, and which serves as a marital frame of reference. It bears emphasis that O'Hara does not seek his standards of marital conduct at the country club, but from the middle-class Pennsylvania-Dutch stock. If Julian can be considered the victim of one particular thing, it is of Caroline's hardness. Even as she grieves for him, she recognizes that she would have failed him, that it is well for both of them that he killed himself: "But this time she knew that she would not have come back this afternoon, and he had known it, and God help us all but he was right. It was *time* for him to die."

O'Hara believed that all good fiction is good social history, and *Appointment in Samarra* was superb social history. (The author he returned to most often for reading pleasure throughout his life was Arthur Conan Doyle, for he admired the Sherlock Holmes stories as a record of English life.) In the early part of his career O'Hara insisted on his position as a social historian; but later, as this designation was increasingly applied by critics as a term of denigration, he developed ambivalent feelings about it: "I deny that I am a social historian; I am a novelist, and a social historian only incidentally. Nevertheless my novels do partake of the elements and classification of social history, and behind my decision to make a novel is the question, can I say what I want to say about my times as well as what I want to say about my people, my characters?"[16]

Toward the end of his Hollywood stint, in August 1934, O'Hara met actress Zita Johann, who was enjoying success on Broadway and in Hollywood. Her stage credits included *Machinal* (1928) and Barry's *Tomorrow and Tomorrow* (1931); and she had appeared in a string of forgettable movies in 1933 and 1934—*The Mummy, Luxury Liner, The Man Who Dared, The Sin of Nora Moran* and *Grand Canary*. O'Hara followed her to New York in the fall. They dated steadily for six months, and Winchell announced in his column that "John O'Hara and Zita Johann are having an appointment in Samarra." O'Hara talked about marriage, but she demurred. In addition to the fact that she was not in love with him, Zita Johann was put off by his touchiness. Once on a date with him she pulled a blank on his name and was unable to introduce him to a friend. The only name she could think of was

Irving Thalberg. She thought the incident was funny, but O'Hara was hurt. She was not particularly impressed by his new success as a novelist, and did not respond to his ambitions. After they broke up, he told her that he had planned to dedicate *Butterfield 8* to her. The actress, who was doing very well on her own, was not devastated by the information.*

O'Hara's emotional life was extremely active in 1934, for he was still considering remarriage to Pet while seeing Zita and dating other girls. In 1935 he would become engaged to still another young lady. New York and Hollywood were full of beddable females, but O'Hara needed the order and permanence of marriage.

BACK FROM HOLLYWOOD in September 1934, O'Hara returned to the Pickwick Arms. Apparently he was in doubt about how much money *Appointment* would earn, for he applied for the job of writing the sports department for *The New Yorker*. Only one column on football, probably a sample piece, was published in September. In 1935, when he was planning an auto trip to the South and Northwest, he offered to write a series of travel pieces for the magazine. This project, which was declined, was probably only partly motivated by financial considerations; he also wanted to keep his name in print.†

The publication of *Appointment* revived O'Hara's hopes for a Yale education, and in 1934 he investigated the possibility of entering the university in an accelerated program with the goal of becoming a psychiatrist. He also talked about his desire to become a ship's doctor. Just possibly he felt that he had proved himself as a writer and now could try to prove other things. Another result of *Appointment* was a form from *Who's Who in America*. Although he hadn't quite fulfilled his boast to his father that he'd be included in it before he was thirty (the 1936–37 volume appeared after his thirtieth birthday), he was satisfied that he had come close enough.

When it became apparent that *Appointment* was going to be a success, Harcourt, Brace scheduled an O'Hara collection, *The Doctor's Son and Other Stories*, which was published in 2,000 copies on 21 February 1935. Despite work on *Appointment* and the Hollywood stint, O'Hara published twelve stories in 1934, including his best stories to date, which appeared in *The New Yorker*: "It Must Have Been Spring" (21 April), "Sportsmanship" (12 May) and "Over the River

---

* O'Hara included a mention of Zita Johann in the novel.

† In the mid-Thirties the magazine was paying him 10¢ per word, so that ten 2,000-word casuals—a successful year—brought $2,000.

and Through the Wood" (15 December). Clearly, the discipline of writing *Appointment* enlarged the scope of his short fiction, for these three are his first published pieces that are developed stories—not vignettes or dramatic monologues. "Over the River and Through the Wood" is a frightening story about loss of dignity. A once-rich man, now a visitor in the home he formerly owned, goes into the room of his granddaughter's guest to offer her cocoa. But he has misheard; she did not say "Come in"; the girl is naked. "Mr. Winfield instantly knew that this was the end of any worthwhile life he had left."

Of the thirty-seven stories in *The Doctor's Son*, all except the fifty-four-page title story had been previously published. It had been written in 1933, and had almost certainly been polished in the intervening time. "The Doctor's Son" is a key work in the O'Hara canon because of its relationship to the Gibbsville cycle, because of its autobiographical content, and because it is a superb novella—a form O'Hara did not return to for twenty-five years. "The Doctor's Son" is an initiation story. Like Hemingway's "Indian Camp" and "The Doctor and the Doctor's Wife," it initiates a boy into the realities of death and adult behavior. Against the background of the slaughter of the 1918 flu epidemic, fifteen-year-old Jimmy Malloy learns that death can be arbitrary and that nice women can be adulterous. The story obviously has strong personal elements, although O'Hara was only thirteen—not fifteen—at the time of the epidemic, and took a less active role in it than does Jimmy. Its depth is provided by the exploration of the relationship between Dr. Malloy and Jimmy: the boy's pride in his father's ability and position; the father's disappointment in his son's rejection of a medical career; and their estrangement because they are too much alike.

The Doctor's Son required a second printing, which was good for a collection by a one-book novelist during the Depression. The reviews were generally friendly—especially that of John Chamberlain in the *Times*—but indicate that the stories had not really made much impact when they originally appeared in *The New Yorker*. There was a certain reluctance to designate them as short stories because of their form; however, the title story made a strong impression and carried the volume. Some reviewers and readers were surprised to discover that John O'Hara could write a long story. O'Hara was probably gratified by the review in *The Journal of the American Medical Association*, which called it "medical realism to the highest degree."

After a short stay at the Pickwick Arms, O'Hara shared digs with Quentin Reynolds in late 1934, probably at 114 East 53rd Street—with an out-of-work ship's steward O'Hara employed as butler. A gregarious, hard-drinking man, Reynolds had played football and been a heavy-weight boxer at Brown. A former sports reporter, he became an associate editor for *Collier's* in 1934. The butler disapproved of his masters' idleness, because all the work they did consisted of typing. O'Hara had asked a Tammany connection to get him a low license plate number for the Ford, and the politician supplied D-69, which allowed O'Hara to complain that he kept finding strange women sitting in the car. During January–July 1935 he shared the ground floor at 103 East 55th Street (between Park and Lexington avenues) with John McClain. The apartment was large enough so that McClain was able to sublet rooms to other friends, including Charles Frazier, who had worked with O'Hara on *Time*. Among the conveniences of this establishment were a butler and a thriving brothel across the street. Frazier remembers comparatively little partying and a great deal of writing by O'Hara, who was then beginning *Butterfield 8*.

In December 1934 John attended a party given by Billy Rose at his Casino-de-Paree night club where he met Ruth Sato, a Japanese showgirl. They joined McClain, sportswriter Jimmy Cannon and showgirl Colette Francis as a late-night group, favoring the Stork Club and the Abbey. At this time John was also dating Toni Sorrell, an actress-model, and showgirl Dorothy Van Hest.[17] During the Thirties he also had a serious affair with a married but separated woman. He saw a good deal of Ruth Sato in 1935, and the rumor about his Japanese wife got back to Pottsville and endured. Ruth's working hours made her available for late visits while he was writing. A telegram to the night club at which she was working ordering a delivery of opium meant that John wanted her to bring hot chocolate and cookies at four A.M., at which time he would read dialogue from *Butterfield 8* to her. It was his lifelong custom to read dialogue aloud—usually to himself—to make sure it sounded right. Once he got Ruth to go with him to inspect an apartment that was for rent so he could check the layout for use in his novel. She was doing very well, even holding down two jobs, and was put off by what seemed to be his clumsy attempts to impress her: . . . my man will serve; my real percale sheets; I bought you this bracelet at Saks Fifth Avenue. He was amused to learn that "Hara" in Japanese was a large valley—by extension the cleavage between a woman's breasts—and began signing his notes to Ruth "Johnu Hara."

A close friend in the Thirties was Robin "Curly" Harris, a writer and public-relations consultant, who was often in his company when O'Hara was drinking hard. One night they left the Stork Club and O'Hara began chasing a man up Park Avenue in a rage, but stopped short when he remembered that the cop on this beat was a crack shot;

O'Hara didn't want him to think he was engaged in a criminal activity. A favorite pastime for O'Hara was target shooting, and Joe O'Hara remembers his spending a good deal of money at the Sixth Avenue shooting galleries.

In February of 1935 O'Hara negotiated a contract for his second novel with Harcourt, Brace, calling for a $1,000 advance and $50 per week during February–April. On the day *The Doctor's Son* was published, 21 February, he was in Florida, planning to see Hemingway in Key West and write there, but he did not go "because of people visiting Hemingway." Instead, O'Hara paid court in Miami to a showgirl who turned out to be a lesbian. He remarked ruefully that they had to wear double-breasted suits and smoke cigars before he could recognize them. O'Hara stopped off to visit Fitzgerald in Baltimore during this trip and invited fourteen-year-old Scottie Fitzgerald to dinner, but her father vetoed the date.

O'Hara's editors at Harcourt, Brace were Charles A. Pearce and Samuel Sloan. Initially, he worked more closely with Cap Pearce and kept in touch with him about *Butterfield 8*. In April, John was working on the novel at the Oceanside Inn in East Sandwich, Massachusetts, where he grew a beard while completing the first 25,000 words. He wrote the first draft rapidly and then revised it, which was unusual for him. While on Cape Cod he attended a house party in the Berkshires at which he met Barbara Kibler of Columbus, Ohio, a Wellesley sophomore with whom he fell in love. During the spring he had several dates with her in Boston.

By May 1935, John O'Hara was enough of a celebrity to be quoted in a feature on the Lindbergh kidnapping, "Why They'll Never Forget the Trial of the Century," in *Hearst's International-Cosmopolitan*— despite the fact that he had not covered the Hauptmann trial. In June he escorted Tallulah Bankhead to the Louis-Baer fight, on which he won $1,500 in bets that were not paid off. On the Fourth of July 1935, O'Hara resumed drinking—after exactly two years on the wagon— at a Long Island dinner party given by the Charles Paysons (the sister and brother-in-law of John Hay Whitney). Shortly after this occasion he left for Europe on the *Conte di Savoia*, planning to finish the novel on shipboard and mail it from Genoa. He won the ship's rifle-shooting contest with a score of 57 out of a possible 60, but *Butterfield 8* was not completed when the ship docked. O'Hara went from Genoa to Florence to Paris, where he finished the novel at the George V and dispatched it on the *Berengaria*. The last page of the final typescript is dated "(Exactly 2 o'clock p.m., August 5, 1935/Paris, France)." That the writing of *Butterfield 8* had presented difficulties is shown by the existence of two incomplete typescripts underlying the setting copy. The novel also underwent some bowdlerization; the copy-edited typescript shows deletion of sexual material, at least some of which was presumably nonauthorial. In 1935 O'Hara was not allowed to print "f——" or refer to sexual organs.* He sailed home on the *Normandie* in August and again won the rifle-shooting contest, receiving a clock which he dropped on the dock. On the *Normandie* O'Hara met Charles (Chad) Ballard, a member of the Yale class of 1937. Chad was traveling with his father, Edward Ballard, a successful promoter who owned the Haggenbeck-Wallace Circus, the plush West Baden Springs Hotel, and gambling houses in Florida and French Lick, Indiana. O'Hara was impressed by the elder Ballard (who had started out cleaning saloons). During 1935 and 1936 O'Hara and Chad pub-crawled on the Yale student's New York trips. When Sherman Billingsley gave a thirty-first-birthday party for O'Hara at the Stork Club in January 1936, Chad attended along with Walter Winchell, Leonard Lyons, John McClain and Curly Harris. The party ended with a quarrel between O'Hara and Winchell about whether Winchell had gotten him his job on the *Mirror* in 1929.

O'Hara's thirty-first-birthday party, Stork Club, 1936. Left to right: Walter Winchell, O'Hara, John McClain.

* O'Hara donated the typescripts to Yale in 1944.

Butterfield 8 was published on 17 October 1935 to mixed reviews.* Again John Chamberlain was respectful in the *Times*, but most reviewers were shocked. O'Hara's old employer Heywood Broun wrote a harsh article, charging the novel with irrelevance and—what must have hurt—complaining that O'Hara had failed to differentiate the characters' speech; they all talked the same, Broun stated. Hemingway provided the publisher with a statement—"John O'Hara writes better all the time"—which was never used. The review that angered O'Hara the most was Clifton Fadiman's in *The New Yorker*, with the snide title "Disappointment in O'Hara." Although he included comments that the publisher used in ads, Fadiman stated that he did not have "the slightest interest" in O'Hara's characters:

Everything about them—their adulteries, their conversations, their lusts, their yearnings—seems so small that one wonders how Mr. O'Hara, generously gifted, intelligent, witty, can possibly care to spend so much of his time with them.

I still think that the path he so brilliantly struck out for himself in "Appointment in Samarra" is bound to end in a blind alley, and I think "Butterfield 8" proves it.

Fadiman's review hurt because it dismissed O'Hara's material and discounted his future. O'Hara took this personally, feeling that *The New Yorker* had betrayed him; and he developed a permanent grudge against Fadiman. Because Fadiman was a Book-of-the-Month Club judge, O'Hara refused to offer his books to them—thereby proving that he was prepared to suffer in the purse for his feuds.† O'Hara's reaction to hostile criticism in *The New Yorker* was repeated with greater intensity in 1949 when Brendan Gill's review of *A Rage to Live* appeared.

Butterfield 8 is John O'Hara's only *roman à clef*. Gloria Wandrous was obviously based on Starr Faithfull, and readers in 1935 were supposed to make the connection. The body of Starr Faithfull was found at Long Beach, Long Island, on 8 June 1931. The autopsy revealed that she had been drugged and that she had sustained injuries before drowning. She was twenty-five years old, drank heavily and was promiscuous. As a schoolgirl she had been debauched by Andrew J. Peters, the wealthy former mayor of Boston. At first her death was

---

* O'Hara had originally intended to use Jimmy Walker's remark that no girl was ever ruined by a book as the epigraph for this novel.

† Years later O'Hara vetoed a large-type edition of *Appointment* because it was proposed by a man who he believed owed him money.

thought to be suicide; but as more evidence about her life was un-covered, the theory developed that she had been thrown from a ship. The case was never solved, and the newspapers—especially the tab-loids—gave it prominent coverage during the summer of 1931.

O'Hara had seen Starr Faithfull around speakeasies, but did not know her well. He had had no part in covering the story, for he was not working for a newspaper at the time of her death. But he had read her diaries—and even had them in his possession for a while. It is not difficult to see why the Starr Faithfull case appealed to him. He wanted to consolidate the success of *Appointment* with a second novel, and Starr Faithfull provided ready-made material; moreover, it was New York material. Writing a novel about New York would show that his muse was not restricted to Gibbsville. The only link between *Butterfield 8* and his earlier work is Jimmy Malloy, the doctor's son, who was now a reporter in New York. The question immediately arises about the degree to which Jimmy Malloy is John O'Hara; and the answer, again, is that Malloy is fictionalized O'Hara—not straight autobiography. Malloy and O'Hara share the same background and the same ideas (Malloy on unassimilable Micks, for example). O'Hara obviously recognized the risk of depending too heavily on Malloy, of writing a Malloy saga, and after utilizing him as the protagonist of his next novel, *Hope of Heaven* (1938) used him only once again in a major work, *Sermons and Soda-Water*, twenty-two years later. Malloy was a dangerous gimmick because it was too easy to write about him.

In 1960—twenty-five years after the novel was published—O'Hara wrote an introduction for the Modern Library *Butterfield 8*, which was never used. This statement connects the novel's impetus with his boyhood feelings about New York and wealth, the metropolitan image of success:[18]

So my approach to New York was conditioned very early by a fantastic ignorance of money matters, so that when I finally did get there, to work and live, and in spite of the fact that my father had died just about broke—my attitude was that of defenseless optimism. New York would take care of the newcomer. Well, New York did, but not in my optimistic use of the phrase. Within two years I was literally starving, by which I mean that for one three-day stretch I went without anything to eat. The experiences of those first two years did not make a banker of me, and they were not all as disillusioning or as difficult as those three days. But you never quite get over the de-grading, debasing experience of going hungry (Henry R. Luce chose that particular moment to dun me for $50 I owed him). You learn to see things very plain, and not only things but people, and not only *people but a city. Six years after I arrived in New York I was the author of a highly successful first novel and was already at work on Butterfield 8, in which I was determined to make plain what I had seen.*

I was, of course, helped by fact. This is my only roman à clef, *taken, as it was, from the headlines of a newspaper story, plus a great deal of digging, plus a slight personal acquaintance with the pathetic girl whom I call Gloria Wandrous. The book was a shocker to the literary cocktail party set that I have never had any part of, and who have written me off almost annually for the past twenty-six years. The story of Gloria Wandrous had appeared as fact in the newspapers, along with her excerpted diary that could not all be printed either in a newspaper or a novel. If anything, I toned the story down, and I can be reasonably certain that my novel was read with relief by some clubmen and litterateurs who were mentioned in the original diary. The novel was not highly regarded artistically, and the Pulitzer Prize that year went to Josephine W. Johnson for Now in November. (The drama prize went to Zoe Akins for The Old Maid.)*

Now, a quarter century later, I look upon the book as I do one of those old New York buildings that are pictured in the Sunday News. The novel is not remarkable for the differences so much as for the similarities to 1930 in 1960. A gentleman whom I shall describe as a noted historian—and he is just that—told me two years ago that Butterfield 8 is the one novel that historians covering that period must read. When I consider what the Toynbee School feels about mere fact in history, I am inclined to believe that my novels may all be as reliable as the work of the formal historians of our time. Unfortunately we novelists must also strive for readability as well as for verisimilitude. Or is that so unfortunate?

Butterfield 8 extends the panoramic technique of *Appointment*— the use of groups of characters to represent different socioeconomic strata—which works less well for New York than for Gibbsville. New York is too big to be encapsulated in terms of representative characters. *Butterfield 8* does not convey to the reader a sense of knowing the structure of New York, as *Appointment* does for Gibbsville.*

---

* *Butterfield 8* provides an example of O'Hara's approach to realism. He tried hard to get every detail right in his fiction, but when a rare factual error was pointed out to him after a novel was published he let it stand. Perhaps he felt that the printed material had achieved a life of its own. In *Butterfield 8* there is a description of Gloria Wandrous studying the bulging jock of Weston Liggett in his crew photo. Press agent Russell Maloney told O'Hara that crewmen didn't wear jocks, which was confirmed by Hobart Weekes, a *New Yorker* editor who had rowed for Princeton. O'Hara was furious, but didn't revise the description. It was the start of a feud with Maloney.

O'Hara had a profound distrust of metaphors. Early in his career he worked out and adhered to the principle that all metaphors are imprecise and that a reliance on them becomes a form of authorial cheating. The best-known enunciation of this principle came in *Butterfield 8*, when the author analyzes Weston Liggett's sense of guilt after Gloria's death:

There comes one time in a man's life, if he is unlucky and leads a full life, when he has a secret so dirty that he knows he never will get rid of it. (Shakespeare knew this and tried to say it, but he said it just as badly as anyone ever said it. "All the perfumes of Arabia" makes you think of all the perfumes of Arabia and nothing more.* It is the trouble with all metaphors where human behavior is concerned. People are not ships, chess men, flowers, race horses, oil paintings, bottles of champagne, excrement, musical instruments, or anything else but people. Metaphors are all right to give you an idea.)

O'Hara's deliberate bareness of style contributed to the critical opinion that his work lacked depth or richness. But stylistic complexity is not synonymous with art, and stylistic simplicity is not contemptible. There is art in precision and economy.

Despite its cool critical reception, *Butterfield 8* got off to a good sales start—probably because it received word-of-mouth publicity as a sexy book. The first printing of 15,000 copies sold out in two days, and a second printing of 10,000 was required; however, the second printing was sufficient until Grosset & Dunlap did a cheap reprint in 1937. O'Hara's royalties from Harcourt, Brace in 1935 for three books amounted to $8,502.53.† An amusing footnote to the reception of *Butterfield 8* was provided when a few hundred copies of the novel were accidentally bound in the covers for a life of John Wesley published by Columbia University Press.

By October 1935 O'Hara was planning to marry Barbara Kibler, and Adele Lovett gave a party on 28 October for his friends to meet her. Among the guests were Joe and Mary O'Hara, Ernest and Pauline Hemingway, Deems Taylor, Jed Harris, Richard Watts, Hoagy Carmichael, George and Ira Gershwin, Burgess Meredith, Robert Benchley, Tallulah Bankhead, Marc Connelly and John McClain. If the plan

---

* In point of fact, the *Macbeth* phrase does not include a metaphor.

† This figure may not include total earnings for the year, but only what O'Hara withdrew from his royalty account.

Ernest Hemingway and O'Hara with Sherman Billingsley, Stork Club proprietor.

was to impress the Ohio girl, it must have succeeded. Hemingway later described O'Hara on this evening in his *African Journal*: ". . . remembering joyously the white-edged evening tie he had worn at his coming-out party in New York and his hostess' nervousness at presenting him and her gallant hope that he would not disintegrate."[19]

O'Hara wrote to Fitzgerald describing Barbara as "5′3, dark, beautiful figure . . . her family are nouveau rich and Protestant. You would like her. Dottie will hate her. . . ." He added that her family "are against me."[20]

In December O'Hara drove to Ohio with his brother Eugene and John McClain. After dropping McClain off at Marion, John and Eugene went to Columbus to meet Barbara's family. This visit produced problems with the Kiblers, some of which John blamed on Eugene's behavior; Barbara's parents had already been disturbed by the sexual frankness of *Appointment* and *Butterfield 8*. The brothers probably drove from Columbus to New Orleans.

Meanwhile O'Hara was developing an English following, which grew throughout his career. In 1935 Faber & Faber published *Appointment*, which required nine hardcover printings by 1965. However, Faber regarded *Butterfield 8* as too hot for them. Until well after

World War II English publishers were more conservative about sexual material than their American colleagues, because the English authorities were very strict. English rights went to Chatto & Windus, which set a bowdlerized text in proof and then canceled publication because the Lord Chamberlain was active just then. Although an English-language edition of *Butterfield 8* was sold on the Continent by Albatross in the late Thirties, the novel was not published in England until 1951.

In 1935 O'Hara's short-story output fell off to eight, of which six were in *The New Yorker*. Two of these stories were among his best: "The Gentleman in the Tan Suit" and "Portisan on the Portis"—the latter of which grew out of the double-talk he and Jimmy Cannon (Jimmy Shott) liked to fool around with. The prize-fight manager of the story is based on Hymie Caplin, whose company O'Hara enjoyed at that time.

The way in which men's clothing functions as part of O'Hara's technique is demonstrated with particular complexity in "The Gentleman in the Tan Suit." In this story the secretary to a Wall Street executive—who is accustomed to well-dressed men—on meeting her brother-in-law for the first time is immediately struck by his awful clothes. She quickly discovers he has behaved with patience and generous understanding in the matter of her sister's sexual ignorance. Here the man's clothes, which at first appear significant, do not matter at all. The young husband is a decent man—no matter what he wears. But since the story is told from the point of view of his sister-in-law, the reader shares the impact of her recognition that the man in the too-light, wrinkled tan suit is indeed a gentleman.

Barbara Kibler broke off the engagement early in 1936. O'Hara took it hard, informing Curly Harris that he was considering suicide. Harris told him that finding another girl was a much better idea. The end of the romance was more than the end of love to O'Hara: it portended isolation. The feeling that he was doomed to loneliness triggered his deepest bouts of despair. By April 1936 O'Hara was in Hollywood looking for work. He reported to Fitzgerald: "I was in love with a girl, as I wrote you; she gave me the air, and on the rebound I got a dose of clap. I apparently suffer more in the head than in the cock, and much more than most men."[21]

IN THE SPRING OF 1936 Belle Mulford Wylie was flying from New York to California when she heard O'Hara being paged at Newark Airport and watched to see who responded. A great admirer of his

To Belle

who somehow got
home from the Tango
after observing a man
in Wichita and seeing
and again seeing the man
from Newark Airport who
loves her in 1945

The Man

27 East 79

O'Hara's inscription to Belle in *Pipe Night* (1945),
referring to their first meeting.

work, Belle had remarked—before she met him—that she wanted to
marry John O'Hara. He noticed her on the plane and tried to pick
her up at one of the stops, but Belle was too shy to respond. At the
Wichita airport O'Hara saw Richard Watts and told him that there
was a swell girl on the plane. Belle was going to Hollywood to visit
her sister Lucilla, who was married to director Henry Potter. Lucilla
gave a party for Belle, to which Belle asked her to invite John O'Hara.
Placed next to Belle at dinner, he turned to her and said, "Now let me
see—you're from New York, and went to Brearley and St. Timothy's
and studied at the Traphagen School of Design." He was correct.* They
left the party together and stayed out till dawn. O'Hara's inscription to
Belle in *Pipe Night* nine years later indicates that he took her to the

---

* O'Hara frequently surprised people with his knowledge of their backgrounds on a first meeting. When he was introduced to Mrs. Ring Lardner, he
said, "The former Ellis Abbott of Goshen, Indiana?"

Tango, a gambling ship anchored off Long Beach—from which she apparently had to get home on her own.

The daughter of a prominent New York obstetrician, the late Dr. Robert Hawthorne Wylie, Belle was the right girl for John O'Hara. Her close friends described her as a "warm, radiantly attractive girl" with a strong personality and high ideals—affectionate and intelligent. She was twenty-three (born in December 1912), five-six and slender, with naturally curly bouffant hair and a faintly Oriental cast to her eyes. Belle read widely, was an excellent dancer, and was interested in fashion—she had modeled and liked to design her own clothes. She even belonged to a Yale family.

Belle Wylie had a cogenital heart disorder.

John and Belle dated during her summer stay in California, often playing tennis at the West Side Tennis Club. There is a report that they decided to elope to Mexico during this summer, but got cold feet. Meanwhile O'Hara was unemployed. Good Hollywood jobs were not forthcoming in 1936. The best offer O'Hara received was $250 per week, which he declined because it would establish his Hollywood value on a low level and would mean that he would have to work on junk pictures. He discussed his problem with Clifford Odets and director Lewis Milestone, who were working on *The General Died at Dawn* for Paramount.

"Will $50 per day for a few weeks solve your problem?" asked Milestone.

O'Hara reacted indignantly. "I will not put pen to paper for a few pennies. I thought I made that clear."

"You certainly did. But I'm not asking you to write. Will you act for $50 per day?"

"What will I play?"

"A corrupt newspaperman," said Odets, "who could be bought for a bag of salt."[22]

The gag developed because the hero, a foreign correspondent in China, played by Gary Cooper, was named O'Hara. One of O'Hara's three speeches was "Hello, O'Hara," addressed to Cooper. The joke went around the studio that this take had to be reshot because Gary Cooper reacted by turning to Milestone and saying, "But *he's* O'Hara."

The friendship between O'Hara and Clifford Odets became extremely close, and they spent a great deal of time arguing politics. O'Hara was amused by the reversal of his usual role in a friendship because Odets was even more volatile than he. "It was he, the Jew, and not I, the Irishman, who would shake his fist in the other's face. It was I, the Irishman, not he, the Jew, who kept the peace."[23]

O'Hara at right behind Madeleine Carroll.

O'Hara with director Lewis Milestone on set of *The General Died at Dawn*.

After a short stay with Dorothy Parker and her husband, Alan Campbell in April 1936, O'Hara settled at 10735 Ohio Avenue in West Los Angeles, drawing an allowance of $300 a month from his Harcourt, Brace royalties. He intended to study American history and French at UCLA, which was nearby, but did not act on the plan. By May he had decided to write a short novel—about 20,000 words—for fall publication. The title was "So Far, So Good"—taken from the first and last words of the work. He informed Cap Pearce of his plans:

It's not a Hollywood story, but it is Californian. It would be about the size of Early Sorrow, Mario & the Magician, and those other Mann books. I want to do it because I want to do it. Butterfield 8 (remember?) made money, but you weren't really behind it, now were you? But anyway, a piece of advice Scott Fitzgerald gave me after he read it, and has repeated since, is that I ought to do a book that is practically a bucolic idyll, only I must believe in the bucolic idyll and the reason for doing it is that the staccato stuff ought to be saved for an effect, rather than used throughout a novel. Badly quoted, but the idea is somewhere around there. One more fast-moving, realistic novel, and nobody will listen to what I have to say; they'll be too sure of what to expect, etc.[24]

O'Hara subsequently clarified the "bucolic idyll" term by explaining that "the difference between other novels (by the same author) is in the fact that there is some hope for the characters."[25] He promised the final typescript around 1 August, and when pressed for a catalog description replied:

The story, such as it is right now, has to do with three young persons; that is, under thirty all three; two males, one female. . . . In the first draught on the first page and the pages immediately following we discover one of the young men counting a large sum of money and then hiding it in various places throughout his abode. One of the males is a Pennsylvania Dutchman, the other a Jew, and the girl is Californian. The story is romantic, middle class to a low degree, and there is a slight, but only slight touch of plot.[26]

There was to be a simple and apparent "secondary, or allegorical, meaning." This summary obviously applies to a working version of *Hope of Heaven*, although the allegory is not apparent in the published work. Pearce responded enthusiastically, declaring that "any publisher would be a lunatic not to publish what you want to write whenever you want to write it."[27] The lunacy clause did not, however, cover another volume of stories. O'Hara wanted to follow *Butterfield 8* with a collection, but Pearce put him off with the explanation that the time wasn't right.

O'Hara missed the August 1936 deadline he had set for "So Far, So Good." In September he explained to Pearce that he was still trying to get one of the characters right:

Two of the characters, the girl and the young Jewish lad, come out all right. But the third character, the young Pennsylvanian just doesn't sound like anyone I want to be known as the creator of. He is a tough one for these reasons: he is discovered on the first pages of the book in a thoroughly dishonest act. Now I have been able to justify this act (to some extent) and to reconcile it with certain other things he does later in the story—but the horrible part is that I find myself writing about two (and sometimes three) different persons. I find myself writing about one person who does the dishonest thing, and then writing about a totally different guy who does something pretty darn good. To bring it pretty close to (my) home I read over the stuff and discovered that I was writing about two of my brothers. That's bad, because the character is supposed to be only one person. If it isn't one person the story's no good.[28]

It was unusual for O'Hara to tell an editor so much about his problems with a work-in-progress, for he resisted collaborative relationships with editors. But "So Far, So Good" was presenting unexpected difficulties, for he was stuck on a main character—which is serious in the case of an author who prided himself on his ability to create characters. This book stalled O'Hara's novelistic career and nearly halted it. "So Far, So Good" was not completed until late 1937—more than a year behind schedule—by which time it had developed into *Hope of Heaven*. O'Hara solved the problem of the split character, Don Miller, by diminishing his role and bringing in Jimmy Malloy as narrator. The basic conception of the story changed from a "bucolic idyll" to one notably deficient in hope. The title *Hope of Heaven* indicates that there is little hope for the characters on earth.*

O'HARA DROPPED IN at the Trocadero almost every night. One Sunday he heard an unknown named Judy Garland sing and made a point of telling the proprietor, Billy Wilkerson, that she was great. Chad

---

* When the novel was reprinted in *Here's O'Hara* in 1946, the final bleak chapter was inadvertently omitted, thereby giving *Hope of Heaven* a less hopeless ending. This blunder was repeated in the Avon paperback edition.

Ballard was in California during the summer of 1936 and at the club introduced O'Hara to a Yale classmate, Alfred Wright, Jr.—thereby setting up a close friendship. Wright was a good deal like John Mc-Clain: handsome, charming, popular with men and women, and a good drinker. After graduation from Yale in 1937, he had a successful career as a writer with the Time organization. For a long period Al Wright was one of O'Hara's favorite drinking companions.

O'Hara remained in California between early 1936 and the spring of 1937—with at least one trip back to New York. He managed to find only short-term movie jobs: a treatment of Joseph Dineen's *Murder in Massachusetts* for Goldwyn and a treatment of an unidentified property for Jean Arthur or Miriam Hopkins at MGM. At this time he talked about the possibility of visiting the Orient or Mexico. He was on and off the wagon, and his drinking spells provided some examples of how difficult he could be. He had developed a mild crush on Alice Faye—whom he had never met—and prevailed on Curly Harris and his wife to arrange a dinner date. O'Hara arrived drunk, and Miss Faye left. The next day a chagrined O'Hara prevailed on Mrs. Harris to phone the actress to listen to his telephone apology —whereupon O'Hara got on the phone and abused her for being pompous. On another occasion he and writer Allen Rivkin were at the Clover Club, a posh gambling joint, where Rivkin met a girl he had known in St. Paul. She asked who was with him; and she asked to be introduced because she was an O'Hara fan. When the girl told O'Hara she had read his books, he snarled that he didn't think people in St. Paul could read and why didn't she go back to her table and let him alone. Rivkin returned her to her party and called John an uncouth son-of-a-bitch. O'Hara admitted it, said nothing more about the incident, and they went into the gaming rooms.[29]

O'Hara played a great deal of tennis in Hollywood. One day he was at the bar of the West Side Tennis Club ordering his favorite St. James Scotch when a man said, "With a twist of lemon, right?" The other St. James drinker was Gilbert Roland. After they introduced themselves, Roland said, "I understand you know my man Hemingway," and a long conversation followed. Roland was one of the strongest tennis players in the movie colony. O'Hara enjoyed playing with him, although he wasn't in Roland's class and never took a set. The actor, however, loved anagrams. A deal was made: Roland would play three sets with O'Hara if O'Hara would play anagrams. The friendship was long and close. O'Hara gave one of the toasts at Roland's wedding to Constance Bennett in 1941 and stood godfather to their daughter

Lynda.[30] During this second Hollywood stint O'Hara's regular companions were James Cagney, Clifford Odets, Sidney Skolsky, Lewis Milestone, Oscar Levant, Mike Romanoff, Cedric Hardwicke, Lothar Mendes, Gilbert Roland, Peter Lorre, and Robert Benchley—a group that gathered at the bar of the Beverly Wilshire Hotel. At that time Benchley was acting in comedy shorts, and his bungalow at the Garden of Allah was a center of alcoholic conviviality. Benchley was, in the words O'Hara later used in the dedication of *Five Plays*, "the best of company."

For a while John McClain shared a bungalow with Benchley. Every evening after six, what they called the "drop-in trade" would arrive. The regulars included O'Hara, Fitzgerald, Dorothy Parker, John Steinbeck, Roland Young, Donald Ogden Stewart, Mike Romanoff, Humphrey Bogart, Monty Woolley, Herbert Marshall, Irene

Michael Romanoff and John O'Hara, Romanoff's, Hollywood.

Selznick, Charles Lederer, Charles Brackett, Eddie Sutherland and Charles Butterworth. The group would move on to a late dinner at Chasen's or Romanoff's.*

In 1936 O'Hara's published story output dropped to what was a low level for him: five stories, of which three were in *The New Yorker*. The magazine's rejections brought about his first attempt to break with *The New Yorker*, in an undated letter to Wolcott Gibbs:

JOHN O'HARA
10735 OHIO AVENUE
WEST LOS ANGELES, CALIFORNIA

Dear Wolc:

      Thank you for your letter. The pieces which you have just rejected, the one about the kid and his father, called FIFTEEN DOLLARS, and the other one, PRETTY LITTLE MRS. HARPER,† are cases in point. When I have paid off the money I owe The New Yorker I will write no more pieces for it. You and Mrs. White, as it happens, were right about FIF-TEEN DOLLARS. The father was only and simply glad his son had a good girl. The other one was just as obvious, but you happened not to like it.

      You can tell Ross about my decision, and also tell him not to bother about answering my let-ter. My only regret now is that I have to give you pieces to pay off what I owe.

                  Yrs.

                  John

Please don't use my name in any advertising.

9 rejects 4 acceptances.) since July

To Wolcott Gibbs, 1936.

* O'Hara had been one of the investors when Prince Mike Romanoff was seeking backing for his restaurant, and enjoyed remarking that he put up more money than Jock Whitney. Romanoff and O'Hara had first met in New York speakeasies and retained a lifelong affection for each other.

† "Pretty Little Mrs. Harper" appeared in the August 1936 *Scribner's;* but "Fifteen Dollars" remained unpublished.

The break was patched up somehow—or ignored—for O'Hara continued to appear in *The New Yorker*. The best story of 1936 was "Saffercisco," which is about a successful movie star who has fallen in love with a young married actress and decides to call on her husband to explain that he wants to marry the girl. At the end of a drunken conversation the actor learns that she is in "Saffercisco" with still another man.

In the spring of 1936 John also picked up some money by writing a pair of Hollywood articles for the King Features Syndicate: "Movie Fans Like Me Should Know All!" and "Cesar Romero and the Three Dollar Bills," the latter a reminiscence of the time they were both broke in New York.

A revealing fact is that although O'Hara was a writer of the Thirties, he was not a Depression writer. His political ideas at this time were strongly liberal, but he never turned his hand to proletarian literature. Indeed, he was frequently criticized for the political irrelevance of his work and for his fascination with the kinds of people Fitzgerald wrote about.* O'Hara never shouldered the burden of liberal guilt, probably because he didn't feel guilty. After all, he had been hungry before and after October 1929. Moreover, the liberals he identified with and who shaped his political thinking—Dorothy Parker, Robert Benchley and Heywood Broun—enjoyed the good life. Hollywood was full of party-liners who would have liked to educate O'Hara, but a couple of visits to their "study sessions" left him bored and unimpressed. His politics were emotional rather than doctrinaire; and his closest brush with outright political activity took a highly O'Hara-esque form: at one point in the Thirties he considered the possibility of shooting Hitler, but abandoned the idea because it would put an end to his writing.[31]

O'Hara's position on literature as a class-warfare weapon is revealed by two projects that interested him in 1936: a dramatization of Steinbeck's *In Dubious Battle* and a movie of *The Great Gatsby*. He discussed the play with Steinbeck and producer Herman Shumlin, but dropped the project because he recognized that it was not his material. O'Hara was never able to work successfully with another writer's plots and characters—which is one of the reasons why his Hollywood career was unexceptional. O'Hara's response to the politics of the Depression is revealed by his feelings about Fitzgerald's

---

* Fitzgerald pasted in his scrapbook reviews of *Appointment* and *Butterfield 8* that compared them to his work with a caption: THE CROSS OF JOHN O'HARA.

career, for he had been "shocked and probably frightened" by the poor reception of *Tender.*

I was politically to the left of Fitzgerald, but it was no more my nature to write a proletarian novel than it was for John Steinbeck to write a novel about Hobe Sound, or Fitzgerald to write a documentary about Pacific Grove. Because I was involved with the New Deal I attempted a dramatization of In Dubious Battle, *but I abandoned the project when I found that in those moments of truth when a writer must believe what he says, a thing is not finally true because another has said it is true. . . . I was seeing Odets almost daily, giving money and lending my name to liberal causes, and I had worked with my hands and been miserably poor. Yet I could not, or stubbornly would not, write a novel that depicted all men in Brooks Brothers shirts as fascists and all men in overalls as crusaders for freedom, decency and truth. My memory of fascists in overalls and genuine liberals in button-down shirts was always getting in the way, whenever I was tempted to follow the trend of the proletarian propaganda novel, and thereby escape the fate of Fitzgerald.*[32]

The *Gatsby* movie probably interested him more than did the Steinbeck play; it was his kind of material. Paramount owned the screen rights to *Gatsby* but had no plans for it.

The reason I wanted to write a talking-picture version of the Fitzgerald novel was that I had seen the silent version and had admired it enormously. . . . But even now I can remember my exultation at the end of the picture when I saw that Paramount had done an honest job, true to the book, true to what Fitzgerald had intended. My favorite Fitzgerald novel had not yet been written, but the movies had done right by Our Boy with the best he had written to date. Roughly ten years later I was sure that I could do an even better job through the new camera techniques and audible dialogue.[33]

O'Hara wanted to write a script for Clark Gable and tried to acquire the rights from Paramount, acting through an intermediary. The price was too high, and he tried unsuccessfully to get Fox to buy the rights for him.

In 1937 nine O'Hara stories appeared in *The New Yorker,* of which two were superb: "Goodbye, Herman" and "Price's Always Open"—a quintessential O'Hara story and one of the peaks of his achievement with the short story. "Price's Always Open," which probably derived from O'Hara's stay on Cape Cod while working on *Butterfield 8,* demonstrates his ability to reveal the social structure of a community through one setting—here a diner patronized by the summer resort people and the townies. The author's sympathies are with the local boy who attends Holy Cross and loves the cruel WASP rich girl. In general O'Hara believed that the wealthy WASPs represented the best in American life, but his attitude toward the class was complex. Generalizations about his alleged snobbery or social-climbing do not obtain, any more than do generalizations about his pro-Irish bias. He created villainous Irishmen and corrupt poor boys, as well as a gallery of worthless aristocrats. Even before he wrote his big novels, he demonstrated an astonishing range of characters and settings—probably a greater range of material than is found in any other American writer. The only generalization that holds is that he created his characters one at a time and portrayed decency and cruelty on every level of American life. Nevertheless, it is indisputable that he found the rituals and appurtenances of upper-middle-class and upper-class life endlessly interesting. John O'Hara admired high personal standards and often found these codes at the upper levels of society, where wealth and training had developed them.

In a number of O'Hara's stories the economical prose and tight control of detail troubled readers who were accustomed to having the message spelled out for them. These readers regarded him as an experimental or obscure writer. For example, *The New Yorker* received letters from readers about the 1937 story "Give and Take," which ends with: "Then he went out, and the bow on his hat-band was on the wrong side of his head." The readers wanted to know what that sentence meant; and some of the *New Yorker* people, including Gibbs, claimed that the point was lost on them. "Give and. Take" describes the relationship between a schoolteacher and her grown son, an unsuccessful promoter and poolroom loafer. He boasts of his contacts with important people while shaking his mother down for twenty dollars. She knows and the reader knows that he'll never succeed with his fast-buck schemes, that he'll always be a bum. Although he is greatly concerned about his appearance—which is part of the equipment for a hustler—he doesn't know how to wear a hat properly. That detail symbolizes his life; it is the objective correlative of his failure. The point should be obvious, and the readers who missed the point did so because they were used to nonfunctional detail in fiction and could not believe that O'Hara was writing so deliberately and accurately.

WHEN O'HARA STARTED "So Far, So Good" in the spring of 1936 he had a contract with Harcourt, Brace for three novels, the first of which was to be about Hollywood, but as far as can be determined none of these novels was started. While he was wrestling with "So Far, So Good," the full-scale Hollywood novel was on his mind. He wanted to spend a year in Ireland, but decided that the book would have to be written near a good film reference library—in California or New York.

These plans changed after he met Belle Wylie.

IV

Belle

BELLE WYLIE was in Europe during March–May 1937. When she returned, O'Hara came East. On their first New York date he took her to the Onyx Club, a jazz spot on West 52nd Street, where she cried because the building was the house she had grown up in.

The Wylie family had a home at Quogue, on the south shore (Atlantic Ocean side) of Long Island, and in the summer of 1937 O'Hara rented a cottage there. He took an immediate and permanent liking for Quogue, a community where the affluent lived well but unpretentiously. Belle's family was close—she had two brothers and three sisters—and O'Hara made a point of being on his best behavior with Mrs. Wylie.

In the fall of 1937 O'Hara was living at the London Terrace, 470 West 24th Street, in the Chelsea district of Manhattan.* He completed *Hope of Heaven* (the published form of "So Far, So Good"), with the final pages being written at the Benjamin Franklin Hotel in Philadelphia. During the Thirties he would sometimes hole up in a hotel to do a writing job.

He needed money and unsuccessfully tried to break into the high-paying *Saturday Evening Post*. His contact there was Joseph Bryan III, a friend who had married Katharine Barnes, a member of the Whitney clan. When *The New Yorker* rejected his profile of Walter Winchell, O'Hara offered to rewrite it for the *Post*, informing Bryan that he would provide 5,000 words for $1,000.[1] The offer was declined, but in March 1938 O'Hara considered trying to write a serial novel for the magazine.

That fall, Belle was O'Hara's steady date. Her friends recall that he would frequently phone late at night asking her to meet him at some night club, and she would unprotestingly dress and go. They eloped to Elkton, Maryland, on 3 December 1937.† The marriage

---

* He had this apartment for some time and seems to have sublet it while he was out of New York.

† O'Hara was so strapped at this time that he had to borrow $900 marriage money from his brother Tom.

Belle Mulford Wylie, Nice, 1937.

certificate gives O'Hara's age as thirty-two and Belle's as twenty-four.
He listed his occupation as reporter and the Algonquin Hotel as his
residence. When Belle phoned the news to her mother, Mrs. Wylie
let out a shriek, but there were no mother-in-law problems for O'Hara
this time. He and Mrs. Wylie became fond of each other.

Belle O'Hara's devotion to her husband assumed legendary dimensions among their friends. She accommodated herself to his drink-

ing and working habits, protected him from distractions, unobtrusively interposed herself in his professional problems when necessary, and never complained or criticized him in anyone's hearing—even when he was in his black alcoholic moods. In those days his life ran on a forty-eight hour drinking/working cycle. He would awake at noon or later to eat his breakfast and spend the afternoon with friends in bars; Belle would join him for dinner, and a night of drinking would follow (on his part, not Belle's: one drink lasted her a long time). The next day was devoted to ministering to his hangover, and late that night he would write. Then the cycle would begin again. There are conflicting accounts about whether O'Hara wrote on alcohol. His friends have reported their surprise that he could leave a bar full of whiskey and go home to write, but they are almost certainly mythologizing. He claimed that he never wrote when he had been drinking, and there is no question about the fact that he went on the wagon for his novels.

Belle was called "saintly" and "angelic" by some of their friends, to whom O'Hara seemed a domineering husband—especially when he was drunk. However, Kate Bramwell, her close friend from St. Timothy's, and Belle's sister Winifred Gardiner, believe that Belle was in control of the marriage—and that it was what she wanted. She was quietly unconventional and loved the drama and excitement of life with John O'Hara. Belle believed in her husband's genius and was determined to do everything in her power to help him. She endeavored to cut off anything that would upset him or interfere with his work; and she was in control of everything except his drinking, which she stubbornly coped with. Belle Wylie O'Hara was not dominated: she was strong, serene and secure.[2]

O'Hara's drinking was not simply heavy (he may have reached a bottle a day at his peak), it was also unpredictable. He might drink all day without showing it until one more drink turned him into a profane fighting drunk. One night at a Hollywood party Winthrop Sargeant met O'Hara for the first time and found him a pleasant fellow who insisted that Sargeant take his car to run an errand; when Sargeant returned, perhaps an hour later, O'Hara was roaring drunk and challenging every "Yale son-of-a-bitch" in the room to fight.[3] Belle tried to discourage his association with heavy drinkers, and she worried when he was with Dorothy Parker or Al Wright, with whom he tended to overdrink. As bartender, Belle unobtrusively limited his intake by pouring a layer of whiskey over a spoon into the top of a highball so O'Hara would think that the drink was strong when he took the first swallow.

Shortly before publication of *Hope of Heaven*, Wolcott Gibbs published an article, "Watch Out for Mr. O'Hara," in *The Saturday Review of Literature* (19 February 1938). In this largely anecdotal summary of O'Hara's career, Gibbs expresses what seems to have been *The New Yorker* party line on O'Hara's development as a short-story writer: that his elliptical techniques too often resulted in cryptic stories.

Unfortunately not many of them could be printed in a magazine whose readers had no special interest in experimental prose, and consequently these were rather thin days for the author. Gradually, however, these stories acquired substance and Mr. O'Hara lost much, though by no means all, of his earlier passion for indirection.

This judgment combines respect with condescension, treating O'Hara as though he had more talent than he knew what to do with. Gibbs implied that O'Hara had failed to fulfill his promise and warned that he might become merely a successful novelist unless he disciplined himself. He closed with expressions of high hope:

If, on the other hand, he can contrive to write about the things he authentically hates—waste and hypocrisy and the sadness of potentially valuable lives failing, but not without some dignity, because they were not born quite strong enough for the circumstances they had to meet— and if he can write about them with the honesty and understanding which he possesses in as great a measure as anyone writing today, then he will certainly be one of our most important novelists.

Gibbs's if-prediction was realized, although he did not really sound as though he expected it to be. Indeed, when it did come true and O'Hara became "one of our most important novelists" in 1949 with *A Rage to Live*, Wolcott Gibbs and some of his *New Yorker* colleagues did not take pleasure in O'Hara's achievement. The two photographs accompanying this essay provide an insight to O'Hara's public image at this time—or, at any rate, the image that journals such as *The Saturday Review of Literature* gave him: one shows the author in white bucks and a tweed jacket looking like an overage Yalie, and the other shows him at the Stork Club.

While *Hope of Heaven* was in press, John and Belle honeymooned at the Lovetts' home in Hobe Sound, Florida—which was authentic O'Hara territory. In April 1938 the O'Haras sailed for Europe on the *Paris*. A surprise fellow-passenger was Helen Ritchie Petit O'Hara.

Pet suggested that she accompany John and Belle, but her offer was declined. After a tour of France, John and Belle settled in London in May. The plan was to spend a year abroad, but a cold snap without central heating persuaded the O'Haras to leave before fall.

While in London they took a three-month lease on a flat at 52 Chesil Court in Chelsea, which the Morley Kennerleys found for them. Kennerley, an editor at Faber & Faber, O'Hara's English publisher, was a Yale-educated American and the son of New York publisher and auction-gallery owner Mitchell Kennerley. The two couples saw a good deal of each other and Mrs. Kennerley was impressed by the fact that nothing O'Hara did seemed to upset Belle. Once Belle asked her to recommend a good dry cleaner because John had come home with lipstick on his tie. Although O'Hara liked England and approved English standards of conduct—it has been remarked that he privately saw himself as an English squire—he was not a social success in London. He was off the wagon, and his drinking behavior did not sit well with the English. Thirty years later, in 1967, at the Foyles luncheon in London marking paperback publication of *The Lockwood Concern* he remarked, "On my earlier visits, while I was still a young man, I gave what might be called a series of private lectures in such cultural institutions as the Ivy restaurant, the Savoy Grill, the 400 Club, Quaglino's, l'Apéritif, the Savage Club, and various locals in S.W. 3. My comments on your manners and customs were not always well received."[4] The Chesil Court flat was near Sigmund Freud's home; although O'Hara greatly admired Freud, he never worked up the courage to call on him. He did not produce much work in London, and only three published stories can be credited to this period— "Richard Wagner: Public Domain?," "A Day Like Today" and "No Mistakes." One of O'Hara's abortive projects was a Reporter-at-Large piece on Scotland Yard, which he proposed to *The New Yorker* but does not seem to have worked on.

Hope of Heaven WAS PUBLISHED on 17 March 1938. The short novel did not represent an advance in O'Hara's career, and the critics said so. The plot chronicles the affair between Jimmy Malloy, now a Hollywood scriptwriter, and Peggy Henderson, a bookstore clerk with communist convictions. Don Miller, a young man from The Region who has been forging traveler's checks, asks Malloy for help. Miller's activities bring Peggy's long-lost father, an investigator who is following the trail of checks. At the end of the book, after Henderson accidentally kills his son during a scuffle, Peggy breaks her engagement to Malloy and drifts into despair. Many reviews took the tone of disappointment or I-told-you-so. Fadiman in *The New Yorker* repeated his view that O'Hara was a greatly gifted writer who was wasting himself on worthless characters, and complained about excessive detail: "Let others write ads for Brooks Brothers, Mr. O'Hara; you go ahead and be a novelist." This piece of advice prompted O'Hara's wisecrack that if Fadiman wore a Brooks suit, he would immediately be spotted as a spy. Heywood Broun revised the position he had taken on *Butterfield 8* and predicted that O'Hara's work would improve as his view of humanity deepened. Charles Poore, writing his first O'Hara review in the daily *Times*, took much the same approach as Broun. The Sunday *Times Book Review* piece by Louis Kronenberger was respectfully unfavorable.

All the praise was for O'Hara's style; his material disturbed reviewers. O'Hara was puzzled and hurt by the failure of *Hope of Heaven*, for he was convinced that it represented a clear advance over his previous work. In 1941 he commented, ". . . the book I worked hardest on, worked longest on, and feel was the best written, made buttons, and I had thought it would be a really big success."[5] The novel was not a total flop for the Depression year 1938, selling 13,000 copies. When he inscribed a copy for his young daughter some seven years later, he wrote: "Dear Wylie/This is my best/J.O'H."

O'Hara was disappointed in the promotional effort for *Hope of Heaven* and wrote to Pearce and Sloan on 3 May:

But don't infer that I am complaining. I think it is sound business psychology to make the reading public think a book is hard to get. . . . I was thinking along these lines the other day, when we were having a drink at the Savoy with Frank Morley, Morley Kennerley, and Dick Simon. I thought how lucky I was not to be identified with a house like Simon & Schuster. No dignity. Put over all their books by advertising.

In the same letter he reported that he had been taken up by Alec Waugh, who gave a supper party to which

he invited Mrs. O'Hara I as well as Mrs. O'Hara II, not to mention the curator of reptiles at the London Zoo, a Lesbian who loved Butterfield 8 and didn't know anything else I'd written, an illegitimate son of Oscar Wilde (!!!), a lady journalist and other interesting folk. Beebe would have loved it. I didn't. We went to someone's flat and the Lesbian asked all the girls to dance with her. Most of them did. Oh, and Mrs. _____, who wanted everybody to get drunk and start fucking.

O'Hara's description of this party bears on the much-argued question of the accuracy of his reportage of sexual conduct. Whenever his friends charged him with exaggerating or distorting sexual behavior in his work, his reply was something like "You don't notice much, do you?"

After their censorship problems with *Butterfield 8*, the English publishers were nervous about the Home Office reaction to *Hope of Heaven*. A laundered text was published by Faber & Faber in 1939, with thirty-six stories selected by O'Hara, thereby giving him good English exposure.[6]

Kennerley introduced O'Hara to John Hayward, the distinguished bibliographer, and an unlikely friendship developed. Hayward was confined to a wheelchair, had a sharp wit (it was said that he had the nastiest tongue in London) and an interest in the varieties of sexual behavior; the two men enjoyed their long talks. A souvenir of their friendship survives in the form of Hayward's copy of *Butterfield 8*, inscribed by the O'Haras, in which Hayward noted—in his capacity as publisher's reader—the page numbers with passages that were considered censorable in England. This copy also has a drawing by James Thurber of a dog contemplating the list of these pages.[7] Thurber was in London that spring, and O'Hara appears to have resented Thurber's great popularity among the English. On the Fourth of July 1938 some of the Americans in London had a party at which an English guest asked, "What is the Fourth of July?" The question prompted an oration by Thurber that made the Americans so homesick they decided to return to the States—or so the story goes. The details of Thurber's speech are lost in the haze of alcohol and time.

On 10 August 1938 the O'Haras sailed from Southampton, probably on the *Normandie*. The trip had been mostly a vacation.* O'Hara did not work on his projected Hollywood novel, which seems to have been permanently shelved. *Hope of Heaven* died after one reprinting in 1938, so he turned to short stories for ready income. In the second half of 1938 he published seven stories, one of which, "Pal Joey," in the 22 October *New Yorker*, was a key event in his career. The cir-

---

*In London, O'Hara wrote a joking article on English newspapers for the September 1938 issue of *For Men*, an American imitation *Esquire*; a second article on English speech and manners appeared in December.

cumstances behind the creation of Joey Evans were later reported by Earl Wilson in a 1948 interview with O'Hara:

"Well, I'm going to level with you about 'Pal Joey.' You are a guy that's got to be in the eerie, and you heard I wrote it while I was on the sauce. I didn't. I was sober.

* * * *

"My wife and I were back from England. Broke.

"We were living at my mother-in-law's. At 93d and 5th. I tell you 93d and 5th because that's important. Do you feel like another one? I think I had better eat something."

He ordered a sandwich. "I had an idea for a story. I said to my wife I'd go to Philadelphia. Hole up in the Hotel Ben Franklin a couple days, lock myself in, eat on room service. Just work.

"But the night before, we went out, and I got stiff.

"I got up next morning to start for the station, and I am dying.

"Now as we got to the Pierre, at 60th St., I said to the cab, 'Stop here.' I went in. After a drink or two I feel what-the-hell. Better take a nap. I check in."

"Then," said O'Hara, looking down at the table, shaking his head, "began a real beauty. Just getting stiff and passing out. I started Thursday. By Saturday morning I'd drunk myself sober. I picked up the phone and said, 'What time is it?'

"The girl says, 'Quarter after 7.'

"I asked her, 'A.M. or P.M.?' The girl said, 'A.M. and the day is Saturday.' They knew me there.

"At that point remorse set in. I asked, 'What kind of god damn heel am I? I must be worse'n anybody in the world.' Then I figured, 'No, there must be somebody worse than me—but who?' Al Capone, maybe. Then I got it—maybe some night club masters of ceremonies I know."

O'Hara took a cigaret from his handsome gold case. "That was my idea. I went to work and wrote a piece about a night club heel in the form of a letter. I finished the piece by 11 o'clock. I went right home.

"Now, I'd never been south of 60th St.

"I said to my wife, 'I have a confession to make.' "

His wife said, "No, you haven't; you've been to the Pierre."

"How did she know? Instinctively, I guess. The New Yorker bought the story the same day, ordered a dozen more, and then came the play, and the movie. . . .*

"That was the only good thing I ever got out of booze, but mind

---

* There is a mistake here. No movie version of *Pal Joey* was made until 1957.

you, Wilson, I wasn't on a bender at the time I wrote it. I was per-fectly sober! Have you got that down in your notebook?"[8]

Harold Ross was delighted with Joey, and during the war even suggested that O'Hara revive the series with Joey in the navy. Through 1940 O'Hara wrote fourteen Joeys, twelve of which appeared in *The New Yorker*. They were easy to write and easy money—eventu-ally a great deal of money. It has been estimated that the book, stage and movie appearances of Joey Evans earned his creator more than a million dollars.

Although the Joey stories and their spin-offs brought John O'Hara his first great popularity, they are not important in themselves. These stories derive from Ring Lardner's *You Know Me Al* letters and represent only a slight advance over the Delphian and Hagedorn & Brownmiller series of 1928–29. In the long run, they probably de-layed O'Hara's development as a novelist, for their earnings relieved him of the pressure to write; moreover, they gave him a new image with the reading public as an imitator of Lardner and Damon Runyon. This Broadway wise-guy reputation almost certainly impeded the proper recognition of O'Hara's major work.

It is difficult to avoid the conclusion that Ross and the *New Yorker* people were a long time in recognizing how good—how important—John O'Hara was. He was, in point of fact, the one great writer that the magazine developed during Ross's editorship. Many major writers contributed to the magazine, but O'Hara was the only one who matured within it. He was also the star contributor in terms of fre-quency, with 134 stories in the 1928–38 decade. It may not be en-tirely accurate to say that Ross didn't take him seriously: his judg-ment of the writer was complicated by the fact that he was put off by O'Hara. Moreover, Ross never really cared intensely about fiction. Some of the *New Yorker* editors seem to have resented O'Hara's achievements outside of the magazine, and during his greatest years as a novelist some of the old hands at 25 West 43rd Street would remark, "I thought he was a better writer before he stopped drinking."

In 1938 William Maxwell replaced Katherine Angell White as O'Hara's editor at *The New Yorker*, at the time of the Pal Joey stories. O'Hara was again working in Hollywood, and his letters to Maxwell show that the job of editing O'Hara was in part the job of running interference between Ross and O'Hara. The writer felt that Ross's editorial queries were either squeamish or ignorant—that Ross did not have the knowledge to question his details or language. He complained to Maxwell in March 1939:

Then the next proof has a query about cribs. Now how many people know that a crib meant a kind of whorehouse? They exist in only a few places—Reno, New Orleans. On the other hand, Ross ought to know that crib is a derogatory term for a night club, like flea-bag for hotel. I wish to hell there would be an end to this quibbling about my use of the vernacular. Even if people don't get it at first, they will. I was the first person ever to do a piece about double talk, and God knows a lot of people still don't know what it is, but that was several years ago that I did the piece (in The New Yorker), and several things in that piece have become established slang. It is a point of artistry with me. I like being first in those things, but you-all makes me nervous. I'm afraid to put in anything more recent than you tell em casket, I'm coffin. There is a piece I've been wanting to do, or rather a kind of talk called ski talk, but I know it would be no use because the queries would drive me crazy—if it ever got to the query stage. I also have been unable to use the verb to make in the sense of recognizing and/or identifying. Detectives are always saying "I made him the minute I sore him," meaning "I recognized him . . ." But Ross would think the detective was a fairy, I suppose. I remember Miss Fishback had a poem in which she said something about somebody's on the up and up, as tho it meant the person was being increasingly successful in business. It doesn't mean that at all, yet Ross passed it.

O'Hara became bored with the Joey letters, but he continued to produce them because they were easy to write while holding down a Hollywood job. He made it a point of professional honor not to take his screenwriting seriously, for he told Maxwell: "I never work more than 3 hrs a day but I am so much faster than they are accustomed to that my boss laughs at me. 'You'll catch on,' he said the other day. 'I hope you don't,' I said to myself."[9] By contrast he could become intensely emotional about his fiction. When he submitted "Too Young" in the summer of 1939 he wrote Maxwell, "For your information, the cop vs girl part actually occurred in Palm Beach four years ago the day before I got there. A friend of mine saw it happen and I nearly went insane. For months I wanted to kill every cop I saw, and as you see I never have forgotten it."

ONE OF O'HARA's New York drinking friends was Ben Finney, who might be described as a *bon vivant* or a sportsman, though these terms do not convey the respect he enjoyed from his large circle of friends.*

* Shortly before his death O'Hara wrote the foreword for Finney's autobiography, *Feet First* (New York: Crown, 1971).

Both Fitzgerald and Hemingway trusted his literary taste. During the Thirties, Finney and O'Hara were both part of a group—including Benchley, Courtney Burr, Quentin Reynolds and McClain—that gathered at P. J. Clark's saloon on Third Avenue. Finney and O'Hara shared a fondness for elaborately plotted practical jokes, and Finney was in on—but did not participate in—what was intended to be a masterpiece. O'Hara had developed a dislike for Rockefeller Center, so he and the artist Jeff Machamer conceived the plan of bribing the cleaning women in one of the buildings to leave the lights on in certain offices. If all had gone according to plan, the letters SHIT would have lit up the skyline; but the building superintendent got wind of the scheme and foiled it.[10]

O'Hara published eleven stories in 1939, of which five continued the Pal Joey series; seven more Joeys followed in 1940. In the spring of 1939 John and Belle were at 471½ Landfair in the Westwood district of Los Angeles, where he commenced his most successful period as a screenwriter. During March and April he was at RKO polishing *In Name Only* for $750 a week. Richard Sherman received script credit for this film that starred Carole Lombard, Cary Grant, Kay Francis and Charles Coburn. In September, O'Hara was hired at $750 by Twentieth Century-Fox, where he received his first screen credits. Although he did not take his Hollywood work seriously, he nonetheless wanted to succeed at it. He was in it for the money; therefore, he wanted to sell himself at the highest price. At the same time he was cautious about being corrupted by easy money. He remarked that he'd seen too many newspaper rewrite men who thought they were thousand-a-week movie writers. One disciplinary device he applied was to segregate his movie money in California banks and not deposit it with his "real" earnings. As a mere writer he was never in the big Hollywood money. During this period O'Hara turned down a job as a movie producer because "I was one of those lucky people who always knew what they wanted. And what I wanted is what I am: a nonstarving author who is allowed to do the best he can. . . . if I had saved my money . . . I would have no sense of urgency about writing."[11] O'Hara delighted in a comment by the wife of a producer-director on the simplicity of Spencer Tracy's life: "He lives just like a $1,000-a-week writer." One extravagance that O'Hara allowed himself with Hollywood money in 1941 was the purchase of his first great car from John McClain: a 1932 Murphy-bodied boattailed Duesenberg Speedster.[12]

At Fox he worked on two Darryl F. Zanuck productions, *He Married His Wife* and *I Was an Adventuress*, between 18 September

O'Hara's Duesenberg Speedster.

and 6 December. For *Wife* he was teamed with Sam Hellman, Darrell Ware and Lynn Starling on a screen story by Erna Lazarus and Scott Darling. A romantic comedy starring Joel McCrea and Nancy Kelly, and directed by Roy Del Ruth, it was not a major film. O'Hara enjoyed the appearance of Cesar Romero and Roland Young in supporting parts, since Romero was an old friend and Young was a more recent drinking pal. However, he found collaborating with three other writers irksome, for he was a confirmed loner in his work. On *I Was an Adventuress* he was teamed with two writers, Don Ettlinger and Karl Tunberg. This romantic melodrama about an international confidence woman—played by Zorina—was directed by Gregory Ratoff. Peter Lorre, one of O'Hara's close friends in Hollywood, was in it. His work on these films brought O'Hara two screen credits and a raise to $1,000 a week for his next Fox assignment. Between 2 January and 5 April 1940 he worked on a Betty Grable musical, *Down Argentine Way*, but did not receive a screen credit.

Producer Collier Young, one of O'Hara's Hollywood friends, shared his interest in *Who's Who in America*. They invented a game of pretending to be people in that reference work. Once when the O'Haras and the Youngs were driving to Palm Springs for a weekend, the men started the game in the car; and O'Hara stayed in character for the weekend as he pretended to be a Midwestern hardware manufacturer.[13] O'Hara also enjoyed convincing Ivy League alumni that

The Bachelors Ball (Los Angeles)
Jan. 26, 1940

John and Belle.

he had attended their colleges by displaying minute knowledge of the traditions and organizations.

O'Hara had met Budd Schulberg through Dorothy Parker in Hollywood in late 1936 or early 1937. An intense friendship developed, and for a while they saw each other almost every day. Both were keenly interested in politics, and Schulberg became O'Hara's favorite late-night drinking companion in Hollywood. Stanley Rose's book-shop on Hollywood Boulevard was a writers' club in the late Thirties. Schulberg was a regular there, along with William Saroyan, Nathanael West and John Fante; but O'Hara was only an occasional visitor. After publication of *Hope of Heaven*, Rose did not make O'Hara feel welcome, for Rose believed that he had treated the model for Peggy Henderson unfairly in the novel.

During some of their long discussions, O'Hara commented to Schulberg, "There's about as much chance of that as a Jew getting into Palæopitus," referring to a student leadership group at Dartmouth. It was typical of O'Hara to know this detail of Dartmouth life and to employ it in a discussion with a Dartmouth graduate.

Schulberg replied, "John, that's not quite as impossible as you think. A Jew can get into Palæopitus."

"I don't believe it," O'Hara said.

"Oh, for Crissake, John, take a look at this," said Schulberg, flipping his Palæopitus key across the room, where it fell on the floor.

"What kind of Palæopitus member are you, to throw your key on the floor?" was the response.[14]

Although Schulberg found himself on the O'Hara blacklist a few times, he enjoyed a special influence over O'Hara at the peak of their friendship and was able to handle him on difficult occasions. One night Belle phoned Schulberg with the information that John was in trouble at the Mocambo. He got to the night club and found O'Hara holding off eight or ten people who were getting ready to beat him up. Schulberg walked up to him and said, "Let's go, John." O'Hara left peacefully with him. On the occasions when O'Hara and Schul-berg arrived drunk, Belle would prepare Underwood's clam chowder, O'Hara's specific for the ills of alcohol.

Schulberg experienced some classic examples of O'Hara's loyalty and touchiness. When Schulberg—a serious boxing fan—couldn't afford to attend the first Louis-Conn fight in June 1941, O'Hara gave him a ticket for the fight and a plane ticket to New York. Although O'Hara is supposed to have been annoyed when Schulberg gave him a carbon copy, instead of the ribbon copy, of *What Makes Sammy Run?* to read, he championed the book when it was attacked by

Hollywood people and wrote a public letter about *Sammy* which was used on the dust jacket. Some of the friends—and former friends—of John O'Hara invented the game of trying to top each other's O'Hara anecdotes. Budd Schulberg won the competition. In 1951 when he was on the O'Hara blacklist he found himself at the bar of "21" next to O'Hara, who ignored him. But when someone came up to Schulberg and began abusing him for *The Disenchanted*, O'Hara growled at the man, "Nobody can talk to a friend of mine like that"—while still cutting Schulberg. The members of O'Hara's blacklist did not always know why—or even if—they were on it. Schulberg thinks he qualified either because he mistreated O'Hara's Mercury or because O'Hara disliked *The Disenchanted*.

O'Hara also met William Saroyan at Stanley Rose's bookshop. Later they found themselves at adjacent tables at a Hollywood gathering on behalf of the Scottsboro Boys. When O'Hara asked Saroyan where he'd found the people he was with—a group of high-paid screenwriters—a long conversation ensued that marked the beginning of a lasting, but not close, friendship. While Saroyan was in the army during World War II, his wife Carol became friendly with Belle, and the couples occasionally dined together after the war. On one occasion when the O'Haras and Saroyans were with the Michael Arlens, Arlen found it necessary to tell O'Hara to stop using strong words at table. Saroyan was amused to see O'Hara comply with the rebuke. Like other writers, William Saroyan was fascinated by O'Hara's writing habits, because at that time O'Hara was still working well while drinking heavily and pursuing an active social life.

John amused me profoundly by his addiction to form and status, but I could never feel that that addiction really diminished him in any way as a writer. He was a worker, and a worker has only that reality . . . . I think O'Hara was one of the loneliest souls I have ever seen, although we gather that he at least affected the opposite. His preoccupation with the most intimate relations between male and female suggests the extent and depth of his separateness, isolation, and essentially inconsolable despair about a failure to heal loneliness. . . .[15]

In September 1939, Harcourt, Brace published the second collection of thirty-five O'Hara stories (including four Joeys), *Files on Parade*. Although it did not have a long story or an important previously unpublished story, *Files* required three printings in 1939, which was more than respectable since it was a law of publishing that short-story collections didn't sell.* O'Hara addressed himself to this law in the foreword, in which he paid tribute to the stories of Lardner, Hemingway, Parker and Faulkner. The foreword was a late addition and had to be tipped into the first printing of *Files*. It was the first in a line of prefatory statements he would supply for his story volumes and strikes the tone that characterized these statements: I know my craft, and I am good at it; I am totally committed to my work, and I take enormous satisfaction from it; any reader who doesn't like my work can go to hell. This position put off readers and reviewers who liked authors to come on Heepish. The foreword to *Files* may be regarded as O'Hara's first proclamation of his view of the literary establishment, which set the pattern for his relationship with the prize givers for the next thirty years. He wanted their awards, but he'd be goddamned if he'd ask nicely. Demand, yes; but not humbly tug his forelock. It was his responsibility to write well; it was the critics' responsibility to recognize his merit.† The crankiness of this foreword may have owed something to the fact that O'Hara had just gone on the wagon after his first serious ulcer attack; but he resumed drinking, to Belle's great distress. In the covering letter to editor Sam Sloan he reported insomnia and loss of appetite. He admitted that he was flinging down a gauntlet: "If you object to it I won't put up a fight, but it just possibly might annoy some of the boys like Fadiman enough to cause a tiny controversy, which would keep the book alive."[16]

O'Hara dedicated *Files on Parade* to his mother, marking the formal end of the estrangement resulting from his marriage to and divorce from Pet. Thereafter he was a devoted and generous son.

During 1939 O'Hara proposed two ambitious nonfiction projects for *The New Yorker*. In May he tried out on Ross the idea of a three-part profile of "a 1939 Babbitt," which seems not to have been encouraged. The outbreak of the war in Europe moved him to consider writing his recollections of 1914–1918, but he dropped the plan. His rate had increased to 13¢ per word, with a 3¼¢ bonus after a certain

---

* O'Hara's later volumes helped to modify this law.

† A puzzling aspect of O'Hara's management of his career was his opposition to having his stories reprinted in anthologies—or even in textbooks. Although a number of his stories were nominated for the annual "best stories" volumes, he consistently refused permission, except for "My Girls" in *O. Henry Memorial Award Prize Stories of 1937*. O'Hara realized that such appearances provide good visibility for an author because the public tends to be impressed by the "best short stories of the year" selections; but he had no respect for the selection process and felt that publication of his stories in these collections would somehow diminish their value as literary properties. His refusal to have his short stories in American literature textbooks was a blunder: he remained largely untaught in colleges while students were exposed to lesser writers.

number of stories had been sold in one year. His request for a raise to 20¢ per word was declined.

F. Scott Fitzgerald had moved to Hollywood in the summer of 1937, and John and Belle saw him during 1939–1940. The O'Haras hosted regular blackjack and poker games at their 342 Midvale home, to which Fitzgerald sometimes came with Sheilah Graham. Late in 1939 or early in 1940 Fitzgerald invited the O'Haras to lunch at his Encino home, "Belly Acres," on the Edward Everett Horton estate. O'Hara later published a recollection of this day:

O'Hara with F. Scott Fitzgerald, Hollywood, 1940. *Photo by Belle O'Hara*

He was terribly nervous, disappearing for five and ten minutes at a time, once to get a plaid tie to give my wife because she was wearing a Glen plaid suit. Once to get a volume of Thackeray because I'd never read Thackeray, another time to get some tome about Julius Caesar which he assured me was scholarly but readable—but which he knew I would never read. Then we went out and took some pictures, and when we finished that he suddenly said, "Would you like to read what I've written, but first promise you won't tell anyone about it. Don't tell them anything. Don't tell them what it's about, or anything about the people. I'd like it better if you didn't even tell anyone I'm writing another novel." So we went back to the house and I read what he had written. He saw that I was comfortable, with pillows, cigarettes, ash trays, a coke. And sat there tortured, trying to be casual, but unhappy because he did not know that my dead pan was partly due to my being an extremely slow reader of good writing, and partly because this was such good writing that I was reading. When I had read it I said, "Scott, don't take any more movie jobs till you've finished this. You work so slowly and this is so good, you've got to finish it. It's real Fitzgerald." Then, of course, he became blasphemous and abusive, and asked me if I wanted to fight. I saw him a few times after that day, and once when I asked him how the book was coming he only said, "You've kept your promise? You haven't spoken to anyone about it?"[17]

The book was *The Last Tycoon*. The photos Belle took that day included the picture of Fitzgerald sitting on a chair with O'Hara perched on the arm—Fitzgerald looking ill and O'Hara looking plump —that O'Hara later had on the wall outside his study in "Linebrook."

When a Hollywood trade paper attacked Miss Graham in the spring of 1940, Fitzgerald phoned O'Hara to ask for help when he went to beat up the editor. O'Hara explained that it was a bad idea to fight with a newspaperman.

"In other words, you're saying no," said Fitzgerald.

"If you insist on going, I'll go with you, but I don't want you to go and I don't want to go with you."

"That's all I wanted to know," he said. "I thought you were my one real friend in this town. I'll get Eddie ———. He's diabetic and he doesn't get into fights, but he's a gentleman."

Fitzgerald did not carry out his plan, but "he never telephoned me again."[18]

EARLY IN 1940 playwright George Oppenheimer approached O'Hara about obtaining an option for the stage rights to the Joey stories.

O'Hara's initial reaction was that it was a bad idea, but the more he thought about it, the more he liked it. He wrote to Richard Rodgers:

I don't know whether you happened to see any of a series of pieces I've been doing for The New Yorker in the past year or so. They're about a guy who is master of ceremonies in cheap night clubs, and the pieces are in the form of letters from him to a successful band leader. Anyway, I got the idea that the pieces, or at least the character and the life in general could be made into a book show, and I wonder if you and Larry would be interested in working on it with me. I read that you two have a commitment with Dwight Wiman for this Spring but if and when you get through with that I do hope you like my idea.[19]

The letter reached Rodgers in Boston where he and Lorenz Hart were trying out *Higher and Higher*. Rodgers wired John to come East as soon as possible, which he did after he finished his work on *Down Argentine Way*.

Back in New York the O'Haras lived for a while on Sutton Place in an apartment with a view of the East River. This apartment is the setting for the familiar anecdote about O'Hara scanning the river with binoculars and checking the yachts against the *Social Register*. The O'Haras' return to New York marked a resumption of close relations with his mother. Katharine Delaney O'Hara left Pottsville in 1940 to share an apartment at 107 University Place with her daughters Mary and Kathleen.* She became active in church work and the New York Foundling Hospital. John and Belle were regular visitors. Mother and son frequently engaged in memory battles about The Region. Katharine O'Hara's recall was as confident as her son's, and she did not hesitate to challenge his version of an event. O'Hara was proud of his mother's wit and often brought his friends to meet her. He would be angered on the rare occasions when his more worldly friends failed to behave with complete decorum. He was not amused when John McClain brought along a current girl friend and patted her on the leg saying, "There'll be more if you're a good girl." When Kathleen left after marrying designer Robert Fuldner in 1944, Aunt Verna Delaney moved into the apartment. Verna and O'Hara were fond of each other; there is a family tradition that Verna once had literary ambitions and was one of the first people to encourage his writing.

* Martin, James and Eugene O'Hara remained in Pottsville. After 1942 Mary, Joseph, Thomas and Kathleen were in the New York area.

John's closest sibling relationship was with Tom, who was eight years younger. He had encouraged Tom's journalistic ambitions and was proud of his success. After a stint as a copyboy on the New York *Daily News*, Tom went to work as a reporter on the Philadelphia *Evening Ledger* and moved to the *Trib* in 1942 as a political reporter. John and Tom saw each other regularly in New York, usually meeting at Bleeck's for long conversations.

Rodgers and Hart were the perfect collaborators for John O'Hara on *Pal Joey*. In addition to his prodigious musical gifts, Richard Rodgers was a highly competent organizer and businessman. Lorenz Hart was the ideal lyricist for *Pay Joey* because it required the cynical-realistic lyrics that he wrote better than anyone else. An alcoholic with an almost compulsive interest in low life, Larry Hart knew the world of Joey as well as O'Hara did. At Rodgers' recommendation George Abbott was asked to direct the show. He accepted, but not without private doubts about the material. At one point early in the project Rodgers offered to find another director if Abbott wanted to step out, but he remained.

As a result of working with them, O'Hara developed strong

Richard Rodgers and Lorenz Hart.

affection for both Rodgers and Hart, although the friendships were as different as the men themselves. It was Rodgers' determination that held the team together. Abbott and O'Hara didn't care for each other, and the director was annoyed by what he regarded as O'Hara's absenteeism during production. Abbott expected the author to be on hand at the theater for instant rewriting. Moreover, Abbott thought there was too much dialogue in the script, and O'Hara resented even necessary tinkering with his work.

When Hart died in 1944 O'Hara wrote a tribute in which he indicated the delicate relationships among the collaborators:

In due course the show went into rehearsal and I went into what might be termed a decline. My work, I figured, had been done, and I had made up my mind not to be that perennial Broadway nuisance, The Author, so I stayed away from the theatre. Then one morning at an hour when most respectable people are at work I heard doorbells and the high-pitched voice of my Finnish maid. Before my tired brain could summon the adequate oaths the door of my darkened bedroom was flung open and a voice was saying, "Get up, Baby. Come on, come on. You're hurting George's feelings." It was, of course, Larry. He had made the trip all the way from his Dutchess County home to Central Park West to take me to rehearsal that morning. And why? Because I was hurting George Abbott's feelings. . . . I'll never forget the awed and grudgingly admiring expression on the face of my maid, who had fully expected to see Larry thrown down the brief but steep penthouse stairs. And I may say that Larry knew that he was taking that chance. It was my show, Dick's show, his show, but when it became necessary to get me to the theatre Larry put it up to me on what seemed the only reasonable basis: I was hurting Abbott's feelings.[20]

O'Hara was late in delivering the book for the show, and Hart's lyric "If they asked me I could write a book" was a comment on O'Hara's tardiness. Rodgers nudged him with a telegram: SPEAK TO ME JOHN SPEAK TO ME. The book was a new work. Although it drew on the ambiance of the Joey series, the play used only two of the fourteen stories—"Bow Wow" and "A Bit of a Shock." The main plot of the play, Joey's involvement with Vera and the related blackmail attempt by Ludlow Lowell, was new. Comparison of an early script with the published script reveals that the plot toughened in revision. The working script hints at Joey's regeneration by Linda, suggesting that he may even end up driving a truck for her brother-in-law. The final version is decidedly unsentimental, for it ends with Joey in pursuit of a new mouse. The only other important difference between the two versions concerns the manner in which Vera handles the blackmail.

In the early script she defeats the blackmailers with a photo of her husband and Gladys *in flagrante delicto*, whereas in the published form Vera uses her influence with the police commissioner.

While *Pal Joey* was in the works, O'Hara realized another one of his ambitions when *Newsweek* hired him to write a weekly column. From the time he had been the F.P.A. of the Pottsville *Journal* with "After Four O'Clock," he had wanted his own big-time column—and he wrote five other columns during his career. "Entertainment Week," for which he was paid $1,000 each, was open-ended; *Newsweek*'s announcement stated that O'Hara would "roam the entire entertainment world." The first column, a memorial to George Gershwin, which appeared on 15 July 1940, set the style and mood for the series, for it combined personal experience with strongly stated opinions. It included the often-quoted statement "George died on July 11, 1937, but I don't have to believe that if I don't want to."* Unfortunately, O'Hara sometimes appeared to be boasting or name-dropping, as when he described how he once corrected George Gershwin on the playing of "Do Do Do." O'Hara relished having his column, for he had many strong opinions and liked the opportunity to publish them. But somehow the column never jelled, never achieved a format. He was always readable, yet some weeks he had nothing special to say and lacked the ability to write entertainingly anyway.

The 9 February 1942 "Entertainment Week" column included the first appearance in print of the now-famous anecdote of the time when Hemingway, James Lardner and Vincent Sheean were pooling their funds during the Spanish Civil War and trying to figure out what to do with the extra money. Hemingway said, "Let's take the bloody money and start a bloody fund to send John O'Hara to Yale." O'Hara's comment was: "It's a mean little story, but (and?) it shows what my friends think of me."†

At this stage of his career John O'Hara was ardently liberal, and

---

*In 1959 O'Hara sent this wire to Ira Gershwin: AFTER 22 YEARS I STILL DONT BELIEVE IT.

†Vincent Sheean's recollection of this episode is that Hemingway's exact words were: "The thing for us to do is to pool our resources and send John O'Hara to Yale." Sheean had intended to use the anecdote in his 1939 book *Not Peace but a Sword*, but omitted it because he thought it would set off one of O'Hara's "savage rages." He subsequently told it to O'Hara, whose response was "pretty outrageous, but later on I heard from various people that he used to tell the story himself. So it's hard to tell what he thought." O'Hara later told interviewer Don Schanche that when he heard the wisecrack it "was the first time I knew Hemingway had any real envy of me."[21]

a few of the "Entertainment Week" columns reflect this conviction. On 12 August 1940 he used the film *Pastor Hall* to attack the Nazis; and two weeks later he denounced the Dies Committee and Hollywood blacklists. Two columns that attracted attention were the 2 December 1940 statement that Shakespeare's plays are boring ("What is more, I don't even admit that they're good to read") and the 17 March 1941 review of *Citizen Kane*, which he called the best movie ever made. O'Hara became convinced that by denouncing the attempted suppression of *Citizen Kane* he had incurred the enmity of William Randolph Hearst and suspected Hearst of attempting to smear him as a communist. When *Newsweek* dropped "Entertainment Week" in February 1942 after eighty-four weeks (and $84,000), O'Hara believed that Hearst was responsible.

While the show was in rehearsal, the fourteen Joey stories were published as a book by Duell, Sloan & Pearce in October 1940. Sam Sloan and Cap Pearce had left Harcourt, Brace to form a new publishing house with Charles Duell, and O'Hara went with them.* *Pal Joey*, the story volume, required only two printings in 1940, although it later became a steady seller in paperback.† Edmund Wilson used the publication of *Pal Joey* as the handle for a retrospective assessment in *The New Republic* (11 November 1940). Expressing disappointment in O'Hara's failure to fulfill the promise of *Appointment in Samarra*, Wilson asserted that the two subsequent novels lacked purpose or meaning because "Mr. O'Hara has never really had his bearings since he abandoned the subject of Gibbsville, Pa."

Pal Joey went into rehearsal at the Biltmore and Longacre theaters in New York on 11 November 1940, and the play opened in Philadelphia on 11 December to encouraging but rather shocked reviews. The critics recognized that *Pal Joey* represented a new development in the American musical theater. There was a strong plot line—not just a series of song cues—and the songs were integral. It has been called the first realistic American musical. The circumstance that Joey is a heel—or anti-hero, in critical language—and the sexual innuendo seemed powerful stuff in 1940. The newspaper *PM* previewed it as "the dirtiest show you ever hope to see." Much of the credit for the alleged "dirtiness" belonged to Hart, whose lyrics perfectly matched the characterizations.

---

* The files of Duell, Sloan & Pearce have been lost; it is therefore impossible to reconstruct the details of O'Hara's relationship with the firm.

† The book and lyrics for the show were published by Random House in 1952.

*Couldn't sleep and wouldn't sleep
Until I could sleep where I shouldn't sleep.*
—*"Bewitched"*

*A canopy bed has so much class
And so's a ceiling made of glass.*
—*"In Our Little Den"*

The cast was strong: Gene Kelly (Joey), Vivienne Segal (Vera), Leila Ernst (Linda), Jack Durant (Ludlow Lowell) and June Havoc (Gladys). *Pal Joey* was Hart's favorite among his shows. Two of the songs Rodgers and Hart created for it eventually became standards— "Bewitched, Bothered, and Bewildered" and "I Could Write a Book." But in addition there were numbers that perfectly suited the action and atmosphere of O'Hara's book, such as "Zip" and "In Our Little Den of Iniquity." John O'Hara always got a kick out of hearing the songs from *Pal Joey* played, and on several alcoholic occasions insisted they be played.

Budd Schulberg—who was correcting proof on *What Makes Sammy Run?* at the time—baby-sat with O'Hara during the tryout of *Pal Joey* in Philadelphia, where they shared a suite at the Warwick Hotel. One night at the Pen and Pencil Club someone began abusing O'Hara about *Appointment*; he was ready to fight, but Schulberg got him out of the place. There were occasions when O'Hara and Schulberg had to take care of Lorenz Hart, who would disappear when he was drunk. Once they found Hart in an after-hours joint and took him back to the Warwick, but Hart refused to leave the cab and went into a fetal position. O'Hara and Schulberg picked up the diminutive lyricist by the arms and carried him into the hotel.*

The O'Haras' party of friends at the Philadelphia opening included Kathy O'Hara, Tom O'Hara and his wife, Ransloe Boone (the old friend from the Pottsville Purity League), the Gilbert Millsteins and Schulberg. Millstein, a great O'Hara admirer, was working with Tom on the *Evening Ledger*, and Tom asked John to invite him to the opening. Describing himself as "awe-struck" on this occasion, Mill-

---

* The copy of *The Disenchanted* that Schulberg later inscribed to O'Hara recalls their Philadelphia sojourn:

> Standing in the Warwick lobby the other evening, John, a flood of old, good memories swept in, set to music by Dick, and remembering many good times and much good advice. I knew I would have to send this book off to you with my sincere respect—pegged a helluva lot higher than you seemed to think that last afternoon in 21. So here it is, with affection and admiration for you and Belle always.
>
> Budd

Oct. 28, 1950

stein recalls O'Hara as sober and very quiet after the performance—clearly greatly satisfied with the show.

Pal Joey opened in New York on Christmas night 1940 at the Ethel Barrymore Theatre, and Richard Rodgers' recollection is that "Approximately one half of the first night audience applauded wildly while the other half sat there in stony, stunned silence."[22] On opening night O'Hara was sick to his stomach—it is not clear whether the cause was nerves, alcohol, or food—and vomited out the window of a cab.

Brooks Atkinson of the *Times* was appalled. He began his review with "If it is possible to make an entertaining musical comedy out of an odious story, 'Pal Joey' is it"—and ended with "Although 'Pal Joey' is expertly done, can you draw sweet water from a foul well?" There were admiring notices from Richard Watts, Jr., in the *Herald Tribune*, Burns Mantle in the *News* and John Lardner in *Newsweek*. Wolcott Gibbs wrote a restrained favorable review in *The New Yorker*. The best notice came from Louis Kronenberger in *PM*, who said it was "the most unhackneyed musical show since *Of Thee I Sing*."

If O'Hara had been unenthusiastic about the rehearsal chores for his show, he thoroughly enjoyed the job when it was done. He liked being the author of a Broadway hit, and his 2½ percent cut of the house—plus his *Newsweek* salary—made him affluent for the first time in his life. He and Belle took an apartment at 8 East 52nd Street, near Cartier's, and O'Hara invested in a bar called The Cloop in honor of Joey's term for his night club. In the show Melba, the reporter who does the "Zip" strip number, orders St. James Scotch, O'Hara's favorite brand. The importer of this whiskey took the mention as a compliment and began sending cases of St. James to the theater for O'Hara. This was during the war when all brands of Scotch were hard to get, St. James particularly. When O'Hara failed to acknowledge the gifts the importer stopped sending them. A mutual friend checked with O'Hara, who knew nothing about the cases of St. James. Investigation revealed that an assistant stage manager had been appropriating the Scotch, and the playwright contemplated assault and battery.

O'Hara's comments on his play in "Entertainment Week" contributed to his reputation for crankiness. On 27 January 1941, for example, O'Hara explained that he had not bothered to attend the opening of *Mr. and Mrs. North* because the author of this play, Richard Lockridge, had knocked *Pal Joey* in his capacity as theater critic for the *Sun*. A typical O'Hara act came when the cast of *Pal Joey* was changed, which prompted him to write in his column, "Under the present circumstances I caution you against going to see 'Pal Joey.'" Rodgers and Abbott were nonplused.

The success of *Pal Joey* may have been impeded by the 1941 ASCAP battle with the radio networks, which prevented songs by ASCAP members from being played on the radio. Therefore the *Pal Joey* songs did not achieve wide exposure at this time. In the long run this situation operated in favor of the show, for the songs seemed fresh when *Pal Joey* was revived in 1952.

Between the Philadelphia tryout and the New York opening of *Pal Joey*, F. Scott Fitzgerald died in Hollywood on 21 December 1940. Schulberg and O'Hara were separately approached by Scribner's to consider completing *The Last Tycoon*, and both thought it was a rotten idea. Apart from his regret for the death of a great writer whose work had influenced him, O'Hara was angered by the patronizing obituaries—especially by Westbrook Pegler's grave-dancing column. When *The New Republic* invited him to contribute to its Fitzgerald symposium in 1941, O'Hara wrote "Certain Aspects," in which he described Fitzgerald as "a *right* writer." Writers usually respect those qualities of other writers' work that they try to achieve in their own; and O'Hara noted that Fitzgerald was the first writer who had excited him: "The people were right, the talk was right, the clothes, the cars were real, and the mysticism was a kind of challenge."[23]

A favorite resort for O'Hara in the early Forties was Nick's, a club in The Village featuring Dixieland jazz. One night the writer George Frazier was introduced to him by cornetist Bobby Hackett. O'Hara scrutinized Frazier and said, "Sit down and have a drink—you're wearing a Brooks Brothers shirt."*

Jerome Weidman witnessed the kind of considerate act O'Hara was capable of when a shy older man who was an admirer said that he'd like to have O'Hara's autograph but was afraid to ask the unpredictable writer. Weidman urged the old gentleman to write to O'Hara, and O'Hara replied with a formal letter. "John had caught the flavor of the old man from his letter, and he had answered in kind: a courtly, gracious, beautifully mannered epistle that could almost not be called a letter and might have been written with a quill."[24] Weidman was also one of the many friends who were surprised by O'Hara's transition from charmer to ugly drunk when he took the one extra drink. One Sunday night in 1941 Weidman and his fiancée, Peggy, were dining at the "Sixty-Eight" restaurant on lower Fifth Avenue with the Louis Kronenbergers when John and Belle came in. The O'Haras joined the party, and John was at his best telling funny stories about his recent stint in Hollywood, where he claimed he had

---

* Frazier became one of O'Hara's staunchest admirers, and peppered his columns and articles with laudatory references to O'Hara's work.

been paid $2,500 per week to change the title of *The Glamour Girls* at Twentieth Century-Fox. Weidman asked O'Hara if he remembered the day John took him through the Fox writers' building and showed him Aldous Huxley's office. Weidman recounted how O'Hara had said, "The son-of-a-bitch knows everything there is to know, and in *Point Counter Point* he has written the greatest novel I have ever read, and look: to Darryl Zanuck he's no different from Zane Grey on his left and Rex Beach on his right." But O'Hara had taken that extra drink. He glared at Weidman and snarled, "Any son-of-a-bitch who says I ever read a goddamned novel in my life is going to have to come outside!" Weidman pacified him, and the friendship continued.

The author of *Pal Joey* became a sort of celebrity in 1941. He appeared at least twice on *Information Please*, but suffered from radio fright and said little. This program was one of his mother's favorites, and he obtained a recording of one of his appearances because she had not been able to listen to it. In April he played the banjo-mandolin on Bing Crosby's radio show. He also appeared on a sports quiz program in 1941. One newspaper cartoon feature even announced that he was working as a trick rider in a Texas circus.

Between March and July 1941, O'Hara was back at Twentieth Century-Fox working on *Moontide* at $1,250 per week. Since he obviously didn't need the money, it would appear that the assignment itself was attractive to him. He worked alone on the screenplay for Willard Robinson's novel. *Moontide* was Jean Gabin's first American film and was intended to launch him as a Hollywood star. Fox tried to make it a major production, assigning Mark Hellinger as producer and Archie Mayo as director. The female lead was Ida Lupino, and the cast included Thomas Mitchell and O'Hara's good friend Claude Raines. A mood film dealing with the cleansing love between a drifter and a defeated waitress, *Moontide* was set in a Southern California fishing village. The novel ended bleakly, but the movie had to have a happy ending. Although it was good enough to be nominated for an Academy Award, *Moontide* was not a hit. Part of the trouble was that Hellinger was trying to produce a serious film while feuding with Zanuck, who wanted a box-office success. Hellinger remarked, "Every time I try for art, I fall on my prat." Given the conditions of movie writing, it was impossible for O'Hara to work without interference. He received sole screen credit, but both Hellinger and Nunnally Johnson revised his script.

Pay Joey had a run of 374 performances, closing 29 November 1941. The success of this show encouraged O'Hara to plan other stage ventures. As early as December 1940 he was working on a play about a country doctor, with Walter Huston in mind for the lead. He also discussed a possible dramatization of *This Side of Paradise* with Maxwell Perkins. In the fall of 1941 it was announced that he was working on a play with music, set in Florida, and Rodgers and Hart had been promised first refusal.

The war years were bad for John O'Hara. Although he was thirty-six years old in 1941, he tried to enlist in the army and the Marines. Both turned him down for ulcers and bad teeth.* He tried to obtain a navy commission through his friend James Forrestal, Undersecretary of the Navy, and asked Robert A. Lovett, Assistant Secretary of War for Air, for the same help. Forrestal displayed great generosity in responding to these calls on his time. O'Hara delighted Forrestal, and the busy government official was always ready to help him. On 23 December 1941 he suggested that O'Hara apply to Naval Intelligence or "Donovan's office," promising to help in either case. At this time O'Hara offered to donate his Duesenberg to the navy as a VIP car. By 18 February 1942 he was experiencing marked anxiety at his civilian status and wrote describing: "A strong sense of guilt and futility, and on the fiscal side, impulsive, unplanned, and sometimes extravagant donations to various Causes."[25] Forrestal replied that he would try to find him the right place in the war effort. Then in July 1942 O'Hara made the request that Forrestal obtain clearance for him to visit a plane factory in order to research a musical about the swing shift that he planned to work on with Rodgers and Hart. In the same letter O'Hara requested a seconding letter for the Racquet and Tennis Club† and a character reference for the Civil Air Patrol. Forrestal acceded to all three requests, but the musical project did not develop.

O'Hara was intensely patriotic, but he was also motivated by the desire to participate in the greatest game in history. His friends were having brilliant wars: Al Wright as a decorated naval aviator, John McClain in intelligence, Joe Bryan in the navy and Quentin Reynolds and Joel Sayre as war correspondents. But O'Hara couldn't even obtain a good assignment as a correspondent. He tried to do the next best thing and serve in some civilian capacity. In spring 1942 he had the resounding title of Chief Story Editor of the Motion Picture Division of the Office of the Co-ordinator of Inter-American Affairs, where he worked on propaganda films "without compensation." The head of this organization was Nelson Rockefeller, and O'Hara's immediate superior was John Hay Whitney, who left for a captaincy in

---

* Friends who asked him why he didn't have his teeth attended to were told that it was a waste of money because he was going to die soon.

† O'Hara never achieved membership.

Air Intelligence. O'Hara experienced a series of health problems, including piles, and took a leave of absence. While recuperating at Quogue he took flying lessons with the intention of joining the Civil Air Patrol and considered having his teeth pulled in order to try for a commission in the Army Specialist Corps. In the fall of 1943 the army turned O'Hara down for limited service waivers, and he thought about trying the Merchant Marine and the Red Cross.*

The war was like college all over again. Glamorous things were happening, and John O'Hara was left out. His friends were being tapped for the military equivalent of Bones, but he couldn't even matriculate. The closest he came to military service was when—through the pull of friends, and with the endorsement of Forrestal—he joined the OSS on 23 November 1943 and was sent to a training camp in Virginia where he grew a beard and took the code name "Doc." Less than a month later, on 18 December, he resigned because "he wasn't able to pass the medical examination."[26] He may have been sent home with pneumonia. His own explanation for his resignation was that he realized he wasn't physically strong enough to take responsibility for other men's lives.

O'Hara remarked that it took a world war to keep him from writing, for his heretofore prodigious output dwindled markedly: in 1942 he published only one story, and nine in 1943. One of the 1943 stories, "Graven Image," is the archetypal O'Hara story of snobbery and exclusion. A high government official is interviewing a Harvard classmate seeking a Washington position. All goes well until the applicant mentions that he is relieved to find that the Undersecretary does not carry a grudge because he wasn't elected to Porcellian:

> *"I don't know why fellows like you—you never would have made it in a thousand years, but"—then without looking up, he knew everything had collapsed—"but I've said exactly the wrong thing, haven't I?"*
>
> *"That's right, Browning," said the Under Secretary. "You've said exactly the wrong thing. I've got to be going." He stood up and turned and went out, all dignity.*

The point of "Graven Image" is not simple. Browning is a self-defeating snob, but the Under Secretary is defeated by his insecurity.

---

* O'Hara allowed four of his books to be printed without royalty in the Armed Services editions that were given to servicemen: *The Doctor's Son, Butterfield 8, Pal Joey* and *Pipe Night*. He also donated a play, "Is This the Army, Mr. Jones?" to a service publication, *Revue Sketches Vaudeville Comedy Acts* (1943).

The wounds of exclusion have not healed, and consequently he does not wear his success well.

In 1943 O'Hara persuaded Ross to give him an office on the twentieth floor of the *New Yorker* building. He didn't really need a place to work, for he had always worked at home, and Belle saw to it that there were no distractions; however, O'Hara relished the symbolic effect of this office, for it meant that he had a special relationship with the magazine.* At this time he was considering a return to newspapers as a columnist or correspondent, and unsuccessfully applied for a war correspondent job on *Collier's*.

During 1944 O'Hara started work on a novel, which he predicted would be published in 1945. It may have been the inception of *A Rage to Live*, which was not published until 1949. He applied for a University of Minnesota writing fellowship for the novel in 1944, but was apparently turned down.

One night in spring 1944 the John Herseys, the Vincent Sheeans, Joel Sayre, Paul de Kruif and Ernest Hemingway and Martha Gellhorn were in the back room at Tim Costello's bar on Third Avenue. The Hemingways left early. When the others left, O'Hara was standing on the sidewalk, very drunk, and he said to them, "Nice people!" Hersey learned that while he had been with the group in the back room, O'Hara had come into the bar. Costello told him who was there. Muttering angrily that he hadn't been invited, O'Hara hooked his blackhorn walking stick on the bar and began drinking. Some time later, Hemingway, on his way out, spotted O'Hara and pounded him hard on the back, with which he had been having trouble, and said, "When did you start carrying a walking stick?"

"That's the best piece of blackhorn in New York City."

"It is, is it? I'm going to break it with my bare hands."

"Fifty says you can't."

Hemingway took the bet and said, "Not only that, but I'm going to break it over my own head." He did. In the course of one night O'Hara had been excluded, painfully pounded, and deprived of a prized possession. Costello saved the pieces of the blackhorn and mounted them over the bar.†

---

* O'Hara probably had an office at *The New Yorker* again in 1946.

† This account is based on John Hersey's recollections. After the episode became the property of literary gossip, it developed permutations in retelling. In December 1959 *Holiday* published a letter from O'Hara correcting a version included in an article on Costello's. O'Hara noted that although Hemingway promised to replace the blackhorn stick, he never did; but John Steinbeck gave him one on O'Hara's fifty-first birthday. The account above differs in certain details from that in Carlos Baker's *Ernest Hemingway: A Life Story*.[27]

O'Hara finally got into the war in the summer of 1944 as a *Liberty* correspondent attached to Task Force 38 in the Pacific. He took no pride in his connection with this magazine and produced only one piece that was published, "Nothing from Joe?"—an appeal for mail to servicemen. Nonetheless he enjoyed his simulated rank of lieutenant commander and purchased an elaborate kit at Brooks Brothers. In August and September 1944 O'Hara was on the carrier *Intrepid*. Although he freely talked about how frightened he was at sea, the *Intrepid* was not under attack while he was aboard; and he missed the Battle of Leyte by a month.

Correspondents were not permitted to keep war journals, but personal diaries were allowed.* The first entry in O'Hara's navy diary is dated 25 July 1944, and the final entry is for 27 September. The entry for 16 August 1944—the tenth anniversary of *Appointment in Samarra* and therefore an occasion for stocktaking—reveals better than anything else O'Hara wrote how much he needed Belle: "I am sometimes beset by the fear that when I finish this masochistic task my life will be over. That, however, is almost certainly up to Belle. As, indeed, it has been for seven years." The intensity of dependence revealed in this statement is impressive, for it is an outright admission that life without her would be insupportable. O'Hara often remarked that no outsider can really know what happens in somebody else's marriage. Certainly no outsider could have understood his need for Belle. Friends saw him order her around and occasionally make her

Belle with John in correspondent's uniform, 1944.

Aboard the *Intrepid*, 1944.

the target for verbal abuse when he was drunk; they saw her unpro-testingly endure his rages and public scenes; they speculated about how long she would put up with him. But no outsider could accurately judge the nature of the shared need between John and Belle. In grossly oversimplified terms, he needed Belle's loyalty and support and the regularity she provided for his life; and she needed his need of her.

The diary is full of his longing for Belle: "I met Belle on a Wednesday, although I first saw her on a Tuesday or maybe it was still Monday. Yes, I guess it was still Monday. . . . I trust that I shall see her again the very first Monday that comes along. A man in love with his wife talking to himself." On 28 August 1944 he sketched a perfect day at home:

How to start the day: It is about 10:30 a.m., and we get up. Lydia has breakfast ready on the terrace. We read the paper & the mail, which includes a fat cheque from some magazine and an urgent plea to polish off a picture for Goldwyn in N.Y. Plenty of milk & cream at break-fast. No mail from Belle because she will be right across the table from

---

* On 14 September John O'Hara made an entry in his navy diary for his biographers: "This rare book—I can just see future scholars, the gifted curious, who will know how many semi-colons I used in Pal Joey (none), picking up this little journal reverently. 'Think of it,' they will say. 'Nineteen-forty-four. The beginning of his Middle Period. Let's see, who was President then?' (Franklin D. Roosevelt was, dear Scholar, and he was my man.)" The navy maintained service records for correspondents, but the file for O'Hara is missing.

me. I take a shower, letting the water run full strength as long as I like. Then I use 3 towels to dry myself. Then I put on my new Glen plaid suit, white Brooks shirt, black silk tie and black Peal shoes, gray hat. I kiss Belle and give her a lingering pat on the behind and am off in a taxi to discuss a radio deal with Mark [agent Mark Hanna]. Lunch at the Ritz with Gibbs or Sayre or Thurber or Norris or Sloan, where Betsey Whitney comes over and asks us to dinner with the Barrys that night. Then I go to the club [Player's Club] and win $34 at gin and $20 at backgammon and $5.50 at pool. Home for tea with Belle and Amanda, who leaves . . . in time for us to dress for Betsey's. The big topic of discussion is the lifting of gas rationing, effective tomorrow. We go to Larue's via 21, and then home. That's the way to start a day. We know how to finish it.[28]*

While at sea O'Hara lost twenty pounds; he was on the wagon and eating regular meals, which almost certainly had some bearing on the fact that Belle became pregnant—after seven years of marriage—in the fall of 1944 immediately after his return from the Pacific. O'Hara was surprised as well as pleased, for he had believed that he was sterile. Moreover, this chance for fatherhood removed whatever lingering guilt he felt about Pet's abortion.

After his return in October 1944, O'Hara wrote Forrestal, now Secretary of the Navy, that he was planning a book called "How to Take an Island"—a combination of fact and fiction using one Marine enlisted man to lend human interest to the material. He planned to use movie technique for this book: "cutting in and out and between the gyrene and the operation for which he is being trained without knowing it." O'Hara asked Forrestal to arrange for him to see restricted material and said he would come to Washington to discuss the book. Like the plane-factory play, this project was abandoned.

O'Hara's next appeals came in October and December 1946, when he asked Forrestal to arrange help for a play he wanted to write about a scientist who had been involved in developing the atom bomb. He was not interested in technical information, but wanted background material on the bomb project. The final O'Hara request that survives in the Forrestal papers came in March 1948 when he asked for details about how a man would have received a navy commission in World War I, for use in *A Rage to Live*. Again Forrestal complied.

O'Hara wrote Frank Sullivan a letter in November 1944, admitting that although the *Intrepid* had not seen action while he was aboard, he was scared most of the time. He had been asked to go out again by Forrestal but had declined because he didn't want to leave Belle during her pregnancy. "But I don't know; if they ask me again I may do it, because what they want me to do is all right and I might as well be doing it. I don't seem to be able to write anything more than 2000 words long, in spite of several good ideas."[29]

While waiting out Belle's pregnancy, O'Hara got back to work on stories. In 1943–44 he published six outside of *The New Yorker*. Working with Mark Hanna—the first and only literary agent he ever had—he sold four short-shorts to *Collier's* and two stories to *Good Housekeeping* (which paid him $1 per word). These stories are not good, and he abandoned the attempt to become a commercial writer. In 1945—after the only year since 1928 in which he had not appeared in *The New Yorker*—he returned to the fold with six stories. On 2 March 1945 O'Hara informed Katharine Angell White: "I have been leading *The New Yorker* for more than ten years, and I am not going to be moved into the back of the book again, not even to help out with a gerrymandering makeup." O'Hara felt keenly that *The New Yorker* was not according his work proper respect, for in the same month he wrote to Mrs. White from the Bel Air Hotel in Beverly Hills complaining about editorial tampering with "Conversation in the Atomic Age": "After all these years the boys still try to punctuate my dialogue, losing, for example, the effect of long breathless sentences." Two years later, in 1947, he sent Mrs. White a one-sentence letter—"My pieces don't run second"—which was a response to the placement of "The Dry Murders" in the 18 October 1947 issue.[30] She replied that an O'Hara story *had* run second, firmly explaining that the make-up of the magazine was an editorial matter, not an authorial concern.* She added that there wasn't any significance to the lead position—that the placement of a story right after "Talk" did not indicate that it was the most important story in that issue. O'Hara was not persuaded.

In March 1945, Duell, Sloan & Pearce published *Pipe Night*,† which included seven previously unpublished stories. It was more successful than any O'Hara story collection up to that time, and was reprinted five times in 1945. The excellent sale for *Pipe Night* was in part a response to O'Hara's fame as the author of *Pal Joey*, and the volume also appealed to a public that had not been offered an O'Hara book since *Pal Joey* in 1940.‡ But the principal reason for the success of the

---

* The O'Hara story had followed a humor sketch by S. J. Perelman and a Vladimir Nabokov poem.

† A pipe night is a meeting of a club at which entertainment is provided by the members.

‡ O'Hara repeated two stories from *Pal Joey* in *Pipe Night*, probably to capitalize on the public's recognition of this character.

collection is that it included some of O'Hara's most brilliant stories: "Bread Alone" (1939), "Too Young" (1939), "A Respectable Place" (1940), "Graven Image" (1943), "Now We Know" (1943) and "Where's the Game" (previously unpublished). It is noteworthy that the most powerful of these stories have nothing to do with affluent society. "Bread Alone" is about a Negro car washer and his son; O'Hara was gratified when Richard Wright told him it was the only story about Negroes by a white author that he liked. "Where's the Game?" describes the cruel rebuff suffered by a Bronx furniture salesman when he tries to get into a poker game. In "A Respectable Place" the proprietor of a family bar in New Haven is forced out of business when he commits the blunder of allowing the Police Benevolent Fund to pay for the damage done when a drunken cop shoots up his place; after the police reprisals begin, he unsuccessfully tries to return the money: "The following Saturday night all drinks were on the house. This was strictly against the law, but Matty knew he wasn't going to open up again." Probably the most memorable of these stories is "Now We Know," the account of how an Irish switchboard operator and a Jewish bus driver fall in love through their brief encounters on his bus; he is unhappily married, but there is nothing he can do about it— except change his route.

Pipe Night was accorded one of the most encouraging and respectful reviews O'Hara had received—and perhaps the most prestige-giving. Lionel Trilling's front-page review in the 18 March Sunday New York *Times Book Review* placed O'Hara in the Howells-Wharton-James-Proust school and asserted that he was more perceptive than either Dreiser or Lewis:

More than anyone now writing, O'Hara understands the complex, contradictory, asymmetrical society in which we live. He has the most precise knowledge of the content of our subtlest snobberies, of our points of social honor and idiosyncrasies of personal prestige. He knows, and persuades us to believe, that life's deepest emotions may be expressed by the angle at which a hat is worn, the pattern of a neck-tie, the size of a monogram, the pitch of a voice, the turn of a phrase of slang, a gesture of courtesy and the way it is received. . . . For him customs and manners are morals.

The *Pipe Night* jacket photo of O'Hara is interesting. He had regained the weight he had lost in the Pacific and was tending toward portliness. When he arrived at photographer Katherine Young's third-floor studio for the sitting, he was puffing and remarked that he'd have to give up something. The heavy tweed suit and tattersall waistcoat

O'Hara at time of *Pipe Night* (1945).

he chose for this photo accentuated his bulk and made him look like a cross between an Irish country squire and "The Rich Boy." When Al Wright married Nancy Cochran in Boston in 1945, O'Hara was a groomsman; during the reception he was approached by a Boston dowager who said, "I've been wondering who you were, and now I know—you're one of the detectives hired to watch the gifts." He was annoyed that she didn't recognize the author of *Pal Joey*, and doubly annoyed to be mistaken for an Irish cop.

BELLE GAVE BIRTH to a daughter, Wylie Delaney O'Hara, at Harkness Pavilion on 14 June 1945. O'Hara was a nervous expectant father. The night before the birth he asked Curly Harris to keep him company. Harris and Belle's sister, Winifred Gardiner, went out to dinner with him. After Winnie departed, O'Hara fell asleep at LaRue's; Harris left him there, which O'Hara regarded as disloyal behavior. After the birth, the forty-year-old father celebrated. That evening Frank Sullivan found him at the Player's Club.

I knew he had to be at the hospital the next day so I got worried lest he over-celebrate. With the help of a loyal taxi driver from around "21", who had been taking him the rounds all afternoon, I got him to start for home. He came along, but unwillingly, and on the way uptown he glared at me and said I was a Jew Fascist. I broke down at that and laughed so hard that O'Hara got laughing too—and we got him home, to the apartment the O'Haras had at that time in the East Seventies [27 E. 79th Street].[31]

At the time *Pipe Night* was published O'Hara had not written a novel for seven years and may have thought that he was finished as a novelist. He later inscribed a copy for his infant daughter in rather dejected terms: "Miss Wylie—Your old man will be remembered as a short story writer, if at all/With love and love/The old man."

John O'Hara proved to be a devoted father, which surprised the people who didn't know him well. Still convinced that he would soon die, and mindful of the condition of Dr. Patrick O'Hara's estate, he began to plan for Wylie's financial security as an orphan and set the goal of a $100,000 trust fund. Money was a problem in 1945, for the *Pal Joey* and *Newsweek* incomes had stopped. Belle had money of her own, which O'Hara refused to touch. Hollywood was the answer again, and between August 1945 and January 1946 he worked on the *Cass Timberlane* screenplay for producer Arthur Hornblow, Jr., at MGM, probably for $1,000 per week. He told Hornblow that he accepted the assignment because he "wanted to show Red Lewis *how* the story should have been written." The project didn't work out. Hornblow felt that O'Hara worked too slowly, and that his dialogue wasn't speakable. He took O'Hara off the picture and thereby secured a permanent place on the O'Hara blacklist.[32] Hornblow replaced him

Wylie O'Hara and father, Quogue.

with Donald Ogden Stewart, which was an annoyance because Stewart and O'Hara did not like each other. It was probably an additional annoyance to be removed from a Spencer Tracy film, because O'Hara greatly admired him.

In the summer of 1945 O'Hara performed a service for two friends by writing the introduction to *The Viking Portable F. Scott Fitzgerald*. Dorothy Parker was supposed to write it, but after she had selected the material she asked O'Hara to do the introduction. There was a deadline problem, and he wrote it overnight on coffee and brandy. After delivering his copy to the publisher, he passed out on the train to Quogue. The strain came not from the length of the introduction, which was a dozen printed pages, but from the effort to do justice to Fitzgerald. O'Hara provided a generous tribute which stated: "All he was was our best novelist, one of our best novella-ists, and one of our finest writers of short stories."* Coming when it did, this collection

* O'Hara's assessment of Fitzgerald was subsequently compared with his statement that Hemingway was the most important writer since the death of Shakespeare. The two judgments are not incompatible, for it is possible that he regarded Fitzgerald as the best American novelist while at the same time considering Hemingway more important as a literary influence.

with its introduction was a key element in the emerging Fitzgerald revival. O'Hara later rightly felt that his role in the reassessment of Fitzgerald had been insufficiently recognized.

The death of Robert Benchley in November 1945 marked the end of a stage in O'Hara's life. As he later commented, "the party was over." Benchley had been a great deal more than an admired writer and entertaining companion; for O'Hara he was the embodiment of the good life. Benchley effortlessly enjoyed entrée to all the great, good places. O'Hara felt honored by his friendship, and Benchley was genuinely fond of him. A remark attributed to Benchley was, "John, I'm your friend, and all your friends know you're a son-of-a-bitch." They saw a good deal of each other in Hollywood, where the friendship was tested a few times by O'Hara's drunken behavior. On one occasion, at the Garden of Allah, O'Hara playfully jumped on Benchley's back and injured him. Another time, at a party, O'Hara was drunk and demonstrating wrestling holds on various women. When Benchley felt that it had gone far enough he said, "All right, John, let's cut it out." O'Hara replied, "And that goes for you, too," and took a swing at him, knocking the cigar out of Benchley's mouth. Benchley closed the incident by saying that he'd get another cigar if it was the last thing he did. The next day O'Hara remorsefully consulted their mutual friend Mike Romanoff, who advised him to call and apologize, which O'Hara did.[33] The friendship was not impaired. When Benchley died O'Hara asked for his banjo, which he kept in his study along with another souvenir of the days before the party ended—a photo of a trouserless Benchley in the jacket of an admiral's uniform.

In 1946 O'Hara undertook to write an original screenplay for *A Miracle Can Happen*. The movie evolved in production, and by the time it was released as *On Our Merry Way* in 1948, the credits were for screenplay by Laurence Stallings and Lou Breslow, original story by Arch Oboler, material for James Stewart and Henry Fonda by John O'Hara. In format it was one of the episodic movies that were popular after the war. Stewart and Fonda portrayed two musicians who answer the question "What influence has a child had on your life?" A great deal of expensive talent was involved in this film produced by Benedict Bogeaus and Burgess Meredith: Paulette Goddard, Dorothy Lamour, Fred MacMurray and Victor Moore, as well as Stewart, Fonda and Meredith. *On Our Merry Way* was directed by King Vidor and Leslie Fenton. During 1946, O'Hara may also have polished the scripts for *Strange Journey* and *Sentimental Journey* at Twentieth Century-Fox.

John O'Hara's literary stature had not advanced by 1946, and his career seemed to have lost momentum. He had not published a novel since 1938, and was not to publish one until 1949. No longer the brilliant young author of *Appointment in Samarra*, he was a fortyish short-story writer who had not lived up to his early promise. In an attempt to bring him to a new generation of readers, Duell, Sloan & Pearce published an omnibus volume in 1946—unhappily titled *Here's O'Hara*—which included *Butterfield 8*, *Hope of Heaven*, *Pal Joey* and twenty stories. The author wrote a "foreword" in which he wondered why he had not written more about some of his interests: music, pool, horses, doctors, football, the Irish—"Where the hell do I get my material?" After the wartime distractions were over, O'Hara was still unable to work on a novel. He published twelve stories in 1946 and thirteen in 1947, all in *The New Yorker*.

Sam Sloan had died at age forty in March 1945—six days after publication of *Pipe Night*. O'Hara had been closer to Sloan than to the other two partners and he felt unhappy at the firm after Sloan's death. In 1946 the O'Haras met Phyllis and Bennett Cerf at a social gathering, and O'Hara remarked to Cerf that he felt his career was stalled. Cerf replied that he regarded O'Hara as a major writer and that Random House would be proud to publish him. They made a luncheon date at the Tavern, at the conclusion of which they shook hands on the agreement that O'Hara would be published by Random House. Cerf said, "John, this is a great day for me because you are one of the great American authors."

O'Hara replied, "One—who else?"

"Faulkner and Hemingway."

"Well, Faulkner is okay," said O'Hara.[34]

In moving to Random House O'Hara really moved to Bennett Cerf, and the two men commenced an elaborate twenty-three-year game of author-publisher that only they knew the rules for. Although O'Hara had noted in his navy diary that he could never have Bennett Cerf as his publisher because Cerf "thinks he is somebody on his own," it turned out that he was the right publisher for John O'Hara precisely because he was "somebody on his own" and was not seeking vicarious literary success through his authors. He left O'Hara's work alone and used soft answers to turn away the wrath that was often an O'Hara-esque test. Cerf didn't provoke. There is a joke in publishing that there were really twin Cerf brothers: the outside brother who appeared on *What's My Line* and compiled joke books, and the inside brother who ran Random House. The inside Cerf knew what to do with John O'Hara—let him write and don't fight with him.

The first O'Hara title to appear under the Random House imprint was *Hellbox* in 1947 (the title refers to a receptacle in which printers discard type), O'Hara's fourth story collection, which required two printings. *Hellbox*, dedicated to Wylie, had twenty-one stories from *The New Yorker* and five previously unpublished stories. A strong collection, it included "The Decision," "The Moccasins," "Doctor and Mrs. Parsons," "Transaction," "War Aims" and "A Phase of Life." The most brilliant story in *Hellbox* is "The Decision," an understated study of unnecessary futility. When Dr. Francis Townsend graduated from medical school, his uncle had informed him that he could never practice medicine or marry because both his parents died insane: "You won't have to worry about money. I've fixed that at the bank. Give yourself plenty of time to pick and choose. You'll decide on something." For the next forty years Francis does nothing—except quietly drink more than a bottle of rye every day while waiting to go crazy. "The Decision" is as effective a story as O'Hara ever wrote, for there is nothing wrong with Francis Townsend's mind. "A Phase of Life" is an extraordinary story about a couple who operate what can be described as a sex service; the extraordinary thing about it is that O'Hara succeeds in making them sympathetic, or at least understandable. The stories in *Hellbox* are not all harsh. Sentimentality is as strong as despair in O'Hara's writing. "Doctor and Mrs. Parsons" is the moving account of a small-town doctor whose practice diminishes after the town's young doctor returns from war. "War Aims"—one of O'Hara's few attempts to write about his navy experiences—describes a fighter pilot's plans for after the war. The impact of the story comes from the unstated point that the boy may not survive to have his good life.

In JANUARY 1948 O'Hara went on the wagon again to write the novel that became *A Rage to Live*. He was pleased by an invitation to speak to the Yale Elizabethan Club in March, and declined to accept an honorarium "from my friend Gilbert Troxell's Club." The Curator of American Literature, Troxell was married to Walter Camp's daughter and therefore seemed to O'Hara a pillar of the Yale establishment. Belle and O'Hara had started visiting the Troxells in 1944—usually after football games—and O'Hara enjoyed meeting the Troxells' friends among the Yale community. O'Hara's topic at the Elizabethan Club was "Writing: What's in it for me?" In it he gave sound advice to would-be writers, including the financial facts of professional authorship. Although his talk was peppered with wisecracks, he spoke seriously about the loneliness of writing and concluded that the real reward of writing is the writer's self-approval. He couldn't resist telling, with obvious relish, Hemingway's joke about starting a fund to send John O'Hara to Yale, and mentioned that he had a Duesenberg for sale. O'Hara was not a great success on this occasion, for he had rehearsed his talk with gestures, and his presentation seemed too elaborate.*

By June 1948—after about six months of work—O'Hara had written 400 pages of typescript for *A Rage to Live*. He projected another 300 pages, but his working typescript was 962 pages long. It is clear that the novel developed while O'Hara wrote it, as his concept of it grew more ambitious.

In June Cerf and O'Hara began discussing possible magazine serial deals. *Good Housekeeping* and *Collier's* expressed interest, and O'Hara stipulated that first look would cost *Collier's* a nonreturnable fee of $15,000. Cerf replied in some dismay that payment for first refusal was unheard of.[35] The serial rights were not sold. O'Hara was ahead of his time, and payment for such options is sometimes made now. Except for movies and plays and the brief period Mark Hanna was handling his non-*New Yorker* stories, O'Hara acted as his own agent. Like many writers, he thought of himself as a good businessman. His basic tactic was take-it-or-leave-it, which he was able to enforce because his work was so good and so prolific. If somebody wouldn't meet his terms for this property, then somebody else would for another property. Moreover, O'Hara resented the author's position in the publishing set-up and frankly took pleasure in driving hard bargains. He felt that other people were making too much money from the author's labor; the publisher was building an equity in the firm, but the author was not.

The Duesenberg had turned into an albatross. O'Hara had tried to give it to the navy as a VIP car during the war, and in 1948 it was on jacks while he tried to sell it. Although the Doozy had proved to be less than the ideal vehicle for him, it figured in three 1947 stories—"Pardner," "Miss W." and the best of the group, "Transaction." This last story describes the purchase by a screenwriter of a classic car from a Harvard Law School couple in reduced circumstances. The transaction is extremely cordial, and the writer insists on paying an extra

---

* O'Hara was nervous before an audience and did not enjoy his public appearances. However, he found it difficult to turn down invitations from schools. In May 1945 he had addressed the Lantern Club at Phillips Exeter Academy; in May 1953 he spoke to the literary club at Rutgers (stipulating that his friend Scottie Cameron, the librarian, be seated in the front row); and in 1954 spoke to the Pipe & Quill Club at Lawrenceville.

$75 for a spotlight. He leaves with the car and with envy for the couple—they are clearly going to have a good life together. In July of 1948 the O'Hara stable consisted of the Duesenberg, a Mercury, a Standard and an American Bantam. Along with millions of other car buffs he fell in love with the MG-TC. He traded in the Duesenberg for $900 against a red TC and disposed of the Bantam. The TC became a favorite toy and remained in the O'Hara garage while more impressive vehicles—including a Jaguar and a Mercedes-Benz—came and went.

In the fall of 1948 he revived his educational plans by enrolling in the Columbia University School of General Studies. He started History R10 (The History of the United States, 1865–1946) on 15 October and withdrew on the twenty-second. The instructor, Donald Sheehan, recalls that O'Hara complimented him after a lecture on the Mollie Maguires and sent a note when he dropped the course, explaining that he was writing a novel and his work habits were such that he was unable to continue the course. O'Hara developed an affection for Columbia through this brief contact and liked to refer to it as his alma mater. While he was working on the novel, his story output in 1948 fell to two.

That fall O'Hara was also planning a research trip through Pennsylvania in his MG. He hoped to underwrite this excursion by writing an article for *Holiday* on the small Pennsylvania colleges and invited Joe Bryan to accompany him. The first stop was to be Lafayette, and he asked his old Lykens friend Harvey Batdorf, who was with the Lafayette administration, to help with arrangements.[36] Since the father of one of O'Hara's characters was a Lafayette graduate, he particularly wanted to check the college yearbooks. However, the trip fell through, possibly because O'Hara didn't want to interrupt his writing. At this point he was trying to complete thirty double-spaced pages a week.

The first crisis in O'Hara's association with Random House came in November 1948 when he requested an additional $10,000 advance for *A Rage to Live*, offering as security the first draft of a play, *The Farmers Hotel*, written "last year," which he planned to rewrite as a novel. Cerf declined to advance $10,000 and offered $2,500. O'Hara took the $2,500 but indicated his disappointment, which elicited a firm letter from Cerf complaining about his behavior toward Random House—in particular, his refusal to let Donald Klopfer and Robert Haas see the typescript of *Rage*. Bennett Cerf had not yet perfected the fine art of handling John O'Hara, for this letter brought a paragraph-by-paragraph rebuttal from the author:

2. "When you suddenly need a lot of additional money for personal reasons." Are you implying that there is something naughty about needing money for "personal" reasons? Gambling debts? A mistress? What other reasons than personal reasons are there? I need the money for an income-tax payment and to run this household while I am writing a novel by which you presumably will profit personally, and what you do with your personal profit is properly none of my business.

* * * *

4. When you say that you "had to virtually steal the manuscript to read it," you are just about stating it, and my cordiality over the telephone was an example of self-control. It was well-known around your office that I did not want anyone to read the manuscript until it was finished. The construction of the novel is such that it is not fair to the author or to the reader to have the novel read in snatches, with weeks intervening. The manuscript was in your office for safe-keeping, to protect your investment and mine against damage by fire, for instance. . . . What should have been thoroughly understood (and I went along thinking it was) was that my novel was not officially in the office.

5. I don't understand what you are getting at in this paragraph or the two following. If you are saying, under your breath, get another publisher, please say it intelligibly and I'll set about to do exactly that. I recognize and deplore the tactics of accusing your vis-a-vis of the very thing you have done or plan to do yourself, and when you call my previous letter threatening you are employing that strategem. My letter applying for a $10,000 additional advance contained my plan for another book after this novel. No comment was made by you either in your letter that offered a quarter of what I asked for, or in the letter that offered me, as far as I can make out, the door.[37]

Cerf cut off further escalation on 1 December: "Damn it all, if we didn't want you very much indeed, do you think we'd be going through all this sturm and drang? If you think I like it, you're very wrong indeed." *A Rage to Live* was ready in January 1949.*

O'Hara had found the right publisher, but Saxe Commins proved to be the wrong editor for him. Commins was one of the prominent American editors, whose authors included Eugene O'Neill and William Faulkner, so O'Hara was being assigned to the firm's top editor. The

---

* The complete working typescript is dated at the end "7.20 a.m., 18 January 1948." But O'Hara made the common error of forgetting to change years in January. The correct year was 1949, for he had just begun work on the novel in January 1948. A clean typescript was prepared by a professional typist; triple-spaced, it is 1,383 pages long.

problem that developed between the men was over their conceptions of the duties of John O'Hara's editor. Commins wanted to *edit*, to help; but O'Hara didn't want any structural or stylistic help. He regarded editors as proofreaders and production men, not collaborators. Commins expected to enjoy personal relationships with authors, but O'Hara did not encourage intimacy. Moreover, O'Hara felt that Commins was attempting to intrude his own social convictions into the novel.

Early in the retyping stage—at this time O'Hara was still revising his typescripts*—the author had explained to Commins the rules for editing an O'Hara novel:

You'd better get that surgical glint out of your eye, because far from doing any ruthless cutting on the final MS, there will be ruthful additions between now and the submitting of the printers' copy. You are in for some surprises when you see the final MS; extremely minor characters as of Book I, which you may think ought to go, will be popping up all through Book II. I don't suppose any of the critics will be alert enough to notice it, but in this book I have been influenced more by Jules Romains than by any other author. I am inclined to think he is the greatest novelist of our time. However, Harrisburg isn't Paris, and I am confining myself to one volume, you will be relieved to learn.[38]

This letter also states that the title has been permanently set as *A Rage to Live.*† O'Hara had considered at least two other titles—*The Pathless Coast* and *But Not Lost.*

Nevertheless, Commins tried to revise the typescript. He reported that when he attempted to delete some sexual material, O'Hara threw a paperweight, shouting, "You'll never touch a line of mine again!" The paperweight did not hit Commins, so it is doubtful whether O'Hara was aiming at him. A more important issue was the material after the death of Sidney Tate, which Commins wanted to cut drastically. O'Hara was persuaded to excise some thirty pages of typescript dealing with the affair between Jack Hollister, the newspaperman, and Mary Kemper; but he felt that it had been a mistake to yield to Commins.[39] After the publication of *Rage*, O'Hara sent Commins a gold pencil with a note, "By God still talking." Saxe

---

* O'Hara disliked the term *typescript* and always used *MS* or *manuscript* when discussing his typescripts.

† The title and epigraph are from Alexander Pope's *Moral Essays*, Epistle II: "To a Lady": "You purchase Pain with all that Joy can give, And die of nothing but a Rage to live."

Commins handled his next book, *The Farmers Hotel*; but the association was uncomfortable, and Commins came to occupy a permanent position on the O'Hara grudge list. He avoided talking to Commins. When William Faulkner was visiting Commins in Princeton, Belle would call and ask Faulkner to come to the phone so that John could speak to him. O'Hara also avoided shaking hands with Commins when they met.

In the spring of 1949—while O'Hara was still editing and proofing *A Rage to Live*—Joe Bryan invited him to Washington to meet some Intelligence people who were interested in looking him over. He disqualified himself by getting drunk at dinner. The next day Bryan's wife, Katharine, told O'Hara that she was pleased by the way things had turned out, for she thought he should not let outside commitments interfere with his writing. It is puzzling that O'Hara should have been interested in a government job just when he had completed his most ambitious novel up to that time and when he was at the top of his writing form. The idea of being an insider at a powerful and secret organization probably appealed to him, and he may have seen the job as a source for new material.

A Rage to Live was published on 16 August 1949, the fifteenth anniversary of *Appointment in Samarra*, and was an immediate success. By publication day four printings had been ordered, totaling 76,000 copies—and without a prepublication book-club adoption. O'Hara had refused to submit his novel to the Book-of-the-Month Club— partly because he didn't care to have his work passed on in this way, and partly because he didn't want to have anything to do with a panel of judges that included Clifton Fadiman.* However, the judges did discuss the novel, and O'Hara learned that Henry Seidel Canby had denounced it as "vulgar." O'Hara used this information as a reason to change his mind about donating the typescript to Yale, for Canby had strong Yale connections.

Random House knew it had a winner, and spent money on promotion. In addition to an ad campaign, 750 copies of a presentation edition were distributed to opinion-makers. *Rage* was the fastest-selling Random House title up to the time; 104,585 copies were sold in its first two months, with a record one-day sale of 8,140. O'Hara kept score of the reviews and reported in November that seventy-four were "wholly receptive," twenty "unfavorable" and ten "on the fence."[40] Two of the *Rage* reviews had long-range consequences—those in the

* It was ironic that the Random House ads for *Rage* on publication day featured a blurb from Fadiman's review in *The Book-of-the-Month Club News*.

Times and *The New Yorker*. Orville Prescott in the daily *Times* objected to the "sensationalism" and inclusiveness of the novel, concluding ". . . it is only the story of a woman for whom there is a common but unprintable word." Since Prescott was the *Times'* Monday-Wednesday-Friday reviewer, O'Hara decided that hereafter his books would be published when Charles Poore, the Tuesday-Thursday-Saturday critic, would review them. *Rage* also met with disfavor in the Sunday *Times* book review section, where the easily shocked J. Donald Adams protested: "A more meretricious, dull, and pointless story, with equal pretensions, has not been published for a long time."

The situation at the *Herald Tribune* was similar to that at the *Times*. One reviewer, Lewis Gannett, was negative in his response to O'Hara; the other, John K. Hutchens, admired his work.* Gannett was on vacation when *Rage* was published, and it was reviewed by O'Hara's old friend and admirer, Hutchens, who wrote a warm notice that began by calling the novel "a major event of this new season." But even Hutchens had reservations about the characters' absorption with the "adventures of the bed. . . . a prepossession suggesting that they don't think about anything much."

The review that caused the author the most hurt and anger—and actually altered the shape of O'Hara's career—was Brendan Gill's in *The New Yorker*, which compared *Rage* to the *Kinsey Report*. Gill applied the terms "sprawling," "discursive" and "prolix," and indicated that O'Hara was finished as a novelist. "Dr. O'Hara's handy guide to healthy sex practices has been tucked inside the disarming wrapper of the formula family novel, and one result of this odd combination is the loss of the old sure-fire, ice-cold O'Hara dialogue." The review concluded, "It is hard to understand how one of our best writers could have written this book, and it is because of O'Hara's distinction that his failure here seems in the nature of a catastrophe." O'Hara regarded this review as the final betrayal by *The New Yorker*: first Fadiman and now Gill. An intensely loyal man, O'Hara could not understand, much less forgive and forget, what he regarded as acts of betrayal. In certain ways Brendan Gill—who was actually an admirer of John O'Hara's work—was involved in a plot he had not made.

O'Hara had been convinced for some time that Harold Ross and *The New Yorker* were not showing proper respect for his work and for him as a contributor. He was their star fiction writer and had

---

* One night when he was drunk O'Hara had encountered Lewis Gannett at Bleeck's and threw a punch at him which was blocked by another man at the bar who got him away from Gannett. O'Hara was reacting to Gannett's comment that his characters weren't worth writing about.

been a contributor for twenty years. Moreover, his association with *The New Yorker* cost him money, for other magazines paid much better. When *The New Yorker* rejected one of his stories, he regarded that story as dead, if he didn't include it in a collection. By 1948 O'Hara had felt secure enough about his value to *The New Yorker* to act on his long-standing unhappiness about rejections. Early in the year he informed Harold Ross that he wanted a payment—perhaps $200—for every story he submitted, whether the magazine used it or not. Ross said that this stipulation was contrary to policy and refused to negotiate. He privately said that O'Hara had gone crazy. A deadlock ensued. O'Hara tried to reopen communication with Ross by submitting a poem on 7 June 1948: "The enclosed, being a poem, does not mean that I have surrendered or yielded from my position. As far I know, we are just where we were in January, and our stalemate is not affected by my being compelled to express myself in verse."[41] Ross did not yield, and the poem was not used. The situation was deescalated by Ross's gift to O'Hara of a large gold watch from a Third Avenue pawnshop, engraved FOR JOHN O'HARA FROM THE NEW YORKER 25 WEST 43RD STREET BR 9-8200, WITH LOVE AND ADMIRATION."* Although O'Hara appreciated the gag and occasionally wore the watch, he continued to brood over *The New Yorker*'s failure to treat him as a valued contributor. Only three O'Hara pieces appeared in the magazine during 1949, all of which had been submitted before publication of Gill's review of *A Rage to Live*.†

Old *New Yorker* hands are convinced that O'Hara's break with the magazine cannot be attributed solely to the Gill review. The review was the immediate cause, but the staffers feel that O'Hara had decided to terminate his connection with the magazine over the issue of payment for rejected stories. The *New Yorker* staff was as full of intrigues as a harem, and the review of *Rage* may have become involved in one such intrigue. According to one version of the gossip, James Thurber passed the word to O'Hara that Gill hadn't done the review, but that Wolcott Gibbs had written it because he felt that O'Hara's true vocation was for the short story and wanted to discourage him from novel-writing. O'Hara found support for this claim when Gibbs

---

* O'Hara also had a miniature Phi Beta Kappa key with a dunce cap, engraved NOPE NEVER MADE IT.

† When *The New Yorker* was assembling material for a twenty-fifth anniversary volume in March 1949, O'Hara supplied Mrs. White with a list of his five best: "Doctor and Mrs. Parsons," "The Decision," "Walter T. Carriman," "Bread Alone" and "The Last of Haley." He left the final choice up to her, and she picked "The Decision."

wrote him a letter about *Rage* employing the word "discursive."
Since Gill's review used this word, O'Hara's suspicions were aroused.
The unlikely story continues that O'Hara believed Thurber and tried
to force a break with the man for whom he had named Gibbsville,
which Gibbs prevented. This may have been the occasion when
O'Hara is supposed to have ordered a glass of the best brandy to
throw at Gibbs. Another element in the *New Yorker–Rage* crisis may
have been O'Hara's personal resentment of Brendan Gill, who was a
member of Skull and Bones. The Yale factor can never be entirely
dismissed in analyzing O'Hara's relationships. O'Hara also heard
gossip that Gill had said he was going to "get" *A Rage to Live*. What
O'Hara expected—and what was never forthcoming—was an apology
or explanation or some expression of concern from Ross. When Frank
Sullivan raised the matter in a letter, Ross replied:

Left to right: O'Hara, Eleanor and Wolcott Gibbs, Charles Addams.

. . . as for the O'Hara review, I didn't know of my own knowledge, and don't know yet, for I haven't read the book, and I probably wouldn't know if I did read it, for I have read almost no novels in the last twenty years and wouldn't have any standard, and probably would be disqualified by the personal equation, too. But I'll say this: I've asked a lot of people who read the book's opinion, and there are more on the side our review took than the side you take—if things can be demarked that roughly.[42]

Ross's hand-washing cost *The New Yorker* a decade without John O'Hara. There are undocumented reports that Ross invited O'Hara to come back to the magazine through intermediaries. These accounts vary in their details of the conditions set by O'Hara: a large sum of money, a printed retraction, and even the execution of Brendan Gill. The author of the review regretted the trouble he had caused and tried to patch up the quarrel. Gill was with Gardner Botsford, a *New Yorker* editor, when they met O'Hara in the lobby of "21." O'Hara was drunk and obscenely rejected Gill's friendly overtures; both men were ready to fight, but a brawl was averted. Charles Addams recalls another occasion at "21" when Gill tried to buy drinks for the O'Haras and the Addamses, to which O'Hara replied, "You son-of-a-bitch, I wouldn't go to a dogfight with you!"—a favorite O'Hara expression of contempt.

A Rage to Live was the first book by John O'Hara to achieve a huge sale. Random House required eight printings in 1949, plus two for the Book Find Club; Grosset & Dunlap reprinted it in 1950; *Omnibook* magazine condensed it in January 1950; and beginning in 1951 the Bantam paperback sold thirty-three large printings. Four months after publication Bennett Cerf was able to send a silver cigarette box engraved FOR JOHN O'HARA FROM HIS GRATEFUL PUBLISHERS RANDOM HOUSE AND THE FIRST HUNDRED THOUSAND PURCHASERS OF "A RAGE TO LIVE"/CHRISTMAS 1949. It was the first of a string of such tokens presented to an author who loved symbols, badges and awards.* His obvious delight in these things was regarded by unfriendly observers as immature; but, as E. B. White wrote, "It is deeply satisfying to win a prize in front of a lot of people."

John O'Hara was forty-four years old when he published *A Rage to Live*, his most ambitious work up to that time, and the novel that

---

* Thereafter O'Hara received an engraved cigarette box to mark the 100,000th copy of a Random House edition or the millionth paperback copy. At the time of his death there were five of them in his home. At least once O'Hara selected the cigarette box himself to be sure of getting one he liked.

inaugurated the major period of his career. Fifteen years after *Appointment in Samarra* he achieved the form and scope he required for his masterpieces. It is remarkable that this achievement came after an eleven-year dry spell in which O'Hara seemed to have become a spoiled novelist who was unable to handle subjects requiring much more than 2,000 words. The clue to Jules Romains that he gave Commins is worth pursuing. Romains' epic, *Men of Good Will*, covering a twenty-five-year span from 1908 to 1933, was published in France in twenty-seven parts and in the United States in fourteen volumes commencing in 1933. If O'Hara read the preface to the first volume, he found there a rationale for the social novel that he could accept: "But one can at least try to avoid reducing collective life to the dimensions of the individual and the individual consciousness. One can at least try to make his representation of human affairs convey the social multiplicity in which we are immersed a little less imperfectly."[43] Romains explained that certain events or characters in his novels do not lead anywhere structurally; they are in his work because they were in life. However, Jules Romains had a much larger canvas than O'Hara; and adjectives like "panoramic" and "kaleidoscopic" have been properly applied to *Men of Good Will*, which are not appropriate to O'Hara's self-contained novels.

That O'Hara shared Romains' theories about the social novel does not mean that he had no regard for the structure of his own fiction. His longer novels are carefully plotted, and he became increasingly concerned with problems of point of view. Nevertheless, beginning with *A Rage to Live* reviewers had a new set of pejorative terms for his novels: "sprawling," "all-inclusive," "over-documented"—in addition to the old stand-by, "sensational." O'Hara's detractors are convinced that he suffered from a list-making compulsion, denying that there was any artistic intention behind his use of detail. A passage such as the description of the vehicles on the way to the Tate Farm near the beginning of *Rage* causes these critics pain.

It would have been impossible for anyone on the Nesquehela Pike that day to miss the place, no matter what name he knew it by. The real farmers, of course, had not been deceived by the light rainfall of the morning, and they had begun arriving as early as ten o'clock, while the committeemen still were deciding about a postponement. The early ones came in spring wagons and hay wagons and truck wagons, some drawn by draft horses, some by teams of mules, some by mixed teams of horse-and-mule; and the next to arrive were farmers more prosperous than the earliest, and they came in buggies and buckboards and democrats and surreys and barouches and cut-unders. There was even a team of goats from a neighboring farm, a nice turn-out with real leather, not web, harness and a small-size truck wagon. Then a little later came the trucks and automobiles: Ford cars and Maxwells and Chevrolets and Partin-Palmers and Buicks and Hahn trucks and Maccars and Garfords and Autocars and Vims, and a few Cadillacs, Franklins and one Locomobile and one Winton. And all this time there would be farm boys on horseback—some with English saddles, some with stock saddles, some with Kentucky saddles, some with a blanket-and-surcingle, and some bareback—and among these were a few fine saddle horses, bust mostly they were work horses and mules, with one-piece ear-loop bridles and work-harness bridles with laundry rope for reins. And all day long too there were the farm boys with their bicycles, singly and in pairs, but more often in groups as large as twenty in number, causing their own particular sound, which was the hum of the wire wheels, and the sound of one bell quickly followed by twenty other bells. They were the grim ones, these boys, not quite of draft age, breaking the silence in their ranks to call out words in Pennsylvania Dutch, but ironically resembling the Belgian army cyclists, whose cousins the farm boys' cousins had beaten in war. The boys on horseback laughed; the boys on the bicycles had no laughter. Everything was clean and shining: the Dietz lamps on the wagons and trucks and buggies, and the nickel studding on the work harness, and the silver conchos on the stock saddles, and the automobile radiators, and the sprockets on the bicycles, and the snaffle bits and curb chains and the ferrules on the buggy-whips and the painted hooves of the horses and the yellow felloes on the wheels of the cut-unders and the black leather dashboards and the white painted canvas tops of the spring-wagons and the brass-bound hose of the bulb horns and the three-by-six-inch windows in the barouches and the Prest-o-lite tanks and hub-caps of the automobiles, and the scrubbed faces and foreheads of the men and the women and the boys and the girls.

This material is not an arbitrary list of trivia; neither is it filler. It is essential to O'Hara's technique and serves at least two related functions: to establish background, and to convince the reader that the author knows exactly what he is talking about. The development of reader confidence in the author and his material is crucial to literary realism. Nonetheless, there is a class of readers on whom this technique is wasted—indeed, it is anathema to them. John O'Hara wasn't writing for them.

For a novel that was supposedly freighted with sex, *A Rage to Live* adheres to traditional sexual morality. Grace Caldwell Tate is not a nymphomaniac, not a flaming adultress. Up to the time of her husband's death she has sexual intercourse with one other man. The violation cannot be excused by Sidney Tate, who lives by the code that governs the conduct of ladies and gentlemen.

> *. . . you see in this world you learn a set of rules, or you don't learn them. But assuming you learn them, you stick by them. They may be no damn good, but you're who you are and what you are because they're your rules and you stick by them. And of course when it's easy to stick by them, that's no test. It's when it's hard to obey the rules, that's when they mean something. That's what I believe, and I always thought you did too. I'm the first, God knows, to grant that you, with your beauty, you had opportunities or invitations. But you obeyed the rules, the same rules I obeyed. But then you said the hell with them. What it amounts to is you said the hell with my rules, and the hell with me. So, Grace—the hell with you. I love you, but if I have any luck, that'll pass, in my new life.*[44]

The author approves of this judgment, although the point is not simple. Sidney is being inflexible, but he is prepared to pay the extremely high price for rigid adherence to his rules. Author and reader know more than Sidney does—that Grace's affair with Roger Bannon resulted from a physical compulsion and meant nothing to her apart from sexual gratification. Therefore author and reader share a sense of regret that Sidney must behave as he does, although they accept his behavior as consistent with his character.

One of the complaints made against *Rage* was that it was too long, that O'Hara should have stopped after Book Two at page 353. The novel continues for another 137 pages, covering Grace's affair with Jack Hollister after the death of Sidney, and a 1947 "Postlude" revealing that the sixty-four-year-old Grace is in love with a married man. *Rage* continues beyond Sidney's death in 1918 because it is not just an account of Grace's marriage. The novel is a study of Grace, who all her life purchases "Pain with all that Joy can give," and her life goes on after she is widowed.

The most impressive review of *Rage* was written for *Newsweek* by Frank Norris—an old friend who later turned novelist—which compared O'Hara favorably with Tolstoy. Norris must have corresponded with O'Hara about the novel before his review appeared, for on 22 July O'Hara wrote him a significant letter:

> *I have tried to do several things in this book. It may be, in the future final judgment, that I tried to do too many things. One thing I tried to do you caught right away, and you caught it specifically where I had intended it to be caught. One or two other readers at*

Random House caught the general idea of Anna, but did not put a finger on the spot where I wanted it to be caught, namely, of course, the turkey shoot scene. (I have a feeling this is going to be a very long letter, so light up.)

You have to take my word for it that I never read Tolstoy, but I did see Garbo as Anna and I did hear the radio version, and I have enough of a feeling for the Russian school to know what they did, plus a scratchy knowledge. So, quite frankly, I made one effort to make Grace an example of that school, knowing that I had to do her some way besides the way she would have been done by the above authors or I'd have wasted my time.

But being an American, and recalling an early satisfaction with the Tarkington treatment of a Caldwellian family and Fort Pennsyllian town, I also decided that I would write this novel as Tarkington might have written it if this kind of treatment could have been got away with in the time Ambersons was written, and if Tarkington had been somewhat less so totally unlike me in almost every respect. I regard myself as a pretty good man, but I think Tarkington would have preferred to go through life completely a gentleman, not only from Indiana.

I also was strongly influenced in the constructing of this novel by a man whom I regard as the greatest novelist living today, Jules Romains. Indeed, if I thought I had the time I would go on writing about Fort Penn as Romains did about Paris. For instance, I cut out of this book a detailed picture of small-city journalism; enough of it is left to show you what I mean. Romains, you will agree, is closer to me than Tarkington is, despite his preoccupation with the politico-economic details of France. This book will be compared—not always favorably—with Lewis, but the fact is I was not even actively influenced to be contemptuous of Lewis. I might have been, say, ten years ago, but in recent years I have only regarded Lewis as passe, no matter how good he was when he wrote Babbitt.

"The idea that any social situation is likely to blow up in anyone's face at any time" is a good way to put critically what I did with Grace and Bannon. But you must also, as a critic and not merely a reviewer, bear in mind that there is nothing in Grace's background that is inconsistent with her behavior. In fact, let me put it another way: whether I succeeded or not, I did attempt constantly to prepare the reader for that business. Bannon, remember, is totally unlike Brock and Charlie Jay and Sidney and the other boys and young men Grace had known, so that when she did kick up it had to be with a Bannon, a violent fox, if you see what I mean. Some day I will tell you the model for Bannon. (You will never guess.) Aside from certain physical resemblances, I would not have known about the real-life character had I not had an affair with a girl he'd had an affair with, and she told all, in a moment of anger with me. Of course when I say model I do

not mean, either, that Bannon is a photographic copy, but close enough to have suited my purpose. I must insist that sexually Grace had been preparing for a Bannon all her life and that it was merely circumstances that kept her from one earlier in her young womanhood, with either more disastrous results, or less. My feeling now is more disastrous results, such as happened to ———.

You must also give some thought to Bannon, independently of Grace. Then you will be less disturbed in the way you are at present. Bannon is quite a man. A hypocrite, treacherous, a lout, and all that, but not a man whose presence would be ignored, in a room or in a town.

Now what I am about to tell you you are free to use. I have considered the ethics of telling you, and decided that if playwrights can show scripts to G. J. Nathan in advance, I can tell you this, but you must not let on I told you. This: I have employed a device in this novel which I doubt if any critic is going to catch on to. I have given you a complete picture of Grace, the superficial things such as a spottily good vocabulary with a naturalistic use of grammar; her clothes, her drinks, etc. But I also have let you know how she thinks and feels AND YET AT NO TIME DO I, THE NOVELIST, ENTER HER MIND. At no time am I the omniscient, ubiquitous novelist. The God. You read that book and you think you have been inside her thinking moments, but the fact is there is nothing told about Grace that could not have been actually seen or actually overheard by another human being. That, my friend, is a triumph of writing. I am very proud of it, because in my own estimation it makes me really a pro.

I am glad you noticed the medical stuff. That was intentional, too. I also am waiting for anyone to pick me up on the slang of the day. I used several expressions that seem more recent than the time I used them, but I got them right out of Clare Briggs in the NY Tribune. I spent many hours on Briggs alone, plus Grantland Rice.[45]

A Rage to Live was dedicated "To Belle." In her copy O'Hara wrote: "the only human being for whom I have enduring and continued admiration, respect, affection and love John."

WILLIAM FAULKNER once complained to Stephen Longstreet that O'Hara lacked a sense of style because he hadn't read enough. Although O'Hara had been a great reader as a boy and young man, after he became a published author he read surprisingly little current fiction. He said that he couldn't read fiction for pleasure because he read it studiously and critically. Reading a novel was "hard work" for him. When asked for a list of good reading in 1934 he had supplied *Man's*

Fate (Malraux), *Tender Is the Night* (Fitzgerald), *A Farewell to Arms* (Hemingway), *Laments for the Living* (Parker), *The Last Adam* (Cozzens), *The Great Gatsby* (Fitzgerald), *Good-bye, Mr. Chips!* (Hilton), *Round Up* (Lardner), *The Complete Short Stories of Saki* and *The Man Who Knew Coolidge* (Lewis). "These," he noted, "are the books I have read and/or reread in the last six months or so, and, in one way or another, enjoyed reading. Before deciding upon 'The Man Who Knew Coolidge' I considered 'Ann Vickers,' 'Mantrap,' and 'Work of Art'; but 'The Man Who Knew Coolidge' won out."[46] Fifteen years later, in 1949, he responded to a similar request with *The Way of All Flesh*, *Ordeal* (Nevil Shute), *Dusty Answer* (Rosamund Lehmann), *The Last Tycoon*, *The Old Maid* and *New Year's Day*—noting that he had not read any current fiction for more than two years.[47] He was not totally uninformed about the current literary scene, for Belle read widely and briefed him. Most of his day-to-day reading was confined to newspapers, and news magazines, which he read very carefully.

Like most writers, O'Hara had a feast-or-famine income. John

Belle, Wylie and John at Quogue.

and Belle worried about money in different ways: Belle worried about the present and O'Hara worried about the future. Because of his premonition of early death he was concerned about providing for Belle and Wylie. In the forties he signed over *Appointment in Samarra* to Belle, so that the royalties would always be hers. The O'Haras lived well, but not lavishly. The only home they owned was a cottage in Quogue, and he never went in for boats or horses. Nonetheless, their daily expenses were high: a lot of O'Hara's money went over the bar, and they regularly ate at expensive restaurants—although he cared little for food.

In Hollywood O'Hara had become friends with producer Carleton W. Alsop. Alsop should have known better than to try to kid him when he was drinking; nevertheless one night at the Copacabana night club in New York in 1949 he tried a gag. Alsop was sitting on the banquette level; O'Hara was right below him separated by a metal fence or grating. Joe E. Lewis was performing, and as part of his act turned the spotlight on Alsop and talked about him. Alsop then asked Lewis to turn the light on O'Hara, describing him as "America's most famous living author, the author of *The Naked and the Dead*." "Even though John knew it was a blatant rib, he was outraged and tried to pull my leg through the grating and, I guess, snap it off."[48]

A Rage to Live was written at 55 East 86th Street, but Belle wanted to get John out of New York where there were too many distractions and too many bars. He concurred, admitting that it was time for him to make "21" a restaurant and not a career. When Wylie showed a mild asthma condition, the O'Haras began town-hunting. Saratoga Springs, where Frank Sullivan lived, was considered, but was rejected because the winters were harsh and it was a long way from the reference sources O'Hara needed. No serious consideration was given to Pottsville. He wanted a college town for the library facilities and for the people; and Princeton won out over New Haven. O'Hara half-jokingly explained that the wisecracks would have never stopped if he had moved to Yale. He liked Princeton's location between Philadelphia and New York and had the theory that the social structure of a college town is set by the living standard of the full professors. This is not the case in Princeton. As John O'Hara certainly knew, Princeton is full of big money, and its social structure is more influenced by Wall Street than by Prospect Street.

Shortly before the move to Princeton O'Hara ran into Warren Leslie at the Plaza Hotel barbershop. Leslie, then about eighteen, wanted to write, and O'Hara made a point of being friendly to him. After their haircuts, O'Hara invited him to "21" for a drink. After three Scotches O'Hara said, "You've just witnessed an historic moment, Warren."

"What moment?"

"You've just seen O'Hara have his last drink. I've held this bar up long enough." He explained that he had just so much time left and more work to do than he could fit into it. He wanted to do long books and drinking got in the way of big writing jobs, as did living in New York. One of the reasons he was moving to Princeton was so he could stay on the wagon. But O'Hara was not able to stick to his plan then.[49]

In September of 1949 the O'Haras rented a house at 18 College Road West near the Princeton Graduate School. Belle's St. Timothy schoolmate, Kate Bramwell, became her closest Princeton friend. A lively, charming and popular woman, Kate introduced the O'Haras to her friends and provided a place for Belle to visit when O'Hara was working. One of the problems for a writer's wife is that he is always around the house. Belle did a remarkable job of compartmentalizing her family's life. Wylie was not permitted to bother her father when he was writing, and neither one was allowed to worry about Belle, who had grown very thin and drank a mixture of cream and ginger ale to gain weight. Belle became pregnant again in Princeton, and although she had a miscarriage did not go to the hospital because she did not want to upset Wylie.

O'Hara was still drinking and spent many afternoons "slopping it up" at the Nassau Club, playing cards or backgammon. He tried to control his public drinking, but he was drinking heavily. The Barklie

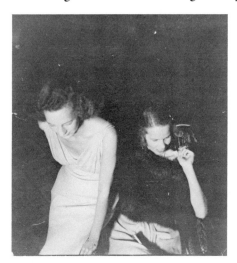

Belle (left) with Kate Bramwell.

Henrys gave dinners which introduced O'Hara and Belle to a cross-section of the Princeton community that it would otherwise have taken them a long time to meet—people from the Institute for Advanced Study, faculty people and wealthy townies.* O'Hara met J. Robert Oppenheimer through Buzz Henry, who was associated with the Institute, and liked him. The Oppenheimers were O'Hara fans, and the custom developed for the O'Haras to go to their home on New Year's Eve. When Oppenheimer lost his AEC clearance in 1954 over his alleged communist connections, he sought O'Hara's advice. O'Hara told him that he was making a mistake in antagonizing the press. Although O'Hara felt that Oppenheimer was going against all the rules, he made a point of walking the length of Princeton Junction station to shake Oppenheimer's hand in front of a crowd at the height of his troubles.

Dean Hamilton Cottier of the English department and art historian Rensselaer Lee became O'Hara's closest faculty friends. When Mrs. Cottier told O'Hara of her admiration for the work of Henry James, he replied, "We're different." He met Albert Einstein, and there are reports of O'Hara and Einstein strolling together licking ice-cream cones. O'Hara's old friend from the *Time* days, Wilder Hobson, was living in Princeton; they saw a good deal of each other during the early Fifties. O'Hara once remarked that Hobson's presence in Princeton had been a factor in his decision to move there. After leaving the Luce organization where he was on the editorial board of *Fortune*, Hobson became associate editor and book critic for *Newsweek*—putting him in the potentially risky position of reviewing O'Hara. The friendship survived this peril, although O'Hara did not always agree with Hobson's critical judgments.

O'Hara was disappointed that the Princeton English department did not respond to his presence by inviting him to appear on campus. *The Princeton Tiger*, the humor magazine, did make him an honorary member of its editorial board in December 1950, and O'Hara subsequently showed his appreciation in 1952 by giving the *Tiger* an unpublished story, "The Favor," which had been written earlier.

Joseph "Pat" Outerbridge, the father of one of Wylie's schoolmates, was to become O'Hara's dearest friend. When O'Hara first moved to Princeton Pat Outerbridge was invited to meet him a couple of times but begged off. He was an O'Hara fan and had the feeling that knowing the author would somehow affect his pleasure in the

---

* Barklie Henry's name is supposed to have provided Hemingway with the names for the lovers in *A Farewell to Arms*.

O'Hara with Joseph W. (Pat) Outerbridge. *Photo by Sister O'Hara*

books. When they finally met at a party, their first conversation was about shaving brushes. As the friendship became increasingly close, Pat sometimes wondered what was in it for John. "He gave me so much more than I could give him."[50] Part of what Pat gave him was undemanding company and a good listener. Pat liked stories and loved to hear John talk about Pottsville.

Although Outerbridge was a serious admirer of O'Hara's work, literature was not the basis for their spontaneous friendship. They felt comfortable with each other, and O'Hara came to rely on Outerbridge's understanding companionship. Outerbridge was an executive of the Homasote Co. in Trenton, manufacturers of wood-fiber building board. Two years younger than O'Hara and a member of the Harvard class of 1929, Outerbridge's great interest was sailing. He had been on the 1928 Olympic sailing team and later participated in blue-water events.

Pat had founded the Kew-Teddington Observatory Society as a parody of a club, to which he could elect his friends. He accorded membership to O'Hara, who was so amused by the concept that he subsequently founded the Hessian Relief Society, complete with an elaborate constitution. A Hessian Relief Society tie was commissioned from Gieves of London, and from time to time O'Hara awarded a tie to a friend to symbolize that he had been granted membership in the Society. Since the founder never called a meeting, the members of the Hessian Relief Society were not sure who else was a member.

In the fall of 1949, John Hersey dined with the O'Haras at the Princeton home of Gerard Lambert, the manufacturer of Listerine. Belle produced O'Hara late, hoping to keep him sober by avoiding the preprandial drinks. Unfortunately, Mrs. Arthur Krock—who had been drinking—provoked O'Hara by telling him that *Rage* was a "fraud." He began drinking fast and became boisterous and musical on the Lamberts' Hammond organ. Hersey had been kidding him all evening about having gone academic at Princeton and was addressing him as "Professor." When the party broke up, he said, "Good night, Dr. O'Hara." O'Hara immediately squared off: "You son-of-a-bitch, you're a friend of Brendan Gill's." Hersey then remembered that the *New Yorker*'s review of *Rage* referred to him as "Dr. O'Hara." There was no fistfight, although the report of one circulated. Hersey and O'Hara saw each other several times after that, and these meetings were friendly.[51]

In February and March 1950 O'Hara took an assignment with the International News Service to cover the mercy-killing trial of Dr. Hermann Sander in Manchester, New Hampshire. Dr. Sander was accused of injecting air into the veins of a cancer patient. O'Hara filed at least fifteen background articles. He was obviously in sympathy with Dr. Sander, and analyzed the New England town's attitude toward the trial. His final article, an account of Dr. O'Hara's last days, was widely syndicated.*

* See above, p. 39. O'Hara's articles were not all printed by the papers subscribing to the INS. Most of his articles appeared in the Boston *Daily Record* (20 February–10 March 1950).

That summer O'Hara announced that he was working on "Observation Car," his first nonfiction book, for 1951 publication. The project was dropped and nothing survives of it.

WHEN HEMINGWAY'S *Across the River and into the Tree*s was published in September 1950, O'Hara wrote his best-known book review for the Sunday New York *Times*. It attracted considerable attention with its lead sentence: "The most important author living today, the outstanding author since the death of Shakespeare, has brought out a new novel." He did not claim that *Across the River* was the greatest work of literature since 1616. Indeed, the review clearly indicated that O'Hara had reservations about the novel. His intention was to reaffirm Hemingway's stature and to demonstrate that any new book by Hemingway merits respect. Probably he was at least partly motivated by his recognition that the novel was not top Hemingway and by a generous desire to counteract the bad reviews it was sure to receive. O'Hara also made a point of rebuking *The New Yorker* for its recent Hemingway profile by Lillian Ross. But whatever O'Hara's intentions were, Hemingway was not pleased. On 11 September 1950, the day after the review appeared, Hemingway wrote to General C. T. Lanham that the praise was embarrassing and that O'Hara couldn't understand the novel because he hadn't known the kind of people Hemingway had known.[52] The review generated controversy, and on 1 October the *Times Book Review* devoted a full page to letters agreeing and disagreeing with O'Hara's estimate of Hemingway.

Rather surprisingly, the review appears to have soured the relationship between the authors. Hemingway resented O'Hara's assumption of the right to defend him; and O'Hara was disappointed by Hemingway's failure to show appreciation for the review. In 1954 O'Hara made three comments in print that escalated the bad feeling with Hemingway. In his "Sweet and Sour" column in April, O'Hara commented on the bums and hangers-on Hemingway associated with and suggested a life plan whereby Hemingway would come to New York once or twice every five years. "He would be given a suite of rooms without a telephone in some rich friend's house and a guest card at the Racquet Club." The result would be to rid him of the barnacles. "Then the Nobel people would have no excuse for passing him over in favor of a historian with an occasional neat turn of phrase." In October—at the time of the announcement that Hemingway had won the Nobel Prize, O'Hara wrote in his *Collier's* column: "You read, probably, that Ernest Hemingway is going to write and act in a film about a safari . . . . If it should turn out that he doesn't like his acting, he will have nobody to shoot but himself. If he *does* like his acting, God help American literature!" And on 24 December O'Hara used his *Collier's* column to rebuke Hemingway for the ill grace with which he accepted the Nobel Prize. Hemingway was enraged by these comments.*

When the news services phoned O'Hara for a statement on Hemingway's death in July 1961, he said:

As an artist he was unique and irreplaceable. I can't think of any other author in history who directly influenced so many writers.
On the personal side, he inspired enduring affection.[53]

On 7 December 1950 the Bennett Cerfs gave a party for the new Nobel laureate, William Faulkner, to which the O'Haras were invited. It was the first meeting between the two writers, and O'Hara tried to teach Faulkner the Swedish for "thank you." O'Hara wanted to mark the occasion and impulsively gave Faulkner his cigarette lighter, which had been given to him by Philip Barry. Faulkner said thanks and casually pocketed it. Cerf and Belle saw O'Hara's expression freeze, and knew that he was about to explode. Belle got John to leave the party. The next day Cerf mentioned the incident to Faulkner, who said, "What do I want with his lighter? It was engraved for him." Either Faulkner was being extremely opaque, or he was unfamiliar with the Yankee ritual of gift-giving. He asked Cerf to return the gift to O'Hara, but Cerf knew that would start a feud. Faulkner was per-

---

* With Hemingway's approval Harvey Breit attacked O'Hara's work as a columnist in *The Writer Observed* (1956):

> I am distressed particularly by John O'Hara's prose and notions in his role as columnist-journalist. As good a novelist and short-story writer as Mr. O'Hara is, that is how poor a journalist he is. His prose, though appearing casual, is in fact careless; his facts go unchecked; his biases are so rampant that contradictory arguments under his nose are overlooked. By his decisive use of the word "class" to denote his highest praise, Mr. O'Hara is on his way, if he persists in his course, to become the Toots Shor of Literature. Yet the novelist has the crucial qualities of a first-class journalist: the savage eye, the sure ear, the economical prose. Since Mr. O'Hara does not introduce these gifts into his journalism, one is forced to the conclusion that he does not regard his job as a demanding one. He fits only too well, I fear, the category that considers journalism a hack job, in which the superior man need only be minimally engaged. The real challenges are overlooked, and the rewards are trivial.

suaded to write a thank-you note, but he left the lighter with Cerf. O'Hara never found out.*

After a year at 18 College Road West, the O'Haras moved next-door to number 20. Summers were still spent at Quogue, where the O'Haras first lived on the Wylie property and then purchased a beach cottage on Dune Road. O'Hara never learned to swim, but he played a good deal of inconsistent golf. Visitors at Quogue were impressed by the fact that "he wrote all the time." Charles Addams summered close by at Westhampton, and the O'Haras and the Addamses were congenial. O'Hara particularly enjoyed the cartoonist's classic cars and occasionally offered Addams cartoon ideas. One evening the O'Haras were attending a party at the Addamses' house, during the course of which O'Hara was enjoying a fireworks display being put on at a nearby house. When O'Hara learned that the place belonged to a man he didn't like, he turned his chair around so he couldn't see the show.

Rage WAS FOLLOWED on 8 November 1951 by *The Farmers Hotel*, which was revised into a short novel from a play written in 1946–47. The title of this book involves one of the familiar anecdotes about John O'Hara's touchiness. He had originally planned to call it *A Small Hotel* as a compliment to Rodgers and Hart. He called on Richard Rodgers to tell him, but the composer pointed out that the title of his song was "There's a Small Hotel." O'Hara was angered by what he considered Rodgers' failure to be properly pleased: "When I want you to name

The house at Quogue.

* This account differs in certain ways from the report by Joseph Blotner in *Faulkner: A Biography* (1974).

a book for me, I'll let you know." Sentimental gestures meant a great deal to him, and he was hurt when other people failed to respond to them. The friendship further deteriorated as the result of Rodgers' failure to consult O'Hara about summer bookings for *Pal Joey*.

The Farmers Hotel depicts a spoiled idyll—perhaps a delayed reaction to Fitzgerald's 1936 advice that O'Hara should write a "bucolic idyll." A group of snowbound travelers representing various social strata come together in a Pennsylvania country hotel and enjoy harmony until one of them violates the order and then murders two others. The hotel was probably based on one in Cressona, where the O'Hara family had stopped to water the horses on trips to Dr. O'Hara's farm.* The author was proud of the allegory, which exists on two levels. The obvious meaning is that there are destructive elements anti-pathetic to social order—that there are people who are not fit to live. The secondary allegorical meaning is political, with Joe Rogg, the murderous truckdriver, standing for Russia or Joseph Stalin. Further political meaning—if any—is not clear. In any case, readers seem to have missed the political allegory, although the dust jacket tried to point them in the right direction: "John O'Hara now turns to a parable

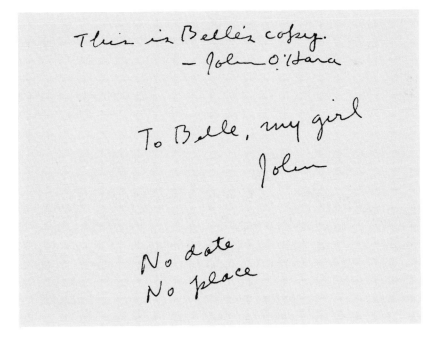

Inscription in *The Farmers Hotel* (1951).

* On pp. 97–98 of *The Farmers Hotel* O'Hara repeats the description of a Pennsylvania-Dutch meal from p. 78 of *Rage*.

of our times . . . *The Farmers Hotel* is a story that projects itself far beyond the simple frame in which it is concentrated and contains implications as wide as the reader's own imagination."

The reviews were mixed, with the most perceptive appraisals coming from Charles Poore in the *Times* (the book was published on a Thursday) and Sterling North in the New York *World-Telegram*, both of whom detected the allegorical intention.[54] The reviewers were generally troubled by the violent ending and complained that the author had not prepared for it in terms of the mood of his story. The *New Yorker*'s brief mention was: "It's all wonderful, except for the odd, violent ending, which is where the contrariness comes in, and with which we will not quarrel, because, of course, it could easily have happened like that, and perhaps it did." If this notice was intended as a conciliatory gesture, it did not succeed.

Elizabeth Janeway's Sunday *Times Book Review* (11 November 1951) response to *Farmers Hotel* complained that O'Hara failed to prepare the reader for the violent end: "O'Hara has not been able to turn coincidence into Fate." John Steinbeck was angered by this review and wrote to O'Hara on 26 November: "Have you found too that the same people who kicked the hell out of 'Appointment' when it came out—now want you to write it over and over?"*

The Farmers Hotel required only two Random House printings in 1951. Although the 1952 Bantam paperback edition did not sell well, there was a delayed reaction when it was reissued in 1957, for it required eighteen Bantam printings by 1970. The paperback ran into censorship problems because Joe Rogg used the word *fuck*, causing it to be banned in Detroit.

The play version of *The Farmers Hotel* was performed on television in January 1952 on *Robert Montgomery Presents* with Thomas Mitchell as innkeeper Ira Studebaker, and by the Actors Studio Workshop in 1954. In July 1954 Cheryl Crawford produced a one-week tryout at the Cecilwood Theatre in Fishkill, New York. This summer stock production featured Fred Stewart as Ira Studebaker; he also directed it and had staged the Actors Studio performance. Although the play was well received by the Cecilwood audiences, a Broadway production did not result—partly because of O'Hara's resistance to rewriting. His position was that since the theater people could not guarantee that their tamperings would make the play a hit, he would

---

* Steinbeck also wrote a letter of protest to the *Times*, which was printed on 2 December.

stick with what he had written. In the case of *The Farmers Hotel* he was particularly concerned about tampering with his allegory.

The Farmers Hotel was dedicated to Philip Barry, who had died in 1949. Their friendship had survived Barry's shocked response to *Appointment in Samarra* and grew stronger. Even though O'Hara was impressed by Barry and proud of his friendship, their relationship had been tested when O'Hara asked Barry to put him up for the Century Association in New York. Barry explained that he was reluctant to act because O'Hara would probably be blackballed, in which case O'Hara would expect him to resign—and Barry did not want to resign. O'Hara persevered, and Barry proposed him for membership. As anticipated, somebody gave O'Hara "the cough drop." When Barry failed to resign from the Century in protest, O'Hara refused to speak to him for a time. (O'Hara subsequently achieved membership in 1955.) O'Hara was gratified when he was designated an honorary pall-bearer for Barry (with Robert A. Lovett, Dr. Dana Atchley, Gerald Murphy, Lawrence Langner, Arthur Hopkins, Charles Addams, John P. Marquand, Artemus L. Gates, Robert E. Sherwood, Edgar Scott, William Lord, Harold Freedman and Lorenzo Semple). Barry left an unfinished play, *Second Threshold*, that O'Hara expected to see through production. After Ellen Barry, the widow, asked Robert E. Sherwood instead, O'Hara never spoke to her again.

O'HARA'S INTEREST in the theater had revived. There was a 1952 dramatic venture, *The Searching Sun*, which he wrote for the Princeton Theatre Intime and Community Players. He had been working on a novel when the local amateur groups asked him for a play. "I'd got 20,000 words on it a couple of times, but I wasn't satisfied with it. I'd done the opening ten times. Finally I decided to make it a play and try it out here."[55] Set on Long Island, *The Searching Sun* deals with a stage couple. The husband is having an affair with his wife's daughter by a previous marriage and promises to leave with her. But he breaks his promise when he is offered a good part opposite his wife. The girl commits suicide, and her stepfather-lover then kills himself too. The author intended to direct the play, but relinquished the job to John Capsis. O'Hara's brief stint as director gave him the opportunity to test his ideas about casting and rehearsals. Instead of having the actors study their lines alone, he had them read the play together. "Before long, by association I guess, they began to memorize the lines and pick up the cues automatically." Belle worked on the costumes.

The Searching Sun opened 7 May 1952 for a ten-day run at Princeton University's Murray Theatre. The Trenton *Times* headlined its review JOHN O'HARA'S PLAY DESTINED FOR BROADWAY; but *The Daily Princetonian*, the undergraduate paper, called it "an unbelievably poor piece of incompetent writing."[56] The play did not make it to Broadway.

John O'Hara's relationship with the theater was a long series of disappointments, apart from *Pal Joey*. He worked on at least sixteen plays between 1940 and 1970; although there were several announcements of impending Broadway productions, none of them made it. As well as it can be reconstructed, the thirty-year inventory is as follows:

Untitled tragedy about a country doctor ruined by drink, intended for Walter Huston (1940–41). Announced in *Times*. No surviving text.

Untitled musical set in Florida, intended for Rodgers & Hart (1941). Announced in *Times*. No surviving text.

Untitled musical about defense plant (1944–45). No surviving text.

Untitled play about atom bomb scientist (1946). No surviving text.

The Farmers Hotel (play version written in 1946–47). Summer stock tryout in 1954 at the Cecilwood Theatre in Fishkill, New York. Published as novel in 1951. Included in *Five Plays*.

Untitled musical about Toulouse-Lautrec, intended for Rodgers & Hammerstein (1949). Announced in *Times*. Possibly begun in 1946. No surviving text.

Untitled play based on Henry Luce (1950). Draft in O'Hara papers.

Dramatization of *Appointment in Samarra* (1952), to be produced by Alexander Cohen and Robert Joseph. Announced in *Times*. No surviving text.

The Searching Sun (1952). Amateur production in Princeton 1952. Included in *Five Plays*.

Untitled musical intended for Robert Alton and Elia Kazan (1953). Announced in *Times*. No surviving text.

Untitled tragedy, intended for Ethel Barrymore (c.1953–54). No surviving text.

The Sisters (1954–55). Also titled *You Are My Sister*. Announced in *Times* for 1955 production by Robert Aldrich and Richard Myers. Draft in O'Hara papers. Published as novel *Elizabeth Appleton*.

The Way It Was (1957). Musical intended for Irving Berlin. Included in *Five Plays*.

Far from Heaven (*Far from Heaven and Thee*) (1962–63). Tragedy about New York politician, intended for Jackie Gleason. Final draft in O'Hara papers. Later considers rewriting as a musical.

Untitled play about husband-and-wife publishing team (1963). Announced in *Times*: "Spanning the last twenty-five years, the drama follows the progress of the publishing house and the individuals involved." Possibly related to untitled story posthumously published in *Good Samaritan* as "Harrington and Whitehill." No surviving text.

Veronique. Included in *Five Plays*.

The Champagne Pool. Included in *Five Plays*.

Untitled comedy (1967). "Just to have a play on in London before I die." No surviving text.[57]

Apart from John O'Hara's disinclination to submit to doctoring, his plays failed to make it to Broadway because most of them are not real plays. They are dramatized novels or dialogue for novels. Surprisingly, his talent for writing dialogue did not guarantee the success of his plays or movie scripts. O'Hara's genius was essentially novelistic, and much of his achievement depends on the kinds of background and detail which are not transferable to the stage. He seems to have reluctantly recognized his deficiencies as a playwright, for in the later years he wrote plays with little hope of production: to take his mind off the critical reception of his latest novel, he said. O'Hara's own taste in drama is shown by a list of his favorite plays he provided *Theatre Arts* in 1957: *Pal Joey, Holiday, Chee-Chee, The Petrified Forest, Journey's End, Street Scene, Serena Blandish, Our Town* and *Of Thee I Sing*.[58]

Pal Joey was twice a success. The original production ran for 374 performances in 1940–41. In January 1952 a revival opened at the Broadhurst Theatre and enjoyed a run of 540 performances, the longest Broadway run a musical revival has had. Produced by Jule Styne,

Leonard Key and Anthony B. Farrell, it starred Harold Lang as Joey and returned Vivienne Segal as Vera Simpson. The reviews could hardly have been better. Even Brooks Atkinson of the *Times*, who had used the word "scabrous" in 1940, joined the show's admirers. *Time* went so far as to declare that *"Pal Joey* is a twentieth-century *Beggar's Opera*, which may conceivably be revived when *South Pacific* and the lost Atlantis are one." John Lardner pointed out in his *Look* column that the original *Joey* had probably prepared the way for *Guys and Dolls*, and that the success of *Guys and Dolls* had probably helped the revival of *Pal Joey*.*

O'Hara was particularly pleased by the awards *Joey* received—the first his work had ever won. It was designated best musical by the New York Drama Critics' Circle and the Donaldson Award Committee. In addition, *Joey* received Donaldson Awards for best actress (Vivienne Segal), best direction (David Alexander), best supporting actress (Helen Gallagher), best dancer (Harold Lang), best book, best score, best lyrics, best dance direction (Robert Alton), best scenic designs (Oliver Smith) and best costume design (Miles White). Altogether *Joey* won eleven out of sixteen musical categories, a record to that time. Gold keys and scrolls were presented to the Donaldson winners. O'Hara framed his scroll and wore the key on his watch chain.

Joey went on to become one of the standards of the musical theater, with a laundered London production in 1954, road companies, and New York re-revivals in 1961 and 1963—as well as summer stock. In 1957 a film version starring Frank Sinatra, Rita Hayworth and Kim Novak was made by Columbia.

IN THE SUMMER of 1952 Mary Leigh Pell, the daughter of Quogue friends of Belle's family, joined the O'Haras as a live-in baby-sitter for Wylie. Lili Pell (now Mrs. Robert F. Whitmer, III) returned for the summer of 1953. She and Wylie became very close, and Lili's name for her charge was "The Play Queen," in recognition of the child's regal ways. Mrs. Whitmer's description of the O'Hara domestic situation is that Belle built separate compartments around her daughter and husband. Neither was neglected, but they didn't intrude on the attention each received from Belle.[59] As a result, Wylie and her father were probably faintly intimidated by each other. O'Hara was a devoted father, but he worked all the time—even during summers at

* Random House published the libretto and lyrics for the show in August 1953.

Quogue. He was still drinking, but he and Belle were careful to prevent Wylie from seeing him drunk. As might be expected of a writer-father, O'Hara made up stories for Wylie—in particular, a continuing saga about a maiden lady and her friends and animals in Kenya. These stories were suspended when the Mau Mau troubles destroyed Wylie's belief in the material, which her father saw as confirmation of his theories about literary realism. He also wrote and illustrated poems for her.[60]

O'Hara was unwilling to vote for either Eisenhower or Stevenson in 1952, but he turned Republican to vote for Eisenhower in 1956—partly as an expression of his dislike for Stevenson. He did not, however, undergo a conversion to the far right. O'Hara regarded Joseph McCarthy with contempt. When he attended the Army-McCarthy hearings in Washington, McCarthy noticed O'Hara chatting with Senator W. Stuart Symington and found out who he was. McCarthy made a point of speaking to O'Hara, who was then writing his *Collier's* column. O'Hara laughed at him. A similar experience had occurred in 1934 when he saw Huey Long walk through Washington's New Willard hotel accompanied by his bodyguards. The tableau was so much like a gangster movie that O'Hara burst out laughing, which caused one of the gunmen to come over to O'Hara and behave menacingly until Long called him off. "Long knew exactly why I was laughing. McCarthy would never have known. Huey Long had the makings of a major villain; McCarthy was only the liberals' nightmare."[61] Nonetheless in 1954 O'Hara took McCarthy seriously enough to plan a project "to put McCarthy in his place."[62]

On 15 December 1952 O'Hara delivered a "Welcome to the New Citizens" for the naturalization ceremony in Wilmington, Delaware, at the invitation of Judge Paul Leahy, an old friend. A patriotic man who later kept an American flag in his study, O'Hara spoke about his own family's mixed origins and recalled the melting pot of The Region, where the announcements and Holy Gospel at Roman Catholic services were read in English, German, Polish and Lithuanian: "One faith, four languages, but no confusion of tongues, and Americans all."[63]

The publication of *A Rage to Live* and the revival of *Pay Joey* renewed interest in O'Hara's earlier work. The Modern Library added *Butterfield 8* and *Appointment in Samarra* in 1953, the latter "With a New Foreword by the Author." A side effect was that *Appointment* became an attractive theatrical property. Several producers tried to acquire the stage rights, and Jack Skirball of Gold Seal Productions bought the movie rights for $55,000 plus 5 percent of the profits. Gold Seal had an oral agreement with RKO, which was canceled when

Gold Seal was unable to deliver Gregory Peck as Julian English. The movie rights reverted to the author. In May 1953 *Appointment* was adapted for television on *Robert Montgomery Presents*—which had already done *The Farmers Hotel*—directed by O'Hara's friend Herbert Bayard Swope, Jr. Although the production staff worried about possible difficulties with the O'Hara temper, there were none. He liked Irving Gaynor Neiman's script and encouraged him to depart from the novel. With considerable trepidation, Swope invited O'Hara to the final run-through. When it was over, Swope heard a noise "like a car motor running" coming from John O'Hara, who was crying and unable to speak. In the euphoric glow of the occasion Swope was granted stage rights to *Appointment*, but O'Hara subsequently changed his mind. The live television production received excellent notices; and Montgomery's performance as Julian English and Margaret Hayes' as Caroline were praised. In December of 1953 Robert Montgomery tried to obtain the stage rights for himself, and the discussions resulted in a permanent estrangement between O'Hara and Montgomery. One of the symptomatic difficulties between them involved Montgomery's telephone manners: his secretary would call O'Hara and then put Montgomery through. This custom always annoyed O'Hara, no matter who did it, and he had made a point of breaking Bennett Cerf of the habit. During the Fifties there were rumors that O'Hara would himself adapt *Appointment* into a play, but the project does not seem to have progressed beyond the planning stage. By 1959 he was in the position to set the nonnegotiable price of $1,000,000 on movie rights for *Appointment*. Paul Newman was prepared to meet this figure on a participation basis—part front money and the rest as a share of the profits; but O'Hara insisted on a flat million. He was in a perfect position to hold out by then: he didn't need the money, and in any case he was in an 80 percent tax bracket. He liked the idea of being the first author to demand a cool million for a single property.

ON 20 AUGUST 1953 John O'Hara came in to New York from Quogue on his way to attend a Little League banquet in Williamsport, Pennsylvania. It later turned out that he had the wrong date. He felt ill and decided to return to Quogue, but became so sick in the cab on the way to Pennsylvania Station that he went to his mother-in-law's apartment on East 63rd Street instead. No one was there, and O'Hara began vomiting heavily. Winnie Gardiner, Belle's sister, happened to drop in after dinner and found him lying on the bathroom floor. She called a doctor, who took O'Hara's tie to his office to analyze the vomit

stains. The doctor found blood and had O'Hara taken to Harkness
Pavilion by ambulance. An ulcer had penetrated his stomach wall.*
Late that night Lili Pell returned to the Quogue cottage and found
Belle distraught but planning to drive to the city. She persuaded Belle
to wait until morning. O'Hara required blood transfusions and was
in the hospital for a week; Belle remained there with him. James
Thurber was also there with his wife, who was undergoing eye
surgery, and the two men amused themselves by exchanging notes.

His doctors gave O'Hara notice that continued drinking would
certainly kill him, and he went on the wagon—at least for a year, he
thought. He spent September recuperating at Quogue. Without alcohol,
O'Hara felt a need to keep busy. *The New Yorker* was closed to him

O'Hara at Quogue.

* Shortly before this hemorrhage O'Hara had suddenly experienced great
fear while flying in a small plane between Fisher's Island and Martha's Vineyard.
He subsequently regarded that feeling as a premonition of death.

by his own decision, and he still felt that he couldn't write short stories for other magazines, so he returned to column work and signed with the Trenton *Sunday Times-Advertiser* for a weekly book column, "Sweet and Sour." In the first column, which appeared 27 December 1953, he made it clear that he would take an open-ended position on his subject and would not write book reviews as such. Most of the twenty-seven columns have nothing to do with books, although they are sprinkled with references to writers. The best columns are auto-biographical—for example, a loving recollection of Grandfather Delaney's store occasioned by "a book called *Country Store,* by Gerald Somebody," which O'Hara admitted he had not read. O'Hara could be embarrassing to read when he dealt with his own stature and his treatment by the literary establishment. In the March 1954 "Sweet and Sour" column he complained about Yale's neglect of him and revealed inside information about the election procedures of the National Institute of Arts and Letters: "I'm not supposed to know this, but I have been put up by Philip Barry, Deems Taylor, Chauncey Brewster Tinker, Struthers Burt, William McFee and Louis Unter-meyer." O'Hara was right in feeling excluded, but a column in the Trenton *Times-Advertiser* was not the right place to protest. For a painfully sensitive man, he sometimes displayed little sensitivity about his public statements. The worst part of this response was that it let his enemies see that they had succeeded in injuring him.

"Sweet and Sour" is a valuable reference for O'Hara scholars because it provides facts about his career that exist nowhere else. On 30 May 1954 he listed the publications he had written for, among which were *Carnival, For Men, The Strand, Today—in New York,* the Brooklyn *Daily Eagle, The Hampton Chronicle* and *The Fire Islander.** The final column explained:

. . . all but two were written during the time of the greatest tragedy that has happened in my life, really the only tragedy. Nobody can survive two tragedies. Of that I shall say no more, but I reluctantly admit that much because the pieces have been generally in a frivolous tone and I want the young to realize that writing is, among other things, an act, like a vaudeville act. If you are a pro, you keep going. If you are not a pro, you get the hell out. For that reason, I am grateful for this job. I could not have worked on a novel or a play, but these essays—and that's what they are, even though you may be ac-

---

* *Carnival* and *Today—in New York* (distributed by hotels) have not been located. No O'Hara short story has been identified in *The Strand*; and his "article on the martini cocktail" has not been found in *For Men.*

customed to Addison—were just the right kind of work to have to do.

The column closed with O'Hara's projection of his future work. He had at that time three plays in the hands of producers and intended to keep writing plays until he had three hits. Then he would try for three successful television scripts. After his novel in progress was published in 1955, he planned to return to his narrative poem; then he wanted to try to obtain a commission to write the libretto for an original American opera. He did continue writing plays, but the television, poem and opera projects were dropped. The columns appeared for six months and were published as a volume by Random House in October 1954, dedicated to Belle's sister Winifred. Sales of *Sweet and Sour* were poor, and the first printing was eventually remaindered.

Pet died in October 1953, still using the name Helen O'Hara. After her divorce she had tried magazine work and had operated her own perfume manufacturing company. During the war she had served with the Red Cross in England and France. O'Hara was saddened by her death, for there had been no bitter feelings after the marriage ended. He wanted to attend the funeral, but decided not to because of the possibility of a scene with Mrs. Petit.*

During 1953 O'Hara considered an unlikely project, a history of the Street and Smith publishing company for its one-hundredth anniversary. He was interested in the impact of pulp fiction—especially the Alger books—on the American mind. Gerald Smith, the son of one of the founders, was a Princeton resident and knew O'Hara. Smith and Arthur P. Lawler, vice-president of Street and Smith, met several times with him to discuss their plans for the volume. They were unable to get a commitment from O'Hara, and the assignment was given to his former roommate, Quentin Reynolds. Still in need of busy-work while he was off the bottle, O'Hara signed with *Collier's* for a second column, "Appointment with O'Hara," which began in 1954.

BELLE FREQUENTLY CAME to Kate Bramwell's to rest on her couch during the fall of 1953, for she was not well. She tired easily; her color was bad; she experienced shortness of breath and occasional dizziness. Her body was retaining fluids, and she seemed bloated. Belle kept this from John as much as possible. One afternoon she told Kate of

---

* In 1954 Pet's uncle, David Mahood, donated $500,000 to Wellesley for the Helen Ritchie Petit Library.

her concern at the news that Katharine ("Sister") and Joe Bryan had separated: "Sister needs somebody to take care of."

On 12 December 1953 O'Hara made a sentimental trip to Pottsville. The *Journal* had folded in September after 128 years, and the former employees held a reunion banquet. It was a satisfying occasion. O'Hara, who was accompanied by Belle, was the principal speaker. He enjoyed seeing Walter Farquhar and Kit Bowman again, and was photographed with David Yocum—who had fired him twice in 1927.

On New Year's Eve the O'Haras were invited to dinner by the Oppenheimers. Although she felt weak in the driveway, Belle insisted on going in, but they left early. The next day John and Belle attended the annual party given by Mrs. Edgar Palmer. When they arrived Belle was dismayed to find that the ladies' coatroom was upstairs, for she didn't feel strong enough to climb stairs. She mentioned her distress to Kate Bramwell, who told her to tell John; but Belle didn't want to worry him. The next day she went to Princeton Hospital for observation. O'Hara didn't know how sick Belle was, but she probably realized she was dying. On the evening of 9 January 1954 O'Hara answered the phone and was told that Belle had just died of acute auricular fibrillation. He went into another room to tell his eight-year-old daughter— who had already sensed that her mother was dead. When Wylie said she wouldn't be able to go on living, he replied, "We'll have to." He was stunned but determined to control himself for Wylie's sake. He did not fall apart. Although a doctor prescribed whiskey that night, he didn't take a drink. Symbolically, he poured a bottle of whiskey into the kitchen sink. John O'Hara didn't take a drink for the rest of his life.

Belle Mulford Wylie O'Hara died at forty-one. Six years later her husband wrote her obituary: ". . . I met a fine girl, and in December of that year we were married and we stayed married for sixteen years, until she died. As the Irish would say, she died on me, and it was the only unkind thing she ever did to anyone."[64]

V

Sister

BELLE WYLIE O'HARA'S funeral was attended by 700 people. After the burial service in Quogue, Kate Bramwell said, "John, I know you and Wylie are going to be all right. I feel Belle wrapped a cocoon around both of you until she felt you could do it on your own. She got the show on the road—and then she left." He nodded, thinking about it. But the days after Belle's death were terrible for O'Hara, who grieved as emotional people grieve. He talked of suicide. His life, which had fallen apart without Belle, had to be reconstructed on a day-by-day basis. Friends were kind. At least two, Hamilton Cottier and Barklie Henry, were concerned that he might be short of cash and offered him loans. O'Hara didn't need money, but he was deeply grateful. Belle's family offered to raise Wylie, but he did not want to give her up. Lili Pell left Smith College to become her companion.

As a father—particularly after Belle died—O'Hara was concerned about teaching Wylie his code of personal conduct, built around values that he had grown up with: honesty, duty, respect for elders, the rewards of work. Although he had resisted some of these values in his own youth, he affirmed them in his maturity. He always kept his word to Wylie and once instructed Lili, "Never break a promise to a child." He shared in Wylie's successes and was delighted when she won a prize at Miss Fine's school for a Halloween costume in which she was inside a book entitled *Screech and Glower*. He was carefully proper in Wylie's presence and watched his language. The use of the word "snot" in a Scrabble game with eight-year-old Wylie brought Lili a look of rebuke from O'Hara.

O'Hara was fortunate to have deadlines to meet, for these jobs helped him to organize his life. In addition to the weekly Trenton *Times-Advertiser* column, "Sweet and Sour," he was writing "Appointment with O'Hara," which appeared in *Collier's* biweekly between 5 February 1954 and 28 September 1956. Devoted to the entertainment world, this column usually consisted of short items—most of them about television. O'Hara always was at his best when reminiscing about The Region, as in the column about Christmas in Pottsville. "Appointment with O'Hara" was terminated after sixty-eight appearances (at a reported $1,000 per column) when O'Hara refused to excise comments he had written about a plane crash.[1] The *Collier's* columns were not collected in book form.

O'Hara sometimes phoned his mother a couple of times a day. She grieved for his grief, and talking with her helped him to get through some bad days. His greatest support during that bad time was Pat Outerbridge. In him O'Hara found a perfect companion, for Outerbridge was also on the wagon. John would call him late at night and Pat would come to keep him company—sometimes talking and sometimes sitting in silence. They also took drives all over the Princeton area. The parallel with Arthur McHenry and Joe Chapin in *Ten North Frederick* is obvious, with the big difference that O'Hara was not drinking himself to death. He was learning to live without Belle. O'Hara acknowledged his affection for and gratitude to Pat Outerbridge in several public ways. When Outerbridge was intimidated by the prospect of writing his autobiography for his 1954 Harvard twenty-fifth reunion report, O'Hara wrote it for him.[2] A colliery in *A Family Party* and *Ourselves to Know* is named Outerbridge; and *Elizabeth Appleton* is dedicated to him. O'Hara bought stock in Outerbridge's Homasote Co., which he left to Pat in his will.

Other friends offered to fix him up with women, but O'Hara wasn't interested in having an affair. In the summer of 1954 he took Katharine Barnes Bryan to dinner in New York and began seeing her steadily. O'Hara liked to remember that when he had arrived at Princeton's Trinity Church for Belle's funeral, she was the first person he had seen as he got out of the limousine. They were married 31 January 1955, on his fiftieth birthday. The marriage was not a case of a widower with a child remarrying in desperation. O'Hara had fallen in love again, with a woman who loved him. Despite his unbuttoned bachelor days, he was a monogamous man who wanted the order of marriage. A grudging tribute from people who didn't like John O'Hara was that he must have been nicer than he seemed because he had two good marriages with wonderful women.

Katharine Barnes Bryan—called "Sister" by her friends—was divorced from Joseph Bryan, III, in December 1954. The daughter of Mr. and Mrs. Courtland Dixon Barnes of New York and Manhasset and the grandniece of W. C. Whitney, she had married Bryan in 1930, and at the time of her marriage to O'Hara had three children away at school: St. George, Joan and Courtland. A beautiful woman—with what used to be called aristocratic features—Sister had remarkable personal qualities: warmth of character, a tough mind, a great capacity for loyalty, a direct style of speech, a cocky walk and a quick laugh. She possessed the charm of being really interested in people, and the wisdom that made them value that interest. She loved laughter, and, as Kate Bramwell remarked, O'Hara could always make her laugh. Sister responded to his humor, which often depended on heavy irony. During their engagement Sister and John were invited by the Cerfs to attend Frank Sinatra's opening at the Copacabana, with William Faulkner and Jean Stein. Faulkner was obviously uncomfortable in the night club; moreover, the Cerfs' table was in a spot where the chorus girls—bigger than Faulkner—were bumping him as they came on and off the stage. Sister whispered to John that he ought to change places with Faulkner, and O'Hara replied that she was trying to get him killed before they were even married.

O'Hara told William Maxwell that Faulkner regarded a woman as "somewhere between a donkey and a princess. 'Best day's wuck *yew* evah did,' he said to me about my marrying Sister. I never considered that work."[3] John and Sister were married at her apartment on East 74th Street in the presence of her mother and two sons and John's mother and Wylie. Kathleen Fuldner, O'Hara's sister, visited their mother at the University Place apartment on the day of the marriage and remembers that he sat silently for hours, as though waiting for his mother to tell him something.

Joe Bryan sent a congratulatory telegram to Sister signed FRYING PAN. Bennett Cerf asked O'Hara what he wanted for a wedding present, and the groom stipulated a complete set of the Modern Library. Sister moved into the house at 20 College Road West and energetically set the place to rights. Her furniture arrived from New York with Lydia Tam, who had been the maid for O'Hara and Belle, and a general reorganization was accomplished. Wylie was put on a schedule, and she seemed rather to like it. When Wylie became recalcitrant about piano practice, Sister took lessons to keep her company. In 1956 John O'Hara was named Literary Father of the Year by the National Father's Day Committee, an honor he at first wanted to decline, but Wylie was so disappointed that he decided to accept the medal. He made a short speech in which he paid grateful tribute to Sister. Indeed, Sister was such a success as a stepmother that the relationship was subsequently formalized by adoption.

Like Belle, Sister accommodated herself to John's nocturnal working habits. He went to his study after late television and worked the rest of the night, retiring around dawn to sleep until joining Sister for

Katharine Barnes O'Hara (Sister) with John.

his breakfast and her lunch. The afternoons were devoted to television during the baseball season—which Wylie liked and Sister didn't. Father and daughter were staunch Yankee fans.* When there was no baseball,

* When Yogi Berra hit his 300th major-league home run in August 1959, O'Hara wrote to Wylie at the Ralston Creek Ranch to tell her that he had sent the catcher an inscribed copy of *A Family Party*: "To Lawrence 'Yogi' Berra—on all occasions, but specifically on the occasion of his 300th home run —in admiration."

the O'Haras played Scrabble, over which they waged elaborate arguments. John was a slow player, and Sister did needlework while he was deliberating. He napped before dinner, which was followed by television. He became a mild television addict—*Gunsmoke* was a particular favorite—and traveled with a portable set. He was at his best when he could provide a running commentary on an old movie, such as why one actress was never photographed below the knees (because she had fat ankles). It was a special occasion when *The General Died at Dawn* was on, for O'Hara never tired of seeing his bit part. Sister shared his liking for Quogue, and they golfed together until his back trouble made him give up the game.

The cottage at Quogue was in fact a cottage—an unpretentious beach structure on the dunes overlooking Moriches Bay. O'Hara wrote every day, and worked in the living room. When father and daughter were watching a televised Yankee game, Sister usually fled the premises. So far as O'Hara was concerned, the ocean was for the view only, because he did not know how to swim. He was an indoors man after he quit tennis and golf, but at Sister's urging he would go out and sun himself on the patio. He was not convivial, and some guests were dismayed to discover that little alcohol was provided.

Katharine Delaney O'Hara had been on excellent terms with Belle, and she got along very well with Sister, who enjoyed her humor. In addition to regular visits they were in frequent touch by phone, and once when Sister began a call with "This is Sister" the senior Mrs. O'Hara replied, "This is Mother Superior"—which delighted the Princeton O'Haras.

O'Hara was a demonstrative husband and would give Sister great hugs. Princeton friends were impressed by the open affection they displayed. The O'Haras greatly amused each other, and they shared an enjoyment of the ridiculous. When their Quogue house was broken into, they went to check the place with a policeman and were delayed by the search for Sister's glasses, which were found on top of her head. O'Hara directed the policeman to "Shoot her!"—much to Sister's amusement.

Sister disappointed some people by making a great success of her marriage to the terrible-tempered John O'Hara. With his third marriage O'Hara commenced his major period, publishing eighteen volumes between 1955 and 1970—including *Ten North Frederick, From the Terrace* and *Ourselves to Know*. This period of productivity, unsurpassed in American literature, is even more impressive in view of the fact that it began when O'Hara was fifty. There were a number of reasons for his great achievement, but it is impossible to overrate the effect of O'Hara's tranquillity with Sister and her dedication to his work. Sister, like Belle, structured her life around his work.

IN MAY 1955 O'Hara made his second public appearance at Yale, as the Bergen lecturer.* Speaking before an audience of 200 on "Yale Blue Shoe," he delivered a "plea to each undergraduate not to conform," stating that there was much more conformity in the Fifties than at earlier times. He received a $200 honorarium for this lecture, and a framed photostat of the check went on his study wall.[4] The issue of conformity came to occupy an increasingly large part in O'Hara's thinking, particularly after he converted to the Republican party and experienced reprisals from the liberal establishment. He felt that his books were being reviewed as reactionary documents, rather than as works of literature.

In the spring of 1955 John and Sister went to California where he had a deal with Twentieth Century-Fox to write an original screenplay based on the DeSylva, Brown and Henderson songwriting team for $25,000. They rented a house in Pacific Palisades where O'Hara did his movie work by day and completed *Ten North Frederick* at night, as well as writing his *Collier's* column. It was hard work but the movie assignment was a congenial chore, for O'Hara knew a great deal about show music. Although his work was doctored by two other writers, William Bowers and Phoebe Ephron, when *The Best Things in Life Are Free* was released in 1956 O'Hara's name went above the title, providing a gauge of Hollywood's view of his eminence.† The movie —with Dan Dailey, Ernest Borgnine, and Gordon McRae—was very successful, and Fox offered O'Hara $75,000 to stay on in Hollywood. But he didn't like living in California, and he wanted to do his real work. H. N. (Swanie) Swanson, his Hollywood agent, later worked out a deal with Fox whereby O'Hara would write three scripts in Princeton for $75,000 each. One of the three was an adaptation of Frank O'Rourke's Western novel, *The Bravados*. He approached this assignment with enthusiasm because he liked Westerns and had ideas about frontier life based on the early days of Pottsville. Moreover, he would be working for people he liked. Herbert Bayard Swope, Jr., the producer, had directed the television adaptation of *Appointment in*

---

* O'Hara also went to Pottsville in 1955 to act as a pallbearer for Ransloe Boone, one of the members of the Purity League.

† O'Hara was sufficiently proud of this movie to submit to a taped radio interview for *Monitor* when it was released.

Samarra that so pleased O'Hara; and the production supervisor, David Brown, was an old Hollywood friend. O'Hara wrote the script in September and October 1956, revising it in January 1957. Fox delicately rejected O'Hara's script because it was not considered sufficiently dramatic—there were not enough memorable scenes. Surprisingly, the studio executives regarded the O'Hara dialogue as too static and not suitable for filming. The matter was handled in such a way that there were no hard feelings, and O'Hara remained friendly with Swope and Brown. The film was eventually produced from a new script by Philip Yordan, and O'Hara did not receive a screen credit. The rest of the Fox contract required two originals. One, *The Man Who Could Not Lose*, was delivered in 1957; but the second, *The Matadors*, was never completed. *The Man Who Could Not Lose*—never produced—is a scenario for an O'Hara novel, tracing the career of a crooked financier in the Twenties who flees America and successively becomes an adviser to Mussolini, Hitler and Stalin.[5]

When *Ten North Frederick* was ready, O'Hara refused to work with Commins and told Cerf that he wanted to work directly with him. Cerf persuaded him that he would have to work with an editor because Cerf's other responsibilities would prevent him from giving O'Hara proper attention. Cerf called in Hiram Haydn and Albert Erskine and said that one of them would have to take it on. Haydn begged off, so Erskine was assigned to edit John O'Hara. Erskine was at first worried by the assignment because of the reports he had heard from Commins. As a matter of principle, O'Hara felt obliged to be strict with editors, but there were no blowups with Erskine. The author-editor relationship grew into a very comfortable one over sixteen years, and O'Hara would dedicate the last book published in his lifetime to Albert Erskine.

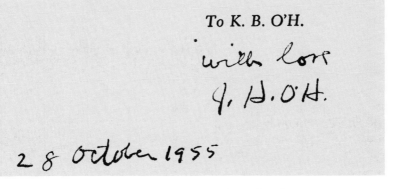

To K. B. O'H.

with love

J. H. O'H.

28 October 1955

Dedication copy, *Ten North Frederick.*

Ten North Frederick*—dedicated "To K.B.O'H."—was published on Thanksgiving Day 1955. O'Hara wanted a day on which Charles Poore would review it in the *Times*; and a Thursday in late November was selected, which happened to be Thanksgiving. O'Hara and his public came to regard it as his day, for thereafter he published eleven books on Thanksgiving. *Ten North Frederick* was his greatest critical and popular success, appearing on the best-seller lists for thirty-two weeks and selling 65,703 copies in its first two weeks.† Moreover, with this novel John O'Hara began to be accorded recognition—though with many abstentions—as a major writer. His hard-boiled wise-guy image metamorphosed into the figure of a testy senior literary citizen. The reviews of *Ten North Frederick* were excellent, but even the most favorably disposed critics found it necessary to defend the novel's sexual frankness, as did Charles Poore in the *Times* and St. Clair McKelway in *The New Yorker*. McKelway was an old friend, and it is difficult to avoid regarding his review as a peace-feeler from the magazine. It was the best review he ever received from *The New Yorker*; McKelway stated that O'Hara's "direct and masculine" treatment of sex set him "apart from, and perhaps even above" Hemingway, Faulkner and Fitzgerald. Even though Ross had died in 1951, O'Hara was not ready to come back to the magazine. He had novels planned and had temporarily lost interest in the short story.

Ten North Frederick‡ was the second Gibbsville novel and came twenty-one years after *Appointment*—a significant fact in view of the popular misapprehension that most of O'Hara's work dealt with Gibbsville.§ The novel is a product of an additional twenty years' brooding over Pottsville/Gibbsville and fills in the picture sketched earlier in *Appointment* and "The Doctor's Son." Nevertheless, it is not a sequel, although Dr. English and Julian appear as minor characters. O'Hara rejected the sequels and continuations that many productive novelists rely on.

---

* The rejected titles for *Ten North Frederick* were *And Not a Stone* (Pope, "Ode on Solitude"), *Thus March We* (Raleigh, "What Is Our Life") and *One Lonely Way* (Landor, "Various the Roads of Life").

† Bennett Cerf's commemorative token was engraved: FOR JOHN O'HARA FROM HIS PROUD PUBLISHERS AND SUPPLIER OF CIGARETTE BOXES/RANDOM HOUSE OCCASION: SALE OF 100000TH COPY OF "TEN NORTH FREDERICK"/LONG MAY HE SLAVE!

‡ Gibbsville's North Frederick Street corresponds to Pottsville's North George Street, a once-fashionable enclave across the tracks from Mahantongo/Lantenengo Street.

§ Four of the novels are set in The Region: *Appointment in Samarra* and *Ten North Frederick* (Gibbsville), *Ourselves to Know* (Lyons), *The Lockwood Concern* (Swedish Haven); *A Rage to Live* is set in the Harrisburg area, out of The Region.

Joseph B. Chapin, the Gibbsville aristocrat who nurtured a secret desire to be President of the United States, provides an excellent example of the O'Hara method of creating character. Paradoxically, the psychological source for Joe Chapin was Franklin Delano Roosevelt, whom Chapin detested. Once this identification is made, the connections are obvious: both were only sons groomed for success by strong mothers; both were handsome men married to plain women; both were crippled in early middle age (although Joe Chapin recovered). In a way, the novel is a what-if study: what if Roosevelt had been a Gibbsville Republican? *Ten North Frederick* can also be seen as a confirmation of O'Hara's own ambitions: just as Joe Chapin at age fifty decided to seek the Presidency, so did John O'Hara at fifty commence his quest for the highest literary stature. Had his 1953 ulcer hemorrhage been fatal, O'Hara's position in the first rank of American literature would have been shaky. Thoughts of failure and death drove him during the last fifteen years of his life, as he wrote his most ambitious novels (except *A Rage to Live*) and all of his long stories (except "The Doctor's Son"). During this period O'Hara expanded the scope and refined the technique of his work as he set about getting it all down against the big deadline.

John O'Hara's structural sense is one of his underrated strengths as a novelist. A favorite technique was to open a novel with a detailed study of a social ritual—the picnic in *A Rage to Live*, for example—and then go back to the beginning of the story and show how the characters introduced in the opening fit into the whole history. Inextricably connected with the structural plan is the increasingly complex treatment of point of view in the later novels. The funeral of Joe Chapin reveals a great deal about O'Hara's mastery of the techniques of fiction. Much of the service is reported through the impressions of Peg and Monica Slattery, who have special angles of vision—the Irish politician's wife and daughter who are outsiders yet possess inside information. It is all information that would have been presented less effectively by an omniscient authorial voice.

One of the themes of *Ten North Frederick* is the futility and private misery of life, even on the best levels of society. Joe Chapin is a failure in almost every way that matters and dies a virtual suicide. The O'Hara view of the privileged class was never simple, although some opaque critics persistently regarded him as an incurable admirer of the rich. Chapin is destroyed by his class loyalties, by his inability to violate the rules he has always lived by. Nonetheless, he demonstrates a certain grace and despairing courage. "Class tells," as Mike Slattery grudgingly admits. If, as the O'Hara canon implies, we are all doomed to disappointment and loneliness, the rich—some of them—have the capacity to live their tragedies with style and class. After Chapin's funeral, Judge Lloyd Williams, a commoner who, the reader will learn, has cuckolded Joe, sums up what he has learned about life: "The safest way to live is first, inherit money. Second, marry a woman that will cooperate with you in your sexual peculiarities. Third, have a legitimate job that keeps you busy. Fourth, be born without a taste for liquor. Fifth, join some big church. Sixth, don't live too long." There are layers of irony in these rules, formulated by a self-made man from a mining patch, who has obtained a good political sinecure. Williams is barely tolerated by the best Gibbsville people, and doesn't care. He has achieved a *safe* life, with no extremes of happiness or misery—and is alive to enjoy it at the funeral of Joe Chapin. Ironically, Williams' rules for safety conform to the life of Chapin, who inherited money, had a sexually satisfactory marriage, was a successful lawyer and a good Episcopalian, and had no alcohol problem—until he deliberately began to drink himself to death.

The Williams rules provide useful insights into O'Hara's degree of adherence to naturalism or deterministic realism. The literary doctrine of naturalism—as illustrated by the work of Zola, Norris and Dreiser—holds that lives are determined by forces of environment and heredity over which people have little or no control. It is impossible to draw firm lines between hereditary and environmental influences, especially in O'Hara's world, but the ironic presentation of Williams' "safest way to live" and the chronicle of Chapin's career show that O'Hara was not an old-line determinist. There is another powerful force that operates in O'Hara's fictional world—call it luck. And the luck of his protagonists is bad. Mike Slattery and Lloyd Williams are safe, but Joe Chapin is a natural victim for bad luck or nemesis. His decent qualities, which the author obviously respects, make Chapin vulnerable.

So far the badges and prizes had been denied O'Hara—except for the *Pal Joey* revival—but in February 1956, *Ten North Frederick* received the National Book Award for fiction.[6] In his acceptance speech O'Hara reminded the literary establishment that their recognition was long overdue: ". . . since 1934 I have been publishing novels and books of short stories in which I told as honestly as I could what I have seen, heard, thought, and felt about a good many of the men and women who populate this country. . . . I have written so accurately and honestly that my overall contribution will have to be considered by future students of my time." What O'Hara called "the dynamite money" began to seem a strong possibility.

O'Hara with Senator John F. Kennedy and W. H. Auden, 1956 National
Book Awards ceremony.

At the press conference preceding the presentation ceremony,
John Cook Wyllie, book-review editor of the Richmond *News-Leader*,
asked about a letter in the *Times* pointing out that there was a North
Frederick Street address in *Ulysses*. O'Hara replied that he had seen
the letter and was interested in the coincidence, but that it was only a
coincidence because he had never finished *Ulysses*.[7] Senator John F.
Kennedy spoke at the NBA ceremony, and John O'Hara, now a
straight-ticket Republican, was photographed with his fellow-Celt, for
whom he would develop strong distrust.

One of the rare attentions that O'Hara received from Princeton
University was the invitation to present the first F. Scott Fitzgerald
Prize for Creative Writing at the annual dinner of *The Daily Princetonian*, on 6 January 1956. By this time O'Hara had reconciled himself to the University's indifference, but the nature of the prize made
it impossible for him to decline the invitation. In making the presentation, he commented on the appropriateness of the Fitzgerald Prize in
view of "Scott's active interest in young authors during his life time."[8]

Random House followed *Ten North Frederick* with *A Family Party*, a long short story that had appeared in *Collier's* on 2 March 1956. The story consisted entirely of one speech at the testimonial dinner for Dr. Samuel Merritt in Lyons, Pennsylvania, in which the speaker, an old friend, recounts the doctor's lifetime of service to the community, and refers to the taboo subject of his wife's insanity. *A Family Party* is O'Hara's first pilgrimage to Lykens, his mother's hometown, where he had good times with the Delaneys. It is also John O'Hara's tribute to his father and to Dr. O'Hara's profession. Lykens/Lyons would later provide the setting for *Ourselves to Know*. Technically, this work is a return to the monologue technique of many of the *New Yorker* stories. The open sentimentality of the story is controlled by the clumsy sincerity of the speaker. O'Hara's letter acknowledging Charles Poore's receptive review in the *Times* clearly reveals his pleasure in praise:

As you have heard me say, I used to write in the hope of appreciation by F.P.A., Dorothy Parker, Scott Fitzgerald, Sinclair Lewis. I would still hope for their approval if they were functioning now. But they're not, and I can tell by the number of times I say to myself, "Charley Poore will like this, Charley Poore will get this," that you have become—I almost said my literary conscience, but that would have been wrong. My professional conscience is no one but me. Instead of calling you my literary or professional conscience I'll put it another way: you, by which I mean your work as a critic, represent the difference between working and working-without-reward. I know how good I am. I know what I can do that no one else can do, because I see them try and I see them when they're not trying. But I cannot honestly accept the artistic article of faith that one writes for oneself alone. It's true to the extent that while writing it I write it my way, but when it's finished it is presented to be read, and that's where you come in.[9]

Although most reviewers were condescending, readers liked it. O'Hara received many fan letters, and the little book of sixty-five pages went through four Random House printings and an appearance in *Reader's Digest Condensed Books* before paperback publication. As befitted a sentimental work, *A Family Party* was published on 16 August (the anniversary of *Appointment* and *Rage*) and dedicated to O'Hara's aunt, Verna Delaney.

The success of *Ten North Frederick* capped by the National Book Award generated new interest in O'Hara's short stories. In 1956 Bantam published *The Great Short Stories of John O'Hara*, seventy stories from *The Doctor's Son* and *Files on Parade*, and the Modern

Library collected thirty-two stories as *Selected Short Stories of John O'Hara.* The background for this Modern Library volume is interesting. In November 1955 O'Hara selected the stories he regarded as his best and wrote a foreword which stated, in part:

> *Most of them were written in the twenty years from 1930 to 1950, during which I believe I wrote more short stories for* The New Yorker *than any other author. Aloofness is not one of my characteristics, so I cannot pretend that I have not been grievously hurt by the magazine, which in commenting on my stories was pleased to call me "the master" but in reviewing my novels was perfectly willing to make fun of me and even to distort what I said by the cheap trick of quoting out of context. The high principles that they peddle in Notes and Comment don't even last till the back of the book. Well, damn their eyes.*
>
> *I don't think I'll write any more short stories. In very recent years I have been made sharply aware of the passage of time and the preciousness of it, and there are so many big things I want to do. But during the Thirties and Forties these stories were part of me as I was part of those nights and days, when time was cheap and everlasting and one could say it all in 2,000 words.*[10]

The collection appeared with an introduction by Lionel Trilling. Whether the decision to drop the O'Hara introduction was made by the author or by Random House is not clear. It seems likely that the publisher regarded the comments on *The New Yorker* as spiteful and wanted to get Professor Trilling's impeccable imprimatur on the volume. His introduction is wholly respectful of O'Hara's gifts as a social observer, but it may misrepresent O'Hara's view of society. Trilling sees these stories as characterized by an "element of almost metaphysical fear" of society and a "delight in its comicality." His insistence on O'Hara's "love of the absurdity of society for its own sake" is inaccurate as applied to the major stories, although this description works for some of the *New Yorker* apprentice pieces—the

---

* These thirty-two stories constitute O'Hara's assessment of his first twenty years as a short-story writer up to the time he temporarily abandoned the form in 1949: "The Decision," "Everything Satisfactory," "The Moccasins," "Doctor and Mrs. Parsons," "Pardner," "A Phase of Life," "Walter T. Carriman," "Now We Know," "Too Young," "Summer's Day," "The King of the Desert," "Bread Alone," "Graven Image," "The Next-to-Last Dance of the Season," "Where's the Game?" "Mrs. Whitman," "Price's Always Open," "Are We Leaving Tomorrow?" "No Mistakes," "The Ideal Man," "Do You Like It Here?" "The Doctor's Son," "Hotel Kid," "The Public Career of Mr. Seymour Harrisburg," "In the Morning Sun," "War Aims," "Secret Meeting," "Other Women's Households," "Over the River and Through the Wood," "I Could Have Had a Yacht," "A Respectable Place."

Delphian sketches, for example. After O'Hara found his major themes in 1931, there is very little social comedy for its own sake in his stories.

Paperback rights to *Ten North Frederick* were sold to Bantam Books for $50,000 advance against a 4 percent royalty to 150,000 copies, 6 percent thereafter (to be shared equally with Random House), and the paperback went through more than thirty-five printings. In January 1957 Detroit Police Commissioner Edward Piggins banned the Bantam and Random House editions from sale as unfit for children and unsuccessfully attempted to have the novel removed from the Detroit public libraries.* Both Bantam and Random House vigorously fought the ban, and Bennett Cerf denounced Piggins before an audience of 3,000 at Michigan State University.† On 14 January 1957 O'Hara delivered a Whittal Lecture at the Library of Congress, and in passing commented on censorship without directly referring to the Detroit case. Although he conceded that organizations had the right to organize boycotts, he refused to "recognize the right of any organization to practice censorship at the source, which is, first of all, the author, and secondly, the publisher."

The Library of Congress lecture, "Remarks on the Novel," was one of three delivered by Irving Stone, Mackinlay Kantor and O'Hara. His lecture was a loose collection of observations on reviews, sales, the reading public and the material of fiction.[11] From Washington the O'Haras drove to Williamsburg, Virginia, where he was contacted by the press for a comment on the Detroit ban and made a surprisingly mild statement, in which he questioned Piggins' educational qualifications for the position of literary censor and suggested that the Detroit police force would be better employed pursuing nonliterary criminals.[12] In March 1957 Circuit Judge Carl M. Weideman granted the publishers a temporary injunction against the police ban on the ground that only the courts can determine if a book violates the law. Piggins declared that the ban was still in force, and the publishers brought a contempt action against him. Finally, in June 1958 Judge Weideman granted the publishers a permanent injunction prohibiting the city of Detroit from interfering with sales of *Ten North Frederick*.[13]

While the Detroit case was breaking, O'Hara received his second

---

* Paperback sale of *The Farmers Hotel* had earlier been banned in Detroit. *A Rage to Live* was in a list of books to be removed from the Illinois State Library in 1953; and in 1955 the National Organization for Decent Literature proscribed *Butterfield 8*.

† John K. Hutchens devoted his 28 February *Trib* book review column to an editorial on Michigan's obscenity laws, with particular emphasis on the *Ten North Frederick* case.

major badge—election to the National Institute of Arts and Letters, of which he was informed on 21 January 1957. This recognition, mattered to him, for he believed that he had been deliberately and improperly excluded from the Institute. Although he cared nothing for literary politics, O'Hara felt that if there was a body that was supposed to represent the best in American literature then he should damn well be in it. This position was an expression of pride in his work. He did not care about his personal popularity among the establishment figures, but he insisted that his work be accorded all the recognition and honor it deserved. His election was managed by John Hersey, whose nomination statement pointedly noted that a body like the Institute can "die of tardiness." A strong group of seconders was available: John Dos Passos, William Faulkner, John Steinbeck, Thornton Wilder, Malcolm Cowley, Robert Penn Warren and Marc Connelly—from which Faulkner and Steinbeck were asked to sign the nomination form. John O'Hara was inducted at the 22 May 1957 meeting of the Institute.

In April 1957 O'Hara agreed to participate in a panel discussion at the Nassau Club in Princeton. The format of the meeting was for two members of the Princeton faculty—R. M. Ludwig of the English department and sociologist G. M. Sykes—to submit questions for the author's advance consideration. O'Hara's nervousness made the session difficult. Professor Emeritus Thomas M. Parrott fell asleep in front of the speakers' table, and woke up to hear O'Hara say that he read three newspapers and as many as ten magazines per day. Parrott said loudly, "Too many," and went back to sleep. O'Hara fumed.

Although O'Hara was not a petition signer, in May 1957 he lent his name to an American Civil Liberties Union statement charging the National Organization for Decent Literature with censorship. The NODL, a Roman Catholic group, had included *Butterfield 8*, *The Farmers Hotel* and *A Rage to Live* among a list of banned books. He was among the 150 prominent figures in literature and publishing who signed the ACLU document.

The Detroit action against *Ten North Frederick* was followed in December 1957 by a censorship case in Albany, New York, when a grand jury investigation indicted Bantam Books, *Confidential* and ten other magazine publishers and newsdealers for conspiracy in the distribution and sale of obscene literature. *Ten North Frederick* was not mentioned in the initial summons; but it immediately became clear that the novel was the reason for Bantam's indictment, and on 13 December 1957 John O'Hara was indicted. He did not appear in court and was not represented by counsel. Bantam's attorneys sought dismissal of the indictment because the jurors had read only selected passages of *Ten North Frederick*—it being a point of law that a book may not be held obscene unless the work is viewed as a whole. The indictments against *Frederick*, Bantam and O'Hara were dismissed in July 1958 by Judge Martin Schenk.[14]

On 17 December 1957—at the time he was under indictment in Albany—O'Hara wrote Malcolm Cowley, President of the National Institute of Arts and Letters, from the Century Association, explaining that he had been informed that his presence in New York State made him "liable to service of papers compelling my appearance in Albany"; therefore he was returning to Princeton and would not attend the Institute dinner that night. The letter closed with an obvious appeal for Institute action: "I am hopeful that I can count on the moral support of the members of the Academy and the Institute. This is a dangerous action affecting not me alone." The next day he was informed by Felicia Geffen, Assistant Secretary for the Institute, that Cowley was abroad but Otto Luening, acting chairman, had read his letter at the dinner. No action was taken, but "the consensus was a sympathetic commiseration with your predicament." The matter rested there until an interview with O'Hara appeared in the 3 November 1958 *Publishers Weekly* in which he stated that "the Institute did nothing about the case. It should have." Miss Geffen responded to this interview on 14 November by explaining to O'Hara—presumably for the first time, according to the records—that the Council of the Institute had agreed to appoint an ad hoc committee to study the problem should the Albany indictment against him hold. He replied that he had not in fact requested Institute action—such action "should have been spontaneous"; that it was never his intention to appear in Albany; and finally: "I beg leave to state that since you wrote me on Institute stationery, in my opinion you took upon yourself, by your censorious tone, a privilege that belongs to elected members of the Institute. If your letter does represent an Institute opinion, I would like to see it signed by an officer of the Institute and I shall then proceed accordingly."

Miss Geffen sent a soft answer, and on 26 November 1958 Malcolm Cowley, the President of the Institute, wrote O'Hara a detailed explanation of the rules governing the Institute's official action in such cases—which required committee study, Council approval and a vote by the membership. Cowley conceded that this procedure was cumbersome and said he was trying to have the rules changed to allow prompter action. O'Hara replied to Cowley on 1 December explaining why he felt that the Institute had failed him:

I never intended to go to Albany, I did not retain counsel. The case, I strongly felt, was for the Guild, the Civil Liberties Union, and, if possible, the Institute to fight immediately, spontaneously and thoroughly. When the charges were brought against me it became, I felt, a much bigger thing than an attack on a single author. Whatever the reasons for the aloofness of the three organizations, the big fact on the record is that they did nothing. It may turn out to be a very unwise decision for American literature, and as though Pearl Harbor had been allowed to pass unnoticed. For the disposal of the case in Albany, although the indictment against me was not pressed, is very unsatisfactory. I was freed on a legal technicality: the grand jury had not read the whole of TEN NORTH FREDERICK but had indicted on isolated passages, and that is contrary to the state law. So no real victory was won; the same situation can be created again in any county in New York State (and many other places), and this time, this next time, if there is one, the local district attorney will prepare his case more thoroughly. The crank letters have started to come in on FROM THE TERRACE, and if there is action again, I am not going to defend unless and until the Guild, the CLU and the Institute forthrightly announce their support of my case. I would be much better off, I think, if the Institute alone backed me; the Guild is ineffectual, the CLU is hardly less so. There is not the slightest doubt in my mind that one reason the Guild and the CLU dragged their feet was their knowledge that I personally have changed my politics, and what price liberalism there?

There is no further correspondence until O'Hara's letter resigning from the Institute three years later, in November 1961.[15]

BEGINNING WITH *Pal Joey* (1957, Columbia), five of O'Hara's books were made into movies: *Ten North Frederick* (1958, Twentieth Century-Fox), *Butterfield 8* (1960, MGM), *From the Terrace* (1960, Twentieth Century-Fox), *A Rage to Live* (1965, Mirisch-United Artists). O'Hara took no part in any of these adaptations, and—except for an abandoned screenplay of *Appointment in Samarra*—never worked on a movie adaptation of his own work. The movie rights brought a good deal of money: $175,000 (announced as $300,000) for *Ten North Frederick* and $100,000 for *Butterfield 8*. O'Hara reportedly declined $500,000 for outright sale of *From the Terrace*, and agent H. N. Swanson worked out terms that satisfied the author: $100,000 front money and a 25 percent participation in the profits for a five-year lease on the novel, plus $50,000 and 25 percent of the profits for each sequel or remake. O'Hara liked the way Swanie handled his movie deals but insisted on setting his own asking prices, some of which were not met. O'Hara wanted $175,000 for *The Farmers Hotel*, $125,-000 for *A Family Party*, $400,000 for *Ourselves to Know* and $600,000 for each of the later novels—"to keep out the grocery clerks." With the exception of *Ten North Frederick* he was not pleased by any of these movie versions—and, indeed, did not bother to see all of them. He did, however, like Philip Dunne's handling of *Ten North Frederick*. Dunne, an old Hollywood friend, wrote and directed the film. The cast included Gary Cooper and Geraldine Fitzgerald as Joe and Edith Chapin, both of whom received excellent notices. Chapin was one of Cooper's favorite roles, and he remarked that he liked playing a part in which he could wear his own clothes. Dunne and O'Hara had a number of associations. Dunne's wife, Amanda, had been a friend of Belle's; Dunne had grown up with the Wylies in Quogue and knew Sister before she married O'Hara. O'Hara and Dunne had both worked at the Office of Inter-American Affairs during the war. Moreover, Dunne appreciated O'Hara's personal qualities: his "tremendous natural courtesy" and "capacity for tenderness." Dunne was the son of Finley Peter Dunne; when he edited *Mr. Dooley Remembers* in 1963, he included John O'Hara among the fourteen dedicatees—the only book dedication O'Hara ever received.

IN 1957 Sister decided that the O'Haras would build their own home, and planned a house for comfort. Since the house was near the junction of Province Line and Pretty Brook roads, it was named "Linebrook"; and O'Hara designed an emblematic letterhead with straight and wavy lines. Although the press half-jokingly came to refer to O'Hara as "the Squire of Linebrook," the house did not qualify as a mansion—certainly not in an area full of more impressive dwellings. It was a house that a Princeton professor who had inherited some money might well have owned. "Linebrook" is a ten-room white brick house in the French provincial style, set on three acres of land about five miles out of Princeton. The effect of the house is of great comfort—bright rooms, comfortable furniture and possessions with association value. The kitchen was run by Thelma Pemberton. What O'Hara called "the home fleet" was berthed in the garage; and it eventually included a Rolls-Royce, a 3.8 Jaguar, a Mercedes-Benz 300 four-door convertible, Sister's Ford station wagon, O'Hara's MG-TC and Wylie's triumph. There were dogs—a golden retriever who seemed to appear only when photographs were being taken, and Sister's poodle called Taxi because he was never around when wanted.

"Linebrook."

O'Hara in MG-TC.

As befitted a sentimental man, O'Hara's part of "Linebrook" was full of memorabilia. In the hall outside his study were a program for the Princeton production of *The Searching Sun*, a photo of O'Hara with Fitzgerald in Hollywood, a photo of O'Hara with Hemingway at the Stork Club,* the award of merit from the National Academy of Arts and Letters, and an original Thurber cartoon of a man playing a violin, captioned "I wasn't worried about my wife when he was just a writer" (probably inspired by O'Hara's amateur fiddling). In his bath were an etching of a coal mine; a Whitney Darrow cartoon of a drunk offering a bottle to a child, who says, "No thank you, I don't drink"; and an Addams cartoon in which a gorilla carrying a female explorer encounters Mrs. Gorilla, captioned, "Uh, Oh." Since the bathroom was the size of an A-deck bathroom on the *Queen Mary*, it included the Cunard lifeboat drill instructions. The study was virtually an O'Hara museum, with memorabilia from every stage of his life: his collection of antique horns; a photo of Wylie and Charles Addams in a Bugatti, of a coonskin-clad O'Hara in a Stutz Bearcat, of young John on his mare Julia, of the racehorse named O'Hara, of the O'Hara Rolls, of Benchley in an admiral's jacket but without trousers, of O'Hara costumed as Hitler; a photostat of the check from Yale for the Bergen lecture; the NBA award; the Donaldson award; caricatures and photos of the *Pal Joey* cast; a photo of O'Hara with Cerf and Cardinal Spellman; a John Held, Jr., drawing; the certificate of membership in the National Institute of Arts and Letters; a school essay by Wylie; the telegram announcing Wylie's election as president of her class at St. Timothy's; a Cape Cod lighter in the fireplace; the certificate attesting that O'Hara had crossed the equator aboard the *S.S. Kaskaskia* on 19 September 1944; a certificate from the New Jersey State Teachers of English; the original Shenton illustrations for *Tender Is the Night*; a horseshoe; a photo of O'Hara dancing with his daughter; a poem by Grantland Rice about Wylie; a pottery ashtray made by Wylie; a photo of O'Hara with Senator John F. Kennedy at the National Book Award ceremony; metal artifacts; an acetylene lantern; a mounted Stewart speedometer (set at 42983—Grace Tate's birthday—by Pat Outerbridge); an antique purser's chest; a leather fireman's bucket for a wastebasket; a bronze head of O'Hara by Joe Brown; a plaque carved

---

* After the death of Hemingway, O'Hara wrote in a review-essay on *A Moveable Feast* (*Holiday*, December 1964): "I loved Ernest Hemingway. At home I have a photograph of us in a night club, taken about thirty years ago, and both of us are looking straight ahead at the camera; but the expression on my face shows the pleasure I took in his company—and I was no unsophisticated kid at the time."

by Bob Fuldner with Conrad's famous credo ("My task, which I am trying to achieve, is, by the power of the written word, to make you hear, to make you feel. It is, before all, to make you see. That—and no more." [Introduction to *The Nigger of the Narcissus*]); engraved silver cigarette boxes (including one presented by John Steinbeck in 1950: "The lonely mind of one man is the only creative organ in the world, and any force which interferes with its free function is the Enemy."); fire extinguishers; model cars; sabers; an Astrolite miner's lamp; decoy ducks; cuspidors; an army paymaster's chest for shoe-polishing equipment; a hurley; Benchley's banjo-mandolin; a violin; a photo of John and Sister taken against the Capitol dome in Washington; lighters; ashtrays; a Zenith transoceanic radio; a fly rod; a buggy whip; a photo of Pat Outerbridge in a Bermuda Ocean race; a large American flag; a framed blackjack hand (nineteen on seven cards); storm-warning signals; a certificate of membership in the United States Naval Institute. The desk was covered with the tools of his trade, and the office model typewriter stood on its own table—with two tear-gas Pen-guns in the drawer.

The study was neither a cluttered den nor a showplace. Everything was neat because O'Hara had become a tidy man in middle age, but it was a working room. It was his safe place where thousands of good words were written every week. He referred to it as his laboratory, and it was also his church—*laborare est orare*. The memorabilia served a dual purpose for O'Hara: they made him feel comfortable and helped to release the flow of memory. When he went into this room every night to do the thing he was born to do, the familiar items charged with emotions became part of the process of literary creation.

O'Hara's study was the working room of a writer who was dedicated to getting things right, so the shelves were stocked with reference books: technical dictionaries, *Who's Who in America*, *Who's Who*, *Burke's Peerage*, two editions of *The Encyclopædia Britannica*, medical books, *Factors in the Sex Life of Twenty-two Hundred Women* (1929), histories of the auto, military reference books, works on Pennsylvania, club yearbooks, atlases, horse books, the 1902 Yale *Classbook*, *Baird's Manual of American College Fraternities*, the *Ayer Directory of Publications*, foreign-language dictionaries, books on music, books on sport. O'Hara's remarkable memory, verging on total recall, relieved him from the necessity of working directly from reference sources. Rather, these tools were available when he wanted to verify his memory. Like nearly everything else in the room, the reference books were comforting presences. It was good to know they were there when needed. Among the books in the "Linebrook" study

O'Hara's study at "Linebrook."

was a copy of the *Yale Banner & Pot Pourri* for 1924, which may have been something more than a reference tool. If O'Hara had gone to Yale after Niagara, he would have entered in the fall of 1924. When he completed a work it went into the wall safe to await publication.* Across the hall from his study was O'Hara's orderly bedroom, with a closet of excellent clothing and a row of treed Peal shoes. On the dresser was a small photograph of Dr. Patrick O'Hara.

An example of how John O'Hara's study was crowded with

* The "Linebrook" study has been rebuilt at the Pennsylvania State University Library, with the actual furnishings, artifacts and books.

memories—and not just memories, but accurately recalled people—as he worked is provided by an unfinished essay about his study at "Linebrook." When the house was being built he had insisted on control over his study and bath. Because the tub was not long enough for him to stretch out in when he took a hot soak after his nightly writing stint, he could not fall asleep and drown. Then the flow of memory:

A man in my home town drowned in the bathtub, and I still remember as his epitaph, the drearily repetitious jokes about his dying a clean death. In fact all I remember about Mr. Halberstadt is that he had two attractive daughters, Mary and Imogene; that he drove a Maxwell, and that he died in the tub. I do remember that the Halberstadts had a big tree in front of their house, in the center of the sidewalk, and you had to walk around it. I happen to be a great lover of trees and I wish to give the Halberstadts full credit for not disturbing their tree, which I think was a horse-chestnut, but I am not able to say whether it was Mr. Halberstadt or his wife who was the dendrophile. Now that I have thought it over and taken myself back fifty years, I incline to the belief that the tree was an oak. If there is anyone who lived in the 1600 block on Mahantongo Street, Pottsville, Pa., and remembers the tree in front of the Halberstadts', I would be glad to hear from him, or her. The Halberstadt girls were like Norma and Constance Talmadge, in that Nim Hal was, like Norma, the prettier, but Mary Hal, like Constance, was the cuter. There was always a bunch of girls on their porch: Elizabeth Fox, Peggy Mould, Margaretta Archbald, Sara Shay, Lucetta Ibach. If there had been a Junior League in Pottsville, they would have been it.[16]

This passage is more than an exercise in nostalgia. The recollection of a man who drowned in his tub fifty years ago elicits the emotions associated with that place in time. The porchful of pretty girls—one of whom John O'Hara loved desperately—is brought to life. The effect is something like that of the author removing the people from a time vault where they have been perfectly preserved.

O'HARA'S PRODUCTIVITY, as well as the fact that he was able to work without rewriting, has led some commentators to assume that he was less than painstaking in his writing. This complaint has been made against other highly productive writers—Trollope, for example. O'Hara was a fast worker compared to most writers, who tend to agonize. Two factors about O'Hara's writing habits must be considered before any judgment about his craftsmanship can be made. The first point is that he knew what he wanted to write before he began writing. More than most authors he worked out material in his head. This ability was part of his special equipment, part of his genius. The second —and perhaps the more important—point about O'Hara's writing is that it was hard work, and that he worked hard at it. He labored over dialogue and customarily spoke it aloud as he wrote. He was also concerned about the visual impressions of his paragraphs on the printed page. Another O'Hara writing habit was to check words in dictionaries as he used them. The *Oxford Universal Dictionary* and *The Random House Dictionary of the English Language* were on a stand next to his desk, and he frequently interrupted his writing to verify the precise meanings of even common words.

On 23 October 1958 O'Hara was awaiting publication of *From the Terrace*, and wrote to Charles Poore expressing his "fatalistic joy that I was able to live long enough to finish it. . . . I like to write, but I have never known such pleasure as I have had with this novel; brutally hard work, sure, but work with a pleasure and a purpose, the pleasure of mastery of my characters and of technique. . . . I have attained a retrospective self-confidence. . . . And it is largely because of what I did and learned and learned about myself in this middle-aged novel." O'Hara published his biggest novel on Thanksgiving Day 1958. In almost 900 pages *From the Terrace* chronicles the career of Alfred Eaton through great success to middle-aged uselessness. Given the Wall Street and government background of Eaton's career, the novel started a guessing game about the identity of the model for the character. James Forrestal was a common identification; but nobody guessed correctly in print. The source for Alfred Eaton was Anthony Eden, and O'Hara built in the name echo as a clue. Although the author did not know Eden, the connection between the former Prime Minister and Eaton is not surprising, given the O'Hara method of character creation: the amalgamation of the psychological pattern of one person with the external qualities of one or more other actual persons. Both Eden and Eaton lost great power and were unable to build new careers; and both married younger women after divorces in middle age.

From the Terrace is John O'Hara's most ambitious novel, for its bulk is matched by its scope. Nowhere else did he lavish so much material on one book: a small Pennsylvania city, Princeton, New York before and after World War I, Wall Street, Long Island, Washington in World War II. The time span is fifty years, and the cast of important characters is large. The sheer quantity and brilliance of the social history in *From the Terrace* may have distracted some readers from its achievement as a character study. Alfred Eaton is a figure hardly touched on in American fiction: the almost-great man who loses his power and dwindles into obscurity and idleness. There are many *de casibus* plots dealing with characters who fall to utter destruction, but that is not the case with Eaton. At the end of the novel he is still reasonably well off and has the loyalty of his second wife; however, he enjoys no respect and has nothing to do. *From the Terrace* was a highly personal work, for in certain ways Alfred Eaton's chronology resembled John O'Hara's. When he wrote it, the author had passed fifty and—like Eaton—had survived a hemorrhage. Viewed from this angle, *From the Terrace* was the author's self-warning and an announcement of his determination to work hard until the end. Seventeen volumes followed.

Believing, rightly, that *From the Terrace* was his masterpiece, O'Hara was hurt by its disappointing reception. John Wain in *The New Yorker* reflected the general response in calling the novel a failure and a "false masterpiece," citing it for lack of selectivity and restraint. Although any theory about a reviewers' conspiracy can be ridiculed, it is clear that the intellectual climate was unfavorable for O'Hara's aims and material. Beginning with *From the Terrace* no O'Hara novel received a predominantly good press.

John K. Hutchens at the *Trib* regarded him as a major figure but manifested a certain nervousness in assessing the O'Hara treatment of sex in *A Rage to Live* and *From the Terrace*. Hutchens' review of *Terrace* brought a mild rejoinder from the author in which he explained that given the fact that sex was a factor in every person's daily life, the space devoted to it in his 900-page novel was not excessive.[17] Hutchens had no reservations about the story collections, and applied the word "master" to O'Hara for his work in this genre.

In addition to Poore and Hutchens, there were other consistently respectful reviewers—Hoke Norris of the Chicago *Sun-Times*, William Hogan of the San Francisco *Chronicle* and Robert Kirsch of the Los Angeles *Times*. Kirsch's review of *From the Terrace* began by making the point that the "essential impact" of the novel is that the reader is not a spectator but is "given direct entry into the world of the novel." He concluded with the flat statement that "John O'Hara more than any contemporary American writer deserves the Nobel Prize." This review elicited a letter from the author, which was published in the Los Angeles *Times* on 28 December 1958:

First I heard about and now I have read your magnificent review of FROM THE TERRACE. You have said what I have been hoping someone would say, not only about this novel but about my work as a whole: ". . . From the very beginning O'Hara has resisted fads and fashions of the novel. He has matured and developed in his craft, writing on the basic assumption that his readers are intelligent enough to understand without facile interpretation or special psychiatric theory. The result is that more than any other American novelist he has both reflected his times and captured the universal, the unique individual for the generations to come." It is important to me to be able to read those words because finally one man, and a man I've never met, has shown that he has known what I've been doing. I have been consciously, deliberately doing it since 1947, when I was getting ready to sit down and write A RAGE TO LIVE. Before that I wrote largely by instinct and from inside myself and my own experience, but in 1947, or maybe 1946, or maybe even 1944—who knows when those things begin?—I consciously brooded about the novel, the construction, technique, etc. As you know, I had a somewhat less than universal success. Eleven years passed between the publication of HOH and ARTL, and the success of the stage show PAL JOEY, which was in that period, almost diverted me into the theater. But I am a novelist and not a dramatist. There is fun and excitement in the theater, but there are too many carpenters and nurses and other helpers, and my conscience kept nudging me. So I returned to the novel, where I belong, and where I shall stay.

This is really an amazing experience. As I read your review I kept saying, "Yes, yes. Attaboy, Kirsch. Oh, you noticed that, too?" And when I came to the last paragraph I said, "He even sensed that." For since 1947 I have not written a line that was not only a line in the novel at hand but also a part of my work as a whole. I want the Nobel Prize, as Joe DiMaggio said in quite another connection, so bad I can taste it. And as long as I live and can be wheeled up to the typewriter, I'll try; by God, I'll try.

When Richard Watts commented in his New York *Post* column (30 December 1958) on the amount of nonfunctional material in the novel, O'Hara sent him a letter declaring an end to their friendship, in which he also rebuked Watts for failing to attend Belle's funeral. Watts was deeply troubled. They met at the memorial service for John McClain in 1967, and the friendship was patched up. Perhaps the occasion reminded O'Hara that there weren't many of his old friends left.

From the Terrace was the fourth successive Pennsylvania novel. It is not set in The Region, although careless readers have assumed that all of O'Hara's Pennsylvania novels have a common locale. Port Johnson in *From the Terrace* resembles Pottstown or Easton more closely than Pottsville. O'Hara never attempted to link his novels into a cycle or saga, but Julian English and Joe Chapin appear briefly in *From the Terrace*, as a sentimental gesture. There is, however, a major episode in Lantenengo County when Alfred Eaton meets Natalie Benziger on a business trip to Mountain City (probably Frackville). Alfred is sent by his Wall Street firm to report on Natalie's father, the superintendent of a coal mine. He falls in love with Natalie literally at first sight, although his marriage to Mary is still apparently sound. It is true that she is unfaithful during Alfred's trip to Gibbsville, but he does not know about her infidelity. Love at first sight is not unusual in O'Hara's work, and his fictional use of it reflects his own sense of love. In "The Girl on the Baggage Truck" (1960), for example, Malloy says to a woman he just met, "I have to tell you this. It may be the wrong time, Mrs. Williamson, and it may be my last, and I know I'll never see you again. But I love you, and whenever I think of you I'll love you."

Although *From the Terrace* sold more than 100,000 copies in cloth, it required only one Random House reprinting.* Like *Ten North Frederick* and *A Rage to Live*, it enjoyed remarkable distribution in paperback, for the Bantam edition went through at least thirty-four printings. It is patently absurd to attribute these paperback reprint sales to John O'Hara's reputation for lubricity. People do not read 500-page or 900-page novels to find a few erotic passages. The prurient can find what they want in more concentrated form.†

While writing his later novels O'Hara was not always sure how they would end. When he began he sometimes had only a general idea of where the story would lead him and let the characters work out their own destinies. For his large-scale novels O'Hara employed Sister

---

* The number of printings is an unreliable gauge of a book's success. In the case of *Terrace* the first printing was 100,000 copies.

† *From the Terrace* became O'Hara's most widely read paperback, with 2½ million copies of the Bantam edition sold by 1966. His other big sellers in Bantam were *A Rage to Live* (two million copies by 1966), *Butterfield 8* (1,800,000)—and surprisingly, *Farmers Hotel* (902,000). The guarantees paid by Bantam rose from $50,000 for *Ten North Frederick* to $185,000 for *Elizabeth Appleton*. The top advance for paperback rights was the $500,000 New American Library paid for *The Lockwood Concern* in 1965, but this figure was almost certainly increased by NAL's desire to take O'Hara away from Bantam. Even more revealing of O'Hara's popularity is the record for his story collections in paperback, since such volumes are usually not considered commercial properties. *Assembly*, *Cape Cod Lighter* and *The Hat on the Bed* sold around a half-million copies each. In 1963 Bantam paid a $25,000 advance for *Assembly*, but by 1966 *The Horse Knows the Way* cost them $100,000. Through 1966 Bantam paid $1,186,750 in guarantees for O'Hara paperback rights; and during this period more than 15½ million copies of O'Hara titles were sold by Bantam.

and Pat Outerbridge as checkers. Sister made notes on the chronology which she referred to while reading the typescript, and Pat was asked to look for factual errors.*

O'Hara asked Barklie Henry, a Harvard alumnus, to arrange for the donation of the typescript for *From the Terrace* to the Harvard University Library. Henry suggested that the typescript be turned over to a Harvard representative at the Random House offices, but O'Hara wanted a more elaborate presentation. A lunch with Dr. Paul Buck, the university librarian, was set up at the Century, after which O'Hara took Buck to the checkroom and gave him two large cardboard cartons containing the typescript and proofs. Buck—who walked with some difficulty—was appalled by the bulk of the material and suggested that it be taken to a nearby rare-book dealer for packing and shipping to Cambridge, but O'Hara insisted that the librarian personally deliver the boxes. With this material O'Hara included a formal letter of presentation which concluded:

For your information, and the information of your successors and other interested parties, the manuscript on yellow paper is the only manuscript that was typed by me. I write directly on the typewriter, and not by hand, and in writing FROM THE TERRACE I put the words down as you see them. From time to time I gave 50-page batches of the manuscript to stenographers for retyping; that is, they made copies of the original; but there are not and never have been carbon copies of the original. The manuscript you now have is therefore unique.

I am glad that this collection is to repose in the Harvard College Library. This is my best novel, and I am pleased that it is now the property of the oldest American university (although I understand that the University of Pennsylvania disputes the claim of oldest American university). In any case I will say that Harvard is the best American university, and this is my best novel.[18]

Buck reported the safe arrival of the material and invited O'Hara to visit Harvard as an honored guest, but the invitation was not acted on.

In 1959 Rider College in Trenton, New Jersey, invited O'Hara to address the students in an evening course on the contemporary American novel taught by Professor Harry D. Sproules, Jr. It had become

---

* Both Pat and O'Hara missed the mistake in *From the Terrace* that placed the Yale and Princeton supporters on the wrong sides of Palmer Stadium. The error was pointed out after publication, but O'Hara let it stand.

his custom to decline such invitations, but O'Hara accepted on the ground of neighborliness. Having taken on the chore, he put a great deal of effort into it, carefully preparing two full lectures. The first lecture, presented in a classroom, created so much interest that the second was delivered at the library before an audience of 200. At the time he thought they were good enough to publish, for a foreword dated 12 November 1959 survives among the O'Hara papers in which he refers to "the two lectures that make up this book."[19] In 1961 he delivered a third lecture at Rider. Although there is nothing to indicate that the lectures were actually submitted for publication, they certainly merit it. The Rider lectures constitute O'Hara's major critical statement.

The subjects of the first lecture were dialogue (which O'Hara invariably spelled dialog), detail and the use of type. Taking the reviewers' commonplace remarks about his mastery of dialogue as a springboard, O'Hara stated that the ability to write dialogue is not the most essential asset for an author. "The basic, indispensable attribute of a novelist is the understanding of character and the ability to understand characters, and they go together. . . . " But the creation of believable characters depends on good dialogue. As a boy he had been impressed by the dialogue of Owen Johnson and Booth Tarkington and learned the lesson that an author who writes bad dialogue cannot be trusted in other respects; he is not first-rate.

Now one of the many experiments I have conducted in my laboratory —and I hope that you realize that I am not being serious when I refer to it as my laboratory—is to put a sheet of paper in the typewriter, think of two faces I have seen, make up a scene, such as a restaurant table or two seats in an airplane, and get those two people in conversation. I let them do small talk for a page or two, and pretty soon they begin to come to life. They do so entirely through dialog. I start by knowing nothing about them except what I remember of their faces. But as they chatter away, one of them, and then the other, will say something that is so revealing that I recognize the signs of created characters. From then on it is a question of how deeply I want to interest myself in the characters. If I become absorbed in the characters, I can write a novel about them and so can any other novelist. A fine novel can be written about any two people in the world—by a first rate novelist. A great novel could be written about any man or woman that ever lived—by a great novelist. But while I have written, and published, short stories that had such accidental beginnings, I do not approach the writing of novels in such casual fashion. As a rule I don't even finish the stories I begin that way, and I deliberately destroy what I have done by giving one of the characters a line of atrocious dialog—humorous, profane, or completely out of character—that makes it impossible seriously to continue. I have killed an hour between the Jack Paar show and bedtime, and I have not been alone.

Good dialogue, O'Hara insisted, is never merely reporting or recording. It is always under the control of the author, who is deliberately using it to create character and advance his story. The author who has mastered the writing—not the recording—of dialogue is always aware of the ways in which a character's social and educational background governs his speech. The best dialogue is not naturalistic; it is controlled. Its accuracy comes from the author's understanding of the relationship between character and the speech of characters.

The dialogue is the first thing that O'Hara checked in the work of other authors, and the second was the accuracy of details. It was his basic rule that meaningful details are in fact meaningful. The author who has mastered his profession understands that he must get the right details, as well as the wrong details, right. For example, the information that a character is wearing a miniature hunting horn instead of a collar pin with a business suit indicates that he is a bit of a fraud. "He could not resist that one vulgarity, and because he could not resist it, he inadvertently proclaimed his dubious standing." O'Hara recognized that such details were overlooked by many of his readers who failed to ask themselves why the fact was important enough for the author to include it. Although he did not state the conclusion in his lecture that readers have been spoiled by authors who did not require them to pay attention, the implication is clear. Careless writers make for careless readers. Not only did O'Hara expect his good readers to pay attention, he required them to have funds of knowledge. When O'Hara mentions a car, he expects the reader to know something about that car, for the author cannot stop and explain. The Franklin, for example, functions not just as a car name, but as a characterizer: "it would be out of character for a Buick type man to own a Franklin." It may well be asked if O'Hara really had the right to expect this kind of knowledge from his readers—most of whom never saw a Franklin. The answer is threefold: first, he expected his best readers to understand his use of characterizing details; second, his own attention to details acted as a disciplining device on his work; third, he was writing for the record. He believed that the authorial intention behind every detail made it difficult for him to violate the integrity of his characters as characters.

The final point in the opening lecture was the effect of type on dialogue and detail. While avoiding typographical tricks and phonetic spellings, beginning with *A Rage to Live* O'Hara used long unbroken blocks of type for descriptions or assemblages of facts. This technique, which became a favorite of his, O'Hara credited to his experience with type as a journalist and to the example of Ernest Hemingway. As a newspaperman he had been required to write short paragraphs, but he developed a feel for the appearance of the type on the page. When he first read *A Farewell to Arms* O'Hara "was so impressed by his paragraphing that I remembered it photographically." The effect of this device is to present "massive blocks of type that by their massiveness prepare the reader for a great collection of facts even before the reader has had a chance to read the words and sentences."

The second 1959 Rider lecture dealt with the "logistics" of the novel—"all the preparatory work that a novelist must do before he starts actual writing." The basic problem is what is an idea for a novel.

I believe that the ultimate, greatest novel of all time will be the one that honestly and completely [sic] the life of one man for one day. The novelist will certain [sic] the best of James Joyce, the best of William Faulkner, the best of Sinclair Lewis, the best of Ernest Hemingway, and, naturally, the best of me. The contribution, or the borrowings from Joyce and Faulkner will consist of the perfecting of what Joyce and Faulkner have done in their tremendous efforts to get down in print the workings of the human brain. More than any other living writer Faulkner comes close to achieving the impossible task of putting the human mind on paper, with a minimum of processing. . . . This perfect novel, then, will be written by a novelist who can do what Joyce and Faulkner have done and do it more coherently. He will possess the sharp eye that Sinclair Lewis had and a portion of his ironic humor. He will write as lucidly as Ernest Hemingway. And from me—although not really from me as much as like me—he will have compassion and vitality and a love of truth.

In his own work, when he had an idea for a novel, O'Hara recognized it immediately as an idea that required the form and length of a novel. He did not try to explain beyond that: he knew that it was an idea for a novel and for nothing else. However, he was able to describe how he worked up this idea so that he could make a novel out of it. In general, he started with a man he knew a great deal about and used his psychological pattern. But, as he explained on other occasions, he did not practice the *roman à clef*—except for Starr Faithful in *Butter-*

field 8. Although there have been many guesses about the sources for the characters in his novels, O'Hara stated that no one ever identified them correctly.

The second Rider lecture included a discussion of the novelist as social historian. "To my way of thinking, the social history that appears in a novel is of importance if it is that kind of novel, but only of secondary importance. When a novel's social-history content begins to take over, the author is in trouble. If the social history part does not relate to his characters, the author is converting himself into historian or journalist." This statement seems surprising coming from John O'Hara: "Social history has absolutely no standing in the world of art as I see it." Nonetheless, he repeated this conviction with increased force, and later devoted much of his 1967 Foyles speech to it. Just as he was upset by the critics who dismissed him as having only a good ear, so was he made defensive by the critics—usually the same ones—who used the designation "social historian" to put his work in a sub-creative category. But his resistance to this designation went beyond resentment of its implied denigration of his work. O'Hara believed that the term "social history" properly referred to studies of social problems and conditions, which he never engaged in. Moreover, such works almost always conform to a social or political or religious doctrine and thereby exclude themselves from the realm of art. This kind of conformity was resisted by O'Hara throughout his career, and in his last years he became increasingly concerned about the pressure that was being applied to make writers submit to it.

Two years later, in 1961, O'Hara delivered a third lecture at Rider College, which built on the second lecture and elaborated on how he made his decision about the subject of a novel and the form it would take. The reviews of his latest books provided the theme for O'Hara's comments. In the intervening period he had published *Ourselves to Know* and *Sermons and Soda-Water*. The critical reception of these works convinced O'Hara that the reviewers were opposed to his long novels because they were lazy—because more time was required to read and review them. He found in the reviews of *Sermons* the warning that his future long novels would not be received favorably: ". . . I am threatened with extinction if I do not conform—note that word—to the 300-page limit." O'Hara explained that the length of one of his novels was not arbitrary, that it was determined by the story idea (usually in the form of a character idea) he began with—and "what opportunities a story offers for my comments on my times." However, in the O'Hara theory of fiction commenting on his times is not the same as writing social history. The distinction may be too fine, for O'Hara was trying to remove a label from his work. "I deny that I am a social historian; I am a novelist, and a social historian only incidentally."

The distinction might have been clearer if he had applied the term "novel of manners" to his work, but he never did. The novel of manners may be defined as a novel in which the essential elements are the customs and conventions of a social class in a particular time and place. The word *manners* is not intended in the narrow meaning of etiquette or deportment, but in the sense of values and codes of conduct. The novel of manners is always realistic, for the behavior of the group is described accurately in detail. It focuses on upper-class (or at least upper-middle-class) groups, requiring characters who have sufficient leisure and education to be concerned with standards of behavior and position. It is frequently—but not always—satiric. The novel of manners has had more distinguished practitioners in England than in America. Indeed, critics have often expressed the theory that this form has not flourished in the New World because American society is not sufficiently complex, or because this country lacks a tradition of manners, or because social mobility is so rapid in America that class lines are blurred. Some commentators have reacted to the idea of an American novel of manners with hostility, charging that it is irrelevant and undemocratic. Nonetheless, American literature has produced the work of Howells, Wharton, Lewis, Marquand and Cozzens.

It is necessary to differentiate the social novel (or novel of manners) from the sociological novel (or problem novel). The sociological novel, as practiced by Steinbeck or Dos Passos, presents a social problem and calls for its amelioration—often recommending a particular action, in which case it may become a propaganda novel, as in the work of Upton Sinclair. If the distinction between the social novel and the sociological novel holds, then it is clear that O'Hara never wrote a sociological novel. He was not indifferent to social problems, and was a concerned liberal in his twenties and thirties. The explanation for his avoidance of problem themes and subjects is simple: they were not his material. Although he had done manual labor—unwillingly—and had experienced poverty, he did not identify with the laboring class and was not moved to write about it. He did not choose to become the literary equivalent of an intellectual in bib overalls.

John O'Hara's devotion to the values and standards of upper-class life earned him the label of snob from many critics. He no doubt was a snob according to some definitions of that word, but snobbishness in itself does not disqualify an author's work from serious consideration. Other critics who respected his ability but disliked his material have attempted to make him respectable by incorrectly insisting that his work was motivated by class hatred. Presumably it is permissible to write about the rich only if you hate them (with the curious exception made for Henry James). But O'Hara did not hate the rich—any more than he worshiped them. He found in their lives a resource for the material that mattered to him: the rituals of social behavior and the ways in which these rituals and the values behind them operate as forces on character. Neither generalization about O'Hara's attitude toward the affluent holds; he created admirable and contemptible characters on all levels of society.

The third O'Hara consideration—after the story-character idea and the opportunities to comment on his times—in determining the length and shape of a novel was technique. He asserted that each of his novels was technically different from the others, and that he set himself new technical problems at the start of each novel. Unfortunately, he did not provide detailed analysis of these technical problems.

The Rider lectures reveal as much about the speaker as they do about his conception of the art of the novel. John O'Hara was hurt by being placed below the salt at the feast of American letters, and he frequently committed the tactical blunder of showing that he was hurt. He never achieved the aristocratic indifference of Faulkner, or even the scathing contempt of Hemingway, that made them invulnerable to criticism. O'Hara was painfully vulnerable and could not conceal it. His response to hostile criticism of his work was reflected in his paradoxical personal conduct. He was at once shy and explosive, generous and inflexible—a sensitive man with an ungovernable temper. Add to this unstable compound his deep pride in his work, and the result is a great writer who could be hurt by the critics he did not even respect. Nonetheless, he never committed the sin of writing to please reviewers. His artistic integrity was total, but it did not protect him against hostile critics. Even though he knew they were trying to hurt him, he allowed them to do it. He craved recognition. O'Hara was entirely secure only when he put the yellow sheets in his typewriter. They couldn't touch him then.

In the fall of 1959 Wylie entered St. Timothy's in Stevenson, Maryland—her mother's school. O'Hara did not attempt to attend St. Tim's vicariously; but he derived satisfaction from the fact that although he had been sent to second-rate schools, Wylie was attending a first-class boarding school. He kept in close touch with her, writing weekly letters of affectionate encouragement and sound fatherly advice. Perhaps mindful of his own father's conduct, he did not play the role of heavy father; he never threatened or reminded Wylie of "all that is being done for you." Instead, he welcomed her to the adult world of responsibility and showered her with support. Any portrait of John O'Hara that does not provide the details of his feelings about his teenage daughter is incomplete. He was fifty-four when Wylie went away to school; the only things that mattered to him were his wife, his daughter and his work. His letters are models of their kind, and Wylie knew they were worth preserving.[20]

[22 September 1959] Welcome to St. Tim's! . . . By the time you read this you will have spent your first night in your new room, or so I imagine, and I am also imagining what your first day will be like. You will be doing and seeing so many new things and meeting so many new faces that you will wonder how so much could be crowded into one day, and you won't have a chance to think about it until you go to bed, the second night. . . . Then, almost without realizing it, you will find yourself a member of a new community.

And that's something I would like to talk about. Just as I am going on a voyage [to London], so are you embarking on a journey that is much more important than my quick trip. Mine will be over in a month, and the real purpose of my trip is to get away from my typewriter and my habits of work in order to get a new perspective and come back, I hope, the better for my holiday. But your journey is more important because you are entering into a new phase of your life. Beginning with the day you read this you will cease to be a child. Your memories, naturally, will all be memories of childhood, the life you have led so far. But each day will be part of the future that you have been looking forward to all your childhood days. You will be assuming new responsibilities, but you will also find that responsibility does not necessarily mean something irksome. Responsibility, and responsibilities, can be a pleasure. The greatest pleasure I have in life is the responsibility of being your father. It is a greater pleasure than my work, which is saying a lot because I love my work. But a man is not born with a love of his work, and he is born with the nucleus of a love for his children, and his responsibility toward them, or toward her, in my case, is only the practical side of that love.

In the Catholic Church you are taught to start each day by dedicating everything you do that day toward the great honor and glory of God. Most Catholics forget that, and none of them remembers it every day, throughout the day. We are all human. But it is possible to copy something from the Catholics that is helpful: as I wrote you two years ago, "to thine own self be true," and if you do that every day you'll be all right. When I stopped drinking I did not say to myself "Quit for a year." I did it a day at a time; get through one day, then repeat it the next. Well, that's more than six years ago. And quite frankly, I still do it day by day. I take those damned exercises every day, not with the thought that I'll be taking them for the rest of my life, but with the thought that I will do them today—and let tomorrow's temptation to skip them take care of itself tomorrow.

I hope you will write me while I am abroad. The address is at the bottom of this so you can tear it off. . . .

I wish you happiness in this new phase of your life. You have come through childhood as a fine person, with wonderful prospects for a wonderful future. You have made Sister love you as though you were her own. And I was born loving you.

[September 1959] This is going to be an odd letter. Not one, but several. This is my first night aboard the Queen Mary, and I have decided that instead of writing you separate letters, I'll write you something every day while I am on shipboard.*

* * * *

I found quite a bit of loot in my stateroom: a handsome book about the Irish from Tracy and Janet; flowers from Mr. and Mrs. Grant; books from Mr. Cerf; hard candy from 21; books and a leather note-pad and scrabble set from Sister; telegrams from Mr. Outerbridge and Mr. Freedman. I was very touched. Then when I went to the promenade deck to reserve my deck chair the asst chief steward said, "You'll be having yours on the terrace?" I honestly didn't know what he meant until I saw the twinkle in his eyes. I thanked him for his little joke and apologized for my obtuseness. So I felt a lot better.

* * * *

Only one girl your age that I've seen. She is traveling with her mother, an attractive woman, and I'll bet anything Ma is taking daughter to school in Paris or Switzerland or Florence. Two or three sexpots in their twenties on board. One is French, traveling with her husband, and my guess is they are returning from their wedding trip. The others? They are taking sexpotluck. Enough for tonight. Goodnight, my love.

* * * *

I know why this trip seems strange: it is the first time I've been on a ship and on the wagon at the same time. As a passenger, that is.

* * * *

I'm sure you will be proud to know that two ladies have flirted quite frankly with your old man. One of them is the French dame; the other, I believe, is English. But the day when I flirt back has long since passed. However, I admit quite frankly that I am pleased when it happens to me. At 54 you better be pleased!

---

* O'Hara sailed alone, meeting Sister in London.

*   *   *   *

I worked yesterday afternoon, did half of a short story, then last night I was so bored with The Devil's Disciple that I went to my state-room and finished the story, which I will send to the Saturday Eve Post. It is a story about a man, his wife, and a younger man, on ship-board.* It was fun to write. It was all invention, and all new yesterday. Not bad, either. I still think you might be a writer. You won't really know for a couple of years whether you want to make it a career, but you have thoughts, you observe well, and you express yourself well, in conversation and on paper. In other words, you already have some of the equipment a writer must have. What you lack now is the desire to write, and nothing anybody says can make you write, any more than anything anybody says can make you stop if you have the desire. The most fascinating thing about writing as a career is that you never stop learning. At 54 I'm still learning; at 74 I'll still be learning; at 94 I'll still be learning. If I'm writing, that is. The first thing you do is learn the basic rules, then as you get more confidence you decide which rules you want to break. In that respect, of course, it is like a lot of other things. . . . You learn the essentials, then you make your own, personal contribution. . . . Every time your Uncle Bobby performs one of those marvelous operations on the heart, he brings to it the skill he acquired as a medical student, as a young doctor, and as a mature surgeon—and then because he is a genius (and he is), he can ignore some rules and create his own. Your Grandfather O'Hara was a great surgeon, make no mistake about that. There are people alive today who would not be alive had it not been for his skill, and his name is still respected and even revered by those who knew what he did. But he did his work a generation before Bobby, and there are hundreds of techniques they know now that they didn't know then. Every surgeon, every composer, every author adds to the knowledge and techniques of his own profession. Next February when my new novel† comes out, there will be reviews that will comment on how different this book is from all my earlier ones. (Mr. Cerf already likes it better than anything I've ever done.) There will, of course, be the usual panning, but practically nothing that was an innovation in writ-ing, music, or art was accepted right away. . . . One time your Grand-father O'Hara was about to operate on an appendix. When he made the incision on the left side the nurses and assistants thought he had lost his mind. But when he completed the incision, that's where the appendix was, and not on the right side. What's more, the patient had a sister who also had her appendix on the left side, and my father oper-

---

* Possibly "Our Friend the Sea," which the *Post* published in 1963. This letter shows that O'Hara had recommended writing short stories before "Imagine Kissing Pete" in 1960.

† *Ourselves to Know.*

*ated on her the same way! . . . You see, you have the stuff, on both
sides of the family. Don't ever forget that, at St. Tim's or anywhere
else. You are as good as they come, and you will be as good as you
make yourself, whether you decide to be a writer or a nurse or an
actress or the mother of triplets.*

[24 October 1959] I inclose a contract for an ad in The Steward.* *The
Linebrook Press is the name of the tiny publishing venture I have
been contemplating. I am going to take some of the money from the
movie sales of* Butterfield 8, A Rage to Live, *and* From the Terrace,
*and use it to establish a publishing firm which will publish books that
ought to be published but that have little or no chance of commercial
success. I have already conferred with Mr. Cottier and when I get
home will do so with Mr. Lee, to ask them to be on the lookout for
authors whom I will publish. Mr. Lee is one of the world's great art
historians, and Mr. Cottier of course has the inside among university
people. So "The Steward" will print my first ad. I expect to lose
money on this venture, but I may do some good.†*

*[December 1959] My trip to Saratoga was very pleasant. At least my
stay there was. . . . Frank Sullivan has always written nicely about
his home town, and the townsfolk used his new book,* A Moose in the
Hoose, *as the excuse for giving him a dinner. . . . Frank himself reminded me that it was like my little Book,* A Family Party, *which
actually I never thought of. The other "famous celebrity" present
besides your old man was Russell Crouse, co-author of* A Sound of
Music, Life with Father, *etc., and he made a nice speech. Mine was
brief, humorous, slightly sentimental, and painless. The best thing
about the trip for me was Frank's being touched by my making the
trip. Well, he is a dear, lovable friend. Asked all about you, hasn't
seen you since you were four years old, but one year he put you in
his annual Christmas greeting in* The New Yorker, *a copy of which
I still have somewhere. It was your second appearance in print; your
first was in* Time, Milestones, *when you were born.*

FIFTEEN MONTHS AFTER *From the Terrace*, O'Hara published another
major novel, *Ourselves to Know*,‡ in February 1960. Set in Lyons, the
counterpart of Lykens, his mother's hometown, *Ourselves to Know*
is technically his most ambitious novel. The technique is that of an
expanded *Great Gatsby*, for the structural relationship between

---

* Wylie's school yearbook.
† The Linebrook Press project was abandoned before it published anything.
‡ "And all our Knowledge is ourselves to know"—Pope, *An Essay on Man.*

narrator Gerald Higgins and Robert Millhouser resembles that between Nick Carraway and Jay Gatsby. Higgins assembles the story from various sources—mainly from Millhouser's own testimony—but invents nothing. Everything Higgins records is given a source, although at one point O'Hara is driven to the extreme of allowing his narrator to communicate with a deceased character. And, like Carraway, Higgins is influenced by the events he records:

> *And so, once again, I take up the story of Robert Millhouser, begging the reader's indulgence for the interruptions, and offering the explanatory assurance that the story behind the story is relevant. I have often wondered, as I watched newsreels of structural workers on skyscrapers and mountain climbers on precipices, what the anonymous cameraman was thinking and doing.*

O'Hara felt that the narrative complexity of *Ourselves to Know* was largely ignored by the critics. Writing to Charles Poore—in a letter never sent—he explained:

> *. . . things that happened a hundred and more years ago could have been passed down in conversations between Moses and Robert and then to Gerald. In relating them I did not exercise my right to omniscience but only my ability to present them without merely stating them. . . . But the unorthodox construction I employ in OTK had not only to justify recollections of an ancient time, but also to justify the kind of probing into Millhouser's mind that was essential to the presentation of this character.*[21]

As a literary term, "point of view" refers to the angle from which the author tells the story in order to direct the reader's response. Although all of O'Hara's novels—except *Ourselves to Know*—employ the unrestricted point of view of the omniscient author, there is considerable flexibility as he makes use of interior monologue and panoramic techniques. Even in *Ourselves to Know* there is great variation in point of view because Higgins functions as a novelist within a novel.*

---

* On 28 January 1963 O'Hara participated in a panel discussion of his works with Profs. Robert E. Spiller and Wallace E. Davies at the Historical Society of Pennsylvania—stipulating that no record of the proceedings be made. One of the comments he made about his technique was that in *A Rage to Live* he deliberately tried to write a novel in which the novelist was absent—in which there was nothing that could not have been observed by someone else. This concept is not clear, but it indicates that O'Hara became increasingly concerned with problems of authorial omniscience and its effect on the reader's "willing suspension of disbelief." His awareness of these problems culminated in the complex structure of *Ourselves to Know.*

The scope of the 400-page novel is large, covering eighty-nine years of Millhouser's life in Lyons, from the 1850's up to 1944. The technical complexities of *Ourselves to Know* are matched by the psychological complexity of Robert Millhouser, an emotionally deficient man who in his fifties, not blinded by love, marries a vicious teenage nymphomaniac in an attempt to stave off emotional starvation. Millhouser knows the marriage cannot endure, that Hedda's willingness to postpone boredom and infidelity will hardly outlast the honeymoon, and seems prepared to let her go. Nevertheless, when she betrays and humiliates him, he murders her as she sleeps, in a final—but unsuccessful—effort to awaken his fury. O'Hara was proud of the compliments on the psychological soundness of the novel that he received from a priest and a psychologist. Nevertheless, general readers were puzzled by Millhouser's folly in marrying so utterly corrupt a girl. The explanation in terms of the novel is that he wanted to make a mistake, that he was—consciously or unconsciously—seeking some experience to shock his emotions into activity, for Millhouser had been rendered incapable of loving by his relationship with his widowed mother. Zilph Millhouser was a largely self-sufficient woman whose love had been given exclusively to her husband. She was not neglectful of Robert; she simply did not love him. Millhouser was also betrayed in friendship; his closest friend, Chester Calthorp, proved to be an extremely active homosexual. Calthorp scrupulously avoided trying to seduce Millhouser—who had been unaware of his friend's appetites and in no way shared them. His complete break with Calthorp, upon the discovery, was both inevitable and emotionally self-crippling.

John Chamberlain's assessment in the *Herald Tribune* was a fair statement of a friendly critic's reservations: "Though it has its fleeting moments of Dostoyevskyan probing, this is fundamentally a social, not a psychological, novel. One never knows precisely what went on in the depths of Mr. Millhouser's soul in the years after the murder. But one does know everything about what the town of Lyons, Pa., thought."

O'Hara was bitterly hurt by the critical response to *Ourselves to Know*, which he regarded as one of his peak achievements. A receptive review by Hoke Norris in the Chicago *Sun-Times* elicited a letter from the author, which was published with O'Hara's permission. After stating and expanding on his refusal to play up to the critics, O'Hara discussed Fitzgerald and Barry as casualties of the politically committed critics of the Depression and spoke about Hemingway's artistic invulnerability.

And where am I? Well, the only thing I'm afraid of is death, which I came close to 6½ years ago. I am afraid I will die before I finish all

*the things I want to do. I have a novel ¾ completed, I am working on
a play that I have been writing for the past two weeks and that I
will finish next week and then return to the ¾ completed novel. The
novel is called Elizabeth Appleton, for the record. But all the time I
am writing these things I am thinking out a big novel, which will be
big in size because it is big in scope—an expression I have never used
before.* If I finish it by the time I'm 60, I will be happy. I don't say
I'll quit then; I'll never quit voluntarily; but I will have said all I now
want to say.*[22]

There can be no argument about the achievement of *Ourselves to
Know* as social history. Lyons is Lykens reconstructed in loving detail;
and the novel is filled with convincing scenes. The account of Robert
Millhouser's successful effort to save the bank, for example, includes
a perfect vignette which catches the character of Gottlieb in one line
of speech:

*On an impulse, while Robert and Ben were dining at the rathskeller,
Ben called the proprietor, Fritz Gottlieb, over to their table. "Fritz,
Mr. Millhouser wants $5,000 cash. He'll give you his I.O.U."
"You want it bick bills or little bills?" said Fritz.*

There is no dedication in *Ourselves to Know*, but Jeremiah MacMahon
—Higgins' grandfather—is a memorial to O'Hara's grandfather, Joseph
Israel Delaney. The sales were disappointing, with only two Random
House printings, totaling 80,000 copies. The Bantam paperback, how-
ever, required seventeen printings between 1961 and 1970.

IN 1960 St. Clair McKelway let it be known at *The New Yorker* that
John O'Hara was writing short stories again, and that he was willing
for the magazine to see them. William Maxwell, who in 1938 had succeeded Katharine Angell White as O'Hara's editor, contacted him.
O'Hara set the condition that Maxwell could read the stories at
O'Hara's house and that his degree of enthusiasm would determine
the next step. On 12 July 1960 Maxwell and his wife went to Quogue
for an overnight visit. He was given three novellas to read. "The first
two I was reasonably sure the *New Yorker* would not want to publish,
and, very much wishing I had not got myself into such a tight situation,
I started to read the third, which was "Imagine Kissing Pete," and

---

* The "big novel" was almost certainly *The Lockwood Concern.*

William Maxwell. *Photo by Con-suela Konaga*

thought it was a masterpiece, and that the New Yorker would want it."[23] Maxwell so recommended to William Shawn, who had succeeded Harold Ross, and the story appeared in the 17 September 1960 issue. Some readers objected to "Pete" 's sentimentality, but it was a true literary event. People argued about it and passed the word that O'Hara was in *The New Yorker* again.

O'Hara obviously wanted to return to *The New Yorker* and to short stories. Once "Pete" and "It's Mental Work" had been accepted, he was cooperative about financial negotiations. When he was leaving for Europe in September 1960 he told Maxwell that he was willing to grant permission for the magazine to proceed with publication of the stories that had been accepted, with the understanding that mutually agreeable terms would be worked out. The price that was paid for "Pete" was $11,000, a figure which gratified O'Hara because *Esquire* had previously offered $1,500 for it.

One of O'Hara's greatest strengths as a writer in his later period was his sense of form or scale. As he remarked in a 1955 interview with John Hutchens after publication of *Ten North Frederick*, ". . . I have an instinct for knowing how much I can do in a certain amount of time, and how much I want to say."[24] This instinct had been slow to develop, and before *Frederick* he struggled with the shape of his novels, feeling more comfortable in the *New Yorker* story format. But in his fifties O'Hara exercised total control over the large novel and several shapes of the story. The most important result of this sense of form and scale was his achievement with the novella.

O'Hara informed Cerf on 7 April 1960 that he was working on *Sermons and Soda-Water*, explaining that ". . . I want to hold on to those readers who like my shorter items. Strategically it is also a good idea, I think, to display some versatility, especially if in so doing I may recapture some readers, and at the same time give those who like my longer books, the newer readers, something to think about." He felt that *Ourselves to Know* would have been better received if it had not appeared so soon after *From the Terrace*, and he planned to use *Sermons* and other short works to space out the publication of his big novels.

On 23 April O'Hara wrote Cerf that he was planning a foreword to *Sermons* explaining:

. . . these are three stories of men and women who were a bit too young to have been disillusioned by World War One. Everybody can understand a war. But it is not so easy to understand an economic revolution; even the experts continue to be baffled by it; and the people of my time never know what hit them or why. When some semblance of order was restored to the domestic economy, we looked about us and the world was already in cataclysm, not much easier to understand than the economic bafflement and over-simplified by the twin villains, Hitler and Mussolini, somewhat complicated by our convenient courtesy to the third villain, Stalin. It is not my intent and not my job to analyze these factors in SERMONS AND SODA-WATER but only to look at some of the people who were affected by them, in the Twenties, Thirties and Forties.

The foreword that appeared in *Sermons* did not address itself to these points.

O'Hara scrupulously referred to the long stories in *Sermons and Soda-Water* and their successors as novellas; he intended this term to describe a particular form of work—a carefully plotted work longer than a short story but shorter than a novel, and requiring little research. He carefully distinguished between his use of the *novella* and the *novelette*, although the terms are usually applied interchangeably. Later, in 1968, he would tell Don Schanche that he was experimenting with a new form, the *novelette*—which, he explained, did not require the tight plot structure of the *novella* or the detail of the novel: "A full unit about 30–38,000 words, tells all you need to know about certain people in certain circumstances so that those people become figures in your personal library."[25] The distinction becomes clearer if "A Few Trips and Some Poetry" (1968) is selected as a specimen of the O'Hara novelette—in contrast, say, to the novella "Imagine Kissing Pete." There is no significant difference in the length of these works, and both cover a large time span. The formal distinction is that "A Few Trips and Some Poetry" is loosely structured and includes the kind of scene that could not have been included in "Pete" or "Fatimas and Kisses." An O'Hara novella was an augmented short story; a novelette was a truncated novel.

"Imagine Kissing Pete," "The Girl on the Baggage Truck" and "We're Friends Again"—under the general title *Sermons and Soda-Water*—made up the O'Hara Thanksgiving book in 1960.* The three-boxed-volumes format was the author's idea; and an unknown number of copies were bound with an extra blank leaf signed by John O'Hara. The three stories are connected by their common narrator, James Malloy; but only two—"The Girl on the Baggage Truck" and "We're Friends Again"—are linked by plot and by the characters. Although they are not the last Malloy stories (he appears in "Fatimas and Kisses" and "A Few Trips and Some Poetry" as well as in short stories), the *Sermons and Soda-Water* pieces are a retrospective view of Malloy from his young manhood in Gibbsville through his wild years to his settled fifties. As O'Hara announced in his "foreword," *Sermons* was a personal reassessment against the history of his own time, written against the calendar.

I have another reason for publishing these stories in novella form: I want to get it all down on paper while I can. I am now fifty-five years old and I have lived with as well as in the Twentieth Century from its earliest days. The United States in this Century is what I know, and it is my business to write about it to the best of my ability, with the sometimes special knowledge I have. The Twenties, the Thirties, and the Forties are already history, but I cannot be content to leave their story in the hands of the historians and the editors of picture books. I want to record the way people talked and thought and felt, and do it with complete honesty and variety. I have done that in these three novellas, within, of course, the limits of my own observations. I have written these novellas from memory, with a minimum of research, which is one reason why the novella is the right form.

This theme is elaborated in "Pete."

* O'Hara seems to have originally planned to include a fourth novella.

After I became reconciled to middle age and the quieter life I made another discovery: that the sweetness of my youth was a persistent and enduring thing, so long as I kept it at the distance of years. Moments would come back to me, of love and excitement and music and laughter that filled my breast as they had thirty years earlier. It was not nostalgia, which only means homesickness, nor was it a wish to be living that excitement again. It was a splendid contentment with the knowledge that once I had felt those things so deeply and well that the throbbing urging of George Gershwin's "Do It Again" could evoke the original sensation and the pictures that went with it: a tea dance at the club and a girl in a long black satin dress and my furious jealousy of a fellow who wore a yellow foulard tie. I wanted none of it ever again, but all I had I wanted to keep. . . . "When Hearts Are Young" became a personal anthem, enduringly sweet and safe from all harm, among the protected memories. In middle age I was proud to have lived according to my emotions at the right time, and content to live that way vicariously and at a distance. I had missed almost nothing, escaped very little, and at fifty I had begun to devote my energy and time to the last, simple but big task of putting it all down as well as I knew how.

And in "We're Friends Again": "A writer belongs to his time, and mine is past. In the days or years that remain to me, I shall entertain myself in contemplation of my time and be fascinated by the way things tie up, one with another."

Gilbert Highet, reviewing *Sermons and Soda-Water* for *The Book-of-the-Month Club News*, complained that the novellas sometimes read more like "fragments of an enormous autobiography" than like independent stories, which he found "embarrassing." Those readers for whom authorial revelations are embarrassing will be put off by some of John O'Hara's best work, for he is usually most effective when dealing with his own deeply felt experiences.

"Imagine Kissing Pete," the novella set in Gibbsville, chronicles the marriage of a couple who slip far down the social ladder and engage in infidelities but who achieve a delayed happiness—in part from the promise of their son. At the end Malloy attends the boy's Princeton commencement but cannot read the program because he is "crying most of the time." The two linked novellas, "The Girl on the Baggage Truck" and "We're Friends Again," deal with a Hollywood actress and a Wall Street man who are connected through Malloy. Like "Pete," they are deeply sentimental stories with a tone of sad acceptance: "What, really, can any of us know about any of us, and why must we make such a thing of loneliness when it is the final condition of us all? And where would love be without it?" Appropriately, O'Hara dedicated *Sermons and Soda-Water* to his wife and daughter, "who sustain me."

Sermons and Soda-Water sold very well for an unusual book, with three Random House printings in 1960. In England, Cresset Press published it in two formats—a three-volume collector's edition limited to 525 numbered and signed copies and a one-volume trade edition. This limited edition was the first for O'Hara, and the idea appealed to him. Bennett Cerf had arranged a deal whereby Cresset Press became O'Hara's English publisher, commencing in 1950 with *A Rage to Live*, and his burgeoning English public was a source of considerable pleasure to O'Hara, who was an Anglophile. In addition to the Cresset editions, his books sold well as paperbacks in England, and at one point he could claim that his books sold more copies in English paperbacks than any other author's.

Though Albert Erskine was not a collaborative editor, there were occasions when his routine editorial duties caused small problems. When Erskine queried the expression "Cloud 90" in *Sermons and Soda-Water*, citing *The Dictionary of American Slang* as authority as the source for "Cloud 7," O'Hara's reaction was: "Cloud 90. And don't cite dictionaries to me, on dialog of the vernacular. Dictionary people consult me, not I them."* Evidence of the tranquil relationship that developed between O'Hara and Erskine is provided by the graceful letter O'Hara sent when his editor achieved middle-aged fatherhood in April 1960:

> *Welcome to the Society of Fathers of Only Daughters—in your case, probably a temporary membership. Thurber, Faulkner, Truman and I come most quickly to mind, but there undoubtedly are others. Those I mention are not likely to become ineligible, but you may have to resign in a year or two.*
>
> *One of the nice things about having an only daughter is that you can make a public slob of yourself in ways that are not permissible if you have a son. It doesn't much matter what happens to a boy; everything matters if you have a girl. Also, you realize early that you are only the custodian of a girl, until she falls in love and then*

---

* As a matter of fact, O'Hara became enshrined in the 1972 Supplement to *The Oxford English Dictionary* as a source for eleven words, including "fuck-up," which appears in *From the Terrace* when a cab driver is complaining about his vehicle (p. 257). O'Hara had originally written "mother-fucker," but Cerf and the Random House lawyers persuaded him to alter it—that was in 1959.

you recede and she becomes independent (of Daddy, that is; not of Mum). So you enjoy your fatherhood while you can, and that is an injunction.

Congratulations to you and to the lady who brought it off.[26]

O'Hara did not enjoy traveling, but Sister did; moreover, she was afflicted by cabin fever in the cold months. In the fall of 1959 the O'Haras took their first trip to Europe—his first since 1938. Thereafter they were regular visitors to Britain, traveling on the Cunarders by preference.* On shipboard he avidly bet on the ship's pool and enjoyed the bingo games. O'Hara usually refused to travel without Sister. When the trip was required for a special meeting with his English publishers or agent, the O'Haras flew. He was pleased to be recognized in London and to be asked for his autograph. He was not a sightseer, and except for business meetings and visits to a few favorite stores—Gieves and Swaine, Adenay, Brigg & Sons, in particular— O'Hara loafed around Claridge's while Sister shopped. He was able to construct a rationale for certain purchases, such as a Jaguar, on the basis that they were paid for out of his English royalty account and so were almost free. The O'Haras attended the London theater, where he sometimes fell asleep. One night the O'Haras were in the same row as Queen Mother Elizabeth, and as they stood up to let her pass the contents of Sister's purse spilled on the floor—to the amusement of all three. He had never employed an agent for his books in America, but O'Hara found it necessary to sign with the Curtis Brown agency in London and enjoyed a very comfortable relationship with Graham Watson of that firm.

ALTHOUGH THE BODY of O'Hara's published literary criticism is not distinguished, he was an astute critic in his correspondence, as can be seen in a September 1960 letter to Maxwell in which he analyzed Hemingway's career:

I would like to continue our discussion of Hemingway, and maybe the best way is to start anew.

We have in Hemingway the most important writer of our time

---

* The chronology of the O'Haras' overseas trips is September–November 1959, London and Scotland; October 1960, London and Paris; February 1963, Bermuda; February 1964, West Indies cruise; March 1964, Bermuda; September 1965, London and Ireland; May 1967, London; October 1967, London; February 1969, London; February 1970, London.

John and Sister aboard the *Queen Mary*.

and the most important writer since Shakespeare. That is the statement I made in the famous Sunday Times review of ACROSS THE
RIVER AND INTO THE TREES. The various circumstances that
have made him the most important are not all of a purely literary
nature. Some are anything but. We start with a first-rate, original,
conscientious artist, who caught on because of his excellence. The
literary and then the general public very quickly realized that a great
artist was functioning in our midst. Publicity grew and grew, and
Hemingway helped it to grow, not always deliberately but sometimes
deliberately. He had an unusual, almost comical name; he was a big,
strong, highly personable man. He associated himself, through his work,
with big things: Africa, Italy, Spain, war, hunting, fishing, bull-fighting,
The Novel, Style, death, violence, castration, and a teasing remoteness
from his homeland and from the lit'ry life. All these things make you
think of Hemingway, and each and all of them add to his importance,
that carries over from one writing job to another. I have a theory
that there has not been a single issue of the Sunday Times book section
in the past twenty years that has failed to mention Hemingway; his
name is a synonym for writer with millions of people who have never
read any work of fiction. Etc., etc. He is the father image of writing
as FDR was of politics.

Now this has not all been good for Hemingway, and Lord Acton's
remark about power can be applied here, substituting acclaim for
power. It is not good for any artist if he does not keep on working
as, for example, Picasso has kept on working. The test of the man, and
possibly of the artist, is what he does after he gets the Nobel prize.
Hemingway, I'm afraid, has not done well in that test. It is not only that
he has rested on his laureate; he might have done better to have rested.
I am told, but I do not quite believe it, that he has several novels in a
bank vault. I believed it for a while—until I saw the Life pieces. I now
believe that he has been wasting his time, which would be okay if he
had decided to quit, to decide that he wanted to write no more, and
stuck to that decision. But there is a cheapness about Hemingway that
I deplore. He likes to get a favorable mention in Leonard Lyons's
column, which is cheapness at its cheapest, and extremely costly to the
man who is willing to settle for it. Hemingway can't stand the quiet of
retirement, and he can't stand the company of the ass-kissers with whom
he deliberately surrounds himself. They don't realize that you can't
win with Hemingway. He will give you an argument on anything, and
he hates you just as much for arguing with him as he does for agreeing
with him; and yet he can't quite reject the toadies. He comes to New
York, makes an ass of himself with Earl Wilson and Toots Shor, then
hurries away to what? To watch bullfighting and, later, to write about
what is to me the most disgusting spectacle in modern Western sports-
entertainment. But the worst spectacle in the Life pieces was not the

bullfighting itself but the collapse of Ernest Hemingway, artist and man.

I do not permit myself to believe that there may never have been any more there than appears in the Life pieces. As a writer I know better. There was always great art in Hemingway, often when he was at his mumbling worst. But in the Life pieces we see our ranking artist concerned with a disgusting spectacle, adopting a son-hero and wishing him dead in conflict with a former son-hero, Dominguin, whom he also wishes dead. He wants to see them die, to be there when they die, and I got the feeling that he particularly wanted Dominguin to die because Dominguin had not been as easy to adopt as Ordonez. Hemingway is afraid to lose Dominguin in life, and rather than lose him in life he wishes him dead. The competition between the two bullfighters, as presented by Hemingway, actually gets us away from the bull ring and could just as well have been a fight with knives between the two son-heroes. It is a terrible thing to get old that way, as Hemingway has done; to feel so strongly about two young men that you want them to kill each other, to play the one you like less against the one you like more—Ordonez against Dominguin. And all the while there is this cheap, vulgar thing I spoke of: the heartiness, the rough play, the feats of strength, the explicit hints of sex orgies, the boy-did-we-raise-hell stuff, did-we-give-it-to-that-cunt, that reminds me of John Ford and John Wayne and Ward Bond on location, and Lucius Beebe's accounts of drinking bouts. There is very little to choose between going out that way and Mr. Eliot's whimper. It's a good thing Gibbs isn't around to write the parody; that would really destroy Hemingway.

The contracts between Random House and John O'Hara called for a fifty-fifty split on paperback royalties, the standard arrangement at the time. Since Bantam was selling more than a million copies of some O'Hara titles, the author came to feel that his publisher's participation was excessive. In February 1961 he decided that it was time to renegotiate and wrote a strong letter to Bennett Cerf. The realities of the situation were such that O'Hara could not lose, for Random House could not afford to turn him down. Under the circumstances his letter was unnecessarily strong. He enjoyed squeezing publishers, for he felt that they tended to underrate the importance of authors; but his basic bargaining tactic of the threat or ultimatum was not required in his dealings with Cerf. The interests of publisher and author coincided; nevertheless, O'Hara obviously enjoyed being difficult in their negotiations.

As you know, I have a full-length novel in my drawer; I have enough stories and more for the collection I plan to bring out next Thanks-

giving; and I am well along the way in a large novel; now past 300 pages.

As you do not know, my mother, who has been in the hospital for three weeks, underwent surgery yesterday. She is 81, and if she recovers it will still be a heavy drain on my finances. It already has been.

I now serve notice on you that the 50-50 reprint deal is a thing of the past, and if you are going to repeat all the answers you had three years ago, don't bother to answer this letter. I know all those answers. You and Donald and whoever else is involved are going to have to come up with a new deal, more favorable to me, and I suggest you use as a working basis the plan outlined in the current Authors Guild Bulletin.

As matters now stand, Random House is getting rich on my money, and I am not getting rich on my money. Your wife and sons will get and are getting the benefit of my work, but my wife and my daughter are not. Your wife and sons are in Random House, I am not; I contribute to the financial well being of Random House; your wife and sons do not. You offered to sell me stock in Random House!

So I want you and Donald et al to sit down, as you refused to do three years ago, and draft a complete new plan that will be to my financial benefit and that of my wife and daughter. Louis Nizer is not in on this; I no longer am a client of Louis Nizer's, because of the way he handled the negotiations three years ago. What you do is submit a plan, then I will show it to a lawyer and tax man, and we can negotiate from there.

If you do not wish to submit a plan, I of course can only take your refusal for its obvious implication.

Although Cerf agreed to negotiate a new formula "that will make you happy," he did not act promptly. O'Hara notified him on 7 March 1961 that after the thirteenth he would feel free to begin discussions with other publishers for *Assembly*. A placating Cerf call no doubt followed, for on 9 March, O'Hara stipulated the new formula: two-thirds of all paperback rights to the author. "As you know, I have not yet signed the SERMONS AND SODA-WATER CONTRACT between Random House and me, but I am an honorable man and although the book was published without a contract, I had not agitated for an increase in my cut of paperbacks; therefore, I will sign that contract on the old basis."

O'Hara's letters to Cerf obscure the affection that existed between them, for many of his letters were written when O'Hara was angry about some publishing or business problem.* Cerf valued O'Hara's personal loyalty. He knew, for example, that O'Hara made a point of watching him on television. During one appearance on a talk show Cerf looked into the camera and addressed a remark to O'Hara. Cerf was pleased when O'Hara phoned the next morning to ask, "How the hell did you know I was watching." Inevitably Cerf was sent to O'Hara's Coventry a few times during their twenty-four-year association, but even these crises had a gamelike quality. Once when Cerf realized that he was on the blacklist he asked O'Hara what he had done and was informed, "If you don't know I won't tell you." O'Hara let him suffer for a suitable period and then let him know that he was forgiven by inviting him to dinner with Oppenheimer, which O'Hara knew would give Cerf pleasure. Loyalty is reciprocal, and O'Hara took comfort from Cerf's pride in publishing him. One clear indication of Cerf's unfeigned admiration for O'Hara is the fact that O'Hara never felt that he was playing second fiddle to Faulkner at Random House. The same thing can be said for the O'Hara-Erskine relationship. After the death of Saxe Commins, Albert Erskine served as editor for both O'Hara and Faulkner without permitting O'Hara to feel neglected.

Over the years O'Hara had been donating his typescripts to university libraries: Yale (*Butterfield 8* and the proofs of *Appointment in Samarra*), Rutgers (*A Rage to Live*, in honor of Robert Kriendler of "21"), Harvard (*From the Terrace*), the University of Pennsylvania (*Ourselves to Know*), Princeton (*Ten North Frederick*). The conclusion that he was fishing for an honorary degree seems unavoidable. In 1961 he gave the typescript for *Sermons and Soda-Water* to Pennsylvania State University in honor of Richardson Dilworth, the mayor of Philadelphia and a Penn State trustee. An additional connection with Penn State was provided by the presence of Professor W. L. Werner, an old friend married to Kit Bowman, who had been a reporter with O'Hara on the Pottsville *Journal*. Werner encouraged him to continue his gifts to Penn State, and O'Hara came to feel that all of his papers should be consolidated there. Penn State does not award honorary degrees, a fact which O'Hara seems not to have known at first; but he indicated that he would appreciate honorary election to Phi Beta Kappa—which was never forthcoming. The university never honored

---

* One of the crises that Cerf had to deal with came when O'Hara tried to use his Random House Air Travel Card in July 1966 and discovered it had expired: "This is absolutely inexcusable, and I hope you chew out the individual responsible. You can start by telling them, or him, that without authors you aint got books, to sell or to keep."

him. After he selected Penn State as the O'Hara repository in 1964, he wrote to the librarians of the institutions to which he had previously given material instructing them to turn the material over to Penn State. He was surprised and offended by their refusal to do so.[27] O'Hara's handling of his papers was no doubt partly motivated by a desire to punish Yale for its ingratitude, for Yale awarded honorary degrees to James Thurber (an Ohio State man) and E. B. White (a Cornell man).* He was deeply hurt by Yale's failure to recognize him or his gifts, so much so that he wrote a bitter letter to the *Yale Alumni Magazine*, which appeared in the November 1962 issue, commenting on the situation.

At the time that O'Hara was making his archival plans, the University of Texas was the most active buyer of literary manuscripts, paying record prices. O'Hara's old London friend, John Hayward, who was serving as adviser to Texas, urged him to sell his papers there. However, O'Hara preferred to give his material to Penn State—taking a tax credit instead of the cash which he did not need. Once he decided on Penn State, O'Hara stuck with his decision, although the university did not overwhelm him with gratitude. O'Hara was tired of the rebuffs from the Ivy League; and that the Penn State arrangement worked very smoothly was due to the efforts of the Curator of Rare Books and Manuscripts, Charles Mann. An admirer of O'Hara's work and an extremely able scholar, Mann handled the paperwork with Albert Erskine and did not pester O'Hara.

O'Hara was offered honorary degrees by three colleges, but twice with strings. One institution proposed a deal whereby he would turn over all income from his next novel, in return for which it would build a library, name it for him and award him an honorary Litt. D. O'Hara rejected this proposal. A second college invited him to become an associate professor in the English department. O'Hara was not interested and tried to decline politely by pointing out his lack of a college degree. He was told, "We'll give you an honorary something or other"—which he found offensive. In 1964 he did, however, agree to accept an honorary degree from American International College in Springfield, Massachusetts, and chartered a small plane to attend commencement. He was prevented from attending by bad flying weather and the college declined to award the degree *in absentia*.[28]

---

* At a Yale alumni function Lili Pell Whitmer asked President Kingman Brewster why Yale had never granted O'Hara an honorary degree. "Because he asked for it," was the reply.

IN AUGUST OF 1961 O'Hara published *Five Plays*—dedicated to Robert Benchley—which included *The Farmers Hotel, The Searching Sun, The Champagne Pool, Veronique* and *The Way It Was*. None of them had reached Broadway, and only *Hotel* and *Sun* had received tryouts. *The Farmers Hotel* had started as a play—possibly a play with music for Rodgers and Hammerstein—and had been published as a novel in 1951 after Joshua Logan declined to direct it. It had been produced once on the straw-hat circuit; then "a prominent playwright" wanted to rewrite it, which O'Hara would not allow. *The Searching Sun* had expired after its Princeton tryout. The best play of the five is *The Champagne Pool*, a comedy about the theater, which has a completely realized character in director Joe Rasmussen. Wisecracking, tough, brilliant and wholly professional, Rasmussen carries the play—although he is not the leading character. In his foreword to the collection O'Hara explained that he wrote this play to "occupy my mind during the days just before and after the publication of a novel, *Ourselves to Know*" —which became a custom for him. *The Champagne Pool* interested several Broadway impresarios, but their dissatisfaction with the third act prevented a commitment to produce it. O'Hara described *Veronique* as "The Village Revisited," for it is based on the time he lived "all over Greenwich Village." Although it seems to start as a comedy, it turns into an analysis of crime and forgiveness. The murder by the jealous homosexual and his offstage conversion to Catholicism is too much burden for the play to carry.

The Way It Was is probably the greatest loss to the theater among these five unproduced plays. It is the book for a musical about The Region and New York in the Twenties. Mary Stewart (born Stukitis) marks the third appearance in the O'Hara canon (*Appointment* and "Mary") of a character based on a Shenandoah beauty. In the foreword to the collection O'Hara recounted the genesis and suspension of the project. The play was written with Irving Berlin in mind, and the two men met January 1957 in New York to discuss a possible collaboration:

. . . he told me he had already written the title song for The Way It Was, *and he handed a couple of sheets of music to a pianist and began to sing. He had not sung three notes before I pricked up my ears. He finished the song and looked at me for my reaction. I said, "Irving, do you mind if he plays the melody, and I'll sing the words?"*

"No, go right ahead. Go right ahead," he said.

So the pianist began to play, and I sang the lyric. But it was not the lyric he had created for The Way It Was. *It was the lyric for* Butterfly, *as he had written it forty years ago. I knew it word-perfect.*

"*You son-of-a-bitch,*" *said Irving.* "*I was warned about you. That song was never a hit. How did you know the lyric?*"

Well, I know a lot of song lyrics, and everybody knows Berlin lyrics. But he was embarrassed, a bit ashamed, I think, to be caught trying to pull a fast one. I honestly didn't mind; Butterfly *or* The Way It Was, *it's a pretty tune; but I knew I had lost Irving Berlin. . . . He said in parting that there were some changes that had to be made in* The Way It Was *before he could work on it, and that he knew I would not make the changes. That gave us both a good out.*

This story (as related in the foreword to *Five Plays*) is virtually the quintessential O'Hara anecdote, the kind other people liked to tell about him, with the familiar elements: the O'Hara total recall, his touchiness and suspicion, his intransigence about revising. Irving Berlin's account of the meeting has the same facts but differs considerably in interpreting them. Berlin was not trying to pull a fast one by salvaging an old tune, for this was a longstanding practice with him. For example, "Easter Parade" was a retread. The "Butterfly"/ "The Way It Was" song was an experiment at finding the kind of music that would be right for the show, an exercise to get in the right musical mood; Berlin had worked up three or four period songs after reading the book. The "son-of-a-bitch" exclamation expressed his surprise that O'Hara remembered an unsuccessful 1921 song—not anger at being caught. The real disagreements that ended the project were about the material. Berlin was troubled about the suicide of Jones and thought that Johnny and Mary should be brought together in a happy ending. O'Hara wanted one story idea expressed through a musical soliloquy, which didn't appeal to Berlin. There was an exchange of polite letters in which they agreed to call off the partnership. Irving Berlin's summary of the episode is that if people really wanted to work together on a theater project they would get together on some basis, but that O'Hara was not really prepared to collaborate.[29] O'Hara continued to consider musical stage projects and in the spring of 1960 approached Cole Porter about working with him on *The Great Gatsby*; but Porter explained that he was too ill to undertake the collaboration.

ON 7 NOVEMBER 1961 O'Hara sent a one-sentence letter to Glenway Wescott, President of the National Institute of Arts and Letters: "I hereby tender my resignation from the National Institute of Arts and

Letters, this resignation to take effect immediately." The sudden resignation was in response to the announcement of the nominations for the Institute's Gold Medal for Fiction that same week: Faulkner, Steinbeck, Katharine Anne Porter and Kay Boyle. He had no quarrel with the selection of Faulkner (who was awarded the medal) or Steinbeck, but he resented the choice of Boyle and Porter when he was not nominated. The Gold Medal for Fiction is awarded every five years, and O'Hara never received it. Wescott wrote expressing regret, and offered to do anything he could to amend the situation: "Please reconsider, if you can do so with honor. In the normal procedure I shall not have occasion to announce your withdrawal until the annual meeting." O'Hara's 13 November reply revealed that his resignation was motivated by self-respect as well as hurt:

A man as sensitive as you will understand what is behind my decision, and I write you this personal letter in reply to the letter of a sensitive man.

My decision stands, and what I say here is in confidence. Twice in the past six years I have been passed over for the Nobel prize—twice that I know of, and I don't know how many other times. But the Nobel people take in the world; the Institute-Academy people take in the work of U. S. citizens only. Not even to be nominated for the fiction prize is a judgment that, considering my work since 1948, I cannot accept with any grace. So I have to separate myself from the organizations that passed that judgment. . . .

An exchange of letters ensued between O'Hara and Malcolm Cowley, in which O'Hara stated that he was adamant about his resignation and intended to discuss the matter in the preface to a 1963 book—which he did not in fact do.[30]

Sermons RELEASED a prodigious flow of short stories. The 1961 Thanksgiving volume was *Assembly*, a collection of twenty-six stories, most of which were written in the summer of 1960 at Quogue, "in two sittings of about three hours each." After an eleven-year absence from the genre, O'Hara was gratified to discover that "I had an apparently inexhaustible urge to express an unlimited supply of short story ideas." Twelve of the *Assembly* stories had appeared in *The New Yorker*, beginning with "It's Mental Work" in November 1960. There is no main theme running through the collection, but the best stories—such as "Mrs. Stratton of Oak Knoll," "The Cellar Domain," "The Pioneer Hep Cat" and "A Case History"—are retrospective (the last three of these are set in Gibbsville). It is a strong collection, with two novellas —"Mrs. Stratton" and "A Case History." The lead work, "Mrs. Stratton of Oak Knoll," studies the quiet struggle of a brave old lady, once very wealthy, to maintain appearances and dignity after her worthless children have consumed most of her money. The chronicle of a bad Gibbsville doctor, "A Case History," closes with a conversation between the doctor and Arthur McHenry (Joe Chapin's law partner):

"Like that piece of tripe Dr. Malloy's son wrote a few years ago," said McHenry.

"Oh, but that was a novel. Fiction. He made all that up."

"But he certainly gave this town a black eye."

"That's what I didn't understand, Arthur. If it was all made up, what are people so sore about?"

"He gave the town a black eye, that's why. And not one damn thing he wrote about actually happened."

"That's what I said. But you as a lawyer, and I as a physician, we know that things like them happened."

"Oh, hell, as far as that goes, I know some things that if young Malloy ever heard about them . . ."

"So do I, Arthur," said Dr. Drummond.

"The Pioneer Hep Cat" is of particular interest because it is about a legendary figure in The Region, the jazz singer Jack Gallagher—here called Red Watson. This story probably resulted from O'Hara's long-standing idea for writing a narrative poem about a jazz musician, which he apparently never progressed with. The most remarkable story in *Assembly* is "The Cellar Domain," which describes the deterioration of the perfect order of a Gibbsville barbershop as the result of one customer's behavior. That kind of situation occurs many times in O'Hara's work: the violation of subordination by some human agent that represents a force inimical to order—as in *The Farmers Hotel*. It bears mention that "The Cellar Domain" again demonstrates O'Hara's ability to master occupations and characters outside his own experience. He knows how—and makes the reader understand how—Peter Durant feels about his shop. With *Assembly* O'Hara commenced the custom of writing forewords for his story collections, in the form of statements about his career, some of which upset the critics—which is what he intended.

Assembly was dedicated to Wolcott Gibbs, who had died on 16 August 1958 (the twenty-fourth anniversary of *Appointment in Samarra*), with the same words that Fitzgerald used in his *Tender Is the Night* dedication to the Murphys: "Many fetes." When Charles

Addams phoned O'Hara to tell him that Gibbs had died, Sister took the message. O'Hara sobbed after she told him.

Between 1955 and 1961 John O'Hara had published seven books, including three major novels; he perfected a new form, the novella; he resumed writing short stories; and, for good measure, he published a volume of plays. At age fifty-six he had created a major body of work and was proceeding with undiminished dedication to his craft.

VI

The Master

O'HARA'S dejected 1945 inscription to Wylie that he would be "remembered as a short story writer if at all" proved to be a poor prediction; nonetheless it is the case that commencing in 1960 he consolidated his position as America's greatest writer of short fiction. In the last decade of his life O'Hara published 139 short stories, novellas and novelettes. Although sheer fecundity is not a gauge of literary merit, comparative figures can be instructive: Hemingway published some 50 stories, Faulkner some 70, Lardner some 115 and Fitzgerald some 160. O'Hara published 374 stories during his lifetime, including such longer stories as "The Doctor's Son," "A Family Party," "Imagine Kissing Pete," "The Girl on the Baggage Truck," "We're Friends Again," "Mrs. Stratton of Oak Knoll," "The Bucket of Blood," "A Case History," "Claude Emerson, Reporter," "The Engineer," "Pat Collins," "90 Minutes Away," "Yucca Knolls," "Andrea," "James Francis and the Star," "A Few Trips and Some Poetry," "Fatimas and Kisses" and "Natica Jackson." He displayed a greater range of material in the stories than in his novels, which focus on the middle and upper classes. The best stories are often about characters on the lower levels of society—shopkeepers, bartenders, barbers, a stableman. The scope of subject matter is accompanied by a remarkable flexibility of form in the post-1960 stories. The early O'Hara stories had been concentrated and virtually plotless, but after his return to the story he experimented with structure as he wrote tight short stories of five to fifteen printed pages, medium-length stories of fifteen to twenty-five pages, and a variety of novellas and novelettes up to a hundred and twenty pages in length. The long stories almost always cover a large time period. The technique of the later stories does not show experimentation—except that O'Hara handles the authorial voice with considerable flexibility. There are few plot tricks, apart from a fondness for withholding a key piece of information until the end of the story. He prefers to tell his stories in straight chronological order, although sometimes the main story takes the form of an extended flashback after an opening scene. Almost always O'Hara relies heavily on dialogue.

The most meaningful difference between the early and late stories, however, is not in the obvious evolution of form, but rather in tone. The angry irony and pain of the pre-*Rage* stories are replaced by compassion and sad acceptance. The late collections are permeated with age, illness, disappointment and death—by blighted expectations and impending oblivion. More often than not, O'Hara's response to his material is one of sympathy. To be sure, his sympathy is often compounded with dismay; it is a sympathy that recognizes the limitations of human character and the unfairness of life, as O'Hara pays tribute to old standards and values: loyalty, love, gratitude, dignity, respect, duty, honor, courage. As Malloy remarks in "In the Silence" (1961), "After you've lived a good many years I don't see how you can be anything but cynical, since all any of us have a right to expect is an even break, and not many get that."

It is too much to claim that John O'Hara's work after 1960 created a new public for the short story; but his collections sold unusually well and were, initially, well reviewed. Again, the critics asserted that O'Hara's genius was really for the short story rather than the novel. Then they complained about his facility, in a line of argument that went something like this: O'Hara was writing so many stories that they must be too easy to write and therefore there must be something wrong with them. Given the fact that story volumes are poor sellers, the O'Hara collections were remarkably successful: *Assembly* (1961)—three Random House printings and eleven Bantam paperback printings; *The Cape Cod Lighter* (1962)—seven Random House printings and three Bantam printings; *The Hat on the Bed* (1963)—four Random House printings and five Bantam printings; *The Horse Knows the Way* (1964)—two Random House printings and two Bantam printings; *Waiting for Winter* (1966)—one Random House printing but eight Bantam printings; *And Other Stories* (1968)—two Random House printings and one Bantam printing.*

THE RENEWED ASSOCIATION with William Maxwell, after an eleven-year hiatus, became increasingly close—and eventually led to the dedication to Maxwell of *The Hat on the Bed* in 1963. O'Hara's business letters to his editor came to be replaced by autobiographical letters in which he sometimes appears to be writing for the record:

---

* *Assembly, The Cape Cod Lighter, Waiting for Winter* and *Pipe Night* have been reprinted posthumously by Popular Library. As of 1975, Bantam could report that over 23 million copies of O'Hara have been sold in paperback.

In a way, of course, the compulsion to write could be said to be a resistance against the inevitable, and by the same token an author who stops writing has given in. The only time in my life when I could not write was during the war. I could write pieces, but pieces are only what they are called—pieces. Even when they are Art. Did anyone ever say that Sinclair Lewis was an artist? William Dean Howells? I don't think so. But Howells was very nearly an artist, and BABBITT was a work of art. I could not produce anything but pieces while the war was on, because the war was too big a distraction, an overabundance of material, a matter, you might say, of life and death, of hotel reservations and gas rationing, of mice and men, of me in all that confusion. Well, now I have got rid of most of the confusion and distractions, no longer feel that my participation will restore order to the world, and ask for nothing much more than time to do my work and once in a while a little pat on the back, the same as you'd give a horse. Or even a mule.[1]

William Shawn's editorial manner was not that of Harold Ross, so O'Hara had little occasion to communicate with him about *New Yorker* policy or proof queries. However, since Maxwell's story acceptances were subject to Shawn's veto, O'Hara did question Shawn's judgment in declining "Mrs. Stratton of Oak Knoll" in a letter written 26 December 1961. This letter developed into a discussion of O'Hara's earlier struggles with the "obtuseness and purity in the exalted echelons" at *The New Yorker*:

Do you know what finally broke the ice for me? The fact that in 1931 Scribner's, then a good magazine, bought a story "Alone" I had not even bothered to submit to The NYer and ran my name on the cover. *Had it not been for that bit of luck I'd still be writing those dreadful little potboilers in the back of the book. And yet as late as 1938 Ross wanted me to make a career of the Pal Joey pieces. (In 1942 he thought it would be a swell idea to have Joey join the Navy and write a modern version of Dere Mabel.)*

Inevitably, Maxwell received a lecture on The Art of John O'Hara, an experience all of his editors had. In this case the occasion was Maxwell querying the repeated use of a character's full name, which struck him as being possibly a mannerism:

4 April '63

I don't think you would try to teach me to write, but I do think that if you had paused long enough to allow one more thought

* *Scribner's* did not run O'Hara's name on the cover of this issue. His name appeared on the cover in July 1932 for "Early Afternoon."

to come, you might not have written your letter. The one extra thought is that I am always, always, experimenting.

Because I write plain, but without the jerkiness of Hemingway-plain, most of what I do of a technical nature is not noticeable. For instance, what I do about blocks of type, or paragraphing. I have been working on that since 1930, which is the year I read A FAREWELL TO ARMS, and I still work on it in every story and all my novels. It would take too long to tell you about it, and it wouldn't make very fascinating reading, but it has to do with technique (mine) of mesmerizing the reader, and is therefore related to the subject of your letter. I want to control the reader as much as I can, and I make the effort in all sorts of ways. (Punctuation is one of them.)

What you tell me about Gibbs's theories did not all originate with Gibbs. Much of it came from me to Gibbs. Much as I loved Gibbs, he had a way of telling me something I had previously told him, and the attributional theories are in that category. It began with a discussion of modifiers ("No, thank you," she said archly.), and went on to "retorted" and "chimed in," etc. Most of the time the dialog should stand on its own, but occasionally the non-modifier rule has to be broken.

The repeated use of the full name, George Denison, George Denison, is not accidental. It would be a damned sight easier just to say George or Denison or he said, or said George, etc. But here again I am fixing that name in the reader's eye, and I am borrowing from, among others, the 19th Century Europeans. Ivan Ivanovitch, a Russian writer would say, every time, as the Irish, in dialog, address each other as John-Patrick, Francis Xavier, etc.

There are times when I want to slow down the reader, almost imperceptibly, but slow him down. I can do that by saying George Denison, in full. I can do it for a greater length of time with a big block of type like the Caporetto retreat. I can make it easier for the reader by filling up that block of type with nouns—rifles, machine guns, tanks, motorcycles, ambulances, and other non-think words—but the reader is still being slowed down. He picks up the pace, is forced to, when I go back to dialog. But since most of the stories I write for The New Yorker are in dialog, I have to use other tricks, and another trick I use is to dispense entirely with the attributive tag. The full name will do that, if used sparingly. By which I mean, George Denison, but not a whole bunch of full names. One of the things that make Hellman unreadable and instantly identifiable is too many proper names, too many capitalized words. Eustace Seligman, Frederick B. Adams, John Hay Whitney, et al., attending a dinner of Les Amis d'Escoffier at the John Dillinger Room of the Hotel des Artistes. I am well aware of that danger.

Finally, I prefer "said John Smith" to "John Smith said," for a

*number of reasons. It is easier on the eye to follow a comma and close-
quotes with a small s than with a cap J. And "John Smith said" is
abrupt and full-stop where I don't want it to be.*

Now let us go out for a smoke.

THE LETTERS to Wylie at St. Timothy's continued as O'Hara tried to
prepare his only child for the responsibility of managing her own life.
In certain ways these letters are among his most self-revealing writing,
for—in contrast to his curmudgeonly public image—they show the
private O'Hara as a loving man who adhered to traditional high
standards of behavior.

*[April 1961] Today I also received two new silver cigarette boxes,
the small rectangular ones that I get for selling a million copies of a
novel.* These are for A RAGE TO LIVE and TEN NORTH FRED-
ERICK, both of which have passed the million mark, and that makes
four so far. They expect the SERMONS AND SODA-WATER trilogy to do that next year, and they are optimistic about OURSELVES
TO KNOW. I am less optimistic about OURSELVES TO KNOW,
but we shall see. My books and for that matter my other work too
have a way of catching on late. It is true that APPOINTMENT IN
SAMARRA and BUTTERFIELD 8 were best-sellers when they first
came out in 1934 and 1935, but BUTTERFIELD 8 lay quiet for many
years (except in England, where it continued to have a moderate sale),
then when the movie came out it came alive again and sold over a
million paperbacks in less than a year! I trust you were as amused as
I was that Miss Taylor got her Oscar, and accepted it, in spite of her
original reluctance to play the part. That, by the way, is a good illustra-
tion of what I was saying in my little lecture when you were home:
you sit at the typewriter with a stack of yellow paper, you go to work,
write your novel, publish it—and 25 years later the hairdressers in
Hollywood are busy as bees, getting the girls ready for the Academy
awards of which the high point was the award to Miss Taylor in a
part that I created in 1935. Of course my name was not mentioned, but
I guess most people are aware that it was not William Faulkner, but
your old man, who wrote BUTTERFIELD 8.†*

---

* In paperback.

† When MGM assigned Elizabeth Taylor to *Butterfield 8* her contract called
for $150,000 per picture. Since she had an offer to appear in *Cleopatra* for a re-
ported $2,000,000, she tried to get out of her MGM commitment. In a public
statement Miss Taylor complained that Gloria Wandrous was "practically a
prostitute." O'Hara's reaction, in a "My Turn" column, was an *ad hominem*
comment on the actress: "Bear in mind, too, the fact that Mrs. Fisher had already
been Mrs. Todd, Mrs. Hilton and Mrs. Wilding, though not yet thirty years
old, and had long since changed her public image from that of the little girl
who loved a horse in National Velvet."[2]

[January 1962] I have been thinking about our conversation of last night, and I hope you have too.

1962, in some ways, is Wylie O'Hara's Year of Decision. Some of the decisions you make this year will have an important bearing on decisions you may want to make several years hence.

For example: suppose that when you are 20 or 21 you should discover that you want to participate in one of the many activities that will be open to young people in the federal or state government. The first thing they will want to know is what education and/or training you have had. Nowadays the minimum, absolute minimum requirement for hundreds of jobs is two years' college, either at a four-year-college or at a junior college.

For another example: you have said that you don't expect to marry before you are 23. Well, that is something you can't be sure of, but suppose you do wait till you're 23. Suppose your fiance-husband is a young man who is taking graduate work at some university—law, medicine, the sciences, government work, etc.—and you and he are living in the vicinity of his graduate school. You may want to do work on the college or the graduate school level yourself, but I assure you you will not be very enthusiastic about it if you have to start as a freshman of 23.

Now I could go on at some length, but the point I am aiming at is this: I want you to think very, very seriously about what you are going to do after St. Tim's. You are not Miss Richbitch. You are not going to be Miss Churchmouse, either, but you must think in terms of being able to earn at least part of your own living. I don't think you are going to fall in love with a dumbhead. I think a dumbhead, rich or not, would bore the hell out of you. Therefore it is extremely likely that the kind of boy you will like and fall in love with is going to be one who uses his brains to earn his living. That almost automatically means that he will be taking either graduate work or special post-college training of some sort. And even if you have children right away, you will want to keep up with him intellectually.

I can tell you from my own experience how important it is to have a wife with whom to discuss one's work. My first wife was a Wellesley B.A. and a Columbia M.A. and a diplomate, I think they are called, at the Sorbonne. Your mother did not go to college, but she could have. Sister and your mother both graduated from good schools and took courses at Columbia and your mother even attended lectures at Oxford without having to enroll there. Both your mother and Sister loved to read and read a great deal, and Sister is multilingual. Both your mother and Sister disliked women's colleges, but they did not dislike higher learning. They formed their dislike of college-girl types thirty years ago. The type has almost vanished, because the kind of girl your mother and Sister were then would be applying for college today. Everybody goes to college.

Now this is what's on my mind: the tentative program you have outlined for yourself does not seem to me very "realistic" in 1962 and 1963 and so on. I am hopeful that you will redirect yourself toward a good college so that you will get those two minimum-requirement years on your record and then be able, three years from now, to qualify for jobs or continue working for a degree. You will not regret having those two years on your record, whereas you might easily regret not having them. As your father I have a duty to point these things out to you. But once I have done that I have to leave the real decision up to you.

I had a wonderful experience at Trenton. I waited on the platform, in case you did not take that train. Right in front of me there was a Pullman car, and I happened to notice that an austere woman was reading SERMONS AND SODA-WATER (the three-volume edition). I knocked on the window, and she was understandably confused until I pantomimed "book" with my hands and pointed to myself. She got it, got all excited, and spoke to her husband in the chair adjoining hers. He was delighted, recognized me right away, and so did a woman who was in the other neighboring chair. Then the people in the other chairs, overhearing the excitement, all laughed and waved to me. So I clasped my hands like a prizefighter, and took off my hat and bowed. I'm sure I'll get a letter from my reader on the other side of the Pullman windows. It was fun.

[28 Feb 1962] I am terribly sorry to hear, from Miss Watkins in today's mail, that Kassie Wilson died. I know how it must sadden you and Patience and the other girls in your class.

When I was about 14 or 15 the phone rang at our house one day. It was the priest who was assistant pastor of St. Patrick's Church, my church, to tell me that a girl named Beulah Keiter had died and that the family wanted me to be a pall bearer. It was all very strange, because Beulah had lived in Pottsville only a few years and had moved back to Williamsport. I can't remember why they were holding the funeral in Pottsville. But this much I do remember: Beulah was one of the first girls I ever kissed. She was a quiet, sexy girl, my age, who wore high heels before other girls did. I was in love with her for a month or so, before she decided she was more in love with a boy named Pat Little, and I decided I was more in love with Catherine Mc-Ginley.

I could not understand why the priest picked me as a pall bearer, until I learned that many years earlier the Keiter family had been friends of the O'Hara family, my father's people, in Shenandoah, Pa., and that the Keiters wanted me because of that old friendship.

All I had to do was meet at the church with five other boys and walk up the aisle as they pushed the casket to the altar rail. As an altar boy I had often served Mass at funerals of people I did not know, but I had only been to two funerals that affected me personally: my favorite Uncle Eugene Delaney's, and my favorite Grandfather Delaney's. But they were family. I cried all through Beulah's funeral, because no one my age had died before and because I had once been in love with her.

In later years I had a couple of dates with Beulah's older sister, and we made out, as your generation says, but she did not seem to have any connection with Beulah. Beulah was separate and distinct, and always has been, all my life. She was my first sadness of that kind.

Why am I telling you this? Because if it's any comfort to you (and Patience and the other girls), Kassie is someone you will always remember with sweet sadness. You will remember her after you have ceased to remember some of your friends who live on. And it is a nice thing to be remembered.

Sadness is a part of growing up, of maturing, of learning to live.

IT BECAME O'Hara's custom to thank reviewers who treated his work respectfully, one of whom was William Hogan of the San Francisco *Chronicle*. In August 1961 O'Hara responded to Hogan's suggestion that he write an autobiography, explaining that he didn't want to take the time away from his fiction. "I have so much I want to write in the freedom of fiction, and that I want to see published while I am alive." Moreover, his autobiography would have to be published posthumously, as well as after the deaths of many of the people mentioned. It would be an enormous work: "For instance, I know the President of the U.S., but I have known his father for many years and consider him a friend of mine, as I do Mike Romanoff and Robert Lovett and Sol Joulwan. . . . I went to St. Patrick's school with Sol, whose father was King of the Syrian colony in Pottsville, Pa. Big Mike, the strongest man in the steel mill. You see what the word autobiography does to me? You also see why I will never run out of material."[3] In this letter O'Hara explained that he was 200 pages into *The Big Laugh* (which began as a novella and "took off"), having suspended work for the summer on *The Lockwood Concern* because he was away from his Princeton research facilities. *The Lockwood Concern* was not published until 1965.

In 1962 Professor Werner of Penn State wrote O'Hara about a

study of him by a former student of Werner's—in which it was stated that O'Hara was wrong when he claimed that his father had once owned five cars at the same time. This charge produced the article which John K. Hutchens published in the 8 April Sunday *Trib* book section, "Don't Say It Never Happened," in which O'Hara identified the five cars and spun off a rejoinder to the critics who had placed him on the wrong side of the tracks. He included, for good measure, an attack on the literary establishment "who hate me. And they better for I despise them."*

An example of O'Hara's sense of loyalty came during the long newspaper strike in 1962. Concerned that John K. Hutchens might be strapped for money, O'Hara wrote him a very tactful letter offering a loan and pointing out that their friendship was so old that there could be no question of impropriety in an author lending money to a critic. Hutchens did not need the money, but he was deeply impressed by the delicacy with which O'Hara handled the matter.[4]

The award of the Nobel Prize for 1962 to John Steinbeck produced mixed feelings in O'Hara. He was pleased for his friend, and considered the award merited. But, inevitably, O'Hara was disappointed for himself.† He had heard through the grapevine that he was being considered by the Nobel committee, and the selection of Steinbeck meant that there would be a waiting period before another American was chosen. O'Hara's congratulatory telegram read, YOU WERE MY SECOND CHOICE. Their friendship was not affected by the Nobel Prize. Indeed, he was distressed by the attacks on Steinbeck following the award. O'Hara analyzed Steinbeck's position with the critics in a 1964 letter to James Gould Cozzens:

Steinbeck has been a friend of mine since 1936, and last year he was badly wounded—trying not to show it, and showing it every minute— by the attacks on him following the Nobel prize. He did not know what hit him. He had been (like you) accustomed to respectful reviews throughout most of his career, and when there was an occasion for jubilation They suddenly turned on him. Of course They are not the same identical They who were reviewing 25 years ago; but the old

---

* Hutchens promised O'Hara that no changes would be made in the article, and he stayed in the composing room while the page was being made up in order to keep his promise.

† O'Hara did not respect the Pulitzer Prize for fiction, which he never received. The works he lost out to provide an instructive gauge of literary prizes: *Lamb in His Bosom* won out over *Appointment in Samarra* (and *Tender Is the Night*); *Andersonville* got the Pulitzer instead of *Ten North Frederick*, and *The Travels of Jaimie McPheeters* instead of *From the Terrace*.

They did not defend Steinbeck as they could have. I happen to know that I have been up for, and passed over for, the Nobel four times. If I ever get it, I know what to expect in the way of angry protest; but Steinbeck was taken completely by surprise.[5]

When Steinbeck later underwent eye surgery, O'Hara drove to Sag Harbor and read to him.

Katharine Delaney O'Hara died of cancer on 13 May 1962 at St. Vincent's Hospital in New York. She was eighty-three. Her son did not regard her as a pathetic figure—despite her years of hardship after Dr. O'Hara's death. He admired her strength of character and felt that she had been happy. O'Hara had developed a theory about God as "the Supreme Ironist," but not in a Hardyesque sense, for he believed that there was some kind of rough justice in life. He later wrote to Maxwell, "Life was fine, death was horrible, it all evened up in the end."[6] Burial was in Pottsville, and was the occasion of John O'Hara's penultimate visit to his birthplace.

AFTER APPLYING the stick to Bennett Cerf, O'Hara would frequently provide a carrot—as in his 18 December 1961 letter expressing satisfaction with the launching of *Assembly*. "You have been a good boy, so I am going to give you a best-seller for May: it is THE BIG LAUGH, a novel about an actor and the Hollywood that is no more. It is not like any Hollywood novel you ever read, and not very much like any anywhere—novel. No one else could have written it. No one." *The Big Laugh*, published in May 1962, was O'Hara's first—and only— Hollywood novel. (*Hope of Heaven* is set in Hollywood, but it is not about the movie industry.) The protagonist, Hubert Ward, is a character who, as the author carefully explains at the start of the novel

. . . tried to be something he was not; who wasted his time, and asked for and got a lot of trouble. As it happens, he was a rascal to begin with, and in a rare surge of perspicacity the people recognized him as such from the start. During his middle period he did nearly everything he could do to behave himself, but he only confused the people and while confusing the people he also confused himself, with results that were predictable because they had been predicted.

Ward's first important movie part is as a cowardly naval officer, and his director remarks, "He's playing the shitheel that he really is, as if he just discovered he was a shitheel." He marries a conservative widow, embarks on a life of extreme respectability—partly as an image-building plan—and falls into this private life so completely that he bores his wife into an affair. After two more bad marriages he is a lonely middle-aged celebrity:

He is Hubert Ward the movie star, and no son of a bitch can take that away from him.
Ha ha ha ha ha.

Although *The Big Laugh* is not an exercise in nostalgia, the quadruple dedication "To David Lewelyn Wark Griffith (1874–1948)/ Rudolph Alphonso Guglielmi di Valentino d'Antonguiela (1895– 1926)/Greta Louisa Gustafsson (1905–)/Roscoe Arbuckle (1887– 1933)" indicates that the novel is partly an attempt to record certain aspects of Hollywood during its golden age. O'Hara did not make his first trip to Hollywood until 1934, but he had worked on movie publicity earlier and had paid attention. Just as Ring Lardner once described his creative process as consisting of listening "hard," John O'Hara paid attention and remembered. The novel abounds in inside dope about the business end of the industry. One of the strongest sequences describes the Simmons house party at Malibu. A powerful movie executive, Charley Simmons is worried about the Depression, and his open concern is getting him into trouble with the other moguls who regard his brooding as weakness or disloyalty. Simmons' tough wife— she is actually his partner—shares this feeling about him and sleeps with Ward as an act of reprisal against her husband. When she tells Simmons, he drunkenly falls to his death from the roof of his house. The struggle for power, the fine lines of executive stratification are admirably presented. But, as is sometimes the problem with O'Hara's adulteresses, Mildred Simmons' behavior is not entirely explicable. She is not in love with Ward, and she clearly understands that he is worthless; yet she violates twenty years of loyalty to her husband and destroys their joint career in order to punish him for what she regards as weakness. Readers who were familiar with the code of such marriages were dubious. When charged with having distorted the sexual conduct of his characters—particularly the women—O'Hara's usual reply was that their behavior was based on his observation.

Inevitably, *The Big Laugh* triggered guesses about who Hubert Ward was based on. As was his custom, O'Hara did not comment, but he seems to have planted a clue in the character's name. However, as has been noted, readers who seek a simple one-to-one relationship between an O'Hara character and an actual person fail to comprehend his techniques for creating characters. Hubert Ward, like all principal O'Hara characters—except Gloria Wandrous and, perhaps, Jimmy Malloy—is a fictional character.

The Big Laugh was the first O'Hara novel that Random House did not have to reprint; however, it required eleven Bantam paperback printings. The comparative failure of this novel is rather puzzling, given the public's appetite for Hollywood fiction and O'Hara's qualifications for writing about Hollywood. It is possible that *The Big Laugh* was penalized for its comparative brevity. O'Hara's public had become accustomed to big novels, and this one was only 300 pages. Moreover, the customers expect Hollywood novels to be full of thinly disguised scandals and crimes. Instead, *The Big Laugh* is a novel without a hero, a thesis novel about a "shitheel." The problem is not so much—as the author anticipated in his preamble—that "the people who want re-generation to be permanent are fanatics for the happy ending," but rather that Hubert Ward does not carry the novel. He lacks that awareness of failure which lends consequence to unheroic protagonists, like Robert Millhouser.

In April 1962 O'Hara announced a volume of four novellas about Gibbsville, to be called *Third Class City*, for Thanksgiving. But the Thanksgiving book that year was *The Cape Cod Lighter*, which almost certainly included these novellas. It is not clear why *The Cape Cod Lighter* proved to be the most popular of the O'Hara story collections, although an obvious explanation is that *Assembly* and the *New Yorker* visibility generated particular interest in this volume. It was jokingly suggested that the book was bought by people who hoped to find out what the title meant. A Cape Cod lighter is a device for starting fires in fireplaces, and the significance of the title seems to be that the stories are about human fires ignited by some outside agency. The foreword to this collection was a rebuttal to the "New Enemies of Fiction"—in particular to two critics he referred to as "Monk Lovechild" (A. J. Liebling) and "Tootsie Washburn" (John Crosby*) in which O'Hara contended that most critics are failed novelists whose judgments are impaired by envy.

Of the twenty-three stories in *The Cape Cod Lighter*, six are obviously set in Gibbsville: "The Bucket of Blood," "Claude Emerson, Reporter," "The Engineer," "Jurge Dulrumple," "Pat Collins" and "Winter Dance." These stories are the strongest in the collection.

---

*In the Forties and Fifties O'Hara and John Crosby drank together at Bleeck's, and O'Hara urged him to go back to his roots in Wisconsin and write a novel. Crosby does not know how he incurred O'Hara's displeasure.

"Winter Dance," about a boy's love for an older girl, came out of O'Hara's memories of Margaretta Archbald. "Pat Collins," a seventy-page novella which brings back Whit Hofman from *Appointment in Samarra*, is a story of male friendship destroyed by sex. Collins, a new arrival in Gibbsville, becomes the favorite companion of Whit Hofman, but this friendship is ruined when Pat's wife sleeps with Whit. Pat holds his wife responsible for spoiling his great friendship—more than he blames Whit. Later, when Pat is befriended by another man, he does not tell his wife: "He could not let her spoil this, he could not let her spoil George Shuttleworth even by knowing about him." Here again is the O'Hara form of misogyny—the feeling that women through their sexuality possess the capacity to upset orderly male relationships. "Misogyny" may be too strong a term to apply to an author who enjoyed the company of women and had two happy marriages. Perhaps O'Hara's feeling is better described as distrust for the disruptive powers of sex.

"Pat Collins" includes a remarkable example of O'Hara's ability to write convincingly about matters outside his own field of experience in the character George Shuttleworth, a wealthy amateur scholar who has been dabbling with a book on Nathaniel Hawthorne for years.

"You knew that Nathaniel spent seven years abroad. Perhaps you didn't. Seven years from 1853 to 1860. . . . He'd done all his best work by then. . . . But I must find out for myself whether European life spoiled Nathaniel or did he flee to Europe when he'd exhausted his talents. That may turn out to be my greatest contribution to the study of Hawthorne. I can see quite clearly how my discoveries might cause me to scrap everything I've done so far and have to start all over again. I've already written to a great many scholars, and they've expressed keen interest."

This speech is perfect. O'Hara caught the mixture of knowledge and dilletantism, the cute reference to "Nathaniel," the elaborate rationalizing for not completing a book.

Assembly and *The Cape Cod Lighter* were combined into a Modern Library Giant, *49 Stories*, in 1963. Since Hemingway's collected stories is entitled *The First Forty-nine Stories*, O'Hara's title seems to invite comparison between the two writers' productivity.

At the beginning of 1963 O'Hara was able to send Bennett Cerf a two-year publishing projection. His letter makes it clear that the author was giving considerable thought to his *career*—not just his output or sales, but the larger matters of his achievement as an artist, and his permanent reputation.

18 Jan. '63

Dear Bennett:

I have decided on my publishing schedule for 1963.

In May I would like to bring out the novel, ELIZABETH APPLE-TON. This is the novel I completed about two years ago and have been holding for the opportune moment. It is a novel about a marriage in a small Pennsylvania college town. The time is the recent past. It will get me no honorary degrees—but then what has?

On Thanksgiving Day I would like to publish a collection of new stories of varying lengths. I have not decided on a title for it, but I will come up with a good one. I may, and I may not, write a Foreword for it.

I have abandoned the novel I almost finished last summer, which I was calling ADAMS LANDING. Recently I reread the manuscript with a view to getting started on it again. It has a lot of good stuff in it. Some very good. But I tried to do too much in too little space and got bogged down in chronologies. There is a lot worth saving, and at some future time I will go back again and see what I want to keep. For the present, however, it is on the shelf.

I have had too many interruptions of a non-literary nature in the writing of THE LOCKWOOD CONCERN. This is already a very long novel. I hope to finish it this year, for publication in 1964, prob-ably the autumn of '64. Another factor in my inability to complete this novel has been the ease with which I write and sell short stories. I sold two last week and I have three more yet unsold. This is not work for me, and I am not deceived by the praise that the stories get. I am the only man alive who could write THE LOCKWOOD CONCERN, who knows the material and how to handle it, just as I was the only one who could have written FROM THE TERRACE, etc.

George Gershwin had an assured reputation with his songs, but he also had to write the Rhapsody in Blue and the other longer pieces, and would have gone on to bigger and better ones if he had lived. You take a tune like MINE, for instance. That's like one of my short stories; it could easily (with a lot of hard work, but easily) become a long piece, but instead of a fugue we have a rich little tune that is only one of many. That is not right. When you have the mastery of your medium that George had (and that I have, let's not kid about that), you simply must not let easy popularity keep you from the big things. There is one of the basic differences between George Gershwin, the composer, and Richard Rodgers, the song writer. Rodgers has to be content with songs, and he now has a song that is almost straight Cole Porter—except that Cole Porter would have known how to hold the melodic line. I refer to THE SWEETEST SOUND, which could also have been written by Jule Styne—and the first six notes were written by Vincent Youmans in NO NO NANETTE. Do you see what I mean? The pleasant little pieces become derivatives; it is only when you do something more ambitious, longer, that you display your unique artistry, your staying powers. Rodgers wrote one successful piece that was longer than a song—SLAUGHTER ON TENTH AVENUE, but even that was quasi-Gershwin, with AN AMERICAN IN PARIS ringing in his ear. I don't want that kind of success.

Yrs,
John

The following year O'Hara invited Cerf and Random House to collaborate in his campaign for the Nobel Prize by doing a better job with the advertising for his books.

CAMBRIDGE BEACHES • Somerset • **BERMUDA**

---

31 March 64

Dear Bennett:

I would like you to check up and tell me when you last ran an ad for THE HAT ON THE BED. I am quite certain that you will find that you did not buy an agate line during the whole months of March and very probably not in February either. This book is not a mystery story, and it needs help. I especially want the book to be selling in May, when I get the Academy medal. The fact that I am getting the medal for my work in the <u>novel</u> is especially gratifying in the light of the success of my short story collections.

You know what I'm after. It's no secret that I am <u>working</u> to get the Nobel. I am not making speeches, or writing letters, or giving interviews, like James T. Farrell and Graham Greene. I am constantly at work, not only quantitatively but also maintaining as high standards as are within my power, and this has been going on for some time.

I have never been an author whom people made excuses for, or in whose work people pretended to see more than is there. The most disgusting recent exhibition of an author as well as his admirers on the excuse-making kick is, of course, Arthur Miller. They got tired of doing it for Irwin Shaw. They cooked Salinger and have turned against him. They will do it to Cheever and Ringo Updike, they've done it to K. A. Porter. They've never alibied for me, so when I get a badge, it means something. It means that the work has prevailed, and that's the way I want it to be. But it deserves support. I would like to see a quote ad written by a man who is not afraid to use the best quotes.

Be home Friday. May see you next week.

As ever
John

In 1963 O'Hara's stories began appearing in *The Saturday Evening Post* as well as *The New Yorker*. No trouble with *The New Yorker* was involved; he was writing more stories than that magazine could publish, and the faltering *Post* was in need of good fiction by authors whose names would sell copies. The fact that he became a *Post* author in the Sixties does not mean he tailored stories to the *Post*. There is no difference in material or treatment between the nine *New Yorker* and five *Post* stories of 1963; any one of them could have appeared in either magazine. O'Hara's work had not changed; the *Post*'s editorial policies had evolved beyond the standards set by George Horace Lorimer. When Clay Blair became editor of the *Post* he made a point of seeking O'Hara's stories as part of a general plan to reintroduce "literary" fiction into the magazine that had published Faulkner and Fitzgerald during its great years. Blair wrote to O'Hara asking for stories. O'Hara replied in some disbelief, setting the conditions under which his work could be seen by the *Post*, which were the same as the conditions he had set for *The New Yorker*. Don Schanche, the executive editor, was assigned to handle O'Hara, and he made his first visit to "Linebrook" in January 1963. "I expected a crusty bastard and found a gracious, charming, warm and friendly man who obviously wanted to talk, which he did for about three hours (in the study) during which we had lunch."[7] O'Hara gave him twelve stories to read, of which Schanche bought four on the spot—"Aunt Anna," "The Glendale People," "Exterior: With Figure" and "The Ride from Mauch Chunk." They worked out the policy that payment for a story under fourteen pages would be $3,000, and $4,000 for a longer story. O'Hara earned $14,000 that day. The first *Post* appearance of an O'Hara story was "The Glendale People," in the 2 March 1963 issue. (On 9 April 1963 O'Hara noted in his "Wafer" diary: "35 years ago this day. My first cheque from The New Yorker—$15.")[8] Thereafter Schanche visited "Linebrook" regularly to read a group of stories and accept those he wanted. This working relationship suited O'Hara ideally, and the two men got along well—so well that O'Hara subsequently granted Schanche the important 1969 interview published in *Esquire*.

In February 1963 O'Hara offered Schanche a play that he had written a year earlier but had not submitted to a producer. It had been written with Jackie Gleason in mind, but O'Hara did not bother to send it to him after Gleason announced that he would never do another Broadway play. The play, *Far from Heaven** is O'Hara's best straight

---

* The title comes from a Catholic hymn: "Mother dear, O pray for me while far from heaven and thee."

drama after *The Farmers Hotel* and traces the attempts of a politician in Manhattan's Chelsea district to regain his power after serving a prison term to cover for the higher-ups in the organization. His defeat is convincingly inexorable as his former stooges desert him at the instigation of the party bosses. Although the protagonist is not an admirable figure, he is the strongest character in the play, and his futile efforts to make a comeback elicit reader sympathy, if only because his opponents are so contemptible. O'Hara did not think that plays made good reading—he said that the dialogue identifications made reading a play too much like watching a tennis match—but he suggested that the *Post* might be able to have somebody else convert *Far from Heaven* into story form, an astonishing concession from a writer who fiercely resisted editorial assistance. When Schanche reported that nobody at the *Post* had the nerve to attempt the job, O'Hara admitted that a man ought to do his own work, and said he would do the conversion himself—but never did. In April 1963 O'Hara considered converting *Far from Heaven* into a musical with Howard Dietz and Arthur Schwartz for Mary Martin, "if she wants to change from the greasy kid parts"; but the project never developed.

Don Schanche required relatively little training in the technique of working with John O'Hara. Nevertheless, when Schanche queried the speech in "The Lawbreaker" O'Hara wrote on 18 May 1963:

One thing you need never worry about in my stories is the dialog. Not to go into another long lecture on The Art of John O'Hara, I may say briefly that I hear the dialog before I put it down on paper. In this case I "heard" Beatrice Kelley. Beatrice was a maid of ours for eight years. . . . She was a Jamaican. . . . In all the West Indies and Bermuda, etc., wherever the English were influential, you get that stilted phraseology, as you quite aptly describe it. You doo nevvah cohnfuse it with a white persohn's speech. . . .

O'Hara was particularly pleased with "The Lawbreaker" and felt he had handled the gangsters well. The story is about the son of a respectable family who becomes a rumrunner in New England and Florida during prohibition. When the mob becomes suspicious of him —wrongly—he quits the business to avoid being murdered. O'Hara wrote Schanche: "I knew some of those people. They were plenty tough, but I am getting a little deeper than the superficial toughness. On the other hand, I fully believed Gatsby until I went to NY and met some of those mob people. Gatsby would not have lasted a week with the ones I met, let alone taken control."⁹ He also liked "The Lawbreaker" because it was an attempt to revise his story technique:

*In the past thirty or forty years there have been very few first-rate short stories that contained action or plot; we who wrote the stories have been influenced by Chekhov, among others, and have been re-acting against the junky plot stories that Littauer at Collier's and Rose at the Post, among others, have insisted upon. That reaction was okay. The plot stories did bear little relation to truth and life. But having been one of the leading practitioners of the oblique and the plotless, I have recently been putting action back into my stories.**

O'HARA TOOK great pride in Wylie's success at St. Timothy's. Her election as class president in May 1962 gave him profound pleasure, as did her acceptance by Bennett College in Millbrook, New York:

[26 February 1963] I am writing you now to tell you how pleased I am, we are, about Bennett. I am particularly pleased because you got in without my having to search around and see where I could use my influence, if any. You got in on your record and the recommendation of Miss Watkins, which is so much better for you than to have me put the pressure on the Bennett trustees—assuming I knew them. Obviously Miss Watkins gave you the highest recommendation, to have them accept you so early in the game, and her fondness and admiration for you (which Patience mentioned to her parents last weekend) is going to continue after you leave St. Tim's. I am so glad I sent you to St. Tim's for the full four years. You would not have got much out of the extra year at Miss Fine's, and you did get a lot out of starting St. Tim's early. So did I. I got a better understanding of Miss Watkins and of the school. It has been an expensive four years, and the best expenditure I ever made (except for the money I paid Dr. Damon to bring you into the world).

[May 1963] Sister is off to Quogue, so I am alone for the rest of the week and I would have been even more miserable if you hadn't tele-phoned. But you did telephone, and that is over. I had a particularly rough time these past few weeks. A week ago yesterday I heard on the radio that Faulkner had been given the Pulitzer prize (instead of THE CAPE COD LIGHTER, which rumor had it would or might get it);

---

* O'Hara's letter was used as a headnote when *The Saturday Evening Post* published "The Lawbreaker" (16 November 1963).

then an hour later my friend Edgar Scott telephoned to say I had been blackballed at The Brook club. The reason? Certain members of the screening committee did not like what I have written about clubs and did not want it to appear that The Brook, by making me a member, appeared to approve of what I had written. Then I also bet on the Kentucky Derby, and my horse, No Robbery, ran out of the money and I had bet him across the board (win, place, and show).

Oddly enough, Louie Gates's suicide did not shock me. Saddened, but not shocked. Although she was unhappy over Geoff's death, and before that, the death of her previous husband, Harry Hopkins. . . . Life with Hopkins was glamorous, meeting Churchill and all those people, but I never felt Louie was really in love with Hopkins. If you are ever disappointed in love, don't marry on the rebound. It seldom works. Marry only for love. Marriage needs love to help both parties through the tough times, and there are tough times in every marriage. Marriage also needs love to get both parties through the good times. Without love, the good times can be meaningless and impermanent. As you must be aware by this time, I got around quite a bit through the years; I had quite a few affairs. But those I remember most pleasantly had some love in addition to the sex and companionship, and in later years the sex recedes in importance, and the affection, or love, is what makes you remember the other person. I am not knocking sex, but the power of it does not last long without love. And in your heart you always know when it is sex alone that attracts you to a person, or that attracts the person to you.

I have seen the graduation present Sister got you. (I don't mean your graduation dress.) It is really beautiful, and you will have it long long after the Spitfire has spat its last spit. Or fire. The 5th and 14th of June will be big days for me as well as for you, because you have made them so.

[28 May 1963] I wanted you to be head of school, captain of the Spiders, tennis champion, and to get your classmates in a crap game in the Sixes Room and win $18,000 so that you could buy me a Rolls-Royce for Christmas.

Seriously, if you think I am in any way disappointed in you, you are out of your little pink mind. I do not want you to be any of the things you are not at the sacrifice of the things that you are: a warm, human, honorable, decent, sensitive girl. Far from being the kind of person who makes a big splash in her, or his, teens, you are entering a future that is so exciting that I believe you sense it yourself, deep down. I believe you sense it because you are having a final struggle, wrenching yourself away from the past. It is almost like giving birth to yourself. Keep this letter and in ten years, or even five, see if the

*old man isn't right. I'll even put the date on this letter. And don't be
afraid of the future. You'll get what you want, if it's what you want.*

THE ACADEMIC NOVEL, *Elizabeth Appleton*, appeared in June 1963,
having begun as a play entitled *The Sisters* or *You Are My Sister* in
1954. The setting is a small college in western Pennsylvania (probably
based on Washington and Jefferson in Washington, Pennsylvania) and
the plot involves academic politics: will Dean John Appleton get the
presidency? However, the novel is primarily a study of marriage
against the background of academia. Elizabeth Appleton is a rich girl
who married a poor graduate student she met when he was a tutor on
Long Island. She has played the academic wife's game carefully, and
after nineteen years of marriage, John Appleton is heir-apparent to the
presidency of Spring Valley College. The weekend that the new
president is to be chosen, the Appletons are visited by her younger
sister, Jean, who has had two divorces and is considering a third
marriage. Jean is seeking guidance from her presumably happily married sister. The truth is that Elizabeth is bored by her husband and has
had an intense affair. She refused to marry her lover because that
would have been destructive to John, for she recognized that her
husband needed her more than her lover did.

John wants the presidency for Elizabeth as much as for himself,
but he fails to get it—partly because the college trustees don't like
having their decision made for them by being offered a logical candidate. They want to exercise the power of decision. The novel is
resolved with the Appletons' understanding that the fact of their
marriage is what matters; it will endure, perhaps firmer than before
their disappointment about the presidency, because of the years they
have invested in it. *Elizabeth Appleton*, then, takes a curiously old-
fashioned position on marriage in view of John O'Hara's image as the
Boswell of infidelity. It makes the point that many good marriages
are maintained by convenience and habit, that the time comes when
it is simply easier to stay married. *Elizabeth Appleton* was the last
O'Hara novel to sell well in cloth, requiring five Random House printings in 1963. It was dedicated to Pat Outerbridge.

Elizabeth Appleton was the first O'Hara novel to present Albert
Erskine with editorial problems. The typescript had serious chronological inconsistencies, for the ages of the characters did not jibe with
the dates of the story. Erskine made an elaborate outline of the story
in order to point out the inconsistencies.

The publication of *Elizabeth Appleton* brought a request from Richard Boeth of *Newsweek* for an interview, which O'Hara declined; but Boeth obtained the intercession of their mutual friend, Wilder Hobson. Four interviews of three hours each for a cover story were arranged on O'Hara's terms: no tape recorders and no note-taking. There was no small talk, but O'Hara did admit to Boeth that he was using *Newsweek* against *Time.** Boeth would leave "Linebrook" with his head full of information, drive out of sight of the house, and make his notes in the parked car. The article appeared in the 3 June 1963 *Newsweek* with the heading JOHN O'HARA AT 58: A RAGE TO WRITE. The subject had no reason to regret his cooperation, for Boeth's article was respectful and accurate.

O'Hara spent less time with Wilder Hobson after his writing schedule increased and his study became the focus of his life. He left "Linebrook" grudgingly. There was no break in his friendship with Hobson, and they had invented a mail game that involved identifying the college of the groom from the names of the ushers in newspaper wedding reports. When Hobson died in 1964 O'Hara worried about his family. He paid Archibald Hobson's prep school bills and bought him a suit when he entered Yale.

AFTER GRADUATION from St. Timothy's in 1963, Wylie entered Bennett College. O'Hara's lingering disappointment about his own lack of a college education made it particularly disappointing for him when his daughter left college after her first year. One of his rare strict-father letters was written in 1963, when he felt that Wylie was not showing proper seriousness about money.

You left this cheque on the table in the livingroom. You will recall that as soon as you asked for your allowance, I went to my study

---

* In August 1964, writing James Gould Cozzens to acknowledge a copy of *Children and Others*, O'Hara expressed his outrage at the 1957 *Time* cover story on Cozzens. "They wanted to do one on me, and I told Luce that after what they had done *to* you and tried to do *for* Herman Wouk, I didn't want any part of them unless Luce himself came down and did the interviewing and wrote the piece. Then, I said, I would know whom to thank." Cozzens and O'Hara never met, although they lived within twenty miles of each other in New Jersey. They respected each other's work, and Cozzens was particularly complimentary about *Elizabeth Appleton*: ". . . Your Spring Valley small college is a wonderfully right, perceptive job."[10]

and wrote out the cheque and brought it in and gave it to you, because you were going to need it the next day in New York.

This cheque is for a larger amount than my entire allowance any year that I was in boarding school. In 1963 it represents approximately the royalty after taxes on the sale of nearly 1,000 books. It is almost twice as much as I earned as a reporter on the Herald Tribune, and I supported myself on that salary. That is, I paid for all my room, board, clothes, and fun on that salary. I had no other income. I therefore take a rather dim view of your casual attitude toward a cheque for $275.

This is, I suppose, your swinging year, and I want you to have a good time. Nevertheless I want you from time to time to give mature thought to certain matters. Every cent, every single cent, that is spent on you, and that you spend, comes out of money that I have earned by hard, hard work. Not one single cent of your mother's or grandmother's money had been touched. Your car, for instance, cost me as much money as I have, after taxes, from the sale of four New Yorker stories. Your year at Bennett will have cost me as much as I netted, after taxes, on the sale of *A FAMILY PARTY.*

As authors go, I am, as I told you, a rich man. But there are not many authors who make nearly as much money as I do, and I do it because I am good and because I work very hard. In the midst of your good time I want you to stop and think once in a while about where the money comes from; not only because it is absolutely necessary for you yourself to get some perspective on your own financial position. When you have finished your education you are going to have to go to work, to earn a salary. I will be 59 in January, and it is just kidding myself to think that I can go on working this hard and earning this kind of money, and I do not often kid myself. At 21 you will be coming into some money, but as I have often told you, it is not going to be enough to make you Miss Richbitch or to permit you to live as Miss Richbitch. I am letting you have a good time now, because this is the time to have it, when you are young. But I would be doing you no favor if I failed to remind you of the hard realities. One of the hardest realities is money and the handling of it. Another is the fact that until you marry, and possibly even after, you are going to be a working-girl. I am very fond of most of your friends, but you must not get into the habit of taking for granted that I am as rich as some of their fathers. I'm not. I have earned as much in one year as you will inherit from your mother's estate. And you will only get the income from your grandmother's trust fund; the principal is held in trust for your children.

Now, and during the months ahead, I want you to direct your thoughts toward your own future, the kind of work you want to do, the kind of man you want to marry, the contributions you can make *to your marriage, and the future wellbeing of your children. I assure you that if you do this you will enjoy yourself more than if you enjoy yourself aimlessly.*

BETWEEN THE TERMINATION of "Appointment with O'Hara" in 1956 and "My Turn" in 1964, O'Hara was without a column, and he obviously missed the opportunity to make public comments on current events. He turned to sending letters to the New York *Herald Tribune*: in addition to nine Letters to the Editor, he sent Red Smith four letters which became sports columns. These *Trib* letters include praise of Edmund Gilligan's "Out of Doors" column, tributes to his friends Rex Smith and F.P.A., a plug for the Yankees, a recollection of sneaking the first female into the Yale Club bar, a comment on Russian policy, a satiric reaction to the news that President Kennedy had banned the *Trib* from the White House. The most important of the public letters were three about television press coverage of the Congress. On 19 September 1962 O'Hara responded to a statement by William S. Paley, in which the CBS president advocated live television coverage of committee hearings in the House and Senate and of the courts. O'Hara asserted that the presence of cameras would promote a circus atmosphere because the people involved would perform for the TV audience.* Richard S. Salant, president of CBS news, replied on the twenty-fifth, commenting on O'Hara's appointment with the eighteenth century. On 28 September O'Hara responded, putting in a good word for the citizens of the eighteenth century: "They produced this nation. CBS produced the $64,000 quiz program." O'Hara's final comment on this question came on 17 April 1963 when the *Trib* published his letter protesting against an NBC "newsreader," referring to the TV people as "working press." The most interesting of the contributions to Red Smith's column was occasioned by the death of fight manager Jack Kearns and the consequent renewal of speculation about whether he had loaded Jack Dempsey's gloves for the Willard fight:

My father was pretty good with his hands, whether he was operating on a man's skull to relieve the pressure on the brain or breaking a Kluxer's jaw for calling him a Molly Maguire. Patrick O'Hara, M.D. could open you up with a scalpel or with a jab and

* In this letter O'Hara committed a blunder in referring to the "Lincoln-Seward debates."

an uppercut. Thus qualified, he had credentials as an expert when he told me about the Willard-Dempsey fight at Toledo.

He and a carload of Pennsylvanians who were the paying guests of Philadelphia Jack O'Brien, attended that fight, and I can add his testimony to the revived controversy.

He told me that when the fight was over he helped Willard leave the arena. Willard, he said, could not see clearly because Dempsey's fists had been soaked in plaster-of-Paris, and my old man led Willard out of the place. In 1919 I didn't understand the plaster-of-Paris bit and so my old man explained it to me; and I have remembered it all these years. That long ago, nearly 45 years ago, I had a first-hand report of what happened to Willard.[11]

The Hat on the Bed, published Thanksgiving 1963, had twenty-four stories—six of which are set in The Region. The longest story in this volume, "Ninety Minutes Away," opens in South Taqua (Tamaqua) but takes place mostly in Philadelphia. A story about a reporter and a corrupt showgirl, it is full of a young man's exuberance at being in a big city during the Twenties. The collection included two remarkable Hollywood stories, "The Glendale People" and "Yucca Knolls"—a long story previously published in *Show Magazine*—which looks back at Hollywood in the Thirties and Forties. The most powerful story in *The Hat on the Bed* is "How Can I Tell You?"—a classic O'Hara story of suicidal despair. Mark McGranville, a car salesman, has a very successful day—two Galaxies and a Thunderbird—yet is unaccountably depressed. The purchaser of the Thunderbird has been patronizing, but not painfully so. Mark is happily married and has no problems; but at two A.M. he gets out of bed and sits with a loaded shotgun until his wife says, "Don't. Please?" He answers, "I won't." His depression is frighteningly convincing just because there is no overt reason for it: his life has turned meaningless. *The Hat on the Bed* required four Random House printings. It did not, however, include the O'Hara foreword that his readers had come to expect. The title refers to the superstition that it is bad luck to put a hat on a bed, but it is misleading to say that all the stories in this volume are characterized by misfortune.

IN FEBRUARY 1964—two years after his resignation from the Institute—O'Hara received notification from John Hersey that he had been selected for the Award of Merit Medal for the Novel by the American Academy of Arts and Letters. Don Schanche was with O'Hara when the call came, and he saw tears coursing down O'Hara's face as he talked to Hersey. This award was a greater honor than the Institute's

John Hersey presenting O'Hara with Award of Merit Medal for the Novel,
American Academy of Arts and Letters, 1964.

Gold Medal, for it had been made to only four other novelists.*
The ceremony took place on 20 May 1964, and Hersey made a graceful
presentation speech that said the things John O'Hara could agree with:
"The stereotype of the successful American writer is one who with
the slipping years becomes dissipated by a sense of failure, by literary
politicking, by alcohol, by envy, by praise or a want of it, by money
or a lack of it. John O'Hara has put all that weak nonsense aside in
honor of his obsession. He goes to his room every night and writes,
and in the pleasure of his work his power grows."† O'Hara had warned
Hersey that he would probably cry during his acceptance speech, and
he did. The speech was short and grateful, but not humble.

At least some *of the liberties that the younger writers enjoy today
were paid for by me, in vilification of my work and abuse of my*

---

* The award was accompanied by a check for $1,000. The previous recipients
had been Theodore Dreiser, Thomas Mann, Ernest Hemingway and Aldous
Huxley.
† The words "he goes to his room" are a reference to the Yale Tap Day
ceremony, and O'Hara no doubt regarded it as a particular compliment.

personal character. . . . These obvious facts need re-stating today because in the context of present-day writing I am regarded as obsolescent, and rightly so. I continue to experiment in every novel that I write, but the experimentation is in techniques rather than in point of view or in principles. There are things that I am for and things I am against, and they have not changed much in thirty years nor are they likely to. The fully rounded irony is that I can expect the same degree of abuse from the new critics for my 1964 conservatism that I got from my critics for my lack of restraint in 1934. But as long as I live, or at least as long as I am able to write, I will go to the typewriter with love of my work and at least a faint hope that once in a great while something like today will happen to me again. We all know how good we are, but it's nice to hear it from someone else.[12]

O'Hara never found it necessary to play Uriah Heep. He was proud of his craft and his achievements; he did not regard modesty as a necessary part of a master's equipment. After the presentation ceremony Charles Mann, the curator of rare books at Penn State, introduced himself to O'Hara, saying that he had made the best speech of the day and that the university was proud to have the O'Hara papers. "Here is another manuscript for the collection," said O'Hara, handing him the speech.

In view of the frequent application of the terms "arrogance" and "insecurity" to John O'Hara, his own self-appraisal in a 1963 letter to William Maxwell merits consideration. O'Hara approached the question by contrasting his own attitude toward literary prizes with Fitzgerald's. Where Fitzgerald could "derive comfort" from the fact that *So Big* won the Pulitzer Prize the year *The Great Gatsby* was published, O'Hara got mad in similar situations. He felt that Fitzgerald possessed a quality of cockiness or personal arrogance that he lacked, whereas O'Hara had greater confidence in himself as a writer. Fitzgerald agonized over his work, but O'Hara felt much more sure of himself at the typewriter. He provided Maxwell with an anecdote illustrating Fitzgerald's arrogance, which is also a superb example of O'Hara's delicate sense of sexual stratification. "He told me about two movie stars that he wanted to invite to a party Belle and I gave for him, implying that he had laid both of them. Well, he had laid one of them, but not the other, and the one he laid he had laid in her dressing-room but not at home."[13]

The Award of Merit Medal caused O'Hara to reconsider his relationship with the Institute, and in the fall of 1964 he dispatched a feeler in the form of an inquiry to John Hersey about the rosette that Ernest Hemingway wore. Hersey picked up the cue perfectly: "But

I propose to you a first-rate solution to the rosette problem: come back." O'Hara replied graciously: "Many thanks for your letter, and for the trouble you have taken. Unlike J. P. Sartre, I have no fear of being institutionalized (or, for that matter, academized). I therefore accept with pleasure and some alacrity your invitation to rejoin the National Institute of Arts and Letters. Not to do so would be churlish, and anyway I made my point when I resigned. The Academy Gold Medal had the effect of binding my wounds."[14] O'Hara came to believe that the Academy awarded him the medal in order to obviate giving him a seat—as his comment to Hersey on being "academized" indicates. When it became clear that he was to be permanently excluded, he ceased to be an active member of the Institute. He was bothered as much by who was in as he was by his own exclusion: "S.J. Perelman has as much right being there as I have driving in the Indianapolis 500."[15] Meanwhile O'Hara was not hurting in the bookshops. By 1964 his publishers estimated that twenty million copies of his books had been printed in twenty languages.

A television network approached O'Hara in 1964 about a program based on Gibbsville, in the hope of creating another *Peyton Place*. He declined this offer, although he liked the idea of a series that would dramatize his stories. For this reason he vetoed Albert Erskine's suggestion that the early story collections be reprinted, because O'Hara thought it would somehow interfere with a TV deal. When Erskine pressed him about reprinting *Doctor's Son*, *Files on Parade*, *Pipe Night* and *Hellbox*, O'Hara replied, "Posthumously, posthumously."

AFTER LEAVING COLLEGE in 1964 Wylie took a secretarial course at the Katharine Gibbs school and worked in New York. It was time for her to start bringing suitors home, and her father objected to one young man who did not treat Wylie with sufficient respect. In 1966 she became engaged to Dennis Holahan. Apart from his personal qualities, Dennis had the right background for the role of John O'Hara's son-in-law: Andover and Yale '65 (where he was a member of the Fence Club). Although his home was Darien, Connecticut, he had family roots in The Region—one of his aunts had been treated by Dr. O'Hara. After Yale, Dennis was commissioned an ensign in the navy at OCS, Newport, Rhode Island. Inevitably, O'Hara had to endure wisecracks to the effect that he had hand-picked a Yalie for his daughter. The wedding ceremony was held on 10 September 1966 at St. Vincent Ferrer's Roman Catholic Church in Manhattan, and was followed by a reception at the Colony Club. John enjoyed the occasion enormously.

When Dick Dilworth saw him at the reception he commented that John looked like Mr. Dooley getting ready to open his saloon on St. Patrick's Day. After the wedding O'Hara wrote Bennett Cerf a high-spirited letter about how Sister wouldn't let him help the bridesmaids with their zippers.

O'Hara missed his daughter when she joined her husband on Guam, and he continued to encourage her intellectual expansion. In March of 1967 he sent her a copy of Sheilah Graham's *College of One*, the account of her education by F. Scott Fitzgerald: "Miss Graham is not too accurate; in this book and in an earlier one she seems to be trying to create the impression that she and I were A Thing. We were not. But apart from that, I thought you might be interested in seeing what Fitzgerald recommended for reading. His recommendations are very sound, I think, and when time weighs heavily on your hands, you can be guided by his taste."*

The Horse Knows the Way—the fourth story collection in four years —appeared on Thanksgiving 1964. John O'Hara had published 101 short stories in four years while writing three novels, as well as plays. With this volume Random House initiated the custom of publishing a limited printing of numbered and signed copies simultaneously with the trade printing.†

The title for *The Horse Knows the Way* comes from Lydia Maria Child's poem, "Thanksgiving Day," which, as every schoolchild once knew, begins "Over the river and through the wood,/To grandfather's house we go;/The horse knows the way/To carry the sleigh/Through the white and drifted snow."‡ The sentimental connotations of the title were partly ironic, since the prevailing mood of the volume has nothing to do with the poem except for evoking a remembered past; however, the title was primarily a reference to the O'Hara Thanksgiving Day publication custom. The foreword to *The Horse Knows the Way* announced, "For a while, at least, this will be my last book of short stories." (Although he did skip 1965, O'Hara published collections in 1966 and 1968.) He explained that at fifty-nine he felt the

---

* O'Hara had been indirectly responsible for *Beloved Infidel*, Sheilah Graham's 1958 account of her association with Fitzgerald. When he was in Hollywood in 1955 producer Jerry Wald suggested that he write a movie biography of Fitzgerald, and O'Hara told him to ask Miss Graham.[16]

† The limitation for *The Horse Knows the Way* was 250 copies, which was raised to 300 for subsequent volumes.

‡ O'Hara also took the title for the 1934 story "Over the River and Through the Wood" from this poem.

responsibility to concentrate his energies on the novel and not "play it safe" with short stories, for the 1964 Award of Merit from the American Academy of Arts and Letters had reinforced "an obligation to the something that is not all you and is not all Art, but is that which does make cowards of us all, and hence the fear." He concluded with the moving declaration, "I have work to do, and I am afraid not to do it."*

Of the twenty-eight stories in the collection, thirteen had appeared in *The Saturday Evening Post* and four in *The New Yorker*. The Region is represented by eight stories—including "Arnold Stone," "The Hardware Man," "All Tied Up" and "Zero." The opening story, "All Tied Up," traces the escalation of an irritation into something destructive when a bank president notices that a teller is wearing loafers to work. The banker and his manager quarrel over the teller, and the bank manager resigns. At the end of the story the bank manager will have to crawl back for his job. Nobody is entirely wrong—not even the inflexible president—but a man's pride has been broken. "Zero" is another story of human destruction. On a bitterly cold night a man meets the trolley on which a girl who has just had an abortion arrives in a small town near Gibbsville. Her married lover can do very little to help her; they quarrel about money, and he slaps her. Then he goes home to his wife, who knows he is involved with another woman, and slaps her. When she threatens to kill him, he states that she'd be doing him a favor:

The strange, simple words shocked her. Whatever else he had said to her, these words she recognized as the truth; at this moment he wished to be dead and free, but not only free of her. More than to be free of her he wished to be free of the other woman. She could think of nothing to say, but she knew that no words of hers could threaten this man with trouble. She was looking at destruction, and she had no part in it.

The way in which a John O'Hara story emerged from his pool of memories and the emotions associated with these memories is revealed by the letter to William Maxwell that accompanied "Zero." The story is not attributed to an actual experience, but it is intimately involved with the author's feelings about a time and place in The Region. When John O'Hara sat at his typewriter in the late-night silence at "Linebrook," the study was crowded.

---

* This sentence was misquoted—even in print—as "I have work to do, and I am not afraid to do it."

In 1922 I was in love with a girl named Gladys Suender, who was known in our set as The Creole. A real beauty, and to some extent the Natalie in FROM THE TERRACE. Her younger sister and husband were here last Saturday after the Yale game, and Jane told me that Gladys is in the hospital and may die. Kidney. Gladys has had a cruel life. A lousy marriage, ending in a desertion; family lost their dough, etc. Anyway, the Suenders lived in Frackville, up the Mountain, the second coldest town in the Commonwealth, next to Snowshoe, Pa. In 1922 the new road had not been completed (a new road which has now been abandoned, by the way) and on one side of the road there was a sheer drop of maybe 500 feet and never room for three cars abreast. So one night I was on my way back to Pottsville after a date with Gladys. If you got going right you could coast six miles in neutral from Frackville into the town of St. Clair. I had my old man's Buick phaeton and I got going right, all right, but half way down I discovered that while I was at Gladys's house the foot brake had frozen tight. So had the hand brake, and I was moving along at about 40 m.p.h. Nothing else was on the road, but sometimes the bootleggers in their Reo Speedwagons would come through in convoy at about that hour and they didn't give a damn about anyone. The only thing I could do, I did, which was to ease the right fenders and running board against the bushes and rocks on the edge of the road, which slowed me down, until I was able to run the car up against the embankment without crashing. I got to St. Clair in second gear. The town Frackville is, of course, the town in ZERO.[17]

Although O'Hara's style (defined as "The arrangement of words in a manner which at once best expresses the individuality of the author and the idea and intent in his mind") offers no challenge to his readers, other aspects of his technique merit the closest attention. In particular, O'Hara's treatment of point of view shows delicate variations in what might be called the voice of fiction. What superficially seem to be monologues are rarely straight monologues, for O'Hara effects a blending of the character's voice with the author's voice. The character's thoughts are controlled by the author's intelligence—so that the attentive reader is simultaneously inside and outside the monologue. In "The Bonfire," a 1964 story that O'Hara particularly liked, a recently widowed young woman realizes how isolated she is as she walks toward a beach party:

It was a long way, and she could make out the figures before she could hear them. She was so close to the ocean that its sounds were all she could hear for the first fifty yards, the first seventy-five yards, the first hundred. And then the voices began to penetrate the sounds of the ocean. She walked on and the voices grew more distinct, the voices of young women and young men, a harsh and frightening chorus of people who did not want her. She stopped to listen. Now she could hear baritone derision and alto contempt and soprano coquetry answered by the baritone derision, and though they were ignorant of her existence they were commanding her to stay away.

The emotions are the woman's; but the presentation and interpretation are O'Hara's. The effect is that of a compound voice.

Most of the novels are structured around O'Hara's voice as controlling intelligence. He is not annoyingly intrusive and only infrequently addresses the reader directly; nevertheless, the point of view and therefore the moral framework of the works are controlled by O'Hara. Since this is the case, it is surprising that one of the familiar denigrations of his work has it that O'Hara is morally callous or indifferent, and that consequently his work lacks a basic vision of what critics like to call "the human predicament." It is difficult to reply to large libels except by protesting that they are lies. Critics who find O'Hara's world lacking in moral framework cannot be enlightened, for what they probably mean is that they reject his standards of judgment. The problem, therefore, is cultural rather than moral or literary. When it comes to understanding O'Hara's work these critics suffer from cultural deprivation. They don't know what he is writing about, and they don't care about his material. They don't share his standards of behavior; therefore, they are incapable of sharing his moral concerns. It was mandatory for these critics to dismiss John O'Hara's work as shallow, to reject his characters as trivial.*

Albert Erskine's duties as John O'Hara's editor came to include the tricky chore of writing dust-jacket copy. O'Hara vetted the material before it was printed, and Erskine handled the assignments so well that only the copy for *The Instrument* was rejected—which the editor revised to the author's satisfaction. O'Hara did not seek an intimate relationship with his editor, but for fifteen years—commencing with *Ten North Frederick*—they had a friendly working relationship characterized by mutual respect. They did not often socialize; but

---

* Writing in the Boston *Evening Globe* after O'Hara's death, George Frazier spoke up for the "O'Hara people": "Naturally, one reason we have this affinity for O'Hara is that he knows about court tennis and custom tailoring and chic clubs, and if Alfred Kazin doesn't like it, why doesn't he review writers who know about stick ball and where to buy a suit with two pairs of pants and a catcher's mitt?" (27 April 1970).

when they were together at parties they enjoyed each other's company, and O'Hara made a point of being gallant with Erskine's warm and lovely wife, Marisa.

It was Erskine who conceived the "stature-enhancing" plan for the limited, signed printings of O'Hara's books. When O'Hara complained about the chore of signing his name 300 times, Erskine worked out the arithmetic for him. Since he received a 15 percent royalty ($2.25 for a $15 book), a 300-copy limited printing earned O'Hara an additional $675—or about $300 per hour. His reaction was, "Not bad." However, O'Hara foiled the production department's custom of sending him extra sheets to sign for spoilage. He counted them as he signed and would quit at the agreed-upon limitation. Although O'Hara cultivated his image as a hard bargainer, his association with Random House was marked by his fundamental trust in his publisher's probity. At least twice Erskine discovered that Random House had an O'Hara book in production without a contract's having been signed.

Although O'Hara refused to submit his books for consideration by The Book-of-the-Month Club and resisted the whole idea of submitting his books for any book club's approval, three of his books were distributed by the Literary Guild—*The Instrument, The O'Hara Generation* and a volume of three novels (*Appointment in Samarra, Butterfield 8, Hope of Heaven*). The three-novel volume involved a perfect example of how well Erskine and Cerf understood their author. When the Literary Guild was negotiating with Random House for this volume, Erskine remarked to Cerf that O'Hara still resented the fact that Doubleday had required a $50 permission fee for the Maugham epigraph to *Appointment in Samarra* back in 1934. Since the Literary Guild is owned by Doubleday, Cerf got them to return O'Hara's $50—in addition to a $50,000 guarantee.

The last important contract letter O'Hara sent Cerf, in December 1964, helps to put their relationship in proper perspective. After sixteen years of being difficult and occasionally outrageous, when O'Hara was putting his affairs in order, he wrote a warm letter in which he acknowledged the significance of the Cerf-O'Hara relationship to him.

14 Dec. '64

Dear Bennett:

Light your pipe and compose yourself. This is to be a contract discussion.

In the contracts which you sent me in August there are points on which I could do a certain amount of nitpicking, and as you said several times over the telephone, all I had to do was scream a little and maybe twist your arm slightly, and you would yield at least some of the points.

But I know that; in recent years our negotiations have been simple and agreeable, and Random House has been reasonable—and so have I. The reason for my delay in signing the contracts has been, it might be said, a more profound one.

You and I have reached an age where we have to take into consideration what I call the terminal truth. As you know, I very nearly passed out of the picture eleven years ago, and although the years since then have been my most productive ones, I have never ceased to be mindful of the precariousness of existence. Naturally I become more, not less, aware of that fact.

The August contracts would tie me up for three books after THE HORSE KNOWS THE WAY. I do not wish to sign any such undertaking. At the moment I have the completed manuscript for a collection of stories to be called WAITING FOR WINTER, of which only two stories have been published (one in The New Yorker, the other in Sports Illustrated). I have even written the Foreword. This book, in other words, is ready to go tomorrow. But I do not plan to publish it until I have published the yet unfinished THE LOCKWOOD CONCERN, which, as you know, is a very long novel. In addition I have a short novel, nearly finished (it will be around 300 pages long), and several novellas. My major concern now is the completion of THE LOCKWOOD CONCERN, which I hope to have ready for autumn 1965.

God willing, I will finish that novel, and you will publish it. But the relationship between Random House and me really comes down to the relationship between you and me. If you should die, God forbid, I may not want to continue with Random House. Random House could elect someone like Alfred Kazin in your place, and where would I be? Your heirs might find it desirable to merge with Simon & Schuster, and where would I be?

On the other hand, what if I should die tomorrow? Sister and Wylie would be committed to Random House for three books of mine, beginning with THE LOCKWOOD CONCERN. That I do not want. I want Sister and Wylie to feel free to negotiate with any publisher in the business. I do not want their hands tied by a three-book contract. . . . Sister and Wylie are well fixed financially and can take their time in choosing a publisher, but I want them to be able to take their time, and to choose. They may choose Random House, but on the other hand they may not.

Therefore I do not wish to sign a three-book contract. One book at a time, from now on.

I believe that THE LOCKWOOD CONCERN is going to be very big. Possibly the biggest in sales of the trade edition, paper-

backs, etc. Already I am being sounded out on a picture deal, and you can imagine what kind of money will be involved there. This brings up another problem.

You have all that money to my credit at Random House. I know, of course, that you have the use of that money while I receive $25,000 a year of it, and in effect I am receiving $25,000 of interest money. (My Wall Street people, by the way, take a dim view of this arrangement.) I have been giving a lot of thought to the idea of making THE LOCKWOOD CONCERN a separate enterprise, outside the existing arrangement between Random House and me. I have all the money I will ever need. My wants are elegant but few. I had promised myself a Rolls-Royce if I won the Nobel prize, but I am reconciled to the conviction that I will never get the Nobel, and I will have to end my days without a Rolls (I could buy one with my English money, but it isn't merely a question of the money). The point here is that I would like to have all the money from THE LOCKWOOD CONCERN made payable to Sister and Wylie while I retain control of the property rights during my lifetime. The novel would be kept separate on the Random House books, and all royalty payments would be made to Sister and Wylie direct. This is where your man Manges can earn his retainer—by suggesting the ways this might be done. Wylie, by the way, will be 21 on 14 June 1966, and her financial matters are in the hands of the U. S. Trust Company. Her legal matters are in the hands of Carter, Ledyard & Milburn, who are also Sister's lawyers.

As you see, I am trying to put my house in order. I will be 60 next month and have lived twice as long as my father said I would. I am trying to achieve peace of mind. I went in to see my father on his deathbed and my mother said to him, "John has a sore knee." My old man said (and they were his last words to me), "Poor John." Later I came to realize that he was not thinking of my sore knee but of what I, the oldest of his eight children, was going to have to face when his tangled finances were revealed. Oh, those German marks he had bought so confidently! Oh, those rows of slum houses! Oh, that failure to make a will!

Well, I daresay I've given you a few things to think about. They are the things I've been thinking about.

> *As ever,*
> *John*

One point in this letter requires attention—the royalty account that O'Hara set up at Random House. When the money began to come in faster than he could spend it, O'Hara allowed it to accumulate in an interest-free account at Random House, drawing only $25,000 per year from it (later increased to $50,000). This annual withdrawal eventually became less than the interest the money would have drawn in a bank account. In effect, O'Hara was lending Random House large sums of money (at his death his royalty account stood at $1,005,401.28) without interest, allowing his publisher to make money on his money. O'Hara's tax situation had some bearing on this matter, for the government was taking as much as 80 percent of his earnings; but there were other options available to him. It was characteristic of John O'Hara to combine hard bargaining with generosity; this came under the heading of loyalty, a key virtue in the O'Hara code of personal conduct.

In a February 1964 letter to Maxwell, O'Hara noted with a mixture of resignation and pride that his 1963 income tax payment would be $135,000. "I wouldn't mind paying $135,000 income tax if I had made $270,000, but I didn't, and that's why I'm a Republican, whatever that is, instead of a Democrat, whatever *that* is.* I can remember my father's anguish when he had to pay $1,500, and *he* thought *I* was a bum, the bum." Although his relationship with Maxwell was tranquil, O'Hara never lost the feeling that *The New Yorker* failed to recognize his stature. When, for example, he wrote a letter in September 1964 correcting the magazine's statement that the race horse O'Hara was named for the Boston track athlete Tom O'Hara, he concluded with a loaded remark: "To get you off the hook a little, there *was* a Boston foot racer named O'Hara years ago. But he was a marathoner, a twenty-five miler. A good distance runner." And so—the clear implication is —is John O'Hara.

In December of 1964 O'Hara began suffering from severe jaw pains. He was unable to chew, and the pain was so bad that he could not sleep for more than two hours at a stretch. He had a complete neurological workup, but the doctors did not find anything wrong. O'Hara worried about the possibility of cancer and considered a return to alcohol if the problem proved to be a malignancy.

O'Hara had promised himself a Rolls-Royce if he won the Nobel Prize, but by 1965 he accepted the fact that he would probably never receive this biggest badge. In April of that year he took delivery on a green Silver Cloud III, for which he paid $17,300. He fell in love with it, and declared he would rather have the car than the Prize. Sister was amused by John's reluctance to have her drive the Rolls. Her later comment was, "You have to exercise the damned thing, like a polo

---

* In "My Turn" O'Hara explained that one reason for his conversion to "independent conservative" was because it was more fun: "But I get my laughs at the expense of the liberals and the intellectuals. As an independent conservative I belong to the Outs, and yet I need not conform to the policies and restrictions of the Outs if I don't feel like it. When I was a New Dealer I had to conform or be banished." (p. 172)

pony." The first state occasion on which the Rolls-Royce was employed was a lunch with Francis Cardinal Spellman arranged by Bennett Cerf. The Cardinal—whose headquarters shared the building with Random House—had complained to Cerf about O'Hara's books, and Cerf replied, "He's one of your boys; why don't you talk to him?" Cerf was nervous about the encounter and asked O'Hara not to embarrass him. When Cerf tried to tell him that Cardinal Spellman should be addressed as "Your Eminence," the reply was, "Which one of us is the Catholic?" At the introduction O'Hara kissed the Cardinal's ring and handed him an envelope containing a check for the New York Foundling Hospital, the Cardinal's favorite charity, in memory of Katharine Delaney O'Hara. Within minutes the prelate and the novelist were deep in reminiscence. They got along splendidly, and nothing was said about O'Hara's books. A bemused Cerf left them while Spellman was showing O'Hara his coin collection.

A photo of Spellman, Cerf and O'Hara was added to the memorabilia collection in the "Linebrook" study. On his infrequent trips to New York, O'Hara would alert Cerf in advance so that a parking space could be reserved for the Rolls-Royce in the courtyard of the Random House building at 457 Madison Avenue. He was unhappy when the firm moved to a new building at 201 East 50th Street, where

Rolls-Royce Silver Cloud III in Random House courtyard, 457 Madison Avenue, 1965. Left to right: Albert Erskine, O'Hara, Bennett Cerf.

there were no parking spaces. From the window of Albert Erskine's office at the new Random House building O'Hara could see the Pickwick Arms, where his career as a novelist began. He became so reluctant to come into the city in his last years that he stopped delivering his typescripts in person, as had been his custom, and dispatched them by Sister.

O'Hara never attempted to conceal his acute pleasure in honors and recognition, so he was gratified by his only invitation to the White House. Ironically it came from Lyndon B. Johnson in 1965, after O'Hara had become a Republican. The occasion was a reception for the National Honor Students on 8 June. Shortly before the reception John Updike—who was to give a reading—spotted O'Hara sitting in the lobby of the Hay-Adams hotel. They had never met, but Updike recognized him from his photos.

"Mr. O'Hara?" he asked.

O'Hara held out his hand and said, "Pull." When Updike hesitated, O'Hara explained, "My back." Updike pulled. "Again," O'Hara said. The second pull got him out of his chair grunting in pain.

When Updike learned that O'Hara was also on his way to the White House, he offered him a ride in the limousine that had been sent for him, since he was on the program. The driver reluctantly allowed O'Hara to ride in the front seat. Updike felt troubled by this violation of subordination and tried to cover up by starting a conversation about Pennsylvania. But O'Hara got going on the number of Updikes residing in Princeton. At the White House, O'Hara devoted his attention to Marianne Moore, and Updike described him as "bending his big ear to her tiny precise voice like a schoolboy listening to a transistor radio he has smuggled into class."[18]

FOR SEVERAL YEARS O'Hara had been referring to the "big book" or two-volume novel that he was working on. On 12 May 1965 he noted in his "Wafer" diary, "Finished Lockwood Concern 7:15 A.M."—after an all-night session. Published Thanksgiving 1965, *The Lockwood Concern* seems to be this ambitious work, although at 400 pages it is not a big book.* It is a condensed big book in that the plan is large—four generations of the Lockwood family from the 1840's to the 1920's.

---

* The *Saturday Evening Post* paid O'Hara for the right to consider *The Lockwood Concern* for prepublication serialization. Although the deal fell through, the fact of the option gave O'Hara a sense of vindication. When he had proposed such an arrangement for *A Rage to Live* in 1948, Bennett Cerf had reacted with dismay.

The "Concern" of the title is used in the Quaker sense of the term: "an obsessive act or thought, or both, of a religious nature." The Lockwood Concern is to found a dynasty in Swedish Haven (i.e., Schuylkill Haven) near Gibbsville. The principal figure in the chronicle is George Lockwood, the head of the third generation; and the novel opens with the completion of what he intends to be the Lockwood ancestral home—with a spiked wall and a hidden staircase, symbolizing his secretiveness and self-isolation. A child is killed on the wall as soon as the house is finished, an obvious ill omen for the house and the Concern it represents. George Lockwood shortly learns that his dynastic ambitions are doomed: his only son (whom he has driven away) is a crook in California and will never return to Swedish Haven; his only daughter is sterile as a result of venereal disease. At the end of the novel George Lockwood, alone in the house, is dying on the secret staircase. There is excellent material in *The Lockwood Concern* about the early days in The Region, but the novel has a disturbing flaw. A question hangs in the reader's mind: why does George Lockwood alienate his only son, who will have to carry on the Concern—thereby destroying it? The novel does not seem to provide any satisfactory answer apart from the possibility that Lockwood is ultimately so cold that he cannot share the Concern and thereby pass it on. As in Faulkner's *Absalom, Absalom!* the character is absorbed with his plan to the exclusion of the human feelings required for its success.

A key moment in O'Hara's world comes in *The Lockwood Concern* when Abraham Lockwood, whose father killed two men, asks an old schoolfriend if his son George will make the Philadelphia Club—

Morris Homestead spoke gently. "No, Locky, he won't. You can spare him that, at least. I'd be very glad to help him elsewhere, but if he ever mentions the Philadelphia Club, discourage him. Memories are too long. When he has a son, the son will stand a good chance. The old-timers will be dead and gone, but some of the same men that don't want you will still be around to oppose your son."

—to which many critics and readers no doubt respond, "Who cares?" Abraham Lockwood cares; Morris Homestead cares; and John O'Hara cares. The next objection is, "Even if they do care, does it really matter?" It is not possible to decree that certain material is irrelevant or precludes serious treatment.* Bullfighters or bootleggers or poor-white trash or even whalers seemed subliterary material until great

---

* See F. Scott Fitzgerald's 1934 introduction to *The Great Gatsby*: "But, my God! it was my material, and it was all I had to deal with."

writers made them the subjects of masterpieces. The issue is not whether O'Hara's material is in itself sufficiently meaningful, but whether he makes it meaningful in his work. This question is in the process of being decided. The returns will probably be a long time coming in, for O'Hara—more than most authors—was writing for unborn generations of readers.

Conrad Knickerbocker's perceptive—but unsympathetic—*Life* review of *The Lockwood Concern* is worth considering because it so well represents a familiar position on John O'Hara.

From Appointment in Samarra 30 years ago through 10 subsequent novels, O'Hara has sounded only minor variations on his solitary theme: the American social order is not capable of bestowing grace on individuals. His version of Gibbsville has never evolved and expanded, as did Faulkner's conception of Yoknapatawpha County. Northeastern Pennsylvania stands frozen in time. The social order about which O'Hara is concerned began to flake away in the 1920s. By World War II it had almost ceased to exist, except in small pockets, as an important part of the national experience. He has completely succeeded in excluding the contemporary mood from his work, which must be comforting to readers who want to be told that the rich put on their pants one leg at a time and that members of the upper crust die disillusioned. But so great is his integrity, his skill, his concern, that he can be forgiven everything except the snide little conviction, so essential to his point of view, that life does not really amount to much. He cannot be forgiven that.

The comparison between Yoknapatawpha County and Lantenengo County—to the disadvantage of O'Hara—became a critical commonplace. One wonders about the ways Faulkner's conception "evolved and expanded" while O'Hara's did not. Critics who complain about O'Hara's treatment of The Region are actually responding to his characters—whom they find narrow—and to his view of life—which they find inhuman. The assertion that O'Hara had the unforgivable conviction "that life does not really amount to much" is a familiar but distorted response. Critics and readers who test literature on the gauge of humanity and endurance will flunk John O'Hara—which is their right. If they want to be told that "man will prevail," they will have to read elsewhere. Although the critic may properly say that he is unable to accept an author's response to life, it is improper for the critic to deny an author his response to life—as Knickerbocker's rejection of "the snide little conviction . . . that life does not really amount to much" appears to do. Moreover, the fact that John O'Hara labored so hard at his craft belies that charge. His prodigious work was an act of faith. He believed that life cheats or beats most of us, which is not the same thing as believing that it does not amount to much.

The Lockwood Concern was dedicated "To Barklie McKee Henry Who Many Times Has Proved Himself A Friend." Although it was unenthusiastically reviewed, this novel sold fairly well, requiring three Random House trade printings in 1965–66, and four Signet paperback printings.* With this novel O'Hara left Cresset Press, his English publisher since *A Rage to Live*, and became associated with Hodder & Stoughton. The English edition went through three clothbound printings (20,890 copies).[19] Publication of the Four Square paperback edition was the occasion of a luncheon sponsored by Foyles bookstore on 3 May 1967 at London's Dorchester Hotel. In a wide-ranging talk that developed from his feelings about his thirty years as a visitor to London, the sixty-two-year-old author paid compliments to the English way of life while very seriously assessing his career. He moved from a discussion of social fiction ("every great writer of fiction was a social historian") to literary awards (he would not swap his Rolls-Royce for the Nobel Prize) to popular acceptance:

> . . . *my books have sold something like 15 million copies, and I could not have attained that circulation if I had not been readable. . . . I still manage to find my books on the current best-seller lists. And do you know why? Because I give them what I want. Not what they want. The author who believes he is going to give them what they want is making a great, great mistake, for the truth is that they don't know what they want. And for an author to attempt to anticipate what they want is an act of dishonesty.*

Perhaps the most significant information he provided about himself was the explanation of the effect of the war years—during which he wrote little—on his career, for after the distractions of the war he found that his resources were "practically unlimited." The guests were amazed to see the American author begin weeping during his address and give his typescript to the chairman, novelist John Moore, to read for him. O'Hara kept in touch with Moore and told Sister that he had not expected to achieve such a close new friendship at that stage of his life.†

---

* Ben Hamilton's review in *The Hampton Bays News*, the local paper for Quogue, no doubt pleased O'Hara: "This is the latest novel of America's greatest living novelist. Since the death of Hemingway and Faulkner, in fact, O'Hara is the only one left who amounts to much."

† One of the guests at the Foyles luncheon was J. Paul Getty, with whom O'Hara chatted about the Duesenberg they had both owned.

While O'Hara was at work on *The Lockwood Concern* he contracted to write a syndicated weekly column for *Newsday*, a Long Island metropolitan newspaper. The guarantee was $1,000 per column for one year. *Newsday* was an unlikely home paper for "My Turn," for it is of the liberal persuasion. At its peak "My Turn" was syndicated in forty-five papers, but editors began dropping it because they disagreed with O'Hara's opinions. At renewal time Captain Harry Guggenheim, the publisher of *Newsday*, proposed that O'Hara write a weekly short story instead of a column. O'Hara commented in his introduction to the collected columns that not even a Guggenheim could afford to pay for a weekly O'Hara story. "My Turn" ran from October 1964 to October 1965.

John O'Hara was miscast as a columnist in the Sixties. He had an abundance of material and the courage to express unpopular ideas, but the tone of "My Turn" is defensive and at the same time truculent —"crusty" was the word that was applied to the column. His old idols had been Heywood Broun and F.P.A., but his column read more like H. L. Mencken's expressions of prejudices meant to provoke trouble. The theme that runs through "My Turn" is one of protest against the liberals' attempts to impose conformity on the nation. O'Hara endorsed Barry Goldwater (because the Lawrence Welk people deserve representation); criticized Martin Luther King; ridiculed the late Joseph McCarthy; attacked the Kennedys, Johnson and Stevenson; defended his right to smoke cigarettes;* opposed too-strict gun control; and rebuked Robert Lowell for rudeness to President Johnson ("When he invites you to the White House, you damn well go").

An extremely revealing column that no doubt baffled many readers came on 13 February 1965, when O'Hara combined comments on the death of Sir Winston Churchill and the closing of Peal's custom shoe workshop.

Winston Churchill, one of a kind, passes out of the picture—probably wearing Peal shoes. Peal, after 173 years, will make no more shoes to order, and I am left without an extravagance. Good men and good things vanish. In the case of Peal shoes, no one will suffer from their disappearance; but we will all suffer, and don't think we won't, from the disappearance of the kind of craftsmen who made the good shoes good. In the brave new world of Bop and Pop and automation there will be no customers for the handmade article. I don't see any new Churchills on the horizon, either.

---

* O'Hara was a two-pack-a-day smoker of L&M cigarettes.

Here is the voice of the Tory squire of "Linebrook"—reminding one of Galsworthy's "Quality"—lamenting the erosion of standards. Not just the passing of good things and great men, but the diminution of life by the passing of human as well as material standards. It is not the case that O'Hara simply grew conservative. At the same time that he turned right, he adhered to the same standards of life that he had always respected—and which were the standards of Dr. Patrick O'Hara. The 18 September 1965 "My Turn" column was O'Hara's position paper on standards of conduct in "the Age of the Jerk." After listing examples of "Jerkism" in America, he made the familiar point that change does not necessarily bring improvement.* His conclusion was bleak, indicating that he felt profoundly isolated from the Sixties: "The total rejection of the standards and principles that we know were good will make it extremely unlikely that honesty and decency will be revived."

The problem for the reader of "My Turn"—and this is true for all of O'Hara's columns—is the inconsistency of tone, almost a violation of decorum, as the columnist mixes issues of high seriousness with personal peeves and even misplaced levity. In urging a policy of isolationism, he wrote: "They could accuse us of passive resistance, but Gandhi made that fashionable. He died by violence, but we all gotta go sometime." In analyzing the encouragement of culture under the Kennedy administration, he stated: "Among his other distinctions, John F. Kennedy was the only President of the United States to ask me for my autograph,† but that was while he was a senator. It was easy to forget that when he became President—and he forgot it." That complaint makes the reader flinch with embarrassment. Such lapses do not occur in O'Hara's fiction, but in his columns he suspended his self-discipline. Although he enjoyed his columns enormously, he did not approach them with complete seriousness. He wrote them for fun and therapy—they were a way of expending anger or relaxing.

When Random House brought out *My Turn* in 1966—with no great enthusiasm—it was dedicated "To Jim Forrestal." The Signet paperback required only one printing, and the book was not published in England.

---

* "The manifestations of Jerkism are all over the place and limited to no class or race. . . . It is Jerkism for a boy to grow his hair like a girl's, and Jerkism for his mother to think it's cute. It is Jerkism for a non-rabbinical student to grow a beard, and Jerkism for a John Bircher to accuse Eisenhower of communism. It is Jerkism to be a Communist, and Jerkism to be a John Bircher." (p. 205)

† At the National Book Award ceremony.

Surprise birthday party for Sister at "Linebrook."

ALTHOUGH HIS work schedule did not permit much entertaining, he relished sentimental occasions, and the O'Haras gave lunches on special days: Sister's birthday, their wedding anniversary and August 16. He took elaborate precautions to surprise Sister on her birthday and usually succeeded. On 31 January 1966, the O'Haras' eleventh anniversary—and his sixty-first birthday—they gave a luncheon party at which Governor Richard Hughes delighted O'Hara by presenting him with JOH-1 license plates for the Rolls. The car provided O'Hara with endless pleasure, and he enjoyed the anecdotes connected with it. A Rolls-Royce attracts attention on American roads; once when the O'Haras were driving to Princeton in old clothes after closing up the Quogue house, he noticed that another driver was apparently studying the occupants of the Rolls. "He's trying to figure out who we are," O'Hara said to Sister, "and has decided that we're the chauffeur and maid."

The year 1965 brought no volume of stories, but O'Hara was back on Thanksgiving 1966 with *Waiting for Winter*, a collection of twenty-one stories. The Region is represented by nine stories, including two novelettes, "Andrea" and "The Skeletons," and the Jimmy Malloy story "Fatimas and Kisses." Set against the background of the family's financial problems after Dr. Malloy's death, "Fatimas and Kisses" presents Jimmy as a Gibbsville reporter and potential alcoholic. The plot deals with a deranged shopkeeper who murders his wife and children, but the story is actually about Malloy/O'Hara's sense of failure and estrangement from Gibbsville. At the end of "Fatimas and Kisses" the reader comprehends that Jimmy will be leaving Gibbsville. When the police chief rebukes him for wasting his education, Jimmy replies that he did not attend college.

> "*Oh, then you're not much better than the rest of us,*" *he said.*
> "*I never said I was, Chief.*"
> "*You never said it, but you act it. Your father was better than most of us, but he didn't act it.*"
> "*No, he didn't have to,*" *I said.*

The longest story in *Waiting for Winter* is "Andrea," which studies the extended and destructive affair between two people who do not realize that they love each other (or perhaps they are incapable of yielding to love)—and sex is not enough. There are two Hollywood novellas, "James Francis and the Star" and "Natica Jackson," and a remarkable short story, "The Way to Majorca," about an unlikely marriage between a fading actress and a homosexual writer who team up for mutual protection. Two of the best stories in the collection, "Leonard" and "Yostie," employ the familiar O'Hara theme of the violation and restoration of order.

In his foreword to *Waiting for Winter* O'Hara explained that the title refers to the fact that he wrote most of the stories in the summer and fall while waiting for novel-writing weather. "Of course it has other implications as well."

In 1966 O'Hara undertook what was to be his last—and best—column, "The Whistle Stop" in *Holiday*. When Don Schanche became editor of *Holiday* in 1964 the magazine had a regular book column by Clifton Fadiman. Schanche changed the heading to "The Wayward Reader" and began using other writers for it. O'Hara contributed three essays before signing on, at Schanche's suggestion, for "The Whistle Stop," which appeared between September 1966 and May 1967. These nine columns are particularly good because most of them are essays—not assemblages of comments. Perhaps O'Hara took special pains with them because he was paid a reported $2,000 each. Three of "The Whistle Stop" columns that made an impression when they appeared were "The Error of Our Ways" (December 1966), an essay on biography; "Reflections of a Non-Travel Writer" (January 1967), a loving re-creation of the trip by trolley and train from Pottsville to Lykens; "When Bands Were Big" (April 1967), a recollection of the bands that made one-night stands all over The Region in the Twenties.

When Caskie Stinnett replaced Schanche as editor of *Holiday* in 1967, there were two O'Hara columns on hand. Stinnett published one and sent the other back; O'Hara dispatched a blunt note, and "The Whistle Stop" was dropped. O'Hara and Stinnett had had difficulties before Stinnett became editor of *Holiday*. Stinnett's comments on *From the Terrace* in *Speaking of Holiday*, a promotional publication, had produced O'Hara's threat to flatten his nose "like a bicycle seat"; and on an earlier occasion during O'Hara's drinking days Stinnett had angered him by closing the bar at a *Holiday* party at "21" before O'Hara was ready to leave.

"The Whistle Stop" terminated in May 1967, but O'Hara subsequently wrote two essays for *Holiday*. His final appearance was "Hello Hollywood Good-bye" (May 1968), prompted by his first visit to Palm Springs since 1941. In 1967 Sister and O'Hara had lunch at the Eldorado Country Club in Palm Desert with the Freeman Gosdens (the Amos of Amos 'n Andy) and Mrs. Dwight D. Eisenhower. The

Gilbert Roland and O'Hara, Palm Springs Racquet Club, 1967.

O'Haras and Mrs. Eisenhower hit it off, and she invited them to her house to meet her husband. The former President was watching a golf match on television with the sound turned off; the men talked for two hours. Describing the occasion, O'Hara admitted that he was "in a fog of euphoria." After returning to the Palm Springs Racquet Club, O'Hara began comparing this visit with his fifteen previous trips to California. The result was a wide-ranging autobiographical statement that included an assessment of his politics during the Thirties when he was a nonconforming New Dealer who couldn't write a proletarian novel.

The Instrument appeared on Thanksgiving 1967. It is the story of Yank Lucas, a gifted playwright who is a rotten human being using women for his work. An ambitious work that does not entirely succeed, The Instrument says a good deal about the creative temperament and the creative process, examining the parasitism of authors and showing how one kind of writer leeches on human relationships for his work. The Instrument is loosely structured for an O'Hara novel, breaking into two sequences: New York during the production of Lucas' play, and Vermont, where he writes a new play. While the play is in rehearsal Lucas has an affair with the star, Zena Gollum, and deserts her on opening night. He then holes up in a small Vermont town to write a play drawing upon his relationship with Zena. At the time Lucas completes this play she commits suicide.

He had not known, however, that he had become the instrument of a creature that he had already destroyed. The splendid irony was in the manner of her revenge. It was sickening to confess to yourself that you would never again do anything as good as this. All those happy confusions of himself with God, those identifications with divinity and genius, and that supreme self-confidence—all of them were as lost as the smoke at Gettysburg, the tears of Gethsemane. He read on rapidly through this obituary of Zena Gollum that was correspondingly the obituary of the talent of Yank Lucas.

Unless, of course, he could find someone else.

Yank Lucas is not intended as everywriter; he is one kind of inadequate writer. There may be some significance in the fact that he is a playwright—the form that O'Hara failed at.

The Instrument sold moderately well despite the fact that it is one of O'Hara's weaker novels. Random House required three trade printings, and it became O'Hara's first book-club volume since *A Rage to Live*. A Literary Guild Selection, it was subsequently distributed by the Dollar Book Club. The Bantam paperback sold nine printings in 1969–70. The novel was not well reviewed by the critics, but at this stage in O'Hara's career the reviews did not matter very much to his public. He was in danger of becoming merely a popular writer, with a following who read John O'Hara as other readers read a new Erle Stanley Gardner. Nevertheless, reviews continued to matter to O'Hara, and he sometimes asked Albert Erskine to read advance reviews to him over the phone. When the clippings came, Sister weeded out the ones that would disturb him.

WHEN AL WRIGHT quit drinking in 1967, O'Hara wrote him:

Welcome aboard the wagon. You are getting aboard at just about the same age I was when I stopped drinking. The only way to do it is completely, and the only way to do it completely is to do it one day at a time. After 13 years I can still taste Scotch and beer, and I still have a recurrent dream about Scotch, in which I am at the bar at 21, order a St. James, am just reaching for it, and Emil takes it away. I have another dream in which I belong to three non-existent clubs, two in NY and one in Philadelphia, to which I go for a sneak drink, but when I get to the Clubs they are all closed. I still have trouble when I travel abroad, especially if I go by ship.

You are going to find that no one who has passed 40 can remain unaffected by two Martinis. There will be constant demands on your tolerance and patience. But there will be no more hangovers, and you will still be alive, be able to sleep better, and your capacity for work will increase. I have often suspected that you have been putting off a book about your wartime experiences. If I am right, now is your chance. You have had a full and rather unique life, you are not a kid any more, and you were not cut out to be one of those amiable halfwits at the Racquet Club bar.[20]

In December 1967 Edward Fox, a boyhood friend, invited John and Sister to a cocktail party at the Pottsville Club. In accepting the invitation O'Hara wrote, "We won't even be in town long enough for me to point out places of interest Sister has not seen on her two previous visits, such as Jack Kantner's Cave, the Charles Baber cemetery, Hughes's Dam, or Quinn's Mule Yard." It was to be O'Hara's last trip home. His back trouble made it necessary for him to remain seated at the party, which prompted some of the guests to privately criticize him for being stand-offish. Although a few people tried to force acknowledgment of friendships that never existed, he enjoyed this reunion.

After the Fox party O'Hara reported to Al Wright on the feelings his visit to Pottsville had generated.

In December I went back to Pottsville to a party which was attended by the people I have known all my life, in a club where my father once lived, on a street where I was born. For the first time since 1927, when I left Pottsville, I had a good time there, recalling people's middle names and old sweethearts and so on. On our way back to Princeton I said to Sister that I enjoyed the feeling of rediscovering my roots, indeed of really discovering them for the first time. At twenty-two I was too young to have anything but roots; at sixty-two the tree that I had become (I fancy myself as a sturdy oak type) was something more than a stick pushed haphazardly into the ground. I have no intention of moving back to Pottsville; we are settled here; but it is nice to know that 130 miles away I have roots some of which were planted two centuries ago.

During the Sixties O'Hara occasionally considered moving to England or Ireland, although he probably suspected that he could not work well outside of America. Taxes certainly had some bearing on this possibility, for he could have saved a good deal of tax money by living abroad; but O'Hara was also motivated by his disgust with the deterioration of American life. Moreover, he liked the people and the climate of Ireland. In 1968 he explained to Al Wright that Wylie didn't need him now that she was married. "She will be 23 in June, and it's more than a year since I've seen her, but she has made her own life, of which I am no longer an essential part. If I were living in Ireland her old man would be conveniently remote. . . ."

Wylie's first child, Nicholas Drew Holahan, was born on Guam, on 26 October 1968. The birth of his grandson elicited a model letter from the author-grandfather.

[29 October 1968] This letter is really to both you and Denny to congratulate you on your joint effort in making me a grandfather, a laudable enterprise. When a man is almost 64 he ought to be able to speak of his grandchild, his grandson. I have the grey hair and the pot belly and the sedentary habits, so the grandson completes the picture of the aging author. Among the thoughts I had after Denny called on Saturday was the idea that I ought to send a telegram to Yale, to enter Nick tentatively with the Class of 1992, but I dismissed the idea as rather impertinent. After all, Nick's father and other grandfather have priority. It did occur to me that Nick would be in a class that is exactly 100 years later than his great-grandfather O'Hara's class at Penn. I also thought of putting Nick up for one of my numerous clubs, but the way things are going who knows what club, if any, will be in existence 25 years from now? My now three-day-old grandson, who probably will never know me, belongs to the present only to the extent that he signifies the existence of your happy marriage; but for that I am grateful to him and to you two. We have had a very full life together, beginning on that hot, hot day in June, Wylie, when you were born, and climaxed on that warm September day two years ago when you and Denny were married. I congratulate you on this baby, and I thank you for having him.

A second grandchild, Belle, was born in September 1969. After Dennis was discharged from the navy, O'Hara enjoyed his grand-children's visits to "Linebrook" and cheerfully served as baby-sitter.

In November of 1968 O'Hara suffered a bad fall—which intensi-fied his anticipation of death—when the O'Haras made one of their periodic visits to the Richardson Dilworths in Philadelphia's Washington Square. O'Hara had known the mayor of Philadelphia since the Thirties, when they struck up a friendship at "21." According to Dilworth, the routine on these weekend visits was for O'Hara to delay announcing his time of departure until he had determined whether

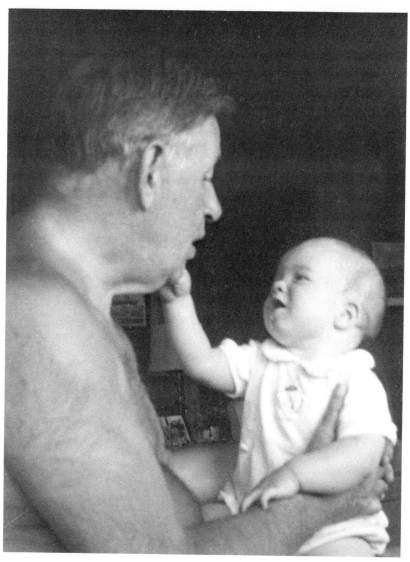

O'Hara with grandson, Nicholas Drew Holahan.

his host was hung over on Sunday. If that proved to be the case, he would depart early—not out of consideration for Dilworth, but because he couldn't endure the company of hung-over people. At noon on Sunday, 10 November, O'Hara decided to leave before lunch and went to get his Rolls from the garage under Hopkinson House. There he fell on an icy ramp and was found by a motorist who took him to the Pennsylvania Hospital. The internist who examined O'Hara assembled a team of a plastic surgeon, an orthopedic surgeon and a neurologist. O'Hara had suffered a concussion that produced amnesia for the fall and his trip to the hospital, and he felt he was not receiving adequate attention. From his private computer bank he recalled that Truxton Hare was president of the hospital's board and had him notified that John O'Hara was being neglected. In addition to the concussion, his elbow was fractured and an eyelid required six stitches. O'Hara suspected that the fall had been caused by a minor stroke, but the neurologist, Dr. Frank A. Elliot, found no evidence of a stroke. He did find that O'Hara was suffering from hypertension and that he had rather extensive vascular disease. Dr. Elliot read him a lecture on the prevention of heart attacks by diet, weight reduction and exercise. O'Hara argued the point with him because he was unwilling to give up his habits—which were, after all, his work habits. Dr. Elliot's conclusion is, "He gave an impression of overwhelming pessimism."[21]

After a few days he was dismissed from the hospital but was unable to drive home—which presented a problem because he did not want Sister driving him when he was ill. Dilworth located a policeman who claimed to be an experienced Rolls chauffeur. He stalled the car in front of the hospital, and John O'Hara said to the mayor of Philadelphia, "You son-of-a-bitch, you couldn't even get me a good driver."

Dilworth had a long experience with the problems of hosting O'Hara, since John and Belle had regularly come to Philadelphia from Princeton to attend the Orchestra during John's drinking period. In some ways Dilworth preferred the drinking O'Hara to the dry O'Hara. The O'Hara of the 1960's radiated disapproval of drinkers and—because of his stomach, throat and jaw conditions—required special feeding, including milkshakes made to his specifications. The Dilworths visited the O'Haras at Quogue and Princeton, and Dilworth commented that O'Hara met guests "as though preparing to repel boarders." He found it difficult to get a drink at lunch. Once when Dilworth had two drinks at an O'Hara party and waited expectantly for a third, his host asked him if he was looking for the free lunch counter.[22]

Another longstanding Philadelphia friendship was with Hope and Edgar Scott, whom O'Hara had first met at Philip Barry's Easthampton house in the late Thirties. Scott had been a classmate of Barry's in George Pierce Baker's Harvard play-writing course, and although he became a stockbroker he remained an ardent theater buff. He became an O'Hara collector, and the author helped him by contributing humorously inscribed copies of translations. O'Hara included a mention of the Scotts in *The Big Laugh*. Edgar Scott successfully put O'Hara up for the Philadelphia Racquet Club and backed him unsuccessfully for the Brook. In November 1962 O'Hara wrote Scott an appraisal of clubs and recognition:

To be denied membership in any club is something less than a life-and-death matter. I'm a man who lost the Nobel prize. I have been up for it at least twice that I know of in the past ten years, but now that they have given it to Steinbeck my chances of ever getting it are gone. There won't be another American winner in the next five years, and nothing I do meanwhile will get it for me. I began pointing for it in 1948, when my work, or my attitude toward my work, underwent a change. Everything I have written since 1948 has had a secondary purpose; I have deliberately attempted to record the first half of the century in fictional forms but with the quasi-historical effect that, say, Dickens achieved. It is all there—or more of it is there than anyone else has put down or will put down. Sinclair Lewis did his share, but then he fell apart. Hemingway didn't do it, Faulkner didn't do it, Steinbeck hasn't done it. Cozzens missed his chance. Mind you, I take nothing away from what they did do that was good, but I really thought I would be judged favorably this year on the basis of what I began in 1934 and rebegan in 1948. Well, I was wrong, and now I have to create a new incentive. So you see I am not very likely to collapse as a result of a club blackball.[23]

O'Hara's professional interest in clubs was reflected in his private life. At various times he belonged to the Century Association, the Coffee House, the Players, the Philadelphia Racquet Club, the New York Athletic Club, the Leash, the Nassau Club, the Quogue Field Club, the Shinnecock Yacht Club, the National Press Club, the Beach Club of Santa Monica, the West Side Tennis Club (Los Angeles), the Metropolitan Club, the National Golf Links of America (Southampton), the Savile Club (London) and the Royal Auto Club. He was blackballed for at least two other clubs he wanted to join, the Brook and the Racquet and Tennis Club of New York.

THANKSGIVING 1968 brought what proved to be John O'Hara's last collection, *And Other Stories*. It was his sixth volume of stories in eight years, during which he had published 139 stories, novellas and novelettes—a body of work on which his reputation could have rested securely had he written nothing else. The foreword again expressed O'Hara's sense of living on borrowed time, and his almost guilty feeling about the self-indulgence of writing stories when there were more important tasks to be done: "I am writing a strange play, and I am well along with a long novel." The play has not been identified; but the novel was either *Lovey Childs* or *The Ewings*, although neither is a long work. *And Other Stories* includes only twelve stories; and seven are of The Region, including the novelette "A Few Trips and Some Poetry," which occupies a third of the volume.* There is nothing tired or careless about the stories themselves, but looking back at the volume one can detect warnings. The dedication "To Bennett Cerf, an amiable man" was well deserved, but it sounds a valedictory note—indicating an end to the twenty-year game of abusing Cerf.† The photo of the author on the back of the dust jacket is ominous: he stands in front of "Linebrook" dragging on a cigarette, and the eyes of an old man peer out from the slack facial skin. This photograph was taken when Alden Whitman came to "Linebrook" to interview O'Hara for the *Times*. Since Whitman was the paper's chief obituary writer, his visit was itself a *memento mori*.[24] O'Hara sent the photo to Albert Erskine with a covering note:

It not only shows me as the rich and stylish country squire, but it also shows me in an act of defiance to the anti-cigarette-smoking bluenoses. Incidentally, the device on my necktie is a ruffed grouse, which is the official bird of the Commonwealth of Pennsylvania. The jacket and waistcoat came from Trimingham's, in Bermuda; the shirt from Brooks and the cap also from Brooks. . . . A great character study, of a great character. Make a nice full-page ad in the Sunday Times book section; the Random House answer to McCall's ad for Capote.[25]

The 120-page novelette "A Few Trips and Some Poetry" emphasized a perplexing aspect of O'Hara's last phase—an apparent fascination with lesbianism that prompted him to make prominent use of it in his final three books. Jimmy Malloy makes his last appearance in "A Few Trips and Some Poetry," which chronicles his long and sometimes messy affair with Isabel Barley, until she finds peace of a sort in a lesbian relationship with a much younger girl. The story ends with a reconciliation and leave-taking between the middle-aged Jim and Isabel, who is dying of cancer. The best stories in the collection are set in the Gibbsville of the Twenties: "The Gunboat and Madge," "We'll Have Fun," "The Farmer" and "The Gangster." "We'll Have Fun" can be singled out for attention because it adds a particularly good character to O'Hara's "Pennsylvania Protectorate," a drunken stableman who retains a certain self-respect. Indeed, all of O'Hara's most memorable stories substantiate his assertion that the art of his fiction

---

* For some stories, such as "How Old, How Young," the reader is certain that the locale is The Region, even though O'Hara does not stipulate the setting. The Region has its own tone or feel.

† O'Hara informed Erskine of the dedication on 6 February 1968: "I will let you convey the news to him. I can't bear to see a grown man cry."

LINEBROOK

~~~~~~~~~~~~

```
      TO BENNETT CERF

In Eighteen Hundred Ninety-eight
(The twenty-fifth of May, the date)
There came upon this mundane sphere
A little lad, so sweet, so dear,
That all alive were moved to say,
"Ah, what a happy, happy day!"
A week went by, he had his bris,
And ever since it's all been bliss.
So birthday greetings to our boy.
Sincerely, John O'Hara, goy.
```

MAY 25, 1968

Author to publisher.

was the art of character creation. Random House did a 50,000-copy first printing of *And Other Stories* and reprinted it once; but only one Bantam printing was required.

In 1969 the Literary Guild proposed a special collection of stories, *The O'Hara Generation*. O'Hara blessed the project but stipulated that the introduction be written by Albert Erskine. The book club selected twenty-one stories; but O'Hara removed "Imagine Kissing Pete," for which Erskine substituted two stories. O'Hara approved the introduction in which Erskine traced the author's development as a writer of short fiction and delivered a rebuke to the academicians and critics who have been clever "at what they think is his expense. . . . Having more publication days than anyone else, Mr. O'Hara has more experiences of this than most." The *Literary Guild Magazine* for July 1969 included a respectful "review" of *The O'Hara Generation* by Louis Auchincloss, who had not been an unreserved admirer of his work.

ONE OF O'Hara's health problems in 1969, in addition to his back, which kept him in almost constant discomfort, was difficulty in swallowing. He went into Harkness for a complete examination, and the problem was diagnosed as a hiatus hernia (a looseness in the hiatus where the esophagus passes through the diaphragm). The doctors also discovered a mild diabetic condition. These two conditions required a special diet, but O'Hara had long since lost interest in food. He uncomplainingly ate whatever Sister told him to eat.

Lovey Childs: A Philadelphian's Story appeared on Thanksgiving 1969. Written during a period of protracted health problems, it is O'Hara's weakest novel. The critics' charges that O'Hara was written out as a novelist, that he was producing novels out of habit, seemed partly justified by *Lovey*. There is a hurried quality about this novel, which had not appeared in O'Hara's previous work. In particular, at 250 pages *Lovey* failed to pass what he called "the hefting test." Bulk had been one of the qualities of his best later novels; but *Lovey*, the shortest novel since *Hope of Heaven* (1937), is a slim work in several ways. If it was in fact the "long novel" O'Hara referred to in *And Other Stories*, then he had lost interest and truncated it—as the abrupt ending seems to indicate.

Lovey Childs had presented unexpected difficulties for O'Hara partway through, and at one point he suspended work on it. Probably the most disturbing symptom of his failing power is a badly handled story detail in the case of Lovey's Main Line family mansion. Two episodes are built around the problems of disposing of the house; yet Lovey retains it, and the reader is given the explanation that her marriage to the wealthy Sky Childs obviated the necessity to sell it. The explanation in the published book is a bit weak, but it passes. However, when Albert Erskine, the dedicatee, read the novel in typescript he was compelled to call the author's attention to the contradiction that the house was actually sold and yet remained in Lovey's possession.* That kind of mistake was ominous. Even more ominous was O'Hara's difficulty in solving the problem, for which he needed Erskine's help.

The plot of the novel deals with a Main Line girl who marries a playboy named Sky Childs, and they become Twenties celebrities. After their divorce Lovey narrowly avoids some sexual disasters before marrying a proper Philadelphia cousin and achieving a stable life. The novel closes with a speech at her twentieth wedding anniversary party:

---

* O'Hara's first reaction to Erskine's queries on *Lovey Childs* was that he could not revise it then; he gave Erskine a novelette about Hollywood, *The Hall-Room Boys*, to publish instead. Subsequently he fixed *Lovey* and withdrew the novelette.

"Why do two people such as Lovey and Francis, as unlike each other as they were, manage to stay together for twenty years? My friends, I am convinced that there's only one reason. Habit. Habit. There's no other explanation for it. That, and the fact that Lovey gave up living in New York, and they both came back to Philadelphia, where they belong."

Lovey Childs increased speculation about John O'Hara's interest in lesbianism, which seemed to be competing with Yale for his attention. A secondary character named Marcy Bancroft, an utterly corrupt girl reminiscent of Hedda in *Ourselves to Know*, seduces Lovey's mother—which unconvincingly leads to the older woman's insanity. Lovey is herself seduced by a lesbian reporter, an encounter which the author describes in considerable detail.*

Lovey Childs was not a commercial or critical success, and was not widely reviewed. Indeed, *Lovey Childs* was not even reviewed in the daily *Times*, for the retirement of Charles Poore meant a change in that paper's attitude toward John O'Hara. He felt that the *Times* had spoiled his Thanksgiving ritual by ignoring his novel, and seriously considered publishing his next book, *The Ewings*, in England before it appeared in America. Random House required only one printing and the Bantam paperback sold two printings.

The year 1969 and early 1970 was a time of health problems for John O'Hara. When he and Sister went to London in the fall of 1969 O'Hara insisted on using a wheelchair at the airports. His back trouble caused steady pain, and his legs sometimes buckled when he stood up. He was still able to work—although the length of his nightly stint had to be shortened—and he completed *The Ewings* on 9 February 1970. Sister had trouble getting John to leave the house, and she would ask Pat Outerbridge to invite him for walks. This assignment was a bit frightening for Pat because O'Hara insisted on walking in the middle of the road and was slow getting out of the way of cars. In March of 1970 O'Hara was feeling better and began taking swimming lessons at the Princeton Y.M.C.A., which he enjoyed.

On the night of 10 April 1970 John O'Hara broke off work on a sequel to *The Ewings* early because he was bothered by pains in the chest and left arm. The last sentence he wrote was on page 74 of the

---

* The reporter was named Virginia Vernon and worked for the New York *Daily News*. After hardcover publication of *Lovey Childs* by Hodder & Stoughton in England, paperback publication was delayed by a libel action initiated by an English newspaperwoman named Virginia Vernon, who had worked for the London *Mirror*. John O'Hara had never known Miss Vernon, and the suit was dropped when she died.

typescript: "Edna had not suspected him, and now his affair with Alicia was a thing of the past." O'Hara reported to Sister that he was going to bed. She looked in on him during the night and in the morning and saw that he was sleeping quietly. When Sister checked at 1:30 P.M. on Saturday, 11 April 1970, John O'Hara was dead in his sixty-sixth year—and after thirty-one books.

AFTER

THERE WERE BULLETINS on the radio. With his pride in inside knowledge, John O'Hara would have angrily admitted that his timing was
off. Saturday afternoon is a bad time for newspaper coverage because
most of the Sunday paper is already locked up. The most important
American obituaries appear in the New York *Times*, and again John
O'Hara was unlucky. The chief obituary writer, Alden Whitman—
who had interviewed him in 1967 as part of his practice of researching
important figures—was not working that day. The *Times* gave Paul L.
Montgomery's story four column-inches on page 1, headlined JOHN
O'HARA DEAD; NOVELIST DISSECTED SMALL-TOWN MORES, and continued
with five columns on the obituary page. There was no page of tributes
from writers and critics, and there was no assessment by one of the
paper's reviewers—which constitutes the full *Times* treatment. The
Pottsville *Republican* does not have a Sunday issue. The Monday paper
(13 April 1970) had a two-column front-page story headlined JOHN
O'HARA RITES SET FOR THURSDAY, and four more columns inside.* John
O'Hara—who paid attention to these things and who wanted all the
badges—would have been profanely disappointed. The sons-of-bitches
were still underrating him.[26]

The funeral service was conducted at the Princeton University
Chapel on 16 April by Dr. Ernest Gordon, the university chaplain.
O'Hara had left no instructions about his funeral, and Sister asked Kate
Bramwell to arrange an Episcopal service. It was not a large turnout—
not like Dr. Patrick O'Hara's funeral, or Joe Chapin's. John Hay
Whitney came with his sister, Mrs. Charles Payson; Random House
was represented by Donald S. Klopfer, Albert Erskine and Mrs. Bennett
Cerf (whose husband was lecturing in California); Joel Sayre, Mrs.
John Steinbeck, former New Jersey Governor Richard Hughes, the
widow of Governor Walter E. Hedge, the Bramwells and Charles

---

* Pottsville's only official tribute to its historiographer is John O'Hara Street
in a low-income housing development.

338

Addams attended; President Robert F. Goheen represented Princeton University; Charles Mann represented Pennsylvania State University; the *Times* sent Alden Whitman; Sister's son C. D. B. Bryan and daughter Mrs. Peter Gates were there; Wylie and Dennis Holahan were present, as were O'Hara's seven brothers and sisters. The chapel was not filled, and the Princeton undergraduates paid no attention to the funeral. After the service the mourners were able to observe the green Rolls-Royce Silver Cloud III with license plate JOH-1 driving away. Burial was at Princeton Cemetery and a headstone was erected with an epitaph selected by Sister: *Better than anyone else, he told the truth about his time, the first half of the twentieth century. He was a professional. He wrote honestly and well.*[27]

The last will and testament of John O'Hara—whose father had died intestate—had been executed 16 June 1967.[28] He bequeathed to his widow his real estate, personal property, unpublished manuscripts and approximately half of his estate in the form of a marital-deduction trust. The remainder of the estate went into a residuary trust for the benefit of Wylie and O'Hara's descendants. In addition, he had set up a trust for his aunt Verna Delaney—who predeceased him—and his sister Mary. There were individual bequests to his brothers and sisters, to Dennis Holahan, and to Pat Outerbridge.

On 13 May 1970 there was a memorial service at Random House. Bennett Cerf spoke movingly about John O'Hara as the "most generally unappreciated author in American literary history," and ranked him with Hemingway, Fitzgerald and Faulkner. The eulogy was delivered by Charles Poore, and Wylie read a letter her father had written to help with her study of history.[29]

WHEN HE DIED O'Hara had completed *The Ewings*. Publication had to be delayed until February 1972 because of estate problems, and the reception was disappointing. The posthumous publication of John O'Hara's last novel should have been the occasion for searching attempts to determine his position in American literature, for retrospective studies of the O'Hara Concern. It was a proper time for grief, for tribute, and for gratitude. The response was restrained and even condescending. Hoke Norris in the Chicago *Daily News* said the right thing: "John O'Hara is dead, and if the novel is dead too, then we are doubly bereaved."

Although *The Ewings* is not a major O'Hara novel, it is clearly better than *Lovey Childs* or *The Instrument*, and merited more attention than it received—apart from any sentimental considerations. Set in Cleveland—the only O'Hara novel about the Midwest—it chronicles the rise of lawyer Bill Ewing in the booming war economy of World War I. Rich, ambitious and hard, Ewing knows where he is going; at the end of the novel he is well on his way to becoming a young tycoon. Certain aspects of Bill Ewing's business career were based on that of a former cabinet officer. *The Ewings* is also a study of marriage. Bill married a college freshman he met at the University of Michigan; and although Edna is a small-town girl, she shares his savvy and ambition. Again, there is an element of lesbianism in this novel, for Bill's very proper middle-aged mother turns lesbian after she is widowed.

The Ewings was dedicated to O'Hara's English agent, Graham Watson. Since his last three books were dedicated to his publisher, his editor and his agent, it is difficult to avoid the conclusion that O'Hara was deliberately settling his debts in anticipation of the big silence.*

The Ewings required only two hardcover printings, but it did well in paperback. Popular Library acquired the paperback rights to all of O'Hara's books for a figure "in excess of $500,000" and began a reprint program with a 500,000-copy first printing of *The Ewings* in 1972. The paperback went into a second printing of another 100,000 before publication date, followed by a third printing.[30]

At the time of his death O'Hara was writing a novel with the working title *Second Ewings*, the only sequel he ever attempted. He was apparently motivated by the televised series on *The Forsyte Saga*, which was attracting great interest. Another explanation for *Second Ewings* is that he felt that he had not been able to make full use of his material in *The Ewings*, which is only 300 pages long and ends rather inconclusively early in Bill's career. The continuation may have been planned as a chronicle of the Ewing marriage, for the principal action in the seventy-four-page opening is Bill Ewing's first extramarital affair.

In 1971 Sister O'Hara and Albert Erskine worked out a plan for several volumes of unpublished or uncollected stories. Some fifty un-

---

* Because O'Hara was a sentimental man who believed that gratitude becomes a man, his dedications merit attention. He dedicated books to Franklin P. Adams, his mother, Robert Benchley, Wolcott Gibbs, Philip Barry, Bennett Cerf, Graham Watson, Albert Erskine, his aunt Verna, his first teacher, Barklie Henry, Pat Outerbridge, Wylie, Belle (twice), Sister, Sister and Wylie, Winifred Gardiner, James Forrestal and William Maxwell; there was also a quadruple dedication to Rudolph Valentino, Greta Garbo, Fatty Arbuckle and D. W. Griffith. Eight of his books carry no dedication: *The Doctor's Son, Butterfield 8, Pal Joey, Ourselves to Know, The Cape Cod Lighter, The Horse Knows the Way, Waiting for Winter* and *The Instrument*.

published stories were found among his papers at "Linebrook." The
first volume was *The Time Element*, a collection of thirty-four stories
selected by Erskine, published on Thanksgiving Day 1972 by Random
House.* All of these stories are from the middle period (thirty-two
were written in the 1940's and two in the Fifties). Of the twenty
previously published stories, fifteen were in *The New Yorker* but
were not collected by O'Hara because his 1949 break with the magazine resulted in a suspension of his short-story work. The remaining
fourteen stories in *The Time Element* were published for the first time
from typescripts that Erskine was able to assign to the period. The
critical reception of the collection was dismal, and the sale was poor
compared to other O'Hara collections. Some 11,000 copies were sold.
A second posthumous collection, *Good Samaritan*, followed on 16
August 1974. It included fourteen stories written in the Sixties, twelve
of which were previously unpublished. *Good Samaritan* was not widely
reviewed, but it sold better than *The Time Element*.

Shortly after the death of John O'Hara, Random House and Mrs.
O'Hara authorized this book. A biography by Finis Farr published in
1973 did not attract much attention in America, but received a prominent review in the London *Times Literary Supplement*. The Pottsville *Republican* ran a series of forty-four installments on "O'Hara's
Roots" by Professor Charles Bassett in 1971–72. Academia has continued to discount O'Hara. During his lifetime only one good short
volume of critical appraisal by Professor Sheldon Grebstein in 1966
and two pamphlet studies were published. There has been scant
scholarly attention since 1970.[31]

A PROCESS OF reevaluation commences after the death of a major
writer. It is never the same process, for it involves an obscure collaboration between the reading public, the critics and the scholars. Sometimes the result is an immediate confirmation of the writer's stature,
as with Faulkner and Hemingway. In other cases a decade or more
is required, as with Fitzgerald. Samuel Johnson stated that "Nothing
can please many, or please long, but just representations of human
nature." John O'Hara pleased millions for forty years. The permanence
of his work is now being determined.

There are no accurate gauges for assaying literary stature. The
evaluation of literature is always impressionistic. Nevertheless, writers

---

* Random House also published on the same day *John O'Hara: A Checklist*,
a bibliographical account of O'Hara's career.

deserve to be judged by their intentions, not just according to the values of other writers or critics. Critics and scholars talk about "universality," but that is a subjective judgment. We elevate our prejudices to universality. The critics are wrong at least as often as they are right when they attempt to assign lasting stature to contemporary writers; the scholars who take responsibility for preserving and reappraising the works of the past almost never alter reputations or rescue masterpieces from oblivion.

Ultimately the permanence of John O'Hara will be determined by whether he is read—and especially by whether he is taught. The professors of English exert great influence by merely exposing students to particular books. In this way classics are made. O'Hara's novels are not on the standard American literature curricula. Professors like works that are susceptible to pedagogical exegesis; but O'Hara's work does not lend itself to that approach, for he set himself the task of eliminating cruces. It is hard to explicate what is clear. Moreover, the professional class has generally been inimical to what it regards as O'Hara's materialism.

What are the grounds for including John O'Hara among the classic American writers? First of all, there is the American-ness of his work: its value as a record of three decades of American life. The unsurpassed accuracy of this record requires that it be accorded respectful consideration for inclusion among the permanently valuable achievements in our literature. Although there are critics for whom "mere accuracy" is contemptible, there also are those who believe that one of the requirements of fiction is to be truthful. O'Hara's detractors employ the tactic of conceding his merits and dismissing them as paltry. A familiar critical cliché is that he achieved only "surface reality"—thereby implying that it was easy to do, and that in devoting himself to "reportorial realism" O'Hara missed the deeper varieties of psychological or spiritual reality. (If "surface reality" is a negligible achievement, perhaps it is worth asking if there is any virtue in its absence.) But "surface reality"—even accepting the condescension of "surface"—is not a mindless reportorial exercise. It presupposes the writer's mastery of his material, for it is mandatory that his meaningful details be really meaningful. John O'Hara was better at using such details than anyone else: he knew exactly what he was writing about. The chief literary benefit of successful "surface reality"—in addition to the pleasure of recognition it affords—is that it conditions the reader to believe in the whole work by making all the other elements more convincing. Good readers learn to distrust writers who are incompetent with details. The more-or-less grudging acknowledgment of O'Hara's "surface reality" is intended to signal the absence of more profound qualities in his work. Fashionable critics look in vain for evidence of his commitment to relevant issues. O'Hara knew that such things have nothing to do with literature. His concern was to write truthfully and exactly about life and people.

It was O'Hara's conviction that readers in the next centuries would turn to his work to find out how Americans lived in the first half of the twentieth century. Nonetheless, there have been objections to his "preoccupation with case histories and social backgrounds," objections which strike at the heart of his method. It is certainly true that "case histories and social backgrounds" are integral to his work; but they are not defects. A writer's preoccupations are defects only when he fails to make them meaningful. Indeed, that is one way to define the writer's chief obligation: that he make his material meaningful to a considerable body of readers. There will always be readers who are indifferent to O'Hara's social history, just as there will be readers who are indifferent to Faulkner's preoccupation with Southern history.

One test of a writer is his ability to create memorable characters. Here again the critics who patronize O'Hara's surface realism assert that his concern with surfaces betokens superficial characterizations. A rebuttal to this charge is the observation that, in O'Hara's own time, he created characters who achieved secure positions in the American literary experience: Julian English, Grace Caldwell Tate, Joe Chapin, Alfred Eaton and even Joey Evans. One surprising flaw in O'Hara's character portrayal is his frequent failure to show his characters actually engaged in their occupations—except for doctors, newspapermen, performers or bartenders. He does not show Joe Chapin practicing law or Alfred Eaton working as an investment banker. Unlike Cozzens, who presents the work of professional men with an impression of absolute familiarity, O'Hara tends to concentrate on the social and sexual activities of his protagonists. This defect is more serious in O'Hara than, say, in Fitzgerald, because the work of men is a crucial aspect of O'Hara's world. O'Hara has been cited for "the tenuous motivation for the behavior of major characters"—a serious charge in the case of a writer who believed that the creation of convincing characters was crucial to the art of fiction, especially in his own work. In particular, critics as well as general readers have challenged the sexual conduct of O'Hara's characters because of their apparently unmotivated adulteries and infidelities. The only possible defense is that this behavior accorded with O'Hara's observation; and he always insisted that he was dealing truthfully with human behavior as he knew it. He might well have employed Stephen Crane's statement: ". . . I understand that a man is born into the world with his own pair of eyes, and he is not at all responsible for his vision—he is merely responsible for his quality of personal honesty."

A related charge brought against O'Hara's work is that it includes "characters whose presence in the tale cannot be fully justified on aesthetic grounds." This criticism can be answered with Jules Romains' observation that life includes characters whose presence in life cannot be fully justified on aesthetic grounds. The writing of fiction is a process of selecting and ordering the materials of life—mostly a process of omission. The issue of how lifelike realistic fiction should be will always remain open. To the extent that a writer undertakes an exact transcription from life, his work becomes less creative. To the extent that he introduces exact causal relationships into his work, it becomes less lifelike. The concept of absolute realism is, admittedly, a delusion, for all writers *connect*—imposing more order on their material than it had in life. That O'Hara's fictional world is occasionally less rigorously connected than other writers' is intentional, and not evidence of his loss of control.

Another way of judging a writer is in terms of his style and technique—with high marks often given to the writers whose work is complex, and therefore purportedly profound. There is no multiplicity of meaning in O'Hara, no ambiguity or ambivalence. His aim was clarity, which is not a spectacular quality. It cannot be said that he was a stylist, for he did not create a style that was uniquely his. Nevertheless, his prose is always recognizable by what he called his "presentation"—the way in which he prepared his material. He presents a world that is identifiably his. A world that has life of its own. This quality, then, may well be what entitles John O'Hara to inclusion among the company of great writers: his work lives.

Related to O'Hara's realism and presentation is his mastery of speech. Even his most splenetic critics admit that he had a great "ear," suggesting that no art is involved in O'Hara's dialogue. (It was all done by ear.) It is worthwhile to recall O'Hara's injunction that writers who cannot be trusted to get the speech of their characters right cannot be trusted for anything else.

Many critics rate literature according to the author's view of "the human predicament," seeking evidence that he provides an ennobling view of humanity. These critics are antagonistic to O'Hara's work—claiming that his characters aren't worth writing about—because he provides no such comforting message. It has not, however, been established that the expression of such ideals is obligatory in great literature. Some of these "humanists" go further and assert

that O'Hara's work offers no standards of conduct, no human values
—ignoring the abundant evidence of his strong commitment to the
values of love, loyalty, duty, honor, pride. In missing—or suppressing—
that evidence, they fail to perceive that John O'Hara approached his
work with a Puritan conscience. He believed in his responsibility to
his genius.

JOHN O'HARA (31 January 1905–11 April 1970) died with his work
done—insofar as this can be said of any writer. For forty years he
wrote truthfully and exactly about life and people, scorning fashion,
to produce a body of work unsurpassed in American literature in
scope and fidelity to American life. He was one of our best novelists,
our best novella-ist, and our greatest writer of short stories.

*I saw and felt and heard the world around me and within my limita-
tions and within my prejudices I wrote down what I saw and felt
and heard. I tried to keep it mine and where I was most successful
it was mine.*[32]

Dedication of O'Hara's study at Pennsylvania State University Library, 1974.
Sister and Wylie with President John Oswald.

NOTES

1. "The Errors of Our Ways"—"The Whistle Stop," *Holiday* (December 1966).

I. *"Tel Arbre, Tel Fruit"**

1. O'Hara's attitude toward his *Who's Who* entries was not compulsive. In the 1944–45 edition he inserted another nonexistent club: "Quogue-Southampton Tuesday Lunch (pres., 1943)." He did not include his 1955 third marriage until the 1960–61 edition.

2. The *Herald Tribune* died before O'Hara. The fact sheet was seen in the newspaper's archives at the New York University Library. O'Hara sent a covering note to Robert Grayson, who was in charge of the *Trib*'s morgue: "I sneezed the other day, so I put together this sheet of biographical material. My Who's Who dossier has been incomplete for years—and so has Who's Who. I naturally want to have this right somewhere, and it won't be in the Times, whose obits are strange indeed. Therefore I am giving you the complete, simple facts as of today, hoping you will not have use for them for at least twenty years, but I had a scare five years ago."

3. O'Hara wrote about Pottsville's autos in "Giants of a Vanished Race," New York *Herald Tribune* (28 September 1930).

4. Michael O'Hara's rank has been variously reported. He resigned a captaincy in his own company to serve as a lieutenant under General Terry until 1863. Though as a civilian he was addressed as "Major," this seems to have been a courtesy title.

5. There are differing accounts of this episode. One version has it that Martin O'Hara fell down a flight of stairs; another report is that the brother who died was Arthur, not Martin.

6. Alice Roarke's family name has been variously reported as Rourke, O'Roark and O'Rourke.

7. Samuel T. Wiley's *Biographical and Portrait Cyclopedia of Schuylkill County, Pennsylvania*, revised edition (Philadelphia: Rush, West, 1893) gives 26 December 1865 as Patrick O'Hara's birth date, but it is probably in error. The O'Hara family believes that 1867 was the correct year.

8. Dr. O'Hara may have gone to Europe before his marriage and again after the birth of his first child, John.

9. Red Smith's column, New York *Herald Tribune* (28 January 1964).

10. Walter S. Farquhar, "Editorial Musings," Pottsville *Republican* (4 January 1953).

11. Foyles speech (3 May 1967), in *John O'Hara: A Checklist* (New York: Random House, 1972).

12. O'Hara to Charles Poore, 7 June 1958, Pennsylvania State University Library. O'Hara's letters to Poore were excerpted in the catalog for *Charles Hamilton Auction No. 56* (1972).

* From La Fontaine's *Fables*.

13. *Sweet and Sour* (1954), p. 113.

14. *Ibid.*, p. 115.

15. Introduction, *The Portable F. Scott Fitzgerald* (1945).

16. Unpublished essay, "Characters in Search"; courtesy of Carter, Ledyard & Milburn.

17. "Don't Say It Never Happened," New York *Herald Tribune Books* (8 April 1962). For an extended reconstruction of Pottsville, see Charles W. Bassett, "O'Hara's Roots," Pottsville *Republican* (20 March 1971–8 January 1972), in weekly installments.

18. *Butterfield 8* (1935), pp. 67–68.

19. Foyles speech (3 May 1967).

20. Don A. Schanche's notes for "John O'Hara Is Alive and Well in the First Half of the Twentieth Century" (*Esquire* [August 1969]). Hereafter cited as Schanche notes. The author is deeply grateful to Mr. Schanche, who generously shared his valuable material.

21. O'Hara to Maxwell, 9 February 1961. There may be significance in the fact that, contrary to his custom, O'Hara dated most of his letters to Maxwell. O'Hara's letters to Maxwell are at the Pennsylvania State University Library.

22. "Memoirs of a Sentimental Duffer," *Holiday* (May 1965).

23. "Dancing School," New York *Herald Tribune* (3 August 1930); "When Dinner Coats Were Tucks and Young Men Toddled," *Herald Tribune* (30 August 1931).

24. "When Bands Were Big"—"The Whistle Stop," *Holiday* (April 1967).

25. "Appointment with O'Hara," *Collier's* (23 December 1955).

26. *Ibid.*

27. O'Hara's letters to Simonds are at the Pennsylvania State University Library. Although they are mostly undated, Simonds kept some of the envelopes, and the sequence can be partly reconstructed from postmarks.

28. *Sweet and Sour* (1954), p. 11.

29. Postmarked 12 February 1934. O'Hara's letters to his brother Tom are at the Pennsylvania State University Library.

30. O'Hara to Simonds, c.28 April 1923.

31. O'Hara to Robert Moses, 4 December 1961. Printed in Moses' column, "Bits and Pieces," *Park East* (17 January 1974).

32. Father Beatty to MJB, 30 June 1972.

33. Pottsville *Journal* (2 October 1950), 5.

34. Russ Green to MJB, 3 November 1972; supplemented by interview in January 1973.

35. *Ibid.*

36. Harvey Breit, "Talk with John O'Hara," New York *Times Book Review* (4 September 1949).

37. "Why Manchester Roots for Its Small-Town Doctor," New York *Daily Mirror* (9 March 1950).

38. "Death Claims Dr. P. H. O'Hara," Pottsville *Republican* (18 March 1925), 1; "Dr. O'Hara Was a City Asset," *Republican* (19 March 1925), 4; "Dr. O'Hara Is Laid to Rest," *Republican* (21 March 1925), 1.

39. Margaretta Archbald Kroll to MJB, 9 July 1971.

40. O'Hara to Simonds, October 1927.

41. O'Hara to Simonds, November 1927.

42. O'Hara to Simonds, possibly December 1927.

II. *The Big Town*

1. "Ninety Minutes Away," *The Hat on the Bed* (1963).

2. O'Hara to Simonds, March 1928.

3. Sirs: Says Grace Gordon Cox, of Boston, under Letters in the January 9 issue of *Time*:

> ". . . There will never be a man on your staff big enough to stand in Lindy's shoes."
> Why not give Robert Emmet Sherwood a job?
>
> —John H. O'Hara
>
> New York City
> Robert Emmet Sherwood's feet fill size 13 shoes. He is editor and cinema critic of *Life*, and author of *The Road to Rome*, highly successful comedy.
> —Ed. (23 January 1928).

4. O'Hara to Simonds, c.April 1928.

5. O'Hara to Simonds, c.April 1928.

6. O'Hara to Ross, c.April 1928. O'Hara's letters to Ross and *The New Yorker* editors are at the Pennsylvania State University Library.

7. Sayre, "John O'Hara: A Reminiscence," Washington *Post Book World* (18 March 1973).

8. Nathaniel Benchley, "The Hard Luck Story of John O'Hara," *Stage*, 1 (February 1941). This article-interview is the source for several familiar anecdotes about O'Hara.

9. "Bleeck's: John O'Hara Recalls a Cave of Journalism Greats," New York *Herald Tribune* (24 April 1963).

10. "Appointment with O'Hara," *Collier's* (13 April 1956).

11. O'Hara to Simonds, c.April 1928.

12. O'Hara remark to Don Schanche; Schanche notes.

13. Beverly, Gary, "A Post Portrait: John O'Hara," New York *Post* (20 May 1959).

14. O'Hara to Simonds, late 1928.

15. *Polly* was a musical with Fred Allen. O'Hara claimed this review in a letter to Don Schanche, 24 December 1964.

16. O'Hara interview for *Time* archives, 1964.

17. "The Hard Luck Story of John O'Hara." See note 8.

18. "A Few Trips and Some Poetry," *And Other Stories* (1968), p. 133.

19. "Cesar Romero and the Three Dollar Bills," New York *Journal* and Chicago *American* magazine section (13 June 1936), King Features Syndicate.

20. O'Hara to Simonds, late 1928.

21. O'Hara interview for *Time* archives, 1964.

22. O'Hara to Alfred Wright, 11 March 1967. At the time of his death O'Hara was working on a play about two partners in a magazine, obviously based on Hadden and Luce.

23. James Thurber, *The Years with Ross* (Boston: Little, Brown, 1959), pp. 129, 135.

24. *Ibid.*, p. 13.

25. MJB interview with Stephen Longstreet, August 1971.

26. Katharine Angell White to MJB, 17 May 1971.

27. Nathaniel Benchley, *Robert Benchley* (New York: McGraw-Hill, 1955), p. 5.

28. *Sweet and Sour* (1954), pp. 4–5. The *Mirror* story was "J. R. Clark Admits Guilt; Faces Life" (24 July 1929).

29. New York *Daily Mirror* (29 July 1929). O'Hara revealed his participation in this stunt in a letter to the New York *Herald Tribune* (29 April 1962).

30. Cain to MJB, 27 April 1974.

31. *The New Republic* (15 January 1940).

32. O'Hara to Simonds, possibly November 1931.

33. "Imagine Kissing Pete," *Sermons and Soda-Water* (1960), p. 65. An earlier comment by Malloy in *Hope of Heaven* (1938) shows the risk of reading the Malloy material as straight autobiography: "My first wife was rich and older than I and divorced, and her friends used to make me feel like a God damn Marchbanks, although I think I really loved her at the time."

34. The marriage certificate gives the witnesses as P. Poveromo and Lawler Hill.

35. O'Hara to Simonds, c.March 1931.

36. "Barrymore's *Real* Ambition," *Screenland* (October 1931) is by-lined John O'Hara. The article, which reads like a publicity release, has no recognizable O'Hara touches.

37. Ads for *Public Enemy* have been located in the New York *Times* (22–24 April 1931). Einfeld also credits O'Hara with the ads for *The Star Witness*, which appeared in the *Times* (1–3 August 1931), after O'Hara quit the job.

38. Cain to MJB, 27 April 1974.

39. The O'Hara-Crichton correspondence is in the Scribners Archives, Princeton University Library. See also Crichton's *Total Recoil* (New York: Doubleday, 1960).

40. Ingersoll to MJB, 30 August 1972. The chronology here is not entirely clear, for by 1931 Ingersoll had moved to *Fortune*.

41. Bergman letter to *Esquire*, CXXII (December 1969), 134.

42. O'Hara ultimately forgave Conrad Richter for invading his material. In *The Lockwood Concern* the town that corresponds to Pine Grove, Richter's hometown, is called Richterville.

43. The short novels published during the 1931–32 contest were Josephine Herbst's *A New Break*, Grace Flandrau's *An Affair of the Senses*, Cornelia Evans Goodhue's *The Cloud of Witnesses*, Sherwood Anderson's *Mill Girls*, Edith Wharton's *Her Son*, Arthur Tuckerman's *Love's a Grown-Up God* and Katherine Anne Porter's *The Cracked Looking-Glass*. There were more than 1,500 entries.

44. O'Hara to Simonds, probably mid-1932.

45. O'Hara to Simonds, probably mid-1932.

46. O'Hara to Simonds, late 1932.

47. Weidman to MJB, 27 March 1972.

48. Mildred Gilman Wohlforth to MJB, 27 January 1973.

49. A typed copy of this letter was provided by Robert Alberts and Oscar Shefler.

50. F. Scott Fitzgerald Papers, Princeton University Library.

51. Fitzgerald Papers (carbon).

52. O'Hara to Crichton, c.May 1933.

53. Fitzgerald Papers.

54. Unlocated clipping, reproduced in *John O'Hara: A Checklist*, p. 104.

55. *Robert Benchley*, p. 5.

56. Foreword to Modern Library *Appointment in Samarra* (1953).

57. *Ibid.*

58. O'Hara to William Maxwell, 16 May 1963.

59. A copy of this book is in the MJB collection.

III. *Success*

1. O'Hara to Tom O'Hara, 9 April 1934.

2. This typescript is now at the Pennsylvania State University Library, where O'Hara decided to consolidate his papers.

3. The galley proofs of *Appointment* are at the Yale University Library.

> . . . he could see the nipples of her breasts and the red circles, big as half a buck. She saw him looking—he couldn't help looking. And she smiled and did the worst thing she could have done to anyone in his state of mind: she sat so that no one could see what she was doing, no one but Al Greco, and she reached in under the dress and cupped the right breast in her left hand, and she smiled at Al Greco and said: "Want some, dearie?" And jiggled the breast up and down. "You're damn right you do," she said, when he did not answer.
>
> * * * * * * *
>
> "What the hell's the matter with you, anyway?" he said.
> "Want some, deeeereeee?" she said. She looked down at the breast in her hand. "Nice. Nice," she said, talking to it like a baby, with exaggerated puckered lips.
>
> * * * * * * *
>
> "Did I what?"
> "Masticate. Come on, don't stall."
> "Yes. From the time I was twelve," she said.
> "You did, really?"
> "Every day of my life. Did you?"
> "Every day of my life. Did you masticate after you fell in love with me?"
> "More than ever. What about you? Did you, after you fell in love with me?"
> "More than ever. Of course there was never a time. I mean I never did really fall in love with you. I always loved you, from the time I was born. Although I began to masticate at the same time. I took one look at Mother when she was getting ready to give me my first meal, and I said to myself, I said. 'Boy, *mas*ticate!' and by God I did."

4. "Appointment with O'Hara," *Collier's* (22 July 1955).
5. "Hello Hollywood Good-bye," *Holiday* (May 1968).
6. On publication day O'Hara wrote to his brother Tom:

> Marg was the one for me; Pet I love actively and deeply, and she fills my waking hours, but all those years with Marg, no matter how much I cheated on her, haven't erased the handwriting on the wall of love, and you may have ten such metaphors by writing to Drawer B, Emporia Kansas. It isn't that Pet is second best. It's just that she's second, that's all. . . . Not that I pine for Marg; Pet is the one I pine for, because she was my wife, and still is, really.

7. Canby, *Saturday Review of Literature* (18 August 1934); Lewis, New York *Herald Tribune Books* (23 September 1934); Lewis, *SRL* (6 October 1934); Crichton, *Life* (January 1935).
8. O'Hara to Mark Schorer, 17 February 1959; *Sinclair Lewis: An American Life* (New York: McGraw-Hill, 1961), p. 351.
9. This ad appeared in several forms and in a number of places—see New York *Herald Tribune Books* (2 September 1934).
10. "Diagram of a Celebrity," Danville *Morning News* (15 July 1935), 4. *Keeping Up with Books*, a book-news advertisement distributed by the Jacobs Book Store (branches in Shenandoah, Pottsville, Hazleton, Tamaqua, Girardville and Frackville), praised *Appointment* in its Summer 1934 issue, but warned that it was a book for "Mature Adults."
11. O'Hara to Farquhar, c.April 1935; Pennsylvania State University Library. In an undated letter—probably acknowledging Farquhar's Pottsville *Journal* article on *Appointment*—O'Hara wrote:

Dear Walter—
> You are a gentleman and a scholar. I hope you're also a good judge of writers. I think that there isn't another soul in Pottsville who knows and understands as you do what that piece did for me. I think that because you know and understand, you wrote the piece. I think I'm good, and Pottsville will think so eventually. But between my conviction and that day when Pottsville realizes my ability, I'll know—as I've always suspected—that the brain behind the Sportitorial is calculating my progress; and the heart that feeds that brain is wishing me well. And by God that means I'm successful already.
> And how could it be otherwise? Who wrote Joe Dark's obit?
> Gratefully
> John O'Hara

12. O'Hara to Murphy, 30 July 1962; collection of Honoria Murphy Donnelly.

13. Julian English's name may have been drawn from that of a Julian Pilgrim who resided on Mahantongo Street. O'Hara wanted an English-sounding family name, like Pilgrim.

14. Unpublished lecture delivered at Rider College, 1959; courtesy of Carter, Ledyard & Milburn.

15. O'Hara to Forrestal, 17 December 1946; Forrestal Papers, Princeton University Library.

16. Foyles speech (May 1967).

17. Ruth Sato recalls that O'Hara was troubled when Winchell announced his impending marriage to Dorothy Van Hest. MJB interviews with Ruth Sato Reinhardt, December 1971 and December 1973.

18. Courtesy of Carter, Ledyard & Milburn.

19. This brutal description reads in full:

> . . . I thought of O'Hara, fat as a boa constrictor that had swallowed an entire shipment of a magazine called *Collier's* and surly as a mule that has been bitten by a tsetse fly plodding along dead without recognizing it and I wished him luck and all happiness remembering joyously the white-edged evening tie he had worn at his coming-out party in New York and his hostess' nervousness at presenting him and her gallant hope that he would not disintegrate. No matter how bad things go any human being can be cheered remembering O'Hara at his most brilliant epoch (*Sports Illustrated*, XXXVI [10 January 1972], 27).

20. O'Hara to Fitzgerald, late 1935; Fitzgerald Papers.

21. O'Hara to Fitzgerald, April 1936; Fitzgerald Papers.

22. Milestone to MJB, 15 July 1971.

23. "Hello Hollywood Good-bye."

24. O'Hara to Pearce, spring 1936; Harcourt, Brace, Jovanovich files. O'Hara did not deal directly with Alfred Harcourt or Donald Brace, but corresponded with Pearce and Sloan.

25. O'Hara to Pearce, Spring 1936.

26. O'Hara to Pearce and Sloan, Spring 1936.

27. Pearce to O'Hara, 1 May 1936.

28. O'Hara to Pearce, c.19 September 1936.

29. Rivkin to MJB, 11 September 1972.

30. MJB interview with Gilbert Roland, August 1971.

31. "Appointment with O'Hara," *Collier's* (13 April 1956) and Schanche notes.

32. "Hello Hollywood Good-bye."

33. "Novelist Likes the Film Translation," New York *Herald Tribune* (18 May 1958).

IV. *Belle*

1. O'Hara to Bryan, May 1937; Pennsylvania State University Library.

2. The author is deeply indebted to Mrs. Gerald Bramwell and Mrs. Henry Gardiner for their recollections of Belle O'Hara generously provided in interviews and letters.

3. Sargeant to MJB, 13 April 1971.

4. Foyles speech (1967).

5. "Entertainment Week," *Newsweek* (4 August 1941).

6. O'Hara included only thirteen stories from *The Doctor's Son*; the remaining twenty-three stories were previously uncollected. See following section, "John O'Hara's Works."

7. MJB collection.

8. Wilson, "It Happened Last Night," New York *Post* (28 March 1948).

9. O'Hara to Maxwell, Fall 1939.

10. MJB interview with Ben Finney, May 1971.

11. "Appointment with O'Hara," *Collier's* (30 September 1955).

12. The first owner of the Duesenberg was Cliff Durant; it then passed to J. Paul Getty and McClain before O'Hara acquired it in 1941.

13. "Author Denies He's Memorizing Whole Book; He's Only Interested in Longer Passages," New York *World-Telegram* (8 March 1941); supplemented by Collier Young's taped recollections.

14. MJB interview with Schulberg, August 1973; Schulberg to MJB, 15 May 1974.

15. Saroyan to MJB, 19 January 1975.

16. O'Hara to Sloan, May 1939.

17. "In Memory of F. Scott Fitzgerald: II. Certain Aspects," *The New Republic* (3 March 1941).

18. Introduction, *The Portable F. Scott Fitzgerald* (1945).

19. Mary Morris and Robert Rice, "How a Musical Is Made," *PM* (22 December 1940).

20. "Some Fond Recollections of Larry Hart," New York *Times* (1944).

21. Sheean to MJB, 9 June 1972; Schanche notes.

22. Richard Rodgers, " 'Pal Joey': History of a 'Heel,' " New York *Times* (30 December 1951), II, 1, 3.

23. "In Memory of F. Scott Fitzgerald: II. Certain Aspects."

24. Weidman to MJB, 27 March 1972.

25. O'Hara to Forrestal, 7 February 1942; Princeton University Library.

26. Ray S. Cline to MJB, 18 June 1971.

27. Hersey to MJB, 21 March 1973.

28. Courtesy of Mrs. John O'Hara.

29. O'Hara to Sullivan, 16 November 1944; Cornell University Library.

30. O'Hara to Mrs. White, c.October 1947.

31. Sullivan to Mrs. John O'Hara, 31 May 1970.

32. Hornblow to MJB, 26 May 1971.

33. MJB interview with Romanoff, August 1971.

34. Cerf oral history notes, Columbia University Library. Supplemented by interview with Mrs. Cerf, May 1974.

35. O'Hara to Cerf, 17 June 1948; Cerf to O'Hara, 18 June 1948. Random House archives, Columbia University Library.

36. O'Hara to Batdorf, 11 September 1948.

37. O'Hara to Cerf, 30 November 1948.

38. O'Hara to Commins, probably Summer 1948. Courtesy of Mrs. Saxe Commins.

39. The original typescript for *A Rage to Live* is at the Rutgers University Library.

40. David Dempsey, "In and Out of Books," New York *Times Book Review* (6 November 1949).

41. O'Hara to Ross, c.7 June 1948. The *New Yorker*'s system of payment became very complicated. Each author had his own word rate, which was higher for the first 2,000 words of a casual to encourage economy in writing; but there was a 25 percent bonus for exceptional pieces. After an author sold four casuals in one year he qualified for a retroactive 25 percent bonus; and there was an additional retroactive 35 percent bonus for six contributions in one year.

42. Ross to Sullivan, 1 October 1949; Cornell University Library.

43. Jules Romains, *Men of Good Will*, I (New York: Knopf, 1933).

44. *A Rage to Live*, p. 245.

45. O'Hara to Norris, 22 July 1949; Pennsylvania State University Library. O'Hara retained a carbon of his letter.

46. New York *Herald Tribune Books* (22 November 1934).

47. New York *Times Book Review* (21 August 1949).

48. Alsop to MJB, 25 October 1973.

49. Leslie to MJB, 12 April 1974.

50. Outerbridge interview with MJB, April 1971. Supplemented by letters.

51. Hersey to MJB, 15 January 1973.

52. Hemingway to Gen. C. T. Lanham, 11 September 1950; Princeton University Library.

53. O'Hara made a record of his statement, which the newspapers did not print accurately. Scrapbook, Pennsylvania State University Library.

54. North (14 November 1951): "More thoughtful readers will understand after a few pages that O'Hara is writing a ferocious little fable for moderns—a fable which will not be appreciated by those leftists who are bright enough to understand its meaning." Poore (8 November 1951) was aware that something was going on in the novel besides the plot, but he was not sure what it was: ". . . I began to suspect some connection with Barry's fitfully profound bouts with Larger Issues. . . . It may be there."

55. William M. Dwyer, "O'Hara Writes Play, Amateurs Stage It," New York *Herald Tribune* (18 May 1952).

56. Thomas C. Matthews, " 'Searching Sun' Terribly Written." *The Daily Princetonian* (8 May 1952). Prof. Willard Thorp of the Princeton English department wrote a letter to *The Princetonian* rebuking Matthews for the review.

57. The list of O'Hara's plays is partly based on information provided by Robert A. Freedman of Harold Freedman, Brandt & Brandt, and on the following newspaper items: Sam Zolotow, "John O'Hara Finds Playwriting Fun," New York *Times* (29 July 1963); Zolotow, "Comedy Premiere Off Till Monday," *Times* (4 November 1949); Lewis Funke, "News And Gossip Gathered On The Rialto," *Times* (20 January 1952); Zolotow, " 'Richard III' Back On Stage Tonight," *Times* (4 December 1953); Zolotow, " 'Late Love' Finds Broadway Haven," *Times* (7 August 1953); Zolotow, " 'Carousel' Seen Prolonging Run," *Times* (7 June 1954); Zolotow, "Premiere Tonight For Play, 'Haven,' " *Times* (13 November 1946); Zolotow, " 'Buy Blue Ribbons' Has Debut Tonight," *Times* (17 October 1951); Zolotow, "Irene M. Selznick Buys Tabori Play," *Times* (21 November 1951); Alden Whitman, "O'Hara, in Rare Interview, Calls Literary Landscape Fairly Bleak," *Times* (13 November 1967).

58. " 'My Ten Favorite Plays,' " *Theatre Arts* (November 1957).

59. Mary Leigh Pell Whitmer to MJB, 23 June 1971 and 11 September 1973. Supplemented by interview, Spring 1973.

60. *Sweet and Sour* (1954), p. 161.

61. *My Turn* (1966), pp. 60–61.

62. *Sweet and Sour* (1954), p. 109.

63. In his speech O'Hara referred to events in The Region during World War I and discussed his grandfather Delaney's career. Unpublished, copy courtesy of Judge Walter K. Stapleton.

64. *We're Friends Again*, p. 64.

V. *Sister*

1. In the summer of 1956 TWA and United planes collided over the Grand Canyon.

2. *Harvard Class of 1929 Twenty-Fifth Anniversary Report* (1954).

3. O'Hara to Maxwell, 16 May 1963.

4. Scott Sullivan, "O'Hara Advises Yale Men To Learn 'Non-Conformism,'" *Yale Daily News* (5 May 1955).

5. MJB interviews with Herbert Bayard Swope, Jr., 1972–73, and David Brown, March 1974.

6. The NBA fiction judges were Carlos Baker, John Brooks, Granville Hicks, Saunders Redding and Mark Schorer.

7. John Cook Wyllie, "Book Editor Keeps An Appointment With O'Hara," Richmond *News-Leader* (22 February 1956).

8. James H. Cohen, "Yegge Honored at Annual Dinner; Gold Gets First Fitzgerald Award," *The Daily Princetonian* (9 January 1956), 1.

9. O'Hara to Poore, 16 August 1956.

10. Courtesy of Carter, Ledyard & Milburn.

11. *Three Views of the Novel* (1957).

12. Louis Cook, "O'Hara Book Naughty, Police Say: It's Banned," Detroit *Free Press* (18 January 1957).

13. The publishers retained Weil, Gotshal and Manges of New York City who appeared with Goldsmith and Rosen of Detroit before Judge Carl M. Weidman on 16 June 1958 in the Circuit Court for the County of Wayne in Chancery (# 555,684 and # 555,685). See Detroit *Free Press* and Detroit *News* (13–14 January, 17 January–22 January, 8 February, 29 March, 9 April 1957).

14. Bantam was represented by Weil, Gotshal and Manges of New York City (Indictment #49, State of New York County Court—Albany County). See Albany *Knickerbocker News* (6 December, 9–10 December, 13–14 December, 19 December, 27 December 1957); New York *Times* and New York *Herald Tribune* (10 December and 14 December 1957, 3 July 1958).

15. O'Hara to Cowley, 17 December 1957; Geffen to O'Hara, 18 December 1957; "As 'From the Terrace' Goes to Press: Appointment with O'Hara," *Publishers Weekly* (3 November 1958); Geffen to O'Hara, 14 November 1958; Geffen to O'Hara, 18 November 1958; Cowley to O'Hara, 26 November 1958; O'Hara to Cowley, 1 December 1958. Archives of the National Institute of Arts and Letters.

16. Untitled; courtesy of Carter, Ledyard & Milburn.

17. O'Hara to Hutchens, c.November 1958.

18. Courtesy of Dr. William Bond, Houghton Library, Harvard.

19. Foreword dated 12 November 1959; courtesy of Carter, Ledyard & Milburn.

20. The author is deeply grateful to Wylie O'Hara Doughty for generously sharing her father's letters.

21. O'Hara to Poore, 27 February 1960; Pennsylvania State University Library.

22. "O'Hara Attacks His Attackers," Chicago *Sun-Times* (3 April 1960).

23. Maxwell to MJB, 4 May 1971.

24. Hutchens, "John O'Hara from Pottsville, Pa.," New York *Herald Tribune Books* (4 December 1955).

25. Schanche notes.

26. O'Hara to Erskine, 29 August 1960; 21 April 1960.

27. William Dix, the Librarian of the Princeton University Library, explained to O'Hara that such a transfer would constitute a precedent that might have serious consequences for libraries (14 October 1964). O'Hara rejected the explanation in an angry reply: "In this matter the only wishes to be considered are those of the author . . ." (17 October 1964).

28. *My Turn* (1966), pp. 195–97.

29. MJB telephone interview with Berlin, October 1972.

30. Archives of the National Institute of Arts and Letters.

VI. *The Master*

1. O'Hara to Maxwell, 9 February 1961.

2. *My Turn* (1966), pp. 180–81.

3. O'Hara to Hogan, 2 August 1961; courtesy of Mr. Hogan.

4. MJB interview with Hutchens, July 1974.

5. O'Hara to Cozzens, 4 August 1964; courtesy of Mr. Cozzens.

6. O'Hara to Maxwell, 4 January 1966.

7. Schanche to MJB, 9 April 1973.

8. O'Hara's pocket diaries are at the Pennsylvania State University Library.

9. O'Hara to Schanche, "Derby Day 1963." O'Hara once told Stephen Longstreet, "I showed Scott how to *really* write about gangsters, with Greco and Charney. Scott didn't know chalk from cheese about real hoods" (Longstreet to MJB, 22 September 1972).

10. Cozzens to O'Hara (15 June 1963); courtesy of Mr. Cozzens.

11. Red Smith's column, New York *Herald Tribune* (28 January 1964).

12. *Proceedings of the American Academy of Arts and Letters and the National Institute of Arts and Letters, Second Series, Number Fifteen* (1965).

13. O'Hara to Maxwell, 16 May 1963.

14. O'Hara to Hersey, October 1964; archives of the National Institute of Arts and Letters.

15. Schanche notes.

16. Sheilah Graham, *The Rest of the Story* (New York: Coward-McCann, 1964), p. 216.

17. O'Hara to Maxwell, 20 November 1963.

18. "Writers I Have Met," New York *Times Book Review* (11 August 1968).

19. Hodder & Stoughton sold 8,200 copies of *Waiting for Winter*, 16,400 of *The Instrument*, 8,500 of *And Other Stories* and 13,000 of *Lovey Childs*.

20. O'Hara to Wright, 11 March 1967.

21. Dr. Elliot to MJB, 10 April 1974.

22. MJB interview with Dilworth, January 1973.

23. O'Hara to Scott, 5 November 1962. Courtesy of Mr. Scott.

24. "O'Hara, in Rare Interview, Calls Literary Landscape Fairly Bleak," New York *Times* (13 November 1967).

25. O'Hara to Erskine, 14 November 1967.

26. *The New Yorker* did not mention O'Hara's death, but *Time* and *Newsweek* both gave it full pages on 20 April 1970.

27. It has been erroneously assumed that O'Hara prepared his epitaph. He made this comment about himself in an interview ("A Writer's Look at His Town, Career and Future," *The Princeton Packet* [23 November 1961]), which became the basis for an AP article by Miles Smith.

28. *Last Will and Testament (dated June 16, 1967) of John O'Hara . . . Carter, Ledyard & Milburn. . . .*

29. *John O'Hara/January 31, 1905/April 11, 1970* (privately printed, 1970).

30. By December 1974 Popular Library had reprinted *The Ewings, Ourselves to Know, The Cape Cod Lighter, Hope of Heaven, The Farmers Hotel* (two printings), *The Time Element* (two printings), *Assembly, Waiting for Winter, Sweet and Sour* and *Elizabeth Appleton*—as well as *Great Short Stories of John O'Hara.*

31. The Pennsylvania State University Library had a memorial exhibit of O'Hara's books and manuscripts, July–August 1970. The *PMLA* annual bibliography of literary scholarship lists nothing for O'Hara in its 1971 issue and two items in its 1972 issue.

32. Schanche notes.

JOHN O'HARA'S WORKS

BOOKS

Reminiscences from "Kungsholm" West Indies Cruise, March 9–March 28, 1934 (Swedish American Line, 1934).

Appointment in Samarra (New York: Harcourt, Brace, 1934).

The Doctor's Son and Other Stories (New York: Harcourt, Brace, 1935). Thirty-seven stories: "The Doctor's Son," "Early Afternoon," "Pleasure," "New Day," "The Man Who Had to Talk to Somebody," "Mary," "Ella and the Chinee," "Ten Eyck or Pershing? Pershing or Ten Eyck?" "Alone," "Coffee Pot," "The Girl Who Had Been Presented," "Mort and Mary," "On His Hands," "It Wouldn't Break Your Arm," "I Never Seen Anything Like It," "Lombard's Kick," "Frankie," "Mr. Cass and the Ten Thousand Dollars," "Of Thee I Sing, Baby," "Screen Test," "Mr. Sidney Gainsborough: Quality Pictures," "Mr. Cowley and the Young," "Never a Dull Moment," "Master of Ceremonies," "Mrs. Galt and Edwin," "Hotel Kid," "Dr. Wyeth's Son," "Except in My Memory," "The Public Career of Mr. Seymour Harrisburg," "Straight Pool," "Back in New Haven," "Salute a Thoroughbred," "All the Girls He Wanted," "Sportsmanship," "In the Morning Sun," "It Must Have Been Spring," "Over the River and Through the Wood."

Butterfield 8 (New York: Harcourt, Brace, 1935).

Hope of Heaven (New York: Harcourt, Brace, 1938). London edition (Faber & Faber, 1939) adds thirty-six stories: "The Public Career of Mr. Seymour Harrisburg," "Sidesaddle," "Saffercisco," "Price's Always Open," "Hotel Kid," "Of Thee I Sing, Baby," "In the Morning Sun," "Can You Carry Me?" "Lunch Tuesday," "Shave," "Portistan on the Portis," "The Cold House," "Days," "Are We Leaving To-morrow?" "Salute a Thoroughbred," "Sportsmanship," "Dr. Wyeth's Son," "Over the River," "Pleasure," "Alone," "Frankie," "The Gentleman in the Tan Suit," "Most Gorgeous Thing," "It Must Have Been Spring," "I Could Have Had a Yacht," "Olive," "Ice Cream," "Brother," "By Way of Yonkers," "My Girls," "No Sooner Said," "Good-bye Herman," "Give and Take," "Peggy," "Straight Pool," "The Doctor's Son."

Files on Parade (New York: Harcourt, Brace, 1939). Thirty-five stories: "Price's Always Open," "Trouble in 1949," "The Cold House," "Days," "Are We Leaving Tomorrow?" "Portistan on the Portis," "Lunch Tuesday," "Shave," "Sidesaddle," "No Mistakes," "Brother," "Saffercisco," "Ice Cream," "Peggy," "And You Want a Mountain," "Pal Joey," "Ex-Pal," "How I Am Now in Chi," "Bow Wow," "Give and Take," "The Gentleman in the Tan Suit," "Good-by Herman," "I Could Have Had a Yacht," "Richard Wagner: Public Domain?" "Olive," "It Wouldn't Break Your Arm," "My Girls," "No Sooner Said," "Invite," "All the Girls He Wanted," "By Way of Yonkers," "Most Gorgeous Thing," "A Day Like Today," "The Ideal Man," "Do You Like It Here?"

Pal Joey (New York: Duell, Sloan & Pearce, 1940). Fourteen stories: "Pal Joey," "Ex-Pal," "How I Am Now in Chi," "Bow Wow," "Avast and Belay," "Joey on Herta," "Joey on the Cake Line," "The Erloff," "Even the Greeks," "Joey and the Calcutta Club," "Joey and Mavis," "A New Career," "A Bit of a Shock," "Reminiss?"

Pipe Night (New York: Duell, Sloan & Pearce, 1945). Thirty-one stories: "Walter T. Carriman," "Now We Know," "Free," "Can You Carry Me?" "A Purchase of Some Golf Clubs," "Too Young," "Joey and the Calcutta Club," "Summer's Day," "Radio," "Nothing Missing," "The King of the Desert," "Bread Alone," "Reunion Over Lightly," "Memo to a Kind Stranger," "The Erloff," "Patriotism," "A Respectable Place," "The Magical Numbers," "On Time," "Graven Image," "Adventure on the Set," "Platform," "Civilized," "Revenge," "Fire!" "The Lieutenant," "The Next-to-Last Dance of the Season," "Leave," "The Handler," "Where's the Game," "Mrs. Whitman."

Hellbox (New York: Random House, 1947). Twenty-six stories: "Common Sense Should Tell You," "Pardner," "Someone to Trust," "Horizon," "Like Old Times," "Ellie," "Life Among These Unforgettable Characters," "War Aims," "Clara," "Secret Meeting," "Drawing Room B," "The Decision," "Somebody Can Help Somebody," "The Pretty Daughters," "Everything Satisfactory," "The Moccasins," "Doctor and Mrs. Parsons," "Wise Guy," "The Three Musketeers," "Other Women's Households," "Transaction," "Miss W.," "Time to Go," "A Phase of Life," "The Chink in the Armor," "Conversation in the Atomic Age."

A Rage to Live (New York: Random House, 1949).

The Farmers Hotel (New York: Random House, 1951).

Pal Joey (libretto and lyrics) (New York: Random House, 1952).

Sweet and Sour (New York: Random House, 1954). Columns.

Ten North Frederick (New York: Random House, 1955).

A Family Party (New York: Random House, 1956).

From the Terrace (New York: Random House, 1958).

Ourselves to Know (New York: Random House, 1960).

Sermons and Soda-Water (New York: Random House, 1960). Three volumes. "The Girl on the Baggage Truck," "Imagine Kissing Pete," "We're Friends Again."

Five Plays (New York: Random House, 1961). "The Farmers Hotel," "The Searching Sun," "The Champagne Pool," "Veronique," "The Way It Was."

Assembly (New York: Random House, 1961). Twenty-six stories: "Mrs. Stratton of Oak Knoll," "The Weakness," "The Man with the Broken Arm," "The Lighter When Needed," "The Pioneer Hep-Cat," "The Sharks," "The Girl from California," "A Cold Calculating Thing," "You Can Always Tell Newark," "The High Point," "Call Me, Call Me," "It's Mental Work," "In the Silence," "First Day in Town," "Exactly Eight Thousand Dollars Exactly," "Mary and Norma," "The Cellar Domain," "The Properties of Love," "Reassurance," "The Free," "The Compliment," "Sterling Silver," "The Trip," "In a Grove," "The Old Folks," "A Case History."

The Big Laugh (New York: Random House, 1962).

The Cape Cod Lighter (New York: Random House, 1962). Twenty-three stories: "Appearances," "The Bucket of Blood," "The Butterfly," "Claude Emerson, Reporter," "The Engineer," "The Father," "The First Day," "Jurge Dulrumple," "Justice," "The Lesson," "Money," "The Nothing Machine," "Pat Collins," "The Professors," "A Short Walk from the Station," "Sunday Morning," "The Sun-Dodgers," "Things You Really Want," "Two Turtle-doves," "Winter Dance," "The Women of Madison Avenue," "You Don't Remember Me," "Your Fah Neefah Neeface."

Elizabeth Appleton (New York: Random House, 1963).

The Hat on the Bed (New York: Random House, 1963). Twenty-four stories: "Agatha," "Aunt Anna," "Eminent Domain," "Exterior: with Figure," "The Flatted Saxophone," "The Friends of Miss Julia," "The Glendale People," "The Golden," "How Can I Tell You?" "I Know That, Roy," "John Barton Rosedale, Actors' Actor," "The Locomobile," "The Manager," "The Man on the Tractor," "The Mayor," "Ninety Minutes Away," "Our Friend the Sea," "The Public Dorothy," "The Ride from Mauch Chunk," "Saturday Lunch," "Teddy and the Special Friends," "The Twinkle in His Eye," "The Windowpane Check," "Yucca Knolls."

The Horse Knows the Way (New York: Random House, 1964). Twenty-eight stories: "All Tied Up," "The Answer Depends," "Arnold Stone," "At the Window," "Aunt Fran," "The Bonfire," "The Brain," "Can I Stay Here?" "Clayton Bunter," "The Clear Track," "The Gun," "The Hardware Man," "His Excellency," "The House on the Corner," "I Can't Thank You Enough," "In the Mist," "I Spend My Days in Longing," "The Jet Set," "The Law-breaker," "The Madeline Wherry Case," "Mrs. Allanson," "The Pig," "School," "The Staring Game," "The Victim," "What's the Good of Know-ing?" "The Whole Cherry Pie," "Zero."

The Lockwood Concern (New York: Random House, 1965).

My Turn (New York: Random House, 1966). Columns.

Waiting for Winter (New York: Random House, 1966). Twenty-one stories: "Afternoon Waltz," "Andrea," "The Assistant," "Fatimas and Kisses," "Flight," "The Gambler," "The General," "A Good Location," "The Jama," "James Francis and the Star," "Late, Late Show," "Leonard," "Natica Jackson," "The Neighborhood," "The Pomeranian," "The Portly Gentleman," "The Skeletons," "The Tackle," "The Way to Majorca," "The Weakling," "Yostie."

The Instrument (New York: Random House, 1967).

And Other Stories (New York: Random House, 1968). Twelve stories: "Barred," "The Broken Giraffe," "The Farmer," "A Few Trips and Some Poetry," "The Gangster," "The Gunboat and Madge," "How Old, How Young," "A Man on a Porch," "Papa Gibraltar," "The Private People," "The Strong Man," "We'll Have Fun."

Lovey Childs: A Philadelphian's Story (New York: Random House, 1969).

The Ewings (New York: Random House, 1972).

The Time Element and Other Stories, ed. Albert Erskine (New York: Random House, 1972). Thirty-four stories: "Encounter: 1943," "Conversation at Lunch," "Pilgrimage," "One for the Road," "The Skipper," "Not Always," "No Justice," "The Lady Takes an Interest," "Interior with Figures," "At the Cothurnos Club," "The Last of Haley," "Memorial Fund," "The Heart of Lee W. Lee," "The Brothers," "He Thinks He Owns Me," "The Dry Murders," "Eileen," "The War," "Nil Nisi," "The Time Element," "Family Evening," "Requiescat," "The Frozen Face," "Last Respects," "The Industry and the Professor," "The Busybody," "This Time," "Grief," "The Kids," "The Big Gleaming Coach," "For Help and Pity," "All I've Tried to Be," "The Favor," "That First Husband."

A Cub Tells His Story (Iowa City: Windhover Press, 1974).

Good Samaritan and Other Stories, ed. Albert Erskine (New York: Random House, 1974). Fourteen stories: "The Gentry," "The Sun Room," "Sound View," "Good Samaritan," "A Man to be Trusted," "Malibu from the Sky," "Harrington and Whitehill," "Noblesse Oblige," "Heather Hill," "Tuesday's as Good as Any," "George Munson," "The Journey to Mount Clements," "The Mechanical Man," "Christmas Poem."

COLLECTIONS

Here's O'Hara (New York: Duell, Sloan & Pearce, 1946). *Hope of Heaven*, *Butterfield 8*, *Pal Joey* and twenty stories.

All the Girls He Wanted (New York: Avon, 1949). Thirty-two stories.

The Great Short Stories of John O'Hara (New York: Bantam, 1956). Seventy stories.

Selected Short Stories of John O'Hara (New York: Modern Library, 1956). Thirty-two stories, with introduction by Lionel Trilling.

49 Stories (New York: Modern Library, 1963). *Assembly* and *The Cape Cod Lighter*, with introduction by John K. Hutchens.

Appointment in Samarra; *Butterfield 8*; *Hope of Heaven* (New York: Random House, 1968).

The O'Hara Generation (New York: Random House, 1969). Twenty-two stories, with introduction by Albert Erskine.

SELECTED CONTRIBUTIONS TO BOOKS

"Is This the Army, Mr. Jones?" *Revue Sketches Vaudeville Comedy Acts . . . Soldier Shows*—Vol. VII, Comedy Sketch Book No. 1 (Washington, D.C.: The Infantry Journal, 1943).

Introduction, *The Portable F. Scott Fitzgerald* (New York: Viking, 1945).

"Remarks on the Novel," *Three Views of the Novel* (Washington, D.C.: The Library of Congress, 1957).

"From Winter Quarters, N.Y.," *Ringling Bros. and Barnum & Bailey Circus Magazine and Daily Review* (1941).

"A Visit to 'Quarters,'" *Ringling Bros. and Barnum & Bailey Circus Magazine and Program* (1948).

"'21' Is My Club," *The Iron Gate of Jack & Charlie's "21"* (New York: Kriendler Memorial Foundation, 1950).

Foreword, *Monster Rally*, by Charles Addams (New York: Simon and Schuster, 1950).

Foreword, *Appointment in Samarra* (New York: Modern Library, 1953).

"Joseph Willets Outerbridge," *Harvard Class of 1929 Twenty-fifth Anniversary Report* (Cambridge: Printed for the class, 1954).

"Long May They—," *62 Quogue Quips* (Quogue, L.I., 1962).

Acceptance of the Merit Medal for the Novel, *Proceedings of the American Academy of Arts and Letters and the National Institute of Arts and Letters Second Series Number Fifteen* (New York, 1965).

Foyles Luncheon Speech (London, 3 May 1967), *John O'Hara: A Checklist* (New York: Random House, 1972).

Foreword, *Feet First*, by Ben Finney (New York: Crown, 1971).

STORIES

"The Alumnae Bulletin," *The New Yorker*, IV (5 May 1928), 101.*

"Overheard in a Telephone Booth," *The New Yorker*, IV (19 May 1928), 77–78.

"Tennis," *The New Yorker*, IV (9 June 1928), 85.

"The Follow-up," *The New Yorker*, IV (7 July 1928), 37.

"Do You Know ——?" *The New Yorker*, IV (14 July 1928), 41.

"Spring 3100," *The New Yorker*, IV (8 September 1928), 56.

"A Safe and Sane Fourth," *The New Yorker*, IV (15 September 1928), 79–82. Delphian.†

"The Hallowe'en Party," *The New Yorker*, IV (22 September 1928), 84–85. Delphian.

"Taking Up Sport," *The New Yorker*, IV (13 October 1928), 58–63. Delphian.

"The Coal Fields," *The New Yorker*, IV (20 October 1928), 85–88. Delphian.

"The Boss' Present," *The New Yorker*, IV (1 December 1928), 56, 58, 62. Hagedorn & Brownmiller.‡

"The Yule in Retrospect," *The New Yorker*, IV (29 December 1928), 40–41. Delphian.

"Theatre," *The New Yorker*, IV (5 January 1929), 70.

"Fifty-cent Meal," *The New Yorker*, IV (12 January 1929), 63–64.

R = Story set in The Region.

M = Jimmy Malloy story.

* The paginations and occasionally the contents differ in the metropolitan and out-of-town editions of *The New Yorker*.

† One of a series of stories about the Orange County Afternoon Delphian Society.

‡ One of a series of stories about the Hagedorn & Brownmiller Paint and Varnish Co.

"The House Organ," *The New Yorker*, V (23 March 1929), 113–14. Hagedorn & Brownmiller.

"Fifteen-Minutes-for-Efficiency," *The New Yorker*, V (30 March 1929), 47–50. Hagedorn & Brownmiller.

"A New Apparatus," *The New Yorker*, V (6 April 1929), 61–64. Delphian.

"Appreciation," *The New Yorker*, V (13 April 1929), 97–98. Hagedorn & Brownmiller.

"Mr. Bonner," *The New Yorker*, V (25 May 1929), 74–75.

"Fun for the Kiddies," *The New Yorker*, V (1 June 1929), 76–78. Delphian.

"The Tournament," *The New Yorker*, V (8 June 1929), 81–83. Hagedorn & Brownmiller.

"Convention," *The New Yorker*, V (15 June 1929), 80–82. Hagedorn & Brownmiller.

"Holes in Stockings," *The New Yorker*, V (22 June 1929), 52.

"Conditions at the Pool," *The New Yorker*, V (6 July 1929), 45–47. Delphian.

"Mr. Rosenthal," *The New Yorker*, V (20 July 1929), 24–25. Hagedorn & Brownmiller.

"The Boss Talks," *The New Yorker*, V (3 August 1929), 43–45. Hagedorn & Brownmiller.

"Unconditioned Reflexes," *The New Yorker*, V (31 August 1929), 58–61.

"Staff Picture," *The New Yorker*, V (7 September 1929), 84–85. Hagedorn & Brownmiller.

"Mauve Starts Early Grid Drill," *The New Yorker*, V (21 September 1929), 101–02.

"Out of the West," *The New Yorker*, V (28 September 1929), 51–52.

"Between the Halves," *The New Yorker*, V (12 October 1929), 85–89.

"The Cannons Are a Disgrace," *The New Yorker*, V (19 October 1929), 105–06. Delphian.

"Halloween Party," *The New Yorker*, V (26 October 1929), 36. Hagedorn & Brownmiller.

"Getting Ready for 1930," *The New Yorker*, V (9 November 1929), 77–78. Hagedorn & Brownmiller.

"Americanization," *The New Yorker*, V (23 November 1929), 81–82. Delphian.

"Merrie, Merrie, Merrie," *The New Yorker*, V (7 December 1929), 98–100. Delphian.

"Memo and Another Memo," *The New Yorker*, V (14 December 1929), 89.

"Beaux Arts," *The New Yorker*, V (25 January 1930), 30.

"Suits Pressed," *The New Yorker*, V (8 February 1930), 28.

"Mr. Cleary Misses a Party," *The New Yorker*, VI (22 February 1930), 90–91. Hagedorn & Brownmiller.

"Delphian Hits Girls' Cage-Game Foes," *The New Yorker*, VI (8 March 1930), 84–86. Delphian.

"The Elevator Starter," *The New Yorker*, VI (15 March 1930), 72.

"On His Hands," *The New Yorker*, VI (22 March 1930), 54–56. *The Doctor's Son.*

"Conversation with a Russian," *The New Yorker*, VI (29 March 1930), 93.

"Little Remembrances," *The New Yorker*, VI (12 April 1930), 96–97.

"Ten Eyck or Pershing? Pershing or Ten Eyck?" *The New Yorker*, VI (19 April 1930), 81–83. Delphian. *The Doctor's Son.*

"A Convert to Equitation," *The New Yorker*, VI (3 May 1930), 97.

"Don't Let It Get You," *The New Yorker*, VI (10 May 1930), 51–52.

"The New Office," *The New Yorker*, VI (17 May 1930), 98–99. Hagedorn & Brownmiller.

"The Girl Who Had Been Presented," *The New Yorker*, VI (31 May 1930), 63–64. *The Doctor's Son.*

"Most Likely to Succeed," *The New Yorker*, VI (7 June 1930), 38–40.

"Paper Drinking Cups?" *The New Yorker*, VI (26 July 1930), 47–49. Hagedorn & Brownmiller.

"New Day," *The New Yorker*, VI (23 August 1930), 38–39. *The Doctor's Son.*

"The Man Who Had to Talk to Somebody," *The New Yorker*, VI (11 October 1930), 77–78. *The Doctor's Son.*

"Old Boy," *The New Yorker*, VI (18 October 1930), 28.

"Varsity Manager," *The New Yorker*, VI (25 October 1930), 87–88.

"Portrait of a Referee," *The New Yorker*, VI (15 November 1930), 80–82.

"John," *The New Yorker*, VI (27 December 1930), 28.

"Getting a Drink," *The New Yorker*, VI (10 January 1931), 60–61.

"One Reason for Betsy's Diffidence," *The New Yorker*, VII (28 February 1931), 65.

"Divorce," *The New Yorker*, VII (11 April 1931), 69–71.

"The Office Switchboard," *The New Yorker*, VII (25 April 1931), 71–72.

"Mary," *The New Yorker*, VII (2 May 1931), 72. *The Doctor's Son.* R.

"Revolt Among the Women," *The New Yorker*, VII (9 May 1931), 73. Idlewood.*

"Papa and Smoking," *The New Yorker*, VII (16 May 1931), 68–69.

"Ninety Cents for a Sardine," *The New Yorker*, VII (23 May 1931), 75. Idlewood.

"Help the Younger Element," *The New Yorker*, VII (6 June 1931), 75. Idlewood.

"Holiday Plans," *The New Yorker*, VII (27 June 1931), 46–48. Idlewood.

"Mort and Mary," *The New Yorker*, VII (19 September 1931), 38–40. *The Doctor's Son.*

"Nancy and Mr. Zinzindorf," *The New Yorker*, VII (26 September 1931), 65.

"Paolo and Francesca," *The New Yorker*, VII (24 October 1931), 56–57. Delphian.

"Let Us Hang On to It," *The New Yorker*, VII (7 November 1931), 56–57. Delphian.

". . . His Partner, Henry T. Collins," *The New Yorker*, VII (28 November 1931), 76–78.

"Alone," *Scribner's* Magazine, XC (December 1931), 647–48. *The Doctor's Son.*

"Coffee Pot," *The New Yorker*, VII (12 December 1931), 54, 56–57. *The Doctor's Son.*

"Ella and the Chinee," *The New Yorker*, VII (23 January 1932), 57–59. *The Doctor's Son.*

* One of a series of stories about the Idlewood Country Club.

"Good Evening, Ladies and Gentlemen . . ." *The New Yorker*, VIII (30 April 1932), 19–20.

"Mr. Cass and the Ten Thousand Dollars," *The New Yorker*, VIII (25 June 1932), 53–55, *The Doctor's Son*.

"Early Afternoon," *Scribner's* Magazine, XCII (July 1932), 25–26. *The Doctor's Son*.

"It Is Easy Enough to Blame Russia," *The New Yorker*, VIII (13 August 1932), 34–36.

"I Never Seen Anything Like It," *The New Yorker*, VIII (3 September 1932), 35–36. *The Doctor's Son*.

"Lombard's Kick," *The New Yorker*, VIII (24 September 1932), 40–43. *The Doctor's Son*.

"Frankie," *The New Yorker*, VIII (8 October 1932), 16–17. *The Doctor's Son*.

"Profiles: Of Thee I Sing, Baby," *The New Yorker*, VIII (15 October 1932), 23–25. *The Doctor's Son*.

"Screen Test," *The New Yorker*, VIII (3 December 1932), 44–48. *The Doctor's Son*.

"Mr. Sidney Gainsborough: Quality Pictures," *The New Yorker*, VIII (17 December 1932), 36–40. *The Doctor's Son*.

"You Need a Rest," *The New Yorker*, VIII (14 January 1933), 57–58.

"Mrs. Galt and Edwin," *The New Yorker*, IX (18 February 1933), 58–61. *The Doctor's Son*.

"Mr. Cowley and the Young," *The New Yorker*, IX (24 June 1933), 31–34. *The Doctor's Son*.

"Never a Dull Moment," *The New Yorker*, IX (8 July 1933), 28–30. *The Doctor's Son*.

"Hotel Kid," *Vanity Fair*, XLI (September 1933), 4b, 4e. *The Doctor's Son*.

"If I Was Brought Up a Holy Roller," *The New Yorker*, IX (16 September 1933), 54–55.

"My Friend in Washington," *The New Yorker*, IX (23 September 1933), 20.

"The Tenacity of Mr. Crenshaw," *The New Yorker*, IX (30 September 1933), 67–68.

"Dynamite Is like a Mill Pond," *The New Yorker*, IX (14 October 1933), 44–47.

"The Public Career of Mr. Seymour Harrisburg," *Brooklyn Daily Eagle* (5 November 1933), magazine section. *The Doctor's Son*.

"Mrs. McMorrow," *The New Yorker*, IX (18 November 1933), 48–55.

"Master of Ceremonies," *The New Yorker*, IX (25 November 1933), 40–43. *The Doctor's Son*.

"Straight Pool," *The New Yorker*, IX (16 December 1933), 38–42. *The Doctor's Son*.

"Pleasure," *The New Yorker*, X (10 March 1934), 70–73. *The Doctor's Son*.

"The Deke Flag," *The New Yorker*, X (24 March 1934), 81–82.

"It Must Have Been Spring," *The New Yorker*, X (21 April 1934), 101–04. *The Doctor's Son*. R, M.

"Sportsmanship," *The New Yorker*, X (12 May 1934), 95–99. *The Doctor's Son*.

"In the Morning Sun," *The New Yorker*, X (14 July 1934), 15–17. *The Doctor's Son.*

"Dr. Wyeth's Son," *The New Yorker*, X (28 July 1934), 25–26. *The Doctor's Son.* R, M.

"Salute a Thoroughbred," *The New Yorker*, X (1 September 1934), 17–18. *The Doctor's Son.*

"Teddy and Ann," *The New Yorker*, X (15 September 1934), 80–81.

"All the Girls He Wanted," *Harper's Bazaar*, #2664 (October 1934), 175–76, 179. *The Doctor's Son* and *Files on Parade.*

"Back in New Haven," *The New Yorker*, X (6 October 1934), 23–24. *The Doctor's Son.*

"Except in My Memory," *Harper's Bazaar*, #2665 (November 1934), 149, 152. *The Doctor's Son.*

"Over the River and Through the Wood," *The New Yorker*, X (15 December 1934), 23–25. *The Doctor's Son.*

"It Wouldn't Break Your Arm," *Harper's Bazaar*, #2667 (January 1935), 138, 140. *The Doctor's Son* and *Files on Parade.*

"You Know How to Live," *The New Yorker*, X (2 February 1935), 20–21.

"I Could Have Had a Yacht," *The New Yorker*, XI (6 April 1935), 19. *Files on Parade.*

"Ice Cream," *The New Yorker*, XI (20 July 1935), 39–41. *Files on Parade.*

"Olive," *The New Yorker*, XI (17 August 1935), 13–15. *Files on Parade.*

"The Gentleman in the Tan Suit," *The New Yorker*, XI (7 September 1935), 21–22. *Files on Parade.*

"Portistan on the Portis," *The New Yorker*, XI (23 November 1935), 17–18. *Files on Parade.*

"Stand-Up," *Collier's*, XCVI (30 November 1935), 17.

"The Doctor's Son," *The Doctor's Son.* R, M.

"Most Gorgeous Thing," *The New Yorker*, XII (7 March 1936), 23–24. *Files on Parade.*

"Saffercisco," *The New Yorker*, XII (11 April 1936), 14. *Files on Parade.*

"Brother," *The New Yorker*, XII (18 July 1936), 23–24. *Files on Parade.*

"Pretty Little Mrs. Harper," *Scribner's* Magazine, C (August 1936), 92–93.

"Little 'Chita," *Esquire*, VI (August 1936), 41, 168.

"Give and Take," *The New Yorker*, XII (13 February 1937), 17–18. *Files on Parade.*

"By Way of Yonkers," *The New Yorker*, XIII (27 February 1937), 28–30. *Files on Parade.*

"Shave," *The New Yorker*, XIII (20 March 1937), 22–23. *Files on Parade.*

"Lunch Tuesday," *The New Yorker*, XIII (3 April 1937), 18–20. *Files on Parade.*

"Peggy," *The New Yorker*, XIII (17 April 1937), 24. *Files on Parade.*

"My Girls," *The New Yorker*, XIII (29 May 1937), 17–18. *Files on Parade.*

"No Sooner Said," *The New Yorker*, XIII (31 July 1937), 13–14. *Files on Parade.*

"Price's Always Open," *The New Yorker*, XIII (14 August 1937), 15–17. *Files on Parade.*

"Good-bye, Herman," *The New Yorker*, XIII (4 September 1937), 17–18. *Files on Parade*. R.

"Are We Leaving Tomorrow?" *The New Yorker*, XIV (19 March 1938), 17–18. *Files on Parade*.

"The Cold House," *The New Yorker*, XIV (2 April 1938), 15–16. *Files on Parade*.

"Days," *The New Yorker*, XIV (30 April 1938), 21. *Files on Parade*.

"And You Want a Mountain," *The New Yorker*, XIV (11 June 1938), 22–23. *Files on Parade*.

"A Day like Today," *The New Yorker*, XIV (6 August 1938), 14–15. *Files on Parade*.

"Richard Wagner: Public Domain?" *The New Yorker*, XIV (3 September 1938), 14. *Files on Parade*.

"No Mistakes," *The New Yorker*, XIV (17 September 1938), 18–20. *Files on Parade*.

"Pal Joey," *The New Yorker*, XIV (22 October 1938), 23–24. *Files on Parade* and *Pal Joey*.

"Trouble in 1949," *Harper's Bazaar*, #2716 (November 1938), 110–11, 130, 132. *Files on Parade*.

"Sidesaddle," *The New Yorker*, XIV (5 November 1938), 21–22. *Files on Parade*.

"Ex-Pal," *The New Yorker*, XIV (26 November 1938), 20–21. *Files on Parade* and *Pal Joey*.

"Invite," *The New Yorker*, XIV (10 December 1938), 27–28. *Files on Parade*.

"Do You Like It Here?" *The New Yorker*, XV (18 February 1939), 17–18. *Files on Parade*.

"How I Am Now in Chi," *The New Yorker*, XV (1 April 1939), 19–21. *Files on Parade* and *Pal Joey*.

"The Ideal Man," *The New Yorker*, XV (29 April 1939), 21–22. *Files on Parade*.

"Bow Wow," *The New Yorker*, XV (13 May 1939), 21–23. *Files on Parade* and *Pal Joey*.

"Can You Carry Me?" *The New Yorker*, XV (3 June 1939), 17–18. *Pipe Night*.

"Reunion Over Lightly," *The New Yorker*, XV (29 July 1939), 25–26. *Pipe Night*.

"Too Young," *The New Yorker*, XV (9 September 1939), 15–16. *Pipe Night*.

"Bread Alone," *The New Yorker*, XV (23 September 1939), 17–18. *Pipe Night*.

"Avast and Belay," *The New Yorker*, XV (7 October 1939), 22–23. *Pal Joey*.

"Joey on Herta," *The New Yorker*, XV (25 November 1939), 19–22. *Pal Joey*.

"Joey on the Cake Line," *The New Yorker*, XV (23 December 1939), 19–20. *Pal Joey*.

"The Erloff," *The New Yorker*, XV (3 February 1940), 22–23. *Pal Joey* and *Pipe Night*.

"Even the Greeks," *The New Yorker*, XVI (2 March 1940), 18–19. *Pal Joey*.

"Joey and the Calcutta Club," *The New Yorker*, XVI (30 March 1940), 30–31. *Pal Joey* and *Pipe Night*.

"Joey and Mavis," *The New Yorker*, XVI (4 May 1940), 21–22. *Pal Joey*.

"A New Career," *The New Yorker*, XVI (13 July 1940), 17–18. *Pal Joey*.

"A Respectable Place," *The New Yorker*, XVI (19 October 1940), 26–27. *Pipe Night*.

"The King of the Desert," *The New Yorker*, XVI (30 November 1940), 16–17. *Pipe Night*.

"A Bit of a Shock," *Pal Joey*.

"Reminiss?" *Pal Joey*.

"The Magical Numbers," *The New Yorker*, XVI (18 January 1941), 18–19. *Pipe Night*.

"Nothing Missing," *The New Yorker*, XVII (14 June 1941), 21–23. *Pipe Night*.

"Adventure on the Set," *The New Yorker*, XVII (15 November 1941), 26–27. *Pipe Night*.

"Summer's Day," *The New Yorker*, XVIII (29 August 1942), 15–16. *Pipe Night*.

"Graven Image," *The New Yorker*, XIX (13 March 1943), 17–18. *Pipe Night*.

"Radio," *The New Yorker*, XIX (22 May 1943), 20–21. *Pipe Night*.

"Now We Know," *The New Yorker*, XIX (5 June 1943), 19–20. *Pipe Night*.

"The Next-to-Last Dance of the Season," *The New Yorker*, XIX (18 September 1943), 22–24. *Pipe Night*.

"Revenge," *Collier's*, CXII (25 September 1943), 21. *Pipe Night*.

"Walter T. Carriman," *The New Yorker*, XIX (16 October 1943), 23–27. *Pipe Night*.

"Memo to a Kind Stranger," *Collier's*, CXII (6 November 1943), 19. *Pipe Night*.

"The Lieutenant," *The New Yorker*, XIX (13 November 1943), 22–23. *Pipe Night*.

"Civilized," *The New Yorker*, XIX (4 December 1943), 32–33. *Pipe Night*.

"On Time," *Collier's*, CXIII (8 April 1944), 72. *Pipe Night*.

"Conversation at Lunch," *Good Housekeeping*, CXIX (July 1944), 28. *The Time Element*.

"Name in the Book," *Good Housekeeping*, CXIX (December 1944), 38, 172–73.

"Leave," *Collier's*, CXIV (2 December 1944), 13. *Pipe Night*.

"Mrs. Whitman," *The New Yorker*, XX (27 January 1945), 20–22. *Pipe Night*. R.

"The Pretty Daughters," *The New Yorker*, XXI (3 March 1945), 24–26. *Hellbox*.

"War Aims," *The New Yorker*, XXI (17 March 1945), 27–28. *Hellbox*.

"Wise Guy," *The New Yorker*, XXI (26 May 1945), 20–21. *Hellbox*.

"Horizon," *The New Yorker*, XXI (23 June 1945), 18. *Hellbox*.

"Life Among These Unforgettable Characters," *The New Yorker*, XXI (25 August 1945), 19–20. *Hellbox*.

"Fire!" *Pipe Night*.

"Free," *Pipe Night*.

"The Handler," *Pipe Night*.

"Patriotism," *Pipe Night*.

"Platform," *Pipe Night*.

"A Purchase of Some Golf Clubs," *Pipe Night*.

"Where's the Game," *Pipe Night*.

"Conversation in the Atomic Age," *The New Yorker*, XXI (12 January 1946), 22–23. *Hellbox*. M.

"Common Sense Should Tell You," *The New Yorker*, XXI (9 February 1946), 20–22. *Hellbox*.

"Doctor and Mrs. Parsons," *The New Yorker*, XXII (23 February 1946), 29–31. *Hellbox*.

"Everything Satisfactory," *The New Yorker*, XXII (23 March 1946), 25–26. *Hellbox*.

"Like Old Times," *The New Yorker*, XXII (13 April 1946), 29–30. *Hellbox*.

"Clara," *The New Yorker*, XXII (27 April 1946), 21–23. *Hellbox*.

"The Decision," *The New Yorker*, XXII (18 May 1946), 23–25. *Hellbox*.

"Secret Meeting," *The New Yorker*, XXII (6 July 1946), 18–19. *Hellbox*.

"The Three Musketeers," *The New Yorker*, XXII (28 September 1946), 25–26. *Hellbox*. R.

"Ellie," *The New Yorker*, XXII (19 October 1946), 29–30. *Hellbox*.

"Pilgrimage," *The New Yorker*, XXII (9 November 1946), 29–32. *The Time Element*.

"One for the Road," *The New Yorker*, XXII (30 November 1946), 37–38.

"Not Always," *The New Yorker*, XXII (11 January 1947), 23–24. *The Time Element*.

"The Moccasins," *The New Yorker*, XXII (25 January 1947), 20–22. *Hellbox*.

"Pardner," *The New Yorker*, XXIII (22 February 1947), 24–26. *Hellbox*.

"Someone to Trust," *The New Yorker*, XXIII (22 March 1947), 31–33. *Hellbox*.

"Drawing Room B.," *The New Yorker*, XXIII (19 April 1947), 25–28. *Hellbox*.

"Miss W.," *The New Yorker*, XXIII (3 May 1947), 29–30. *Hellbox*.

"Other Women's Households," *The New Yorker*, XXIII (24 May 1947), 32–34. *Hellbox*.

"The Lady Takes an Interest," *The New Yorker*, XXIII (28 June 1947), 22–23. *The Time Element*. R.

"Interior with Figures," *The New Yorker*, XXIII (19 July 1947), 22–24. *The Time Element*.

"The Last of Haley," *The New Yorker*, XXIII (30 August 1947), 21–23. *The Time Element*.

"The Heart of Lee W. Lee," *The New Yorker*, XXIII (13 September 1947), 29–31. *The Time Element*.

"The Dry Murders," *The New Yorker*, XXIII (18 October 1947), 33–34. *The Time Element*.

"Eileen," *The New Yorker*, XXIII (20 December 1947), 25–26. *The Time Element*.

"The Chink in the Armor," *Hellbox*.

"A Phase of Life," *Hellbox*.

"Somebody Can Help Somebody," *Hellbox*.

"Time to Go," *Hellbox*.

"Transaction," *Hellbox*.

"Nil Nisi," *The New Yorker*, XXIII (10 January 1948), 23–25. *The Time Element*.

"Requiescat," *The New Yorker*, XXIV (3 April 1948), 27–30. *The Time Element.*

"The Frozen Face," *The New Yorker*, XXV (23 April 1949), 22–24. *The Time Element.*

"The Industry and the Professor," *The New Yorker*, XXV (16 July 1949), 16–20. *The Time Element.*

"Grief," *The New Yorker*, XXV (22 October 1949), 28–29. *The Time Element.*

"The Kids," *The New Yorker*, XXV (26 November 1949), 32–34. *The Time Element.*

"The Favor," *The Princeton Tiger*, LXIII (March–April 1952), 8–10. *The Time Element.*

"A Family Party," *Collier's*, CXXXVII (2 March 1956), 34–36, 38, 40–41, 44, 46. R.

"That First Husband," *The Saturday Evening Post*, CCXXXII (21 November 1959), 23–24, 52. *The Time Element.*

"Imagine Kissing Pete," *The New Yorker*, XXXVI (17 September 1960), 43–134. *Sermons and Soda-Water.* R, M.

"It's Mental Work," *The New Yorker*, XXXVI (26 November 1960), 50–56. *Assembly.*

"Exactly Eight Thousand Dollars Exactly," *The New Yorker*, XXXVI (31 December 1960), 24–26. *Assembly.*

"The Girl on the Baggage Truck," *Sermons and Soda-Water.* M.

"We're Friends Again," *Sermons and Soda-Water.* M.

"The Cellar Domain," *The New Yorker*, XXXVI (11 February 1961), 28–34. *Assembly.* R.

"Sterling Silver," *The New Yorker*, XXXVII (11 March 1961), 38–42. *Assembly.*

"The Man with the Broken Arm," *The New Yorker*, XXXVII (22 April 1961), 42–47. *Assembly.*

"The Girl from California," *The New Yorker*, XXXVII (27 May 1961), 34–42. *Assembly.*

"The Weakness," *The New Yorker*, XXXVII (8 July 1961), 23–29. *Assembly.*

"Mary and Norma," *The New Yorker*, XXXVII (5 August 1961), 22–26. *Assembly.*

"The Trip," *The New Yorker*, XXXVII (23 September 1961), 39–42. *Assembly.*

"Call Me, Call Me," *The New Yorker*, XXXVII (7 October 1961), 56–58. *Assembly.*

"The Father," *The New Yorker*, XXXVII (28 October 1961), 48–49. *The Cape Cod Lighter.*

"Two Turtledoves," *The New Yorker*, XXXVII (23 December 1961), 22–23. *The Cape Cod Lighter.*

"A Case History," *Assembly.* R.

"A Cold Calculating Thing," *Assembly.*

"The Compliment," *Assembly.*

"First Day in Town," *Assembly.*

"The Free," *Assembly.*

"The High Point," *Assembly.*

"In a Grove," *Assembly.*

"In the Silence," *Assembly*. R, M.

"The Lighter When Needed," *Assembly*.

"Mrs. Stratton of Oak Knoll," *Assembly*.

"The Old Folks," *Assembly*.

"The Pioneer Hep-Cat," *Assembly*. R.

"The Properties of Love," *Assembly*.

"Reassurance," *Assembly*.

"The Sharks," *Assembly*.

"You Can Always Tell Newark," *Assembly*.

"Sunday Morning," *The New Yorker*, XXXVII (13 January 1962), 24–26. *The Cape Cod Lighter*.

"The Women of Madison Avenue," *The New Yorker*, XXXVII (10 February 1962), 32–33. *The Cape Cod Lighter*.

"A Short Walk from the Station," *The New Yorker*, XXXVIII (24 February 1962), 32–34. *The Cape Cod Lighter*.

"Money," *The New Yorker*, XXXVIII (24 March 1962), 38–46. *The Cape Cod Lighter*. R.

"The Bucket of Blood," *The New Yorker*, XXXVIII (25 August 1962), 31–62. *The Cape Cod Lighter*. R.

"Winter Dance," *The New Yorker*, XXXVIII (22 September 1962), 34–36. *The Cape Cod Lighter*. R.

"How Can I Tell You?" *The New Yorker*, XXXVIII (1 December 1962), 57–59. *The Hat on the Bed*.

"The Public Dorothy," *The New Yorker*, XXXVIII (15 December 1962), 36–37. *The Hat on the Bed*.

"Appearances," *The Cape Cod Lighter*.

"The Butterfly," *The Cape Cod Lighter*.

"Claude Emerson, Reporter," *The Cape Cod Lighter*. R.

"Jurge Dulrumple," *The Cape Cod Lighter*. R.

"The Engineer," *The Cape Cod Lighter*. R.

"The First Day," *The Cape Cod Lighter*.

"Justice," *The Cape Cod Lighter*.

"The Lesson," *The Cape Cod Lighter*.

"The Nothing Machine," *The Cape Cod Lighter*.

"Pat Collins," *The Cape Cod Lighter*. R.

"The Professors," *The Cape Cod Lighter*.

"The Sun-Dodgers," *The Cape Cod Lighter*.

"Things You Really Want," *The Cape Cod Lighter*.

"You Don't Remember Me," *The Cape Cod Lighter*.

"Your Fah Neefah Neeface," *The Cape Cod Lighter*.

"Saturday Lunch," *The New Yorker*, XXXVIII (12 January 1963), 27–30. *The Hat on the Bed*.

"Agatha," *The New Yorker*, XXXIX (23 February 1963), 33–39. *The Hat on the Bed*.

"The Glendale People," *The Saturday Evening Post*, CCXXXVI (2 March 1963), 34–41. *The Hat on the Bed.*

"John Barton Rosedale, Actors' Actor," *The New Yorker*, XXXIX (16 March 1963), 46–53. *The Hat on the Bed.*

"Aunt Anna," *The Saturday Evening Post*, CCXXXVI (23 March 1963), 50–56. *The Hat on the Bed.* R.

"Yucca Knolls," *Show* Magazine, III (April 1963), 85–100. *The Hat on the Bed.*

"The Ride from Mauch Chunk," *The Saturday Evening Post*, CCXXXVI (13 April 1963), 38–41. *The Hat on the Bed.*

"The Manager," *The New Yorker*, XXXIX (4 May 1963), 42–48. *The Hat on the Bed.*

"Exterior: With Figure," *The Saturday Evening Post*, CCXXXVI (1 June 1963), 54–61. *The Hat on the Bed.* R, M.

"The Flatted Saxophone," *The New Yorker*, XXXIX (1 June 1963), 28–29. *The Hat on the Bed.*

"The Man on the Tractor," *The New Yorker*, XXXIX (22 June 1963), 25–30. *The Hat on the Bed.* R.

"The Locomobile," *The New Yorker*, XXXIX (20 July 1963), 22–27. *The Hat on the Bed.* R.

"Our Friend the Sea," *The Saturday Evening Post*, CCXXXVI (24–31 August 1963), 60–65. *The Hat on the Bed.*

"The Lawbreaker," *The Saturday Evening Post*, CCXXXVI (16 November 1963), 52–54, 58, 62, 64, 68, 69, 70, 72–77. *The Horse Knows the Way.*

"Zero," *The New Yorker*, XXXIX (28 December 1963), 28–32. *The Horse Knows the Way.* R.

"Eminent Domain," *The Hat on the Bed.* R.

"The Friends of Miss Julia," *The Hat on the Bed.*

"The Golden," *The Hat on the Bed.*

"I Know That, Roy," *The Hat on the Bed.*

"The Mayor," *The Hat on the Bed.* R.

"Ninety Minutes Away," *The Hat on the Bed.* R.

"Teddy and the Special Friends," *The Hat on the Bed.*

"The Twinkle in His Eye," *The Hat on the Bed.*

"The Windowpane Check," *The Hat on the Bed.*

"The Whole Cherry Pie," *The Saturday Evening Post*, CCXXXVII (8 February 1964), 32–33. *The Horse Knows the Way.*

"At the Window," *The New Yorker*, XL (22 February 1964), 28–32. *The Horse Knows the Way.* R.

"The Hardware Man," *The Saturday Evening Post*, CCXXXVII (29 February 1964), 46–53. *The Horse Knows the Way.*

"The Victim," *The Saturday Evening Post*, CCXXXVII (14 March 1964), 46–51. *The Horse Knows the Way.* R.

"Arnold Stone," *The Saturday Evening Post*, CCXXXVII (28 March 1964), 52–59. *The Horse Knows the Way.* R.

"The Answer Depends," *The Saturday Evening Post*, CCXXXVII (18 April 1964), 46–51. *The Horse Knows the Way.*

"Can I Stay Here?" *The Saturday Evening Post*, CCXXXVII (16 May 1964), 44–45, 48. *The Horse Knows the Way.*

"I Spend My Days in Longing," *The New Yorker*, XL (23 May 1964), 40–46. *The Horse Knows the Way.*

"His Excellency," *The Saturday Evening Post*, CCXXXVII (11 July 1964), 56–60. *The Horse Knows the Way.*

"The House on the Corner," *The Saturday Evening Post*, CCXXXVII (22–29 August 1964), 64–66. *The Horse Knows the Way.* R.

"Aunt Fran," *The Saturday Evening Post*, CCXXXVII (15 September 1964), 56–57. *The Horse Knows the Way.* R.

"The Tackle," *Sports Illustrated*, XXI (21 September 1964), 108–13. *Waiting for Winter.*

"School," *The Saturday Evening Post*, CCXXXVII (26 September 1964), 56–61. *The Horse Knows the Way.*

"All Tied Up," *The New Yorker*, XL (3 October 1964), 48–55. *The Horse Knows the Way.* R.

"The Bonfire," *The Saturday Evening Post*, CCXXXVII (10 October 1964), 46–53. *The Horse Knows the Way.*

"The Madeline Wherry Case," *The Horse Knows the Way.*

"Mrs. Allanson," *The Horse Knows the Way.*

"The Pig," *The Horse Knows the Way.*

"The Staring Game," *The Horse Knows the Way.*

"What's the Good of Knowing?" *The Horse Knows the Way.* R.

"The Gambler," *The New Yorker*, XLI (1 May 1965), 40–42. *Waiting for Winter.* R.

"The Neighborhood," *The New Yorker*, XLI (15 May 1965), 49–53. *Waiting for Winter.* R.

"The Assistant," *The New Yorker*, XLI (3 July 1965), 22–28. *Waiting for Winter.*

"The Clear Track," *The Saturday Evening Post*, CCXXXVII (24 October 1964), 58–62. *The Horse Knows the Way.*

"Christmas Poem," *The New Yorker*, XL (19 December 1964), 34–39. *Good Samaritan.* R.

"The Brain," *The Horse Knows the Way.*

"Clayton Bunter," *The Horse Knows the Way.* R.

"The Gun," *The Horse Knows the Way.*

"I Can't Thank You Enough," *The Horse Knows the Way.* R.

"In the Mist," *The Horse Knows the Way.*

"The Jet Set," *The Horse Knows the Way.*

"A Good Location," *The New Yorker*, XLI (4 September 1965), 29–31. *Waiting for Winter.* R.

"Leonard," *The New Yorker*, XLII (26 February 1966), 33–37. *Waiting for Winter.*

"Afternoon Waltz," *The Saturday Evening Post*, CCXXXIX (23 April 1966), 56–74. *Waiting for Winter.* R.

"Fatimas and Kisses," *The New Yorker*, XLII (21 May 1966), 44–53. *Waiting for Winter.* R, M.

"Yostie," *The Saturday Evening Post*, CCXXXIX (4 June 1966), 46–62. *Waiting for Winter*. R.

"The Jama," *The Saturday Evening Post*, CCXXXIX (22 October 1966). *Waiting for Winter*.

"The Private People," *The Saturday Evening Post*, CCXXXIX (17 December 1966), 56–72. *And Other Stories*.

"Andrea," *Waiting for Winter*. R.

"Flight," *Waiting for Winter*.

"The General," *Waiting for Winter*. R.

"James Francis and the Star," *Waiting for Winter*.

"Late, Late Show," *Waiting for Winter*.

"Natica Jackson," *Waiting for Winter*.

"The Pomeranian," *Waiting for Winter*.

"The Portly Gentleman," *Waiting for Winter*.

"The Skeletons," *Waiting for Winter*. R.

"The Way to Majorca," *Waiting for Winter*.

"The Weakling," *Waiting for Winter*.

"The Gunboat and Madge," *The Saturday Evening Post*, CCXL (25 February 1967), 64–77. *And Other Stories*. R.

"How Old, How Young," *The New Yorker*, XLIII (1 July 1967), 28–32. *And Other Stories*. R.

"Barred," *The Saturday Evening Post*, CCXL (7 October 1967), 60–62. *And Other Stories*. R.

"The Gangster," *The Saturday Evening Post*, CCXL (18 November 1967), 56–66. *And Other Stories*. R.

"Good Samaritan," *The Saturday Evening Post*, CCXLI (30 November 1968), 62–64, 66, 68–70. *Good Samaritan*.

"The Broken Giraffe," *And Other Stories*.

"The Farmer," *And Other Stories*, R.

"A Few Trips and Some Poetry," *And Other Stories*. R, M.

"A Man on a Porch," *And Other Stories*.

"Papa Gibraltar," *And Other Stories*.

"The Strong Man," *And Other Stories*. R.

"We'll Have Fun," *And Other Stories*. R.

"The Sun Room," *The Saturday Evening Post*, CCXLII (8 February 1969), 40–42, 44, 46, 48. *Good Samaritan*.

"At the Cothurnos Club," *Esquire*, LXXVIII (July 1972), 114–15. *The Time Element*. (This story and "All I've Tried to Be" appear under *Esquire*'s general title, "The Little Mysteries of Pomp and Circumstance.")

"All I've Tried to Be," *Esquire*, LXXVIII (July 1972), 115–16, 162–64. *The Time Element*. R.

"Encounter: 1943," *The Time Element*.

"The Skipper," *The Time Element*.

"No Justice," *The Time Element*.

"Memorial Fund," *The Time Element.*

"The Brothers," *The Time Element.*

"He Thinks He Owns Me," *The Time Element.*

"The War," *The Time Element.*

"The Time Element," *The Time Element.*

"Family Evening," *The Time Element.*

"Last Respects," *The Time Element.*

"The Busybody," *The Time Element.*

"This Time," *The Time Element.*

"The Big Gleaming Coach," *The Time Element.*

"For Help and Pity," *The Time Element.*

"The Journey to Mount Clemens," *The Saturday Evening Post*, CCXLVI (August/September 1974), 62–64, 92–94. *Good Samaritan.* R, M.

"The Gentry," *Good Samaritan.* R.

"Sound View," *Good Samaritan.*

"A Man to Be Trusted," *Good Samaritan.* R, M.

"Malibu from the Sky," *Good Samaritan.*

"Harrington and Whitehill," *Good Samaritan.*

"Noblesse Oblige," *Good Samaritan.*

"Heather Hill," *Good Samaritan.*

"Tuesday's as Good as Any," *Good Samaritan.* R.

"George Munson," *Good Samaritan.*

"The Mechanical Man," *Good Samaritan.* R, M.

ARTICLES & JOURNALISM*

"A Cub Tells His Story," Pottsville *Journal* (2 May 1925), 17.[†]

Review of *Polly*, *Time*, XIII (21 January 1929), 36.[‡]

"Saxophonic Fever," New York *Herald Tribune* (17 February 1929), II, 7.

"J. R. Clark Admits Guilt; Faces Life," New York *Daily Mirror* (24 July 1929), 2, 6.

"Girl Invades Yale Club Bar, Only for Men," by Jean Atherton. New York *Daily Mirror* (29 July 1929), 4. (Ghosted by O'Hara.)

"The Pennsylvania Irish," New York *Herald Tribune* (9 March 1930), II, 7.

"Dancing School," New York *Herald Tribune* (3 August 1930), II, 7.

"The Decline of Jazz," New York *Herald Tribune* (14 September 1930), II, 7.

* O'Hara's contributions to *Today—in New York, Carnival* and *The Hampton Chronicle* have not been located.

† The only example of O'Hara's *Journal* work that has been recovered.

‡ The only *Time* contribution by O'Hara that has been identified.

"Giants of a Vanished Race," New York *Herald Tribune* (28 September 1930), II, 7.

"Jazz Artists," New York *Herald Tribune* (14 December 1930), II, 9.

"A Jazz Leader," New York *Herald Tribune* (25 January 1931), II, 9.

"Jazz from the West," New York *Herald Tribune* (1 March 1931), II, 9.

"Sing Us the Old Songs," New York *Herald Tribune* (9 August 1931), II, 9.

"When Dinner Coats Were Tucks and Young Men Toddled," New York *Herald Tribune* (30 August 1931), II, 9.

"Barrymore's *Real* Ambition," *Screenland*, XXIII (October 1931), 58–59, 116. (Signed John O'Hara, but possibly a studio press release.)

"Home in the Mud," *The New Yorker*, VII (5 December 1931), 16. (Unsigned "Talk of the Town" piece, credited by the magazine to O'Hara and McConnell.)

"$35-a-Week Actress Wonders Why Stagehand Still Gets $90," New York *Herald Tribune* (26 March 1933), VII, 2.

"Football: Up Boston Way," *The New Yorker*, IX (18 November 1933), 30–32.

"Football: Four Downs and a Fumble," *The New Yorker*, IX (25 November 1933), 61–62.

"Football: Requests and Demands," *The New Yorker*, IX (2 December 1933), 52, 54.

"Football: Princeton Visits the Bowl," *The New Yorker*, IX (9 December 1933), 85–87.

"Football: The Coming Boom in Stadiums," *The New Yorker*, X (29 September 1934), 30, 32.

"Good Reading," New York *Herald Tribune Books* (22 November 1934), 17.

"Why They'll Never Forget the Trial of the Century," *Hearst's International-Cosmopolitan* (May 1935), 180. (Comment on Lindbergh case.)

"Movie Fans like Me Should Know All!" New York *Journal* (9 May 1936), Saturday Home Magazine section, 2. King Features Syndicate.

"Cesar Romero and the Three Dollar Bills," New York *Journal* and Chicago *American* (13 June 1936), Saturday Home Magazine section. King Features Syndicate.

"The English . . . They Are a Funny Race," *For Men*, II (September 1938), 47–50.

"Are the English Human?" *For Men*, II (December 1938), 44–47.

"In Memory of Scott Fitzgerald: II. Certain Aspects," *The New Republic*, CIV (3 March 1941), 311.

"Some Fond Recollections of Larry Hart," New York *Times* (27 February 1944), II, 1.

"Nothing from Joe?" *Liberty*, XXI (9 December 1944), 20, 21.

"The Stutz Bearcat," *Holiday*, IV (August 1948), 84, 86–89.

"The Novels Novelists Read, or 'Taking in the Washing,'" New York *Times Book Review* (21 August 1949), 3.

Coverage of the Sander Trial for INS, 20 February–10 March 1950: 14 articles syndicated in subscribing papers, with complete series in Boston *Daily Record*.

"The New Expense-Account Society," *Flair*, I (May 1950), 22–23, 110–11.

"Famous Author Writes of His Early Days on Journal; Is Now Big Literary Figure," Pottsville *Journal* (2 October 1950), 5.

"Quogue," *Hampton Pictorial* (27 July 1951), 8.

" 'Joey' Comes of Age," New York *Herald Tribune* (23 November 1952), IV, 1, 3.

"There Is Nothing like a Norfolk," *Holiday*, XIV (September 1953), 14, 17.

"We Have with Us Today: Mr. John O'Hara," *The Fire Islander* (28 May 1954), 5, 7.

"My Ten Favorite Plays," *Theatre Arts*, XLI (November 1957), 9.

"Novelist Likes the Film Translation," New York *Herald Tribune* (18 May 1958), IV, 3.

"Don't Say It Never Happened," New York *Herald Tribune Books* (8 April 1962), 3.

"Bleeck's: John O'Hara Recalls a Cave of Journalism Greats," New York *Herald Tribune* (24 April 1963), 28.

"The Wayward Reader," *Holiday*, XXXVII (December 1964), 31–34.

"Memoirs of a Sentimental Duffer," *Holiday*, XXXVII (May 1965), 66–67, 118, 120, 122.

"On Cars and Snobbism," *Holiday*, XL (August 1966), 52–53.

"Celibacy, Sacred and Profane," *Holiday*, XLII (August 1967), 28–29.

"Hello Hollywood Good-bye," *Holiday*, XLIII (May 1968), 54–55, 125–26, 128–29.

BOOK REVIEWS

Frederick Ramsey, Jr. and Charles Edward Smith, *Jazzmen: The New Republic*, CI (27 December 1939), 287.

The Portable Dorothy Parker: New York *Times Book Review* (28 May 1944), 5, 29.

F. Scott Fitzgerald, *The Crack-Up*: New York *Times Book Review* (8 July 1945), 3.

Arthur Kober, *That Man Is Here Again*: New York *Times Book Review* (8 December 1946), 7, 59.

Eddie Condon, *We Called It Music:* New York *Times Book Review* (2 November 1947), 6.

Ernest Hemingway, *Across the River and Into the Trees*: New York *Times Book Review* (10 September 1950), 1.

VERSE

"Stars in My Eyes," *The New Yorker*, XV (6 May 1939), 61.

"November March," Red Smith's column, New York *Herald Tribune* (6 November 1962), 25.

COLUMNS

"After Four O'Clock," Pottsville *Journal* (April 1925–1926?). No surviving example.

"Entertainment Week," *Newsweek* (15 July 1940–16 February 1942).

"Sweet and Sour," Trenton *Sunday Times-Advertiser* (27 December 1953–27 June 1954). Collected in *Sweet and Sour.*

"Appointment with O'Hara," *Collier's* (5 February 1954–28 September 1956).

"My Turn," *Newsday* (3 October 1964–2 October 1965). Collected in *My Turn.*

"The Whistle Stop," *Holiday* (September 1966–May 1967).

CONTRIBUTIONS TO "THE CONNING TOWER"

O'Hara quoted, *World* (17 March 1927), 13.

"From the Tower's Attention-Caller," *World* (16 June 1927), 13.

"The Literary Quest," *World* (15 July 1927), 13.

"The Weather and the Public," *World* (15 September 1927), 15.

"The City Hall Plaza Talkers," *World* (1 December 1927), 13.

"The Veteran Reporter Goes Just Slightly Insane," *World* (2 December 1927), 13.

"A Speech by George F. Gabbitry at a Christmas Party, Delivered at, Let Us Say, Scott High, Toledo, Before the Entire School," *World* (13 December 1927), 11.

"The Private Branch Exchange Talker," *World* (16 December 1927), 15.

"Famed Folk Plan Big Fest," *World* (11 January 1928), 19.

"George F. Gabbitry Stops a Little Early for the Wife at Her Literary Club Meeting," *World* (12 January 1928), 15.

"The Man Who Knew Sinclair Lewis," *World* (27 January 1928), 13.

"George F. Gabbitry Settles Once and For All the Democratic Situation—If Any," *World* (13 March 1928), 13.

"Why Dr. Bdrplf. . . ." *World* (16 April 1928), 13.

"Famed Convivial, Hurt, Flags Tower," *World* (19 April 1928), 13.

"Old Fashioned," *World* (28 May 1928), 13.

"Laboratory Stuff," *World* (29 May 1928), 11.

"Christmas Is for the Kiddies," *World* (24 December 1928), 11.

"A Boy Who Made Good," *World* (13 September 1928), 15.

"A Style Sheet Goes to a Copyreader's Head," *World* (13 February 1929), 13.

"Aged Muser Sighs for Old Days," *World* (21 June 1929), 15.

"Conning Tower, I Love You," *World* (26 June 1929), 15.

"The Little Boy Blues," *Herald Tribune* (10 July 1931), 20.

"The Ruling Passion for Accuracy," *Herald Tribune* (20 January 1932), 15.

"Unverbosity," *Herald Tribune* (14 October 1935), 13.

JOHN O'HARA'S WORKS

"Buffalo Wins Belasco Cup" (13 May), 2. Play review.

"Short Turns on Dial" (13 May), 4. Radio.

" 'Wooden Idol' in Cup Trials" (14 May), 2. Play review.

"Ad Club's Ad on Air" (14 May), 3. Radio.

"In Praise of Ballew" (15 May), 4. Radio.

" 'New Freedom' Tourney Hit" (16 May), 3. Play review.

"Chic Sale Takes Air" (16 May), 3. Radio.

"Derby on Air Today" (17 May), 3. Radio.

"New Freedom Wins Prize" (18 May), 3. Play review.

"Radio Tube News" (19 May), 3. Radio.

"Radio and Press Pals" (20 May), 4. Radio.

"Sure—It's a Horse—On the O'Haras!" (21 May), 1, 3. Article.

"What! No Politics?" (21 May), 3. Radio.

"Yes, with Noodles" (23 May), 3. Radio.

"Not Enough Salt on Bar Pretzels" (26 May), 1, 2. Article.

"Race Rehearsal" (26 May), 2. Radio.

"Radios and Gas" (28 May), 6. Radio.

"Lucky Strike Music" (29 May), 6. Radio.

"Radio Gossip in Air" (30 May), 4. Radio.

"Radio Door to Stage" (31 May), 3. Radio.

"Radio Aids Lingo" (1 June), 3. Radio.

"Tennis Racket Skips Pun" (2 June), 1, 3. Article.

"Radio Recollections" (2 June), 2. Radio.

"Mauve Decade Yarn" (3 June), 2. Movie review.

"Derby on Air Early" (4 June), 3. Radio.

"Fans Hear Aviatrix" (5 June), 2. Radio.

"Corinne Griffith Achieves Accurate Characterization in 'Back Pay' " (5 June), 3. Movie review.

"Hill-Billy Songs" (6 June), 3. Radio.

"O'Hara Gets the Air" (7 June), 2. Radio.

"William Powell Wades Through Pain and Prison at Paramount" (7 June), 3. Movie review.

"Novarro Film at Capitol" (8 June), 2. Movie review.

"O'Hara's Ordeal" (9 June), 2. Radio.

"Edmund Lowe's War in Trenches and Night Clubs Shown in Roxy Film" (9 June), 3. Movie review.

"New Star Dawns: Bernice Claire Steals the Lead in 'Numbered Men' " (10 June), 2. Movie review.

"Cuban Band Novel" (11 June), 2. Radio.

---

* Unless otherwise stipulated, all pieces were by-lined "John O'Hara." O'Hara used the by-line "Franey Delaney" for radio reviews, and he was probably also "Dial Spinner." Although he said that he worked for the *Morning Telegraph* twice, only the 13 May–7 July 1930 period has been identified.

"Lois Moran Gets Her Englishman in 'Not Damaged' at the Globe" (11 June), 3. Movie review.

"Russian Cameramen Repeat Triumphs in 'Cain and Artem' at Cameo" (12 June), 3. Movie review.

"Bout on Air Tonight" (12 June), 4. Radio.

"Press Agents Slip" (13 June), 2. Radio.

"Milestone's Genius Makes Spectators See 'All Quiet' via German Eyes" (13 June), 3.

"Oar Race June 20" (14 June), 2. Radio.

"Edmund Lowe Wisecracks, Dolores Del Rio 'Figures' in 'The Bad One'" (14 June), 3. Movie review.

"Capitol Picture Sophisticated" (15 June), 2. Movie review.

"M'Namee Version" (16 June), 2. Radio.

"Silent Film Die Hards Exhorted to Lend Their Talents to Talkies" (16 June), 3. Article.

"Pepper Passes" (17 June), 2. Radio.

"Clara Bow Fan Sea-Sick" (17 June), 3. Article.

Dial Spinner, "Radio Wags Liberal" (18 June), 2. Probably by O'Hara. Radio.

"Secrets Barred in 'All Quiet'" (19 June), 2. Article.

Franey Delaney, "Air Pocket Spotted" (19 June), 2.

"Films' Diaper Days" (20 June), 2. Article.

Franey Delaney, "Mike to Pace Crews" (20 June), 3.

"Terrifying Whales, Comic Penguins Caught by Camera in Byrd Record" (21 June), 2. Movie review.

Franey Delaney, "Pillow Fight on Air" (21 June), 3.

"Critics Disagree" (22 June), 5. Article.

Franey Delaney, "How to Get on Stage" (23 June), 2.

"Marie Dressler 'Funny as Ever' Amidst Woes of Wall Street Crash" (23 June), 3. Movie review.

Franey Delaney, "Song Helps Organ" (24 June), 2.

"'She's My Weakness' Proves Mildly Amusing Fare at Globe Theater" (24 June), 3. Movie review.

Franey Delaney, "Comic Strip Stumped" (25 June), 2.

"'Women Everywhere' Has Exciting Beginning but Lets Interest Die Out" (25 June), 3. Movie review.

"'The Big House' Brings Thrilling Prison Riot to Astor Screen" (26 June), 2. Movie review.

Franey Delaney, "Big Business Boom" (26 June), 3.

Franey Delaney, "Jones Arrival on Air" (27 June), 3.

Franey Delaney, "Mike in Golf Gallery" (28 June), 2.

"'Swing High' at George M. Cohan Theatre a Film for Whole Family" (28 June), 3. Movie review.

"Dandy Outdoor Film" (29 June), 5. Movie review.

"'Czar of Broadway' Finds Death's Disgrace in Pack of Cards at Roxy" (30 June), 2. Movie review.

Franey Delaney, "Radio on Vacation" (30 June), 2.

" 'The Big Fight' Comparatively Good; Has Competent Cast, Happy End" (1 July), 2. Movie review.

Franey Delaney, "For A. M. Thinkers" (2 July 1930), 2.

" 'Juno and the Paycock,' Fine Characterization, Comes to the Cameo" (2 July), 3. Movie review.

Franey Delaney, "Belle Baker on Air" (3 July), 2.

Franey Delaney, "Puff for Mr. Lopez" (4 July), 2.

" 'Holiday' Well Done Version of Barry Play, Comes to Rivoli" (4 July), 3. Movie review.

" 'On the Level' with McLaglen Found as Entertaining Picture at Roxy" (5 July), 2. Movie review.

Franey Delaney, "Radio Odds and Ends" (5 July), 3.

" 'The Unholy Three' " (6 July), 3. Movie review.

Franey Delaney, "Royal Broadcast" (7 July), 2.

APPEARANCES IN PITTSBURGH *BULLETIN-INDEX**

"Joe: Straight Man" (18 May 1933), 4, 12.

Items on Kenneth O'Brien, *Anthony Adverse* and Yale-In-China (1 June 1933), 7.

Item on Geoffrey Hellman (1 June 1933), 4.

Reply to letter about "sports formals" (8 June 1933), 35.

Reply to letter about jodhpurs and reply to telephone call (15 June 1933), 15.

Article on Rhodes Scholars (22 June 1933), 12–13.

Reply to letter about Rhodes article (29 June 1933), 15.

"Plush & Velvet" (6 July 1933), 12.

Replies to letter about *Anthony Adverse* and letter about staff (20 July 1933), 15.

Replies to letter about San Francisco and request for Manhattan addresses (27 July 1933), 15.

"Polo" (27 July 1933), 6–7.

"Torch Singer" (3 August 1933), 12.

Reply to letter about underground travel in New York City (17 August 1933), 15.

* John O'Hara's work was not by-lined, but former staff members have attributed the following to him.

PUBLISHED LETTERS*

Letter to the editor, *Time*, IX (9 May 1927), 6.

Letter to the editor, *Time*, XI (23 January 1928), 1.

* See contributions to "The Conning Tower."

Richard Watts, Jr., "A Defense of the Film Star Who Has to Live His Parts," New York *Herald Tribune* (13 July 1930), VIII, 3.

Letter to the editor, *Vanity Fair*, XXXVI (August 1931), 17.

Stanley Woodward's column, New York *Herald Tribune* (16 January 1938), III, 3.

Letter to the editor, New York *Herald Tribune* (3 March 1938), 16.

Letter to the editor, *The New Republic*, C (25 October 1939), 343.

Letter to the editor, *The New Republic*, CII (15 January 1940), 88.

Letter to the editor, *The New Republic*, CII (12 February 1940), 215.

Letter to the editor, *The New Republic*, CII (29 April 1940), 579.

Letter to Richard Rodgers—Mary Morris and Robert Rice, "How a Musical Is Made," *PM* (22 December 1940), 51, 54; repeated on sleeve of *Pal Joey* recording (Columbia ML 4364)

Letter to Random House on dust jacket of Budd Schulberg's *What Makes Sammy Run?* (New York: Random House, 1941).

Stanley Woodward's column, New York *Herald Tribune* (8 January 1944), 13.

Letter to the editor, New York *Herald Tribune* (7 March 1945), 22.

Charles Poore, "Books of the Times," New York *Times* (1 January 1949), 11; includes excerpt from O'Hara letter.

Dale Kramer, *Heywood Broun* (New York: Current Books, 1949), p. 203. Possible letter.

Red Smith's column, New York *Herald Tribune* (12 June 1952), 31.

Letter to the editor, New York *Herald Tribune* (3 May 1957), 16.

Letter to the editor, *The Princeton Packet* (20 June 1957), 12.

Red Smith's column, New York *Herald Tribune* (31 August 1958), III, 1.

Letter to the editor, *The Princeton Packet* (4 December 1958), 11.

Letter to Robert R. Kirsch, Los Angeles *Times* (28 December 1958), V, 7.

Letter to the editor, New York *Herald Tribune* (22 May 1959), 12.

Letter to the editor, *Holiday* (December 1959), 4.

Letter to the editor, *The Princeton Packet* (17 March 1960), 10.

Hoke Norris, "O'Hara Attacks His Attackers," Chicago *Sun-Times* (3 April 1960), III, 1, 5.

Letter to the editor, New York *Herald Tribune* (5 April 1960), 18.

The George and Ira Gershwin Song Book (New York: Simon & Schuster, 1960). O'Hara telegram, p. x.

Contribution to symposium on teaching creative writing, *four quarters*, X (January 1961), 17.

Walter Farquhar, "Editorial Musings," Pottsville *Republican* (5 April 1961), 4.

Letter to the editor, New York *Times* (5 July 1961), 32.

Letter to the editor, New York *Herald Tribune* (20 August 1961), II, 3.

Letter to the editor, New York *Times* (30 December 1961), 18.

Mark Schorer, *Sinclair Lewis: An American Life* (New York: McGraw-Hill, 1961), p. 351.

Letter to the editor, New York *Herald Tribune* (26 January 1962), 16.

Letter to the editor, *The Princeton Packet* (1 February 1962), 8.

Letter to the editor, New York *Herald Tribune* (29 April 1962), II, 3.

Letter to the editor, *The Princeton Packet* (10 May 1962), 6.

Letter to the editor, New York *Herald Tribune* (5 June 1962), 20.

Letter to the editor, New York *Herald Tribune* (19 September 1962), 24.

Letter to the editor, New York *Herald Tribune* (28 September 1962), 24.

Letter to the editor, *Yale Alumni Magazine*, XXVI (November 1962), 7.

Red Smith's column, New York *Herald Tribune*—Paris Edition (18 January 1963), 9.

Letter to the editor, New York *Herald Tribune* (17 April 1963), 24.

Red Smith's column, New York *Herald Tribune* (28 January 1964), 20.

Red Smith's column, New York *Herald Tribune* (10 June 1964), 25.

"Dept. of Correction and Amplification," *The New Yorker*, XL (19 September 1964), 164–65.

Douglas Watts' column, New York *Daily News* (6 August 1965), 60.

Dorothy Manners' column, New York *Journal-American* (8 April 1966), 12.

John O'Hara: January 31, 1905–April 11, 1970. (Privately printed, 1970.)

Excerpts from letters to Charles Poore, Charles Hamilton Auction Number 56, March 9, 1972 (Item #226).

Joel Sayre, "John O'Hara: A Reminiscence," Washington *Post Book World* (18 March 1973), 2.

Robert Moses, "Bits and Pieces," *Park East* (10 January 1974), 5; (17 January 1974), 5.

SELECTED INTERVIEWS AND PUBLIC STATEMENTS

John McClain, "On the Sun Deck," New York *Sun* (12 April 1934), 29.

"John O'Hara says—," unlocated ad for *Appointment in Samarra* (1934).

John McClain, "On the Sun Deck," New York *Sun* (21 August 1935), 22.

"Backstage with Esquire," *Esquire*, VI (August 1936), 24.

Robert Van Gelder, "John O'Hara, Who Talks like His Stories," New York *Herald Tribune Books* (26 May 1940), 12.

Thomas O'Hara. "John O'Hara Interviewed By Brother at Show Here," Philadelphia *Evening Public Ledger* (11 December 1940).

"Pal Joey Is Just a Boob to His Creator," New York *Post* (8 January 1941), 3.

Lucius Beebe, "Stage Asides," New York *Herald Tribune* (12 January 1941), VI, 102. Interview about *Pal Joey*.

Nathaniel Benchley, "The Hard Luck Story of John O'Hara," *Stage*, I (February 1941), 42.

"Who's Who Gives O'Hara Chance to Startle Strangers," New York *World-Telegram* (8 March 1941).

Earl Wilson's column, New York *Post* (28 March 1948).

Harvey Breit, "Talk with John O'Hara," New York *Times Book Review* (4 September 1949), 11.

David Dempsey, "In and Out of Books," New York *Times Book Review* (6 November 1949), 8.

Benjamin Welles, "John O'Hara and His Pal Joey," New York *Times* (26 January 1951), IX, 2.

"Some Authors of 1951 Speaking for Themselves: John O'Hara," New York *Herald Tribune Book Review* (7 October 1951), 6.

Ward Morehouse, "Broadway after Dark," New York *World-Telegram & Sun* (14 December 1951), 34.

William M. Dwyer, "O'Hara Writes Play, Amateurs Stage It," New York *Herald Tribune* (18 May 1952), IV, 2.

Lewis Nichols, "Talk with John O'Hara," New York *Times Book Review* (27 November 1955), 16.

John K. Hutchens, "John O'Hara from Pottsville, Pa.," New York *Herald Tribune Books* (4 December 1955), 2.

John K. Hutchens, "Authors, Critics, Speeches, Prizes," New York *Herald Tribune Book Review* (12 February 1956), 2, 4.

John Cook Wyllie, "Book Editor Keeps an Appointment with O'Hara," Richmond *News-Leader* (22 February 1956), 11.

Robert L. Perkin, "John O'Hara: Rugged, Talented, Bitter," Denver *Rocky Mountain News* (23 February 1956).

Louis Cook, "O'Hara Book Naughty, Police Say; It's Banned," Detroit *Free Press* (18 January 1957), 3, 11. O'Hara also quoted in 18 January 1957 INS article on Detroit case.

"As 'From the Terrace' Goes to Press: Appointment with O'Hara," *Publishers Weekly*, CLXXIV (3 November 1958), 22–23.

Rollene Waterman, "Appt. with O'Hara," *Saturday Review*, XLI (29 November 1958), 15.

"Talk with the Author," *Newsweek*, LII (1 December 1958), 93–94.

Robert A. Burt and Charles E. Ruas, "Appointment With O'Hara," *Daily Princetonian* (7 January 1959), 2. Includes O'Hara's written replies to questions.

Maurice Dolbier, "What NBA Means to Some Past Winners," New York *Herald Tribune Book Review* (1 March 1959), 2, 11.

A. H. Weiler, "Passing Picture Scene," New York *Times* (31 May 1959), II, 5.

Hal Boyle's column, Associated Press (3 May 1960).

Jack Keating, "John O'Hara World of Yale, Society, and Sex," *Cosmopolitan*, CXLIX (September 1960), 59–63.

Statement on the death of Hemingway, New York *Times* (3 July 1961), 6.

[Miles A. Smith], "A Writer's Look at His Town, Career and Future," *Princeton Packet* (23 November 1961), 1, 4. Revised as AP dispatch.

Lewis Nichols, "In and Out of Books," New York *Times Book Review* (29 July 1962), 8.

Anon. "John O'Hara at 58: A Rage to Write," *Newsweek*, LXI (3 June 1963), 53–57.

Sam Zolotow, "John O'Hara Finds Playwriting Fun," New York *Times* (29 July 1963), 16.

Headnote for "The Lawbreaker," *The Saturday Evening Post*, CCXXXVI (16 November 1963), 53.

"John O'Hara Hears 'Influential People' Selling Bermuda Short," *The Royal Gazette* (20 March 1964), 6.

Note on "The Tackle," *Sports Illustrated* (21 September 1964), 6.

Ray Erwin, "John O'Hara Comes 'Home' to Newspapers," *Editor & Publisher*, XCVII (26 September 1964), 120.

Lewis Nichols, "In and Out of Books," New York *Times Book Review* (29 November 1964), 8.

Arthur Pottersman, "The world, I think, is better off that I'm a writer," London *Sun* (21 September 1965), 3.

James Kerney, Jr., "The Simple Life . . . But in Style," Trenton *Evening Times* (23 May 1966), 13.

Homer Bigart, "Staff of Tribune Sad, Not Shocked," New York *Times* (16 August 1966), 26. Statement on the death of the New York *Herald Tribune*.

Peter Grosvenor, "John O'Hara . . . two blows he had to beat," London *Daily Express* (4 May 1967).

"Mr. John O'Hara," *Foylibra* (June 1967).

Alden Whitman, "O'Hara, in Rare Interview, Calls Literary Landscape Fairly Bleak," New York *Times* (13 November 1967), 45.

Alden Whitman, untitled interview, New York *Times Book Review* (26 November 1967), 5.

Don A. Schanche, "John O'Hara Is Alive and Well in the First Half of the Twentieth Century," *Esquire*, CXXII (August 1969), 84–86, 142, 144–49.

NEWSPAPERS & MAGAZINES

Reporter, Pottsville *Journal*, July 1924–late 1926. No surviving file of the *Journal* for this period.

Reporter, Tamaqua *Courier*, January–March 1927.

Reporter and rewrite man, New York *Herald Tribune*, March–August 1928.

Reporter and checker, *Time*, August 1928–March 1929.

Reporter, *Editor & Publisher*, Spring(?) 1929.

Rewrite man, New York *Daily Mirror*, July 1929.

Critic and radio columnist (as John O'Hara and Franey Delaney), New York *Morning Telegraph*, May–July 1930.

Managing editor (without title), Pittsburgh *Bulletin-Index*, May–August 1933.

Editor, *The Kungsholm Cruise News*, March 1934.

O'HARA AND HOLLYWOOD

1934	12 June–20 August. At Paramount for $250 per week. Worked on scripts for *Dad's Day* and *Soldier Woman* (neither film released with these titles).
1936/37	Acted in *The General Died at Dawn*. Worked on treatments for Goldwyn and MGM.
1939	17 March–13 April. At RKO for $750 per week. Worked on *In Name Only*.
	18 September–6 December. At Twentieth Century-Fox for $750 per week. Worked on *I Was an Adventuress* (screen credit to Karl Tunberg, Don Ettlinger and O'Hara); also worked on *He Married His Wife* (screen credit to Sam Hellman, Darrell Ware, Lynn Starling, Erna Lazarus, Scott Darling and O'Hara). Possibly worked on *These Glamour Girls* at MGM.
1940	2 January–5 April. At Twentieth Century-Fox for $1,000 per week. Worked on *Down Argentine Way*.
1941	24 March–26 July. At Twentieth Century-Fox for $1,250 per week. Received sole credit for *Moontide*.
1945	August–January 1946. At MGM for $1,000(?) per week. Worked on *Cass Timberlane*.
1946	June. Worked on *A Miracle Can Happen* (*On Our Merry Way*) from own original story for United Artists. Received credit for James Stewart–Henry Fonda material.
1946	Possibly worked on *Strange Journey* and *Sentimental Journey* for Twentieth Century-Fox.
1950	Skirball and Manning planning to do *Appointment in Samarra* (have owned rights for four years); not produced.
1955	Spring. Wrote original story for *Best Things in Life Are Free* for Twentieth Century-Fox. Script by William Bowers and Phoebe Ephron.
1956	September. Writes script of *Bravados* for Twentieth Century-Fox, but not used. Part of three-picture deal at $75,000 each. Aldrich planning to produce *Now We Know*; not made.
1957	Writes *The Man Who Could Not Lose*—unproduced original for Twentieth Century-Fox.
1957	*Pal Joey* (Columbia).
1958	*Ten North Frederick* (Twentieth Century-Fox).
1960	*Butterfield 8* (MGM).
1960	*From the Terrace* (Twentieth Century-Fox).
1965	*A Rage to Live* (Mirisch–United Artists).

ABOUT JOHN O'HARA

CRITICISM & BIOGRAPHY

Bassett, Charles W. "O'Hara's Roots," Pottsville *Republican* (20 March 1971–8 January 1972).

Bruccoli, Matthew J. *John O'Hara: A Checklist* (New York: Random House, 1972).

Carson, Russell E. *The Fiction of John O'Hara* (Pittsburgh: The University of Pittsburgh Press, 1961).

Farr, Finis. *O'Hara* (Boston: Little, Brown, 1973).

Gary, Beverly. "A Post Portrait: John O'Hara," New York *Post* (18–22, 24 May 1959).

Grebstein, Sheldon Norman. *John O'Hara* (New York: Twayne, 1966).

McCormick, Bernard, "A John O'Hara Geography," *Journal of Modern Literature*, 1 (Second issue, 1970–71), 151–58.

Schanche, Don A. "John O'Hara Is Alive and Well in the First Half of the Twentieth Century," *Esquire*, CXXII (August 1969), 84–86, 142, 144–49.

Walcutt, Charles C. *John O'Hara* (Minneapolis: University of Minnesota Press, 1969).

SELECTED REVIEWS

Appointment in Samarra (1934)

Anon. "American Life," Springfield (Massachusetts) *Republican* (2 September 1934).

Anon. "Diagram of a Celebrity," Danville (Pennsylvania) *Morning News* (15 July 1935).

Anon. *The Forum and Century* (October 1934).

Anon. "Gibbsville," *Time* (20 August 1934).

Anon. "A Good First Novel by John O'Hara," New York *Times Book Review* (19 August 1934).

Anon. "Pottsville Author Writes First Novel," *Keeping Up with Books* (Summer 1934). Jacobs Book Store.

Anon. *Times Literary Supplement* (7 March 1935).

Bell, Neil. Manchester *Guardian* (12 March 1935).

Blackmur, R. P. "A Morality of Pointlessness," *Nation* (22 August 1934).

Brickell, Herschel. "Country Club Life," *The North American Review* (October 1934).

———. "Mr. O'Hara's Virtues," *The North American Review* (November 1934).

Canby, Henry Seidel. "Mr. O'Hara, and the Vulgar School," *Saturday Review of Literature* (18 August 1934).
Chamberlain, John. New York *Times* (16 August 1934).
Crichton, Kyle. "Contents Noted," *Life* (January 1935).
Fadiman, Clifton. *The New Yorker* (1 September 1934).
Hall, Theo. "Appointment with O'Hara," Washington *Post* (17 August 1934).
Lewis, Sinclair. "Nostalgia for the Nineties," *The Saturday Review of Literature* (6 October 1934).
Mangione, Jerre. "Rootless Tragedy," *The New Republic* (3 October 1934).
Marsh, Fred T. "Appointment in Samarra," New York *Herald Tribune Books* (19 August 1934).
Paterson, Isabel. New York *Herald Tribune* (16 August 1934).
Quennell, Peter. *The New Statesman and Nation* (29 December 1934).
Rascoe, Burton. *Esquire* (October 1934).
Soskin, William. Los Angeles *Examiner* (16 August 1934) and New York *American*.

The Doctor's Son and Other Stories (1935)
Anon. "Straight Reporter," *Time* (25 February 1935).
Benét, William Rose. *The Saturday Review of Literature* (2 March 1935).
Chamberlain, John. New York *Times* (21 February 1935).
Gannett, Lewis. New York *Herald Tribune* (23 February 1935).
Marsh, Fred T. New York *Herald Tribune Books* (3 March 1935).
Walton, Edith H. New York *Times Book Review* (24 February 1935).

Butterfield 8 (1935)
Adams, J. Donald. New York *Times Book Review* (20 October 1935).
Anon. "Speakeasy Era," *Time* (21 October 1935).
Broun, Heywood. "His 'Ayes' Bigger than His Stomach, So Its Escape on a Train to Read More," New York *World-Telegram* (31 October 1935).
Chamberlain, John. New York *Times* (17 October 1935).
Cowley, Malcolm. "Hemingway Mixed with Hearst," *The New Republic* (4 December 1935).
Fadiman, Clifton. "Disappointment in O'Hara," *The New Yorker* (19 October 1935).
Gannett, Lewis. New York *Herald Tribune* (18 October 1935).
Smith, Bernard. New York *Herald Tribune Books* (20 October 1935).
Stevens, George. "Appointment in Park Avenue," *The Saturday Review of Literature* (19 October 1935).
Trilling, Lionel. "Mr. O'Hara's Talent," *The Nation* (6 November 1935).

Hope of Heaven (1938)
Anon. *Times Literary Supplement* (11 February 1939).
Anon. "Tragedy Off Stage," *Time* (21 March 1938).
Fadiman, Clifton. *The New Yorker* (19 March 1938).
Ferguson, Otis. *The New Republic* (13 April 1938).
Gannett, Lewis. New York *Herald Tribune* (19 March 1938).
Kazin, Alfred. "Smeared with Glitter," New York *Herald Tribune Books* (20 March 1938).
Kronenberger, Louis. New York *Times Book Review* (27 March 1938).
Poore, Charles. New York *Times* (18 March 1938).
S., J. "American Tales," London *Times* (17 February 1939).
Stevens, George. "Lucky to Live," *The Saturday Review of Literature* (19 March 1938).

Files on Parade (1939)

Anon. "Heeltalk," *Time* (25 September 1939).

Anon. "O'Hara Gems," *Newsweek* (25 September 1939).

Ferguson, Otis. "O'Hara on Parade," *The New Republic* (11 October 1939).

Pratt, Fletcher. "O'Hara Short Stories," *The Saturday Review of Literature* (23 September 1939).

Rugoff, Milton. "Tough, Tender and Swift Paced," New York *Herald Tribune Books* (24 September 1939).

Schorer, Mark. Boston *Transcript* (7 October 1939).

Van Gelder, Robert, "John O'Hara's Short Stories and other Recent Works of Fiction," New York *Times Book Review* (24 September 1939).

Pal Joey (1940)

Anon. "'Joey' in Print," New York *Herald Tribune* (7 September 1952).

Anon. "Letters of Credit," *Times Literary Supplement* (5 December 1952).

Rothman, N. L. *The Saturday Review of Literature* (26 October 1940).

Rugoff, Milton. "Coarse, Sly, Big Town Wise Guy," New York *Herald Tribune Books* (3 November 1940).

Van Gelder, Robert. "O'Hara's Portrait of a Night-Club Singer," New York *Times Book Review* (3 November 1940).

Wilson, Edmund. "The Boys in the Back Room," *The New Republic* (11 November 1940).

Pal Joey: Musical—1940 Production

Anderson, John. "'Pal Joey' Staged at the Barrymore," New York *Journal-American* (26 December 1940).

Anon. "New Plays in Manhattan," *Time* (6 January 1941).

Anon. "Pal Joey," *Theatre Arts* (February 1941).

Atkinson, Brooks. "The Play: Christmas Night Adds 'Pal Joey' and 'Meet the People' to the Musical Stage," New York *Times* (26 December 1940).

Bronson, Arthur. "The Stage: 'Pal Joey' Full of Snap and Sting," Philadelphia *Record* (12 December 1940).

Brown, John Mason. "'Pal Joey' Presented at The Ethel Barrymore," New York *Post* (26 December 1940).

Gibbs, Wolcott. "The Theatre: Upturn," *The New Yorker* (4 January 1941).

———. "The Theatre: In like a Lamb," *The New Yorker* (13 September 1941).

Keen, J. H. "'Pal Joey' and What a Pal for Abbott," Philadelphia *Daily News* (12 December 1940).

Kronenberger, Louis. "Theater: 'Pal Joey' Brings Holiday Cheer," *PM* (26 December 1940).

Lardner, John. "Sport Week? Nice Going Neighbor," *Newsweek* (6 January 1941).

Lockridge, Richard. "John O'Hara's 'Pal Joey' Is Offered at the Barrymore Theater," New York *Sun* (26 December 1940).

———. "The Stage in Review: The Heeldom of Pal Joey, and the Place of Heeldom on the Stage," New York *Sun* (18 January 1941).

Mantle, Burns. "'Pal Joey' Smart and Novel," New York *Daily News* (26 December 1940).

Marshall, Margaret. *The Nation* (18 January 1941).

Mellor, William B., Jr. "Appointment in Philadelphia," Philadelphia *Record* (13 December 1940).

Murdock, Henry T. "'Pal Joey' Scores Hit at Forrest," Philadelphia *Ledger* (12 December 1940).

Schloss, Edwin H. "Footlights: Pal Joey Sticks Strictly to Top-Shelf Show Now," Philadelphia *Record* (15 December 1940).

Sensenderfer, Robert, "Living Theater: Pal Joey—George Abbott Musical About Night Club Life Has Premiere," Philadelphia *Evening Bulletin* (12 December 1940).

Watts, Richard, Jr. "The Theater: No Longer a Winter of Discontent," New York *Herald Tribune* (5 January 1941).

———. "The Theaters: Night Club Portrait," New York *Herald Tribune* (26 December 1940).

Welles, Benjamin. "John O'Hara and His Pal Joey," New York *Times* (26 January 1941).

Whipple, Sidney B. "Theater: Pal Joey Is a Bright, Gay, Tuneful, Novel/Work," New York *World-Telegram* (26 December 1940).

Pal Joey: Musical—1952 Production

Anon. "The Heel as a Hero," *Life* (21 January 1952).

Anon. "The Theater: Old Musical in Manhattan: Pal Joey," *Time* (14 January 1952).

Anon. "Theater: Review: Pal Joey," *Newsweek* (14 January 1952).

Atkinson, Brooks. "At the Theatre," New York *Times* (4 January 1952).

———. "The Music Master," New York *Times* (13 January 1952).

Brown, John Mason. "In a Class by Itself," *Saturday Review of Literature* (2 February 1952).

Clurman, Harold. "Theatre: The Mighty Have Tripped," *The New Republic* (21 January 1952).

Gibbs, Wolcott. "The Theatre: Fine Low Fun," *The New Yorker* (12 January 1952).

Kerr, Walter. "The Stage: Pal Joey," *Commonweal* (25 January 1952).

Lardner, John. "New York," *Look* (29 January 1952).

M.M. "Pal Joey," *Nation* (26 January 1952).

Watts, Richard, Jr. "Two on the Aisle: More Enthusiasm for 'Pal Joey,'" New York *Post* (13 January 1952).

Pipe Night (1945)

Anon. "Hollywood to 52nd Street," *Time* (26 March 1945).

Anon. *The New Yorker* (17 March 1945).

Fearing, Kenneth. "Perfidies of Life His Concern," New York *Herald Tribune Weekly Book Review* (25 March 1945).

Prescott, Orville. New York *Times* (20 March 1945).

Rosenfeld, Isaac. "Racket or Tragedy," *The New Republic* (14 May 1945).

Sugrue, Thomas. "John O'Hara's 'Little People,'" *The Saturday Review of Literature* (28 April 1945).

Trilling, Lionel. "John O'Hara Observes Our Mores," New York *Times Book Review* (18 March 1945).

Weeks, Edward. *The Atlantic Monthly* (June 1945).

Here's O'Hara (1946)

Hager, Richard. *The Commonweal* (19 July 1946).

Macfall, R. P. "O'Hara Stories from Jazz and Speakeasy Age," Chicago *Tribune* (23 June 1946).

Robinson, Henry Morton. "O'Hara in His Time," *The Saturday Review of Literature* (18 May 1946).

Watts, Richard, Jr. "O'Hara in Omnibus," *The New Republic* (27 May 1946).

Hellbox (1947)

Anon. *Newsweek* (18 August 1947).

Anon. *Time* (11 August 1947).

Burger, Nash K. New York *Times* (4 August 1947).

Butcher, Fanny. "John O'Hara Hard-Boiled and Brilliant," Chicago *Sunday Tribune* (3 August 1947).

Fearing, Kenneth. "A Manhattan Cocktail," New York *Herald Tribune Weekly Book Review* (3 August 1947).

Hansen, Harry. New York *World-Telegram* (4 August 1947).

Jackson, J. H. San Francisco *Chronicle* (4 August 1947).

Johnson, Gerald. New York *Herald Tribune* (4 August 1947).

North, Sterling. "O'Hara's Majority," New York *Post* (7 August 1947).

Sullivan, Richard. "O'Hara Short-Stories: Bright, Bitter, 'Moral,'" New York *Times Book Review* (17 August 1947).

Woodburn, John. "Tattooed Portraits," *The Saturday Review of Literature* (9 August 1947).

A Rage to Live (1949)

Adams, J. Donald. "Speaking of Books," New York *Times Book Review* (11 September 1949).

Anon. *Christian Science Monitor* (22 September 1949).

Anon. *Newsweek* (22 August 1949).

Anon. "The Pennsylvania Story," *Time* (29 August 1949).

Anon. *Times Literary Supplement* (8 December 1950).

Breit, Harvey. "The World O'Hara Made," *The Atlantic Monthly* (September 1949).

Dempsey, David. "In and Out of Books," New York *Times Book Review* (6 November 1949).

Fadiman, Clifton. "A Rage to Live," *Book-of-the-Month Club News* (August 1949).

Fineman, Morton. "O'Hara Proves His Mastery," Philadelphia *Inquirer* (21 August 1949).

Gill, Brendan. "The O'Hara Report and the Wit of Miss McCarthy," *The New Yorker* (20 August 1949).

Howe, Irving. *Partisan Review* (October 1949).

Hutchens, John K. New York *Herald Tribune* (16 August 1949).

——. "On the Books," New York *Herald Tribune Weekly Book Review* (28 August 1949).

——. "On the Books," New York *Herald Tribune Weekly Book Review* (4 September 1949).

Jackson, J. H. San Francisco *Chronicle* (16 August 1949).

Jones, Ernest. "Mr. O'Hara's Panorama," *The Nation* (3 September 1949).

McFee, William. New York *Sun* (16 August 1949).

North, Sterling. New York *World-Telegram* (16 August 1949).

Pickerel, Paul. *Yale Review* (Autumn 1949).

Prescott, Orville. New York *Times* (16 August 1949).

Rago, Henry. *The Commonweal* (16 September 1949).

Rogow, Lee. "Skittish Thoroughbred," *The Saturday Review of Literature* (20 August 1949).

Rugoff, Milton. "John O'Hara Once More on His Home Ground," New York *Herald Tribune Weekly Book Review* (21 August 1949).

Spectorsky, A. C. "Portrait of a Woman," New York *Times* (21 August 1949).

Sullivan, Richard. "Novel Lacks Altitude, but It's Readable," Chicago *Tribune* (21 August 1949).

Watts, Richard, Jr. "New O'Hara Novel a Solid, Brilliant Work," New York *Post Home News* (21 August 1949).

Woodburn, John. "Homesick O'Hara," *The New Republic* (31 October 1949).

The Farmers Hotel (1951)

Anon. "Briefly Noted Fiction," *The New Yorker* (8 December 1951).

Anon. "John O'Hara's Latest Novel Wins Praise," Pottsville *Journal* (9 November 1951).

Anon. *Time* (19 November 1951).

Butcher, Fanny. "Something New under O'Hara Sun," Chicago *Sunday Tribune* (18 November 1951).

Cooke, Alistair. "O'Hara's Joyless, Wonderfully Observed Little World," New York *Herald Tribune Book Review* (18 November 1951).

Gannett, Lewis. New York *Herald Tribune* (12 November 1951).

Jackson, J. H. San Francisco *Chronicle* (21 November 1951).

Janeway, Elizabeth. "Violence in the O'Hara Country," New York *Times Book Review* (11 November 1951).

Kelly, James. *Saturday Review of Literature* (14 November 1951).

Marquand, John P. "The Farmers Hotel," *Book-of-the-Month Club News* (November 1951).

North, Sterling. New York *World-Telegram* (14 November 1951).

Poore, Charles. New York *Times* (8 November 1951).

Sweet and Sour (1954)

Anon. "Page Proof. . . ." New York *Post* (18 October 1954).

D.D. "Chatter by Novelist O'Hara," Kansas City *Star* (23 October 1954).

Duffield, Marcus. "O'Hara-isms," New York *Herald Tribune Book Review* (31 October 1954).

Jackson, J. H. San Francisco *Chronicle* (15 October 1954).

O'Neill, Decker. Louisville *Courier Journal* (17 October 1954).

Perkin, Robert L. "One Man's Pegasus: You'll Like O'Hara," *Rocky Mountain News* (31 October 1954).

Rogow, Lee. *Saturday Review* (13 November 1954).

Williams, Ernest E. Fort Wayne *News-Sentinel* (23 October 1954).

Williamson, Samuel T. "The O'Hara Swath," New York *Times Book Review* (17 October 1954).

Ten North Frederick (1955)

Alexander, Sidney. "Another Visit to O'Haraville," *The Reporter* (26 January 1956).

Anon. "The Best of O'Hara," *Newsweek* (28 November 1955).

Anon. "Member of the Funeral," *Time* (28 November 1955).

Chamberlain, John. *Wall Street Journal* (29 December 1955).

Cooperman, Stanley. "A Flat Sort of Realism," *The Nation* (31 December 1955).

Davis, Robert Gorham. "O'Hara's World of Secret Lives," New York *Times Book Review* (27 November 1955).

Fiedler, Leslie A. "An Old Pro at Work," *The New Republic* (9 January 1956).

Gannett, Lewis. New York *Herald Tribune* (24 November 1955).

Highet, Gilbert. *Book-of-the-Month Club News* (December 1955).

Hogan, William. San Francisco *Chronicle* (28 November 1955).

Kelly, James. "Under the Million Dollars," *The Saturday Review* (26 November 1955).

Kirsch, Robert R. Los Angeles *Times* (25 November 1955).

McKelway, St. Clair. ". . . And Nothing But the Truth," *The New Yorker* (17 December 1955).

Poore, Charles. New York *Times* (24 November 1955).

Rolo, C. J. "Gibbsville, Pa.," *The Atlantic Monthly* (January 1956).

Rugoff, Milton. "Masterly Portrait by John O'Hara," New York *Herald Tribune Book Review* (27 November 1955).

Sullivan, Richard. "Memorable Joe Chapin," Chicago *Sunday Tribune Magazine of Books* (27 November 1955).

A Family Party (1956)

Adams, Phoebe. *Atlantic* (September 1956).

Anon. *New Yorker* (8 September 1956).

Anon. "Our Town," *Time* (27 August 1956).

Dempsey, David. "A Few Well-Chosen Words," New York *Times Book Review* (19 August 1956).

Hogan, William. San Francisco *Chronicle* (16 August 1956).

Kelly, James. *Saturday Review* (18 August 1956).

Kirsch, Robert R. Los Angeles *Times* (21 August 1956).

Poore, Charles. New York *Times* (16 August 1956).

Rugoff, Milton. "O'Hara in Mellower Mood," New York *Herald Tribune Book Review* (19 August 1956).

Sullivan, Richard. "Technical Brilliance Seen, as Usual, in O'Hara Story," Chicago *Sunday Tribune Magazine of Books* (19 August 1956).

From the Terrace (1958)

Anon. "John O'Hara's Panorama," *Newsweek* (1 December 1958).

Anon. "Limited View," *Times Literary Supplement* (23 October 1959).

Bruccoli, Matthew J. Richmond *News-Leader* (19 November 1958; 18 March 1959).

Hicks, Granville. "The Problem of O'Hara," *Saturday Review* (29 November 1958).

Hogan, William. "John O'Hara as the American Galsworthy," San Francisco *Chronicle* (1 December 1958).

————. "O'Hara's New Novel—A Rage to Love," San Francisco *Chronicle* (2 December 1958).

Hutchens, John K. New York *Herald Tribune* (25 November 1958).

Kirsch, Robert R. "O'Hara's Latest Held Magnificent," Los Angeles *Times* (7 December 1958).

Mizener, Arthur. "Something Went Seriously Wrong," New York *Times Book Review* (23 November 1958).

Norris, Hoke. "John O'Hara Gives Us a Big, Big Novel," Chicago *Sun-Times* (30 November 1958).

Poore, Charles. New York *Times* (25 November 1958).

Rugoff, Milton. "O'Hara's Latest, Largest Novel," New York *Herald Tribune Book Review* (23 November 1958).

Sullivan, Richard. "A Dim View of Mankind," Chicago *Sunday Tribune Magazine of Books* (7 December 1958).

Wain, John. "Snowed Under," *The New Yorker* (10 January 1959).

Williams, Ernest. Ft. Wayne *News-Sentinel* (6 December 1958).

Ourselves To Know (1960)

Adams, Phoebe. *Atlantic* (March 1960).

Anon. *Time* (29 February 1960).

Anon. "Time Out of Joint," *Times Literary Supplement* (30 December 1960).

Boroff, David. *Saturday Review* (27 February 1960).

Chamberlain, John. " 'Passions Spin the Plot' in O'Hara's Novel of a Tragically-Fated Man," New York *Herald Tribune Book Review* (28 February 1960).

Dolbier, Maurice. New York *Herald Tribune* (27 February 1960).

Dunlea, William. *Commonweal* (March 1960).

Fadiman, Clifton. *Book-of-the-Month Club News* (April 1960).

Hogan, William. San Francisco *Chronicle* (4 March 1960).

Kirsch, Robert R. "An Experiment by John O'Hara," Los Angeles *Times* (23 May 1960).

Moore, Harry T. "The Murderer Tells His Story," New York *Times Book Review* (28 February 1960).

Norris, Hoke. "Critics Be Damned—It's Vintage O'Hara," Chicago *Sun-Times* (28 February 1958).

Poore, Charles. New York *Times* (27 February 1960).

Sullivan, Richard. "Life as Viewed Under a Low and Sexy Sky," Chicago *Sunday Tribune Magazine of Books* (28 February 1960).

Williams, Ernest. Ft. Wayne *News-Sentinel* (27 February 1960).

Sermons and Soda-Water (1960)

Adams, Phoebe. *Atlantic* (December 1960).

Anon. *Time* (28 November 1960).

Anon. "Dolls and Dollars," *Times Literary Supplement* (13 October 1961).

Anon. "Triple Play by O'Hara," *Newsweek* (28 November 1960).

Bruccoli, Matthew J. Richmond *News-Leader* (14 December 1960).

Dolbier, Maurice. New York *Herald Tribune* (24 November 1960).

Hicks, Granville. *Saturday Review* (10 December 1960).

Highet, Gilbert. "Sermons and Soda-Water," *Book-of-the-Month Club News* (December 1960).

Hogan, William. San Francisco *Chronicle* (24 November 1960).

Kirsch, Robert R. "John O'Hara: Three Novellas," Los Angeles *Times* (7 December 1960).

Moore, Harry T. "The Losing Generation," New York *Times Book Review* (27 November 1960).

Poore, Charles. New York *Times* (24 November 1960).

Rugoff, Milton. "O'Hara Trio, More or Less from Life," New York *Herald Tribune, The Lively Arts and Book Review* (27 November 1960).

Sullivan, Richard. "An Abundance of Nostalgia and Sentiment," Chicago *Sunday Tribune Magazine of Books* (27 November 1960).

Williams, Ernest. Ft. Wayne *News-Sentinel* (3 December 1960).

Five Plays (1961)

Anon. *Newsweek* (21 August 1961).

Anon. *Time* (18 August 1961).

Bruccoli, Matthew J. Richmond *News-Leader* (9 August 1961).

Butcher, Fanny. "The Literary Spotlight," Chicago *Tribune* (6 August 1961).

Poore, Charles. New York *Times* (15 August 1961).

Taubman, Howard. "A Novelist in the Wings," New York *Times Book Review* (20 August 1961).

Assembly (1961)

Adams, Phoebe. *Atlantic* (December 1961).

Anon. "Short but Not Sweet," *Times Literary Supplement* (25 May 1962).

Anon. *Time* (1 December 1961).

Boroff, David. "Chapters of America," New York *Times Book Review* (26 November 1961).

Hicks, Granville. *Saturday Review* (25 November 1961).

Howe, Irving. "The Flaw in John O'Hara," *The New Republic* (27 November 1961).

Hutchens, John K. New York *Herald Tribune* (24 November 1961).

Kirsch, Robert R. "Short Stories Illuminate Virtuosity of John O'Hara," Los Angeles *Times* (6 December 1961).

Spector, Robert Donald. "Assemblage of Stories by a Genuine Craftsman," New York *Herald Tribune Books* (26 November 1961).

Sullivan, Richard. "Narratives Turned Out as on an Assembly Line," Chicago *Sunday Tribune Magazine of Books* (26 November 1961).

Tucker, Martin. *Commonweal* (29 December 1961).

Williams, Ernest. Ft. Wayne *News-Sentinel* (9 December 1961).

The Big Laugh (1962)

Anon. *Time* (1 June 1962).

Anon. *Times Literary Supplement* (7 December 1962).

Boroff, David. "Love Came to Fulfill—and to Destroy," New York *Times Book Review* (3 June 1962).

Harnack, Curtis. "A Morality Fable All Talk and No Moral," Chicago *Tribune* (3 June 1962).

Hogan, William. San Francisco *Chronicle* (28 May 1962).

Marx, Arthur. *Saturday Review* (7 July 1962).

Norris, Hoke. "John O'Hara's Hollywood Novel," Chicago *Sun-Times* (27 May 1962).

Poore, Charles. New York *Times* (29 May 1962).

Spector, Robert Donald. "Life and Times of a Hollywood Cad," New York *Herald Tribune Books* (27 May 1962).

Stanley, Donald. "O'Hara Puts the Finger on a Real Louse," San Francisco *Examiner Highlight* (27 May 1962).

Williams, Ernest. Ft. Wayne *News-Sentinel* (2 June 1962).

The Cape Cod Lighter (1962)

Anon. "Small Town Story," *Times Literary Supplement* (29 June 1963).

Barkham, John. "New Tales by John O'Hara," *Saturday Review Syndicate* (21 November 1962).

Butcher, Fanny. Chicago *Tribune* (2 December 1962).

Gutwillig, Robert. "From Tiny Details, the Big Truth," New York *Times Book Review* (25 November 1962).

Hutchens, John K. New York *Herald Tribune* (28 December 1962).

Kluger, Richard. New York *Herald Tribune Books* (2 December 1962).

Nordell, Roderick. "O'Hara Country," *Christian Science Monitor* (28 December 1962).

Norris, Hoke. Chicago *Sun-Times* (25 November 1962).

Peden, William. " 'Vanity Fair' Updated," *Saturday Review* (5 January 1963).

Poore, Charles. New York *Times* (22 November 1962).

Slavitt, D. R. "The Cape Cod Lighter," *Book-of-the-Month Club News* (December 1962).

Elizabeth Appleton (1963)

Anon. *Time* (7 June 1963).

Anon. "Top-Pop Trollope," *Times Literary Supplement* (14 November 1963).

Boroff, David. *Saturday Review* (8 June 1963).

Geismar, Maxwell. "Who's Afraid of the Professor's Wife?" New York *Times Book Review* (9 June 1963).

Poore, Charles. New York *Times* (4 June 1963).

Ware, Cade. "A Faculty Wife Joins the O'Hara Gallery," New York *Herald Tribune Books* (2 June 1963).

The Hat on the Bed (1963)

Anon. *Newsweek* (2 December 1963).

Anon. *Time* (22 November 1963).

Boroff, David. "A Portrait of America," New York *Times Book Review* (8 December 1963).

Hicks, Granville. *Saturday Review* (30 November 1963).

Keeley, Edmund. "Only a Few Trips from His Small, Tidy Realm," New York *Herald Tribune Book Week* (1 December 1963).

Lewis, R. C. "The Hat on the Bed," *Book-of-the-Month Club News* (February 1964).

Poore, Charles. New York *Times* (28 November 1963).

Pryce-Jones, Alan. "A Prize for O'Hara Fans—24 Short Stories," New York *Herald Tribune* (28 November 1963).

Vidal, Gore. "Appointment with O'Hara," *New York Review of Books* (16 April 1964).

Williams, Ernest. Ft. Wayne *News-Sentinel* (7 December 1963).

The Horse Knows the Way (1964)

Anon. *Newsweek* (30 November 1964).

Anon. "Scheherazade's Thousandth," *Time* (27 November 1964).

Donohue, H. E. F. "Steering Clear of Green Pastures," New York *Herald Tribune Book Week* (6 December 1964).

Elliott, George P. "Exploring the Province of the Short Story," *Harper's* Magazine (April 1965).

Hicks, Granville. "So Long to the Short for a While," *Saturday Review* (28 November 1964).

Kiely, Robert. "John O'Hara's World," *Christian Science Monitor* (17 December 1964).

Mayne, Richard. "Ventriloquism," *New Statesman* (28 May 1965).

Mitchell, Adrian. "Another Appointment with O'Hara," New York *Times Book Review* (29 November 1964).

Poore, Charles. New York *Times* (26 November 1964).

Pryce-Jones, Alan. "O'Hara's Detailed Moments," New York *Herald Tribune* (26 November 1964).

Sullivan, Richard. "Short Stories Before an O'Hara Sabbatical," Chicago *Tribune* (29 November 1964).

The Lockwood Concern (1965)

Anon. "John O'Hara: The Lockwood Concern," *Times Literary Supplement* (28 April 1966).

Anon. "O'Hara Country," *Newsweek* (29 November 1965).

Braybrooke, Neville. "The Judge's Story," *Spectator* (15 April 1966).

Galbraith, John Kenneth. "The Milk Train to Gibbsville," Washington *Post Book Week* (28 November 1965).

Hicks, Granville. "Fences, Finances, and Flings," *Saturday Review* (27 November 1965).

Knickerbocker, Conrad. "The Archaic Sage of Gibbsville," *Life* (26 November 1965).

Meagher, James P. "Switching Back to the Novel Length, O'Hara Says It All Over Again," *The National Observer* (6 December 1965).

Morgan, Edwin. "Unconcerned," *New Statesman* (15 April 1966).

Muggeridge, Malcolm. *Esquire* (November 1965).

Poore, Charles. New York *Times* (25 November 1965).

Schott, Webster. "How to Go to Hell in Style," New York *Times Book Review* (28 November 1965).

Sullivan, Richard. "An Obsession to Be the Top Dog," Chicago *Tribune Books Today* (12 December 1965).

My Turn (1966)

Anon. "Scold in Spats," *Time* (6 May 1966).

Balk, Alfred. "Wrong Turn," *Saturday Review* (14 May 1966).

Kirwan, J. D. "My Turn," *National Review* (23 August 1966).

Maddocks, Melvin. "Brickbats and Mosaics," *Christian Science Monitor* (8 June 1966).

Meagher, James P. "The Weekly O'Hara Comment Is Mildly Sportive," *The National Observer* (25 April 1966).

Waiting for Winter (1966)

Anon. "Behind Closed Doors," *Time* (18 November 1966).

Anon. "Keeping It Short," *Times Literary Supplement* (24 August 1967).

Cook, James E. "Trappings Change, But the Essential O'Hara Is There," *National Observer* (5 December 1966).

Galloway, David. *Spectator* (17 March 1967).

Maddocks, Melvin. "O'Hara—Feedback on the Tape," *Christian Science Monitor* (1 December 1966).

McDowell, David. "The Darkness Ahead," *Saturday Review* (17 December 1966).

Meier, T. K. "Waiting for Winter," *National Review* (16 May 1967).

Price, R. G. G. *Punch* (15 March 1967).

Rogers, Thomas. "Money Talks," Washington *Post Book Week* (27 November 1966).

Schott, Webster. "Carrying On and Getting On," New York *Times Book Review* (27 November 1966).

Williams, Ernest. Ft. Wayne *News-Sentinel* (3 December 1966).

The Instrument (1967)

Anon. "What Love Is and Is Not," *Time* (24 November 1967).

Coleman, John. "The Man Beneath the Skin," *National Observer* (31 March 1968).

Cook, Bruce. "In 'Instrument,' an O'Hara Religious Theme," *National Observer* (1 January 1968).

Davenport, Guy. "With a Long Spoon," *National Review* (30 January 1968).

Dolbier, Maurice. *Saturday Review* (25 November 1967).

Grebstein, Sheldon. "A Tour of O'Hara's Tinsel-Land," Washington *Post Book World* (19 November 1967).

Greenfeld, Josh. "The Playwright Played Wrong," New York *Times Book Review* (26 November 1967).

Lindroth, James R. *America* (13 January 1968).

M., P. "Playmaking by O'Hara," *Christian Science Monitor* (30 November 1967).

Norris, Hoke. Chicago *Daily News* (26 November 1967).

Poore, Charles. New York *Times* (22 November 1967).

Thompson, John. "Old Friends," *Commentary* (January 1968).

Williams, David. *Punch* (10 April 1968).

Williams, Ernest. Ft. Wayne *News-Sentinel* (9 December 1967).

And Other Stories (1968)

Davenport, Guy. "And Other Stories," New York *Times Book Review* (24 November 1968).

Kay, Jane Holtz. *Christian Science Monitor* (19 December 1968).

Lasson, Robert. "O'Hara Without Apologies," Washington *Post Book World* (24 November 1968).

Poore, Charles. New York *Times* (27 November 1968).

Sandberg, Peter L. "Conflicting Passions in Gibbsville, Pa.," *Saturday Review* (30 November 1968).

Weeks, Edward. *Atlantic Monthly* (December 1968).

The O'Hara Generation (1969)

Auchincloss, Louis. *The Literary Guild Magazine* (July 1969).

Grubisch, Thomas. "A Recorder Is Not Enough," The Washington *Post* (16 July 1969).

Hogan, William. "The O'Hara Files Again on Parade," San Francisco *Chronicle* (17 July 1969).

Kirsch, Robert. "Sampler from the O'Hara Generation," Los Angeles *Times* (3 August 1969).

Norris, Hoke. "O'Hara's Pre-World War I Days: Journey into Nostalgia," Chicago *Daily News* (5 July 1969).

Lovey Childs (1969)

Adams, Phoebe. *Atlantic* (December 1969).

Kirsch, Robert. "O'Hara in the Main Line Mainstream," Los Angeles *Times* (5 January 1970).

Meier, T. K. *National Review* (5 May 1970).

Reynolds, Stanley. *New Statesman* (19 June 1970).

Rhodes, Richard. "After Many Adventures Lovey Finally Settled Down," New York *Times Book Review* (30 November 1969).

The Ewings (1972)

Adams, Phoebe. *Atlantic Monthly* (March 1972).

Bell, Millicent. *Saturday Review* (4 March 1972).

Bruccoli, Matthew J. "O'Hara Knew His America," Philadelphia *Bulletin* (27 February 1972).

Cheever, John. *Esquire* (May 1972).

Cole, Barry. *New Statesman* (21 July 1972).

Davis, L. J. "Bill and Edna's Bank Account," Washington *Post Book World* (20 February 1972).

Hogan, William. "Remembrances of Things Past," San Francisco *Chronicle* (7 February 1972).

Kauffmann, Stanley. "A Rage to Write," *The New Republic* (20 February 1972).

Kiely, Robert. "Edna Only Wanted a Spin in Someone's Pierce-Arrow," New York *Times Book Review* (27 February 1972).

Lehmann-Haupt, Christopher. New York *Times* (29 February 1972).

Loukides, Paul. "Posthumous O'Hara Novel Set in Michigan and Ohio," Detroit *News* (16 January 1972).

Mano, D. Keith. *National Review* (3 March 1972).

Norris, Hoke. "R.I.P. O'Hara, ex-V.I.P.," Chicago *Daily News* (25 March 1972).

Waugh, Auberon. "Having It Both Ways," *The Spectator* (12 August 1972).

The Time Element and Other Stories (1972)

Anon. *Saturday Review* (16 December 1972).

Anon. *Times Literary Supplement* (21 September 1973).

Barkham, John. New York *Post* (29 November 1972).

Broyard, Anatole. "Creating Your Own Cliches," New York *Times* (18 December 1972).

Bruccoli, Matthew J. Chicago *Daily News* (16 December 1972).

Oberbeck, S. K. *Newsweek* (27 November 1972).

Good Samaritan & Other Stories (1974)

Barkham, John. Barkham review syndicate.

Bruccoli, Matthew J. Chicago *Daily News* (10 August 1974).

Grau, Shirley Ann. Chicago *Tribune* (11 August 1974).

Moss, Robert F. New York *Times Book Review* (18 August 1974).

Rosenthal, Lucy. *Book-of-the-Month Club News* (Special, Fall 1974).

Wolff, Geoffrey. Los Angeles *Times* (22 September 1974).

Yardley, Jonathan. Miami *Herald* (25 August 1974).

INDEX*

ABOUT THE AUTHOR

MATTHEW J. BRUCCOLI, Professor of English at the University of South Carolina and Director of the Center for Editions of American Authors, is editor of the *Fitzgerald/ Hemingway Annual*. He has written or edited some twenty volumes in the field of American literary scholarship and is a leading authority on F. Scott Fitzgerald. Among his recent books is *The Romantic Egoists*, a pictorial biography of F. Scott and Zelda Fitzgerald, which he edited with Scottie Fitzgerald Smith and Joan P. Kerr. His *John O'Hara: A Checklist* was published by Random House. He is a partner in Bruccoli Clark Publishers.